The Creolization of American Culture

William Sidney Mount and the Roots of Blackface Minstrelsy

Christopher J. Smith

UNIVERSITY OF ILLINOIS PRESS
URBANA, CHICAGO, AND SPRINGFIELD

Publication supported by the Barry and Claire Brook Endowment of the American Musicological Society and by the H. Earle Johnson Fund of the Society for American Music.

First Illinois paperback, 2014

Manufactured in the United States of America
1 2 3 4 5 C P 5 4 3 2 1
∞ This book is printed on acid-free paper.

The Library of Congress cataloged the cloth edition as follows:
Smith, Christopher J. (Christopher John), 1959-
The creolization of American culture: William Sidney Mount and the roots of blackface minstrelsy / Christopher J. Smith.
pages cm. — (Music in American life)
Includes bibliographical references and index.
ISBN 978-0-252-03776-4 (cloth : alk. paper)
ISBN 978-0-252-09504-7 (e-book)
1. Minstrel music—United States—History and criticism.
2. Minstrel shows—United States—History.
3. Blackface entertainers—United States.
4. Mount, William Sidney, 1807–1868.
I. Title.
ML1711.S63 2013
781.640973'09034—dc23 2012050436

PAPERBACK ISBN 978-0-252-08052-4

This book is dedicated to Old Corn Meal,
"Bobolink Bob" Rawley, Juba Lane, John J. "Juba" Clark,
John "Picayune" Butler, Banjo Joe Sweeney,
Thomas "Daddy" Rice, George Dixon, Dan Emmett, Shep Jones,
Robert Nelson Mount, "Ferguson," "Pot Pie" Herbert, Bob Farrell,
Joe Blackburn, John Diamond . . . and all the rest of them.

In memory of Bobby Smith Thomas.

Contents

Preface

THE *CREOLIZATION* IN THE TITLE of this book connotes a process of cultural exchange identifiable in many aspects of antebellum life. In the early-nineteenth-century United States, this exchange was particularly rich and particularly visible in the expressive arts; most specifically, in the sounding and bodily performance genres of participatory Anglo-African music-and-dance. While black-white exchange has long been recognized as a major element in shaping North American vernacular music, the extent, geographic distribution, breadth of time span, diversity, and *terminus post quem* of that exchange have sometimes been misunderstood. Minstrelsy, conventionally understood since the 1840s as a significantly new synthesis of vernacular forms, was in fact not the inception but rather the culmination of an exchange, rooted in the combination of culture-crossing vernacular idioms that significantly predate the first theatrical blackface performances.

The Afro-Caribbean elements whose entry into Anglo-American music-and-dance made both blackface minstrelsy and the creole synthesis possible in the United States can be identified not only in textual descriptions or music notations, but also through reconstruction of performances and in the body vocabularies depicted in a range of iconography. The paintings and drawings of William Sidney Mount, the eponymous focus of this book, present particularly rich, detailed, and reliable portrayals of instrumental music making and dance, and as a result provide particularly solid and comprehensive evidence for the presence of the creole synthesis among the African American and Anglo-Celtic populations he represented.

But Mount's evidence, especially considered in light of parallels between his life experience and those of his musician and artist contemporaries, also confirms the presence of the creole synthesis beyond his own localities of Long Island and of Manhattan's Lower East Side. Contemporaneous demographics, iconography, biography, and other data reveal that analogous conditions, conducive to the creole synthesis, existed in riverine and maritime contexts all over the early-nineteenth-century United States. Evidence for such conditions can be identified from New York, Albany, and Boston in the North; Charleston and Savannah in the Southeast; Cincinnati and Louisville on the frontiers; Mobile, Natchez, and New Orleans on the Gulf Coast; and out into several islands of the West Atlantic and the Caribbean. Therefore, in order to fully understand both the musicological significance of Mount's own works, and of what those works reveal about the Afro-Celtic creole synthesis across the wider realms of U.S. music, it is necessary to situate Mount in a nuanced and overlapping combination of cultural-historical contexts.

The musicological scholarship on blackface minstrelsy is rich but has typically focused on one or another subset of primary-source evidence—most commonly, on either period descriptions or printed sheet music. Conversely, while blackface iconography and antebellum vernacular painting have been widely studied, these studies have tended to employ analytical methods derived from semiotics or art history; as a result, the musicological implications of artworks have not been fully explored.

This book argues that a cross-referencing of evidence—music notations, textual descriptions, iconography, and vernacular art, along with demographics and other primary sources—reveals an Anglo-African cultural exchange that was much wider, more ubiquitous, and more influential than even the specialist blackface scholarship has previously suggested. Such analysis suggests that the conditions for the creole synthesis existed across a wide geographical distribution from as early as the mid-seventeenth century, and thus far predate the moments or locations of origin conventionally attributed to minstrelsy. Seen in this light, nineteenth-century blackface becomes, not a radical new invention, but rather the codification and theatricalization of a cluster of working-class performance idioms that were already familiar from the boundary zones of streets, wharves, decks, and fairgrounds.

Recognizing the wider conditions and distribution of the earliest roots of the creole synthesis conversely helps us situate Mount in a wider range of immediate contexts and experiences than have previously been attributed to him: for example, while he died in 1867, his artistic, musical, and political consciousnesses were formed in a postrevolutionary cultural environment strongly influenced by Dutch, English, Scottish, and Afro-Caribbean musical elements. Similarly, Mount's early manhood in the 1820s made him a witness to the historical moments at which the creole synthesis began to move from streets, decks, and wharves to theatrical stages. In terms of geography, the conditions that brought about the creole synthesis in riverine and maritime environments across the Caribbean and West Atlantic were mirrored in Mount's home regions of Long Island and Manhattan's Lower East Side; that blackface minstrelsy first took root on the theatrical stage in New York City (with Rice and Dixon in the early 1830s, and the Virginia Minstrels in the winter of 1842–43) is a product of unique visibility and reportage, not of unique or atypical conditions.

It is a happy accident that Mount was active as an apprentice, fan, musician, and visual chronicler in this same period. His unique suitability as close and accurate musical and visual reporter raises this happy accident to the level of nearly miraculous, but should not be taken to mean that the creole synthesis occurred only where Mount, the "flash" press, or Charles Dickens were present to describe it. Mount's reportage is uniquely valuable, as we will see—but its range and specificity of detail should not blind us to the copious evidence for the creole synthesis found elsewhere across the West Atlantic.

Mount was born into a creolizing environment, in close maritime proximity to Manhattan, with a strong aptitude and interest for music and a circle of musical acquaintance, into a family whose Long Island and Lower East Side connections (most notably in the person of his musician uncle Micah Hawkins) provided Mount extensive exposure to the street musics of the Jacksonian period. His interest and skills in music, his habit of sketching from life, and his biographical and geographical proximity to cross-cultural environments, all make him a particularly useful and reliable reporter on the musical elements of the creole synthesis. Circumstantial, archival, and iconographic evidence all confirm this reliability.

Additional confirmation of Mount's accurate and informed observation is found in the musical repertoires represented in his personal papers—letters, music manuscripts, autobiographical fragments, and family recollections—that confirm the central role that music played in his life as player, listener, and professional artist. In this area, the materials held by the Long Island Museum of American Art, History, and Carriages and the New-York Historical Society are crucial.

What we know of Mount's biography, interests, experiences, and musical circles encourages us to look for evidence of the creole synthesis not only in these materials (notations, recollections, and so on) but also in the iconographic information contained in his paintings and drawings—the latter almost always sketched from life subjects. The genres of and markets for vernacular and popular art experienced explosive growth with the rise of Jacksonian politics and the opening of the "frontiers," and this market in turn generated artworks (by Mount, but also George Caleb Bingham, Daniel Claypool Johnson, James Henry Beard, and others, all discussed ahead) some percentage of which contain kinesthetic evidence of dance idioms identifiable as creole—and thus, of the "creolization" of U.S. movement vocabularies in the antebellum period.

The book thus follows a gradually tightening focus, situating Mount in nested historical and geographic contexts. We begin with a wide geographic and historical span, gradually tightening in time and space to frame the more immediate context for Mount's own life, works, and potential contributions to the historical record. Following the introduction in chapter 1 of the problem (further enriched by a methodological appendix that surveys the existing literature), chapter 2 identifies elements of the "creole synthesis" throughout the Caribbean and the British colonies of North America, essentially from first black-white historical contact. Chapter 3 tightens the focus again, to the Long Island and Lower Manhattan geographical locations and the postrevolutionary generation into which Mount would be born.

The scene having been set, chapters 4 through 6 address Mount's evidence directly. Their topics include: the material culture and professional experience of the musicians he portrayed (chapter 4); the melodic and polyrhythmic implications of the musical repertoires he collected (chapter 5); and the physical and participatory implications of the dance cultures he depicted (chapter 6). Chapter 6, in addition to addressing the breadth and complexity of the movement vocabularies that reveal the influence of Afro-Caribbean ethnochoreology in Mount's subjects, then opens out the discussion again, referencing analogous examples of iconography, and using the ubiquity of these vocabularies to trace the heretofore unrecognized scope and spread of the creole synthesis.

For some readers, the material on black-white contact and the street roots and theater roots of blackface may be familiar, while less familiar for others. Chapters 1 and 2 thus establish a central narrative, situating Mount in wider chronological and geographic contexts, and exploring the ways in which his life and works illuminate both contexts and musical expression within those contexts. I hope in this fashion to invite the expert to see familiar data in a new interpretive light, and the novice to experience a clear, persuasive, and engrossing storyline.

This book's analysis of specific artworks, situated within a very wide geographic and historiographic range of contexts, helps us see both the concrete evidence and the wider implications of the creole synthesis, not just for understanding the roots of theatrical blackface minstrelsy (arguably, the first American "pop music craze"), but for understanding the ubiquitous, long-standing, and essential aspects of cross-community and class cultural exchange as well, within the wider span of U.S. history. Mount is a particularly rewarding subject for cultural history, but the unusually concrete and detailed visual and biographical data in his case should not blind us to the ways in which his experience reveals that of other less well documented contemporaries, both artists and musicians.

My personal motivation and preparation for doing this scholarship likewise implicate a range of autobiography and activities appertaining to these musical traditions. I have experience as a learner—a participant observer—seeking to cross cultural boundaries in order to acquire a desired musical idiom: as a musician, most of the genres I have played have required me to engage in a degree of quasi-ethnographic activity. I have long-standing research interests in the history of U.S. immigrant groups' use of music as a tool for maintaining and protecting cultural identity—and in the collision of those groups at the roots of American popular culture. In addition, I have experience in the craft of historical performance, which develops practical music-reconstructive methodologies between, and drawing on, both musicology and ethnography: in this sense, as a historical performer I have also been required to engage in the "ethnography of the past" that I undertake in this book. At the same time, I am strongly influenced by the synthesis of methods and perspectives employed by the seminal blackface scholars, W. T. Lhamon Jr., Eric Lott, Dale Cockrell, and William Mahar among others, who identify the semiotic, expressive, and symbolic elements of the idiom, and situate its attraction and immediacy for audiences in the appeal of these factors. Finally, there is an element of the political in my motivation, which derives from my sense that, as with many other musics I have studied and loved, the story of the creole synthesis has largely been omitted from wider musical histories due to prejudices of economic class, social hierarchy, and racial discrimination.

This book arises from all these factors.

My topic and methodology have implications across a range of scholarship. This would include studies addressing the histories of oral-tradition (especially dance) music, and most particularly those for which iconographic evidence is stronger than notated materials. In such cases, wherein historiography infers there was a rich, non-notated, oral-tradition performance practice not fully represented in the written record, reconstruction of the actual sound and kinesthetic experience of the resulting music can be challenging. The methodologies described in this book, particularly those addressing the rhythmic and kinesthetic analysis of iconography, enrich such reconstructions, as the "frozen motion" of the bodies depicted in images can tell us things about how dance rhythm sounded, worked, and felt, and about the social communities it made possible.

In addition, this book provides useful perspectives on the study of American popular culture processes, particularly those by which dance music idioms have migrated and amalgamated across geographical, historical, and ethnic boundaries. Such situations are complex, implicating many different factors, but in these pages I have suggested both a model and a set of tools for addressing these factors to yield more sophisticated and nuanced historical interpretations.

The book creates a historiographic approach to, and a framework for understanding, a group of American popular cultural idioms that arise precisely because of the nature of the (sometimes difficult) interaction between class, race, and cultural exchange in this hemisphere. Beyond my particular historical and geographical example, I would argue that the earliest roots of Appalachian, Cajun, Zydeco, and brass-band musics, for example, might respond well to a similarly multidisciplinary approach to the creole synthesis.

Moreover—and here I am especially indebted to previous blackface scholarship—the book situates the cultural history of conflict between nativist and immigrant groups, and the complexities of those groups' cultural interactions, as embodying a fluid, contested dynamic of appropriation, derogation, emulation, exploitation, greed, theft, and inspiration. It makes clear that, over the history of U.S. culture, the creole synthesis, while unquestionably engaging all these dynamics both positive and negative, has also been a source of empowerment, enrichment, engagement, and positive cultural change. Understanding the dynamics of the creole synthesis thus provides essential insights for understanding the dynamics of American popular culture, and of American cultural identity.

Acknowledgments

THE ORIGINS OF THIS RESEARCH arise from a combination of intuition and conversation: my intuition, as an American musician and long-time practitioner of both Anglo-Celtic and African American vernacular styles, that these immigrant musical traditions might share complex and tightly intertwined social histories. The conversation, on the other hand, took place on a hot day in July 1999 on the shaded porch of an antebellum tavern, built by slave masons, at the old river port of Weston, Missouri: talking with new friends and fellow roots musicians Roger Landes and Chipper Thompson about the Missouri River painter George Caleb Bingham and the New Yorker William Sidney Mount.

My thanks go also to my root musicology teachers J. Peter Burkholder, the late Austin Caswell, Jeffrey Magee, Thomas Mathiesen, and the late George Buelow; and to the remarkable medieval music specialist Thomas Binkley, who located for me an experiential and analytical portal between old music and vernacular music. I am deeply grateful to these giants for their professional example and their personal friendship. I am grateful likewise to my undergraduate professors Robert Prins, Joseph Dyer, and Dianthe Myers-Spencer, who opened for me the world of academic music scholarship, and to the staff of the inaugural class of the New School's Freshman Year Program (1976–77), who first introduced me to the wider pleasures of scholarly inquiry. More distantly, I thank the authors George MacDonald Fraser, Mark Twain, David Halberstam, and Natalie Goldberg, for their shining example, and for teaching me that the very most riveting stories of all are rooted not in fiction but in history.

It has been a pleasure and a privilege to be welcomed into the ranks of musicologists specializing in American vernaculars; special appreciation goes to my friends and rigorous discussants Paul Wells, Dale Cockrell, Jeff Todd Titon, and Scott DeVeaux. This book would likewise have been impossible without the superb work of those scholars who, with insight, rigor, and scholarly courage led the way to a reenvisioning of what blackface was and means: Hans Nathan, W. T. Lhamon Jr., Eric Lott, Dale Cockrell, William J. Mahar, Robert Carlin, and Robert Winans. I have also been inspired by many other great writers on various genres of American music, whose work has been a constant source of emotional engagement and interpretive energy: Peter Guralnick, Lester Bangs, Michael Broyles, Richard Crawford, Elijah Wald, Robert Palmer, Eric von Schmidt, and Jim Rooney, among others.

I here formally acknowledge and personally thank the several anonymous readers who read and commented in detailed and helpful fashion on the manuscript at several important stages. A special thank-you goes also to editor Laurie Matheson of the University of Illinois Press, who has been a calm, supportive, and insightful respondent and sounding board since we first spoke of Mount and blackface minstrelsy. I would also here thank Deborah Oliver for rigorous, sensitive copyediting and Susan Cohen for her expert indexing.

Most centrally among archives and libraries, I thank the staff, board, docents, archivists, and volunteers of the Long Island Museum of American Art, History and Carriages: Eva Greguski, Christa Zaros, and their other colleagues. Appreciation likewise goes to the staff and resources of the New-York Historical Society and to the staff of the Texas Tech University (TTU) interlibrary loan division. The Texas Tech Libraries provided a Gloria Lyerla Research Travel Grant for work with the Mount archive at the Long Island Museum in 2007. I thank the provost and regents of Texas Tech University for a faculty development leave in fall 2007, during which much of the archival work for this book was completed.

Among colleagues and contemporaries, I thank my boss William Ballenger (director), and my colleagues Wayne Hobbs, Thomas Cimarusti, Angela Mariani, and Stacey Jocoy, of the TTU School of Music; I likewise thank my seminar members and research assistants at TTU, most notably Brian Place, Sarai Hughes Brinker, and Shannon Crenshaw. Special thanks go to the irreplaceable and indefatigable Abi Rhoades, administrative coordinator for the TTU Vernacular Music Center, who largely ran the VMC during those periods when W. S. Mount too fully claimed my attention.

For support of the most practical and neighborly sort, I thank the owners, management, and baristas of independent coffee roasters J&B Coffee, of Lubbock, Texas, who provided literally years of congenial, creative, and liberating space to work. I also thank my root performance teachers Larry Baeder, Dean Magraw, and the great David N. Baker—towering giants all—and my brothers and sisters in the worldwide traditions of vernacular music, most especially Roger Landes and Chipper Thompson, for helping light the fire; likewise musician and dancer Sule Greg Wilson of Sankofa Strings and the

Carolina Chocolate Drops, for quick, insightful, and supportive conversations on Jim Crow iconography and choreology.

I thank J. Peter Burkholder, my erstwhile dissertation advisor and continued mentor, and a fearless, articulate advocate for top-quality scholarly prose, and my old buddy and fellow Wobbly Rich Remsberg for massive assistance in image sourcing and permissions.

Finally, and most essentially, I acknowledge the essential and incalculable contributions of Dr. Angela Mariani, who has been with me for every step of several very long journeys, and without whose company, support, empathy, musicianship, example, and love I would never have completed any of them—nor cared to.

The Creolization of American Culture

1 Recovering the Creole Synthesis

The Roots of Blackface Minstrelsy

Body to body, culture is communicated, and the more one identifies with the other person, the more easily there is a transfer of knowledge.
—Rebecca Sachs Norris, "Embodiment and Community"

THIS BOOK USES THE ARTWORKS, letters, sketchbooks, music collection, ephemera, and biography of the vernacular painter William Sidney Mount (1807–1868), and similar materials from some of his predecessors and contemporaries, as a lens through which to see the multiethnic antebellum world that gave birth to blackface minstrelsy, and to recover the roots, sound and impact of that popular music idiom in performance. I argue that the resources, demographics, and conditions for a unique black-white cultural exchange, a "creole synthesis," existed widely across riverine and maritime antebellum United States. Finally, I suggest that, though Mount in his local environments of Long Island and the Lower East Side was uniquely situated to accurately observe and report the creole synthesis, analogous contextual factors and music results were present throughout early-nineteenth-century America. Mount was a man of his times: his family background, professional experience, political and cultural convictions, and overall life trajectory were shared by thousands of other young men born around or just after 1800—including, as we shall see, by seminal blackface architects such as George Washington Dixon (b. 1801?) and Thomas Dartmouth Rice (b. 1808).[1] His experience was thus consistent with that of others of his age, ethnicity, class, gender, and background, and may legitimately be regarded as representative of the wider experience of the first blackface audiences.

However, what sets Mount apart from his contemporaries, vernacular artists such as James Goodwyn Clonney (1812–1867), George Caleb Bingham (1811–1879), and James Henry Beard (1812–1893), is the range and precision of his musical observation. An avid fiddle and flute player and tune collector, and a meticulous visual reporter, Mount was also a close observer at a crucial moment in blackface history. Because of this felicitous combination of aptitude, skills, and timing, the record of Mount's paintings, letters, music manuscripts, and sketchbooks, in its breadth of detail and demonstrable accuracy, opens a musicological window on the first flowerings of antebellum popular music. Looking at Mount's works helps us to recover not only the semiotic meanings but also the performance practices and sounding processes of minstrelsy's Anglo-Celtic and African American synthesis. These materials thus repay elements of ethnomusicological and iconographic interpretation, and such interpretation in turn allows a fundamental revision in our understanding of how and when that creole synthesis came into being.

RECOVERING MINSTRELSY

Dale Cockrell, Eric Lott, William Mahar, Hans Nathan, W. T. Lhamon Jr., and other scholars have documented minstrelsy's urban contexts, published texts, and working-class semiotics, but their work has tended to focus on unpacking cultural meaning, and, in some cases, to depend on the prose record.[2] This has meant, with a few exceptions noted ahead, comparatively little examination of performance practice (both African American and Anglo-Celtic), improvisation, the cross-fertilization of diverse music-and-dance traditions, and, especially, the ways that iconography can help to reconstruct the idiom.

W. S. Mount's life experience, ephemera, and artworks provide contemporaneous, precisely observed documentation on the blackface experience, particularly as regards its constituent performance practice traditions and the ways that those source traditions shaped the music's sound. This integration of diverse-sounding traditions is demonstrated, through the contextualization and analysis of Mount's work, to be far more geographically ubiquitous, far more stylistically distinctive, and far more influential on the wider sound and practice of American dance music, than has been remarked. Mount is of course not the only useful source—similar analysis of works depicting music by other vernacular painters is also productive—but by dint of timing, geography and proximity, personal biography and musical inclinations, and the caliber of his observation and depiction, he is particularly valuable. Recognizing Mount as a useful reliable reporter on antebellum vernacular music helps us situate his precisely observed rural laborers and wandering musicians as part of, not separate from, the urban contexts that have been more commonly and exclusively understood as minstrelsy's birthplace.

EXAMPLES

A few preliminary examples, of the sort to be discussed in detail throughout this book, will confirm Mount's relevance as a visual source for minstrelsy's musicological reconstruction. While he certainly held high ambitions as a portraitist, Mount was also a pragmatic commercial painter, and an inveterate pencil sketcher from life. Those sketches were typically employed, deployed, and transformed in subsequent oils in consideration of his commercial market, but—as with his music manuscripts, his letters, and the oils themselves—they also represent valuable period observation of musical practice.

The earliest biographical anecdotes confirm the reliability of Mount's sketches as precise reportage: "A lady told the tale of his coming into her room while she was amusing herself with a spaniel she had taught to sit upright. Mount took out his sketchbook and essayed to sketch him. Just as he had completed all but the position of one leg, the animal dropped. As he could not be induced to sit again, Mount declared his sketch spoiled. It was in vain that the lady urged him to add the little required from memory. He *would not risk falsehood in a line or a hair*."[3] Mount continued this habit long after his career as a portraitist was essentially over: as his health and eyesight eroded in the 1860s, his painting slowed down and deteriorated, but he never stopped sketching.[4] Mount himself clearly viewed these drawings as essential field notes for later paintings, even prior to those oils having been commissioned or conceived: he often appended notes, initials, and dates to pencil sketches as aide-memoire: "May 1864.—From Ranney. Dear skin Gloves—yellow vest, blue coat, yellow blanket, buff britches."[5] Linkages between Mount's sketches and final paintings help illuminate the creole synthesis, not only as he observed it, but also as it was transformed within his own visual imagination. Despite the tendency among art historians to focus on the allegorical and narrative content of Mount's paintings, those works contain valuable musicological information, as well.[6] The following demonstrate the immediacy of the linkages between sketches and oils and of Mount's potential for recovering the creole synthesis.

A young African American fiddler in *Boy Playing Violin*, a Mount sketch (image 1), depicted sitting on a tavern bench, wearing an agricultural laborer's smock and a rakish slouch hat, is transformed into an Anglo-American fiddler playing for country dancing in *Dancing on the Barn Floor* from 1831 (see plate 1).

Elements of this transracial fiddler may also recur in the iconic African American fiddler in *Right and Left* (1850; discussed in chapter 4, see plate 6).

Image 1. William Sidney Mount (1807–1868), *Boy Playing Violin*, n.d., pencil on paper, 4.5 × 6.875 in., 77.22.209. Credit: The Long Island Museum of American Art, History & Carriages, Bequest of Ward Melville, 1977.

Two Men Dancing, a sketch of an African American dancer accompanied by a (possible) Anglo-American "patting juba" (supplying body percussion), both observed by an Anglo-American listener (image 2), is transformed in *Dance of the Haymakers* (see plate 3) and *The Power of Music*, where the dancer is Anglo-American (*Haymakers*), the musician becomes an Anglo-Celtic fiddler (both paintings), and the listener becomes African American (both).

An interim watercolor study for a painting on a similar topic, *Dance of the Haymakers* (see plates 2 and 3) contains an adolescent African American dancing a caricatured "Jim Crow," who in the final oil is transformed to an African American drummer, while the Jim Crow akimbo body vocabulary is transferred to the white dancers.

The creole synthesis can be located in works by other artists of the period, who can sometimes be linked to Mount: the African American "jumping Jim Crow" in an anonymous sketch labeled *Dancing for Eels, 1820 Catharine Market*, subjected to an effective semiotic analysis in Lhamon's *Raising Cain*, is troped in later lithographs (discussed by Eric Lott in *Love and Theft*), and in a number of images not identified by previous scholarship (see chapter 6).[7] But that same dancer, or a shared model, also influences art by caricaturist David Claypoole Johnston illustrating Mount's uncle Micah Hawkins's 1824 "Backside Albany," the first blackface song published in the United States.

Image 2. William Sidney Mount (1807–1868), *Two Men Dancing*, n.d., pencil on paper, 77.22.347. Credit: The Long Island Museum of American Art, History & Carriages, Bequest of Ward Melville, 1977.

Art historians have recognized Mount as a central figure in the foundation of a U.S. vernacular school.[8] Conversely, musicology has mapped minstrelsy's urban synthesis and its semiotic meaning and recurrence in American popular music, but has not addressed Mount's work in a full-length monograph.[9] Recovering Mount's evidence reveals the ready and extensive musical exchange between rural and urban regions such as Long Island and the Lower East Side, as elsewhere across the States; also, the extensive geographic distribution of specific conditions that made the blackface synthesis possible; and the unexpectedly wide range of "creolizing" activities in the period of the 'teens and '20s, before blackface had ever made its way from the street to the stage. Moreover, we can find in Mount examples of the actual processes by which young white musicians, engaged in a kind of participant observation, learned and replicated African American performance practices, and the degree to which borrowing, appropriation, imitation, and the creole synthesis implicated musical influences traveling between all ethnic groups, both white to black and black to white. Mount is thus a key witness to the roots of American popular music, and his visual testimony transforms our understanding of that music.

AGENCY

Before Hans Nathan's major 1962 work, *Dan Emmett and the Rise of Early Negro Minstrelsy*, blackface was underexamined in the serious study of American music history, in part because of the idiom's ubiquitous and noxious racist caricature.[10] More recent scholarship has helped to nuance our understanding of nineteenth-century white-against-black racism, to demonstrate its varying character and severity in different periods, to reveal the social, cultural, and historical factors that impacted that severity, and to demonstrate the cultural exchange that went on despite it. Beginning approximately with Lott's *Love and Theft* (1993) and Cockrell's *Demons of Disorder* (1997), and continuing with Lhamon's *Raising Cain* (1998) and Mahar's *Behind the Burnt Cork Mask* (1998), this scholarship has usefully complicated monolithic presumptions about what blackface "was," "did," and "meant." These scholars have shown the idiom's piebald roots in European *carnivale*, Afro-Caribbean festival traditions, and U.S. comic theater, and its semiotic strategies of transgression, resistance, and working-class solidarity. Their work has gone a long way toward "rehabilitating" minstrelsy: not disavowing the idiom's racist component, yet also recognizing its significant musical and historical impact.

Not so completely recovered has been agency on the part of the African American musicians who were the source and subject of imitation by white blackface minstrels, or the widespread creolized exchange of which minstrelsy was only the theatricalized, commodified, visible tip of a much larger iceberg of idioms mostly submerged below the horizon of middle-class experience.[11] Some modern analyses of blackface have tended to prioritize unpacking the signification intended by white performers and understood by white audiences; sometimes neglected have been African American perspectives, traditions and performance practice—and thus African American contributions. The creole sounds, practices, and procedures that made minstrelsy possible are the focus of this book.

Scholarly avoidance of blackface at one point led to a simplistic tendency to presume that, because antebellum African American musicians' economic, social, and creative choices were severely limited by discriminatory laws and customs, the musicians must therefore have been "only" the passive victims of white exploitation. Such a presumption misunderstood the sophistication with which disenfranchised creative artists sometimes respond to social or economic restrictions. Emphasis on white intentions and understanding underestimated African American musicians' own agency, when many were in fact skilled negotiators of the boundaries of ethics, economics, and social expectations.

This is precisely why European devotees of *carnivale*, *charivari*, and rough music, like their counterparts among Afro-Caribbean singers, dancers, and magicians, were regarded as marginal members of society: because, for the duration of their performances, they engaged and subverted social boundaries. As so often in the human history of performance, this was typically done in service of creating, in a festival, dance party, political rally, or worship ceremony, a temporary environment of liminality: that is, an "in-between" cognitive space in which existing social pressures could be mitigated or alternate social behaviors tried on.[12] Cockrell, especially, has laid the groundwork for thus understanding minstrelsy as recalling liminality in European carnival behaviors.[13] Similarly, Shane White cites the "striking dynamism and cultural fluidity" of Anglo-African cross-cultural festivals, describing Pinkster, Negro 'Lection Day, Militia Training Day, and (by implication) blackface theater as "a time for excess, for release from the rigors of a northern winter and the everyday exigencies of a slave regime, [adding that] the exuberance exhibited by the slaves—in their clothing, feasting, music, and dance—made the African American participants seems larger than life."[14] Antebellum African American musicians, though disenfranchised by law and custom, were "larger-than-life" symbolic inspirations, and, as a result, were observed, learned from, and (on occasion) imitated by the blackface architects. Certainly unequal treatment was part of the antebellum experience for both slaves and free blacks. It is quite another thing, and an indefensible analytical presumption, to conclude that, because African American musicians were denied power, they were unable to identify, analyze, respond to, and symbolically contest racist strictures.

Like all performers, musicians in both Anglo-Celtic and African American traditions, though marginalized as individuals, wielded considerable powers of signification. As professional singers, players, dancers, and "ritual makers," they understood the semiotics and social psychology of their environments and were capable of manipulating creative arts to negotiate those situations. Presuming their passivity fundamentally misunderstands the ability to symbolically comment on and manipulate social expectations—in Gates's famed locution, "signifyin'"—which is fundamental to the African American tradition.[15] And it ignores the sophisticated symbolic and musical vocabularies, of imitation, caricature, "double-consciousness," and stylistic synthesis, that such musicians employed. African American musicians developed strategies of adoption, assimilation, accommodation, and creative adaptation. If the young white musicians who were the first blackface stars—the prototypical "white boys playing the blues"—intentionally observed, adopted, and adapted alien performance idioms to create economic opportunities, we can insist that black musicians did the same.

We can prove that black musicians observed and imitated white musicians, just as whites did blacks; the exchange that yielded the "creole synthesis" moved in both (indeed, multiple) cross-cultural directions.[16] The evidence begins with the well-documented ubiquity of black musicians, especially fiddlers, playing for white dancing, in all regions and eras of the British colonies and the young republic. Both economy (the ability to get jobs playing for white folks) and aesthetics (the magpie adoption, typical to all vernacular musicians, of useful new sounds) suggest that black musicians were just as much active agents, even if vastly disadvantaged ones, in minstrelsy's creole synthesis, as were white "appropriators." Thus in the antebellum period we find black styles influencing white idioms, and white styles influencing black. Both previous scholarship and Mount's visual evidence demonstrate the back-and-forth nature of this musical interaction, and confirm that the breadth, depth, and distribution of the creative synthesis were much more extensive than has been presumed.[17]

METHODOLOGY: ICONOGRAPHY, ETHNOGRAPHY, AND PERFORMANCE ANALYSIS

In the case of vernacular performance practices predating the age of electronic media, static visual materials yield some of the most apposite evidence, provided that this information is approached with appropriate analytical methodology. Just as in the ethnographic or cultural-anthropological examination of "material culture"—that is, of the physical objects, structures, and tools that a community employs in day-to-day living—study of musical performance's visual iconography produces not only observable detail regarding instruments, techniques, body postures, performance contexts, and so forth, but also deductive insights regarding movement, sound, and meaning. When informed by ethnochoreological theory, and a practical analysis of the mechanics of the dancing and playing body, it becomes possible to reconstruct aspects of rhythm, timbre, texture, and musical usage. Hence, by coupling iconographic analysis (i.e., images) with traditional musicology's objects-based method (i.e., tunes, titles, and texts) we can achieve a surprisingly complete reconstruction of the sound, processes, and meaning of performances. Such multi-faceted analysis, focused on recovering performance processes, is particularly appropriate in considering the oral or aural nature of non-notated musics. Iconography is thus an essential component in reconstructing antebellum performance.

Our interpretation of this music making is comparably deepened through ethnographic analysis of the cultural contexts in which antebellum music was made and heard. Ethnomusicology's analytical techniques are derived from and most commonly employed in the case of fieldwork: that is, the in-person, in-context, face-to-face observation and analysis of the meaning of present-day musical events for participants. But similar techniques can also be employed in a more historiographic fashion: a quasi-ethnographic analysis of a historical idiom's musical behaviors and meaning, for example, can be derived by reconstructing its cognitive contexts and the likely impact of its performance specifics in those contexts. This is the central research technique in the worlds of medieval and Renaissance historical performance: the combination of historiographic reconstruction with contextual observation and interpretation, and the creation of performances based on those combined insights. In the case of early minstrelsy, then, an idiom that predates audio recording but which is reasonably extensively represented in visual sources, iconographic reconstruction of performance practice is quite useful.

Finally, the discipline of performance studies, which draws its literature from cultural anthropology (Turner, Geertz, Goffman, Babcock), folklore (Hymes, Bauman, Glassie, et al.), and drama theory (Schechner, Mukarovsky, and the Prague School), can facilitate the close reading and structural analysis of meaning in past musics.[18] These methodologies analyze performance—whether scripted or improvised, formal or informal, set aside in formal "frames" or as part of everyday interpersonal interaction—as created within webs of signification that in turn implicate complex layers of allusion and meaning. Such analysis permits Cockrell, Lhamon, and Lott, for example, to find both recollections of medieval European *carnivale* on one hand, and foreshadowing of African American jitterbug and hip-hop dancing on the other, in the blackface evidence. However, while performance studies is effective in "teasing out" meaning, it is neither intended nor suitable for the reconstruction of sounding processes.

Hence, in the case of an historical musical repertoire such as early minstrelsy, carried in the memory and the body, dependent on improvisation and synthesis in its execution, and captured more accurately in visual representations than in crude musical notations, we need an integrated set of interpretive tools—derived from iconography, ethnography, and performance studies—if we are to undertake the reconstruction of the sound, practice, and experience of minstrelsy. This book employs the synthesis of ethnographic, musicological, iconographic, and ethnochoreographic tools in order to address the idiom's creole synthesis of music-and-movement, sound, and the body, across boundaries of race, class, geography, and time.

FOCAL THEMES

Reevaluation of early minstrelsy, its contexts, and of Mount's reporting on it, can inform us about a range of topics central to the history of American popular music. Investigation of historical dance requires iconographic analysis. Such analysis, as modeled by Malone, Stearns, Thompson, and Wilson, makes possible multiple layers of insight.[19] Reconstructing the movement vocabularies that iconography has frozen in two dimensions reveals not only how bodies moved through space, but also the rhythmic languages that animated those moving bodies. However, in order to understand the rhythmic languages implicit in iconography, it is necessary to reanimate those images: to recognize that two-dimensional images of dance capture a moment of movement—not necessarily a moment of rest.[20] As Bond and Stinson have said, "all dance is situated in a cultural context;" hence, in order to understand blackface dance, it is mandatory to reconstruct both its movement vocabularies and the creole contexts in which it emerged.[21]

The rewards of such effort are substantial: when successful, reanimation of iconography via synthesis of performance analysis and musical practice reveals the improvisational, non-notated, bodily (and thus sounding) adaptations that black dance introduced to Anglo-Celtic melodic languages. Looking at pictures of blacks dancing to Anglo-Celtic fiddle tunes gives us information about how Afro-Caribbean musical concepts polyrhythmicized both the tunes, the responding bodies of dancers, and U.S. popular music as a whole; it begins to be possible to "hear" how this creolized music sounded in performance. Such information, in addition to recovering its sounding practice, situates minstrelsy's performance synthesis as a precursor to (and foundation of) later Africanizations of American rhythm.

This is why iconographic study of blackface dance is essential. Cockrell, Mahar, and before them Nathan, all provide musical analysis of minstrelsy's published music.[22] But that musical analysis is primarily predicated on analysis of the tunes as they were notated, not as they would have been realized in performance: danced, improvised, and polyrhythmicized. Nathan, for example, goes so far as to suggest that the idiom was overall "straightened-out" and de-Africanized in the 1840s and '50s: his conclusion is that this was a reflection of a gradual *embourgeoisement* of the idiom—that it was regularized so as to be comprehensible and accessible for a middle-class audience in the parlor. But this is to misinterpret the evidence: to assume that sheet music captured the totality of sound in performance. Both logic and the visual and descriptive evidence directly contravene this interpretation, indicating rather the polyrhythmic and polymetric shifting accents that were an essential element of African American improvised performance practice. Even those pieces that in the '40s and '50s were printed in simplified and squared-out versions for bourgeois consumption were often syncopated or "ragged" (as the process was later labeled) in performance. Certainly this rhythmic cutting or ragging was an essential part of the African-creole street performance idiom as it is depicted in period sketches, and in images and descriptions of T. D. Rice, G. W. Dixon (both white), and William Henry "Juba" Lane, the Long Island–born African American dancer witnessed by Charles Dickens.

Mount's pictures of players and dancers help complete this reconstruction. I argue that precisely the same improvisational rhythmic "cutting" described in prose by Dickens, and analyzed in transcriptions by musicologist Charles Keil as "participatory discrepancy," is present in Mount works such as *Dance of the Haymakers*.[23]

Because the majority of musicological studies have emphasized notated sources at the expense of iconography, they have failed to identify the polyrhythmic dance elements that could have been, and were, improvised instead of notated. This book redresses that situation, drawing on iconography, kinesics, and dance theory to argue not only that this creolized approach to rhythm was part of blackface performance, but further that it was precisely these same improvisational, non-notated elements that made creolized dance so exotic, enticing, and engaging to Anglo-Celtic audiences and participants. Musical recovery and analysis of the sounding performance practice of minstrelsy cannot be predicated exclusively on notation, which did and does not capture improvised rhythmic alterations. Those improvisational alterations were what made Anglo and African synthesis possible, and they have made creolized rhythmic elements the backbone of American popular music down to the present day.

I further suggest that, already in the antebellum period, improvisational, performance-based rhythmic procedures were introducing African American body vocabularies into Anglo-Celtic culture: that these dances, as observed, borrowed, imitated, and adapted, were "creolizing" Anglo-Celtic dance long before the 1830s. The pleasurable bodily experience that syncopated dance provided made it a powerfully attractive and effective conduit for cross-cultural exchange. Blackface entailed a complex process, driven by appropriation and opportunism, but also implicating exchange, assimilation, participation, and pleasure.

Iconography, ethnography, and performance analysis help us recover minstrelsy's sound, motion, and bodily appeal. In turn, these, coupled with contextual and historical framing, help us understand its expressive intentions, the sophisticated agency that practitioners, both black and white, brought to bear on its creation, and the engrossing participatory experience that resulted. Musicians, then as now, made conscious choices. Popular musicians made conscious choices in part based on commercial considerations: then, as now, they sought to create music that was susceptible rather than resistant to appropriation, because such susceptibility often represented the surest route to enhanced economic success.

Pragmatic adaptation is at the root of all popular music's mutability, resilience, and durability. Antebellum musicians, white and black, played, danced, and evolved music that would sell, because such music could empower their motion up the economic ladder. That such pragmatism was ostensibly contrary to Romantic ideals of individualism and iconoclasm simply facilitated critical derogation. Nineteenth-century critics despised popular idioms, blackface among them, not just because they sought popularity—after all, so did Mozart and Beethoven—but because they sought popularity without the Romantic artifice of divine inspiration; blackface as working-class defiance of middle-class encroachment is a fundamental and important premise of Lott's *Love and Theft*, for example.[24] It is no coincidence that this same period of Jacksonian democracy marks the first major attempts in the United States to assign to different idioms Romanticism's vision of a hierarchy of cultural and thus social value (for parallels, see Broyles's *Music of the Highest Class*).[25] Minstrelsy ritualized class resistance, and the transgressive appeal that such rituals could have for working-class youth. The reality of this appeal is confirmed, as Cockrell and Lhamon have also shown, by the degree to which cultural arbiters derogated popular music, and the direct relation between the intensity of derogation and the perceived transgression of the idiom viewed. Blackface minstrelsy offered a channel for cultural defiance.

However, viewing minstrelsy only from the perspective of its cultural-semiotic meaning is to deny its immediacy as lived experience. It is to miss the improvisational and participatory elements that fueled the idiom's popularity and recurring ubiquity. Until we recover the sound and the motion of the playing, singing, and dancing body; the performance practice; and the ethnographic context in which that practice occurred, we cannot know what minstrelsy "felt like" to its practitioners, their sources, and their audience. Observing minstrelsy only in terms of its signification neglects the informed expertise, creative choices, and sophisticated agency of both African American sources and Anglo-Celtic imitators. Failure to recognize participants' agency renders them passive, the subject of theoretical interpretations that ignore the reality of participant experience, victims lacking the critical facility or creative cunning to resist or exploit appropriation. But this is a false conclusion: one the present book seeks to counter. Both black and white musicians, African American music's sources and its imitators, including not only the archetypal blackface innovators but also whites in a variety of classes and geographic locations, participated actively, intentionally, and with agency, in the creolization of American popular music.

As a side note, and particularly recognizing the influence of his paintings on the recovery and reconstruction of the historical banjo and its performance practice, it is worth mentioning the information Mount provides on musical instruments and techniques in the period. This information both supplements and nuances our understanding of period instruments, and more importantly of their repertoires, associations, and communities.

FIDDLE

From the colonial through antebellum periods, and in both the Caribbean and what became the United States, the fiddle was the ubiquitous dance instrument, played by both blacks and whites, in both rural and urban settings, in the South and North, and in all situations in which fiddlers combined both Anglo-Celtic and also African American repertoires. This is attested by general descriptions and in the Mount works (depicting black fiddlers and white fiddlers, playing for black dancers and white dancers), but also in both the Mount and Hawkins musical collections (which include notations of both Anglo-Celtic and Afro-Caribbean tunes) and in the various ephemera.

PERCUSSION

Hard-shoe dancing and the use of body percussion ("patting juba," handclapping, and so on) are widely depicted in Mount's work, as both accompaniment to other instruments and also unaccompanied, and as performed by both black and white musicians. Sharing of rhythmic vocabularies between black and white musicians is thus implicit in the visual crossover between Anglo-Celtic clogging and African American dance and in the various renderings of dancers on various resonant surfaces (wharves, barn floors, rain barrels, and so forth). It is more explicit in Mount's portrayals of both blacks and whites supplying "juba"—a percussive language explicitly Afro-Caribbean in derivation.

With the exception of the bones player in that iconic portrait (discussed in chapter 6), percussion instruments are not so widely depicted, but Mount's extensive portrayals of dancing, handclapping, and "juba" carry working-class associations: we may recall here earlier scholarship's linkage of minstrelsy to European "charivari," "noise," and "rough music" and those earlier street idioms' ritualized contestation of public space. The sketch *Dancing for Eels, 1820 Catharine Market* for example, analyzed by Lhamon in *Raising Cain*, is thus "about" not only commerce and cultural exchange, but also "about" the sonic contestation of public space.[26]

BANJO

Of all instruments depicted in Mount's artworks, his renderings of the banjo have been most widely remarked and most extensively unpacked by music scholars (including banjo players and builders). However, the banjo appears in only a few images: most notably, in the iconic *Banjo Player* of 1856 (chapter 4), and the unfinished but beautifully evocative *Banjo Player (in the Barn)*, circa 1855.[27] The relative infrequency of banjos in Mount's catalog is a logical reflection of both his own musical interests (the flute for listening or private music and the fiddle for dancing or public music) and of contemporaneous preference for dance music on the fiddle, from either black or white players.

However, though less central to Mount's catalog in terms of appearances, the banjo's presence in that iconic portrait, and the musicological details that can be derived from it, are extremely important, and merit discussion. It is logical that banjo appears in only a few Mount paintings, and—particularly significantly—almost never in the sketches, which, in contrast to the oils, were drawn from life. Mount sketched what he saw around him: both contextual and visual evidence confirms that the banjo was not part of his environment before the 1850s. This makes the centrality of the banjo in his 1856 masterpiece *The Banjo Player* (discussed in chapter 6) all the more remarkable and significant. Most of the banjo players referenced in New York and in early minstrel culture were whites who had learned from blacks on the various southern and western frontiers. Banjo is thus a tangible example of blackface mobility: of instruments and their accompanying musical languages crossing geographic, racial, and subcultural boundaries. The instrument was iconic in early renditions of minstrel instrumentalists, both the solo singers and dancers such as Sweeney and Emmett and in the context of the classic minstrel quartet of fiddle, banjo, bones, and tambourine.

It is thus logical that, in the 1850s height of the minstrel craze, when Mount was called on to depict black instrumentalists, he selected a player of the iconic banjo. What would not have been expected is that Mount chose to ennoble, rather than caricature, that instrumentalist, and, even more, that his depiction of banjo playing technique should be so precisely musicologically accurate. I say much more about Mount's depiction of a "Banjo Player" in chapter 4, but here I merely observe that the African American teenager (details of whose biography and experience are deepened and nuanced in this book) who modeled for *The Banjo Player* either owned or was lent a gorgeous period banjo and that he played it with impeccable African-derived technique. As I demonstrate, aspects of clothing, physiognomy, performance technique, and new biographical and oral-historical research permit us to reconstruct this story, and the world of African American musical experience it reveals.

OTHER INSTRUMENTS

For Mount, winds (especially tin whistles and simple-system wooden flutes) are principally a signifier of rural, nostalgic, and Anglo-Celtic contexts and experience—just as we would expect, he depicts them as essentially peripheral to dance-music practices. Instead, he ties images of flute playing to women, to his own youth, or boys. Similarly, despite the presence of a handsome boxwood flute in his personal effects, and the same instrument's presence in a self-portrait from 1828.

Mount's own organological experiments revolved around reinvention of the fiddle, not the flute. The association of winds with marginal or boundary identities (e.g., those of the past, or not-yet-mature, or "not-male"), however, connects to the irruptive symbolism of whistling and mimesis of bird song (see here Strasbaugh's and Lhamon's readings of the transgressive power of "Bobolink Bob's" piercing bird whistle).[28] The shared marginality of youths, women, and blacks (and a young self-portraitist) playing tin whistles and flutes would suggest an overlap, in Mount's world, of winds' liminal status in African American and Anglo-Celtic contexts.

Mount provides a few images of and occasional textual references to antebellum brass band music and its role in Long Island communities, particularly in his loving sketches of the Setauket Military Band's various musters (discussed in chapter 6). These large, striking, and beautiful drawings have been addressed by Kevin Scott, who provides a useful symbolic analysis of the subversive black dancers on the periphery of the scenes.[29] The precision and accuracy of Mount's musical observation, coupled with his skilled depiction of bodies at rest and in motion, will permit us to reanimate this militia scene as one in which African American dancers' motion would "cut" or syncopate both march rhythms and the dominant Anglo-Celtic sociology of the scene—just as it would have done in the creole festivals of Pinkster and 'Lection Day (chapter 2). In precisely the same way, I will suggest, the dancing polyrhythm of Jim Crow's dancing body cut (and undercut) the straightforward 2/4 rhythms of Anglo-Celtic fiddle tunes (see chapter 5). And it was thus that the participatory pleasure of African American polyrhythmic dance infiltrated Anglo-Celtic performance culture.

Vocal music does not appear to have been one of Mount's areas of particular interest, though it was a topic relatively well-served by antebellum printers and publishers, and his own papers contain a fascinating cross-section of vocal music prints from the period (discussed in chapter 5). That collection also helps flesh out some biographical lacunae in Mount's New York experience (1824–30): a period he omitted documenting in his various autobiographical sketches but which is extremely important in establishing his credibility as a witness to minstrelsy's birth.

A few songs are present as prints, folios, what look like concert-saloon chorus cards, and the rare handwritten song notation; yet almost all of his sketching and painting on music making depicts instrumentalists—and typically dance-music players. The comparative *absence* of fiddle- and minstrel-tune prints (as opposed to manuscripts) in Mount's collection, and his extensive notation and retention of handwritten transcriptions, confirm the value of his collection in fleshing out the picture of what New Englanders danced to in the antebellum period.[30]

REGIONAL MUSIC COMMUNITIES

Long Island and the Lower East Side were of particular significance in Mount's musical development—that is, the "sources of his musical world." But Mount's evidence also confirms that the two regions, joined by a flow of commerce, travel, and cultural exchange via the waterways of Long Island Sound, shared musical resources. In focusing on minstrelsy's urban "origins" in New York City, the research on minstrelsy has tended to neglect the degree to which minstrelsy's earliest sources (singers and songs, dancers and tunes) were often based in rural and frontier experience. Five Points and the Catherine Wharf may, it is true, be regarded as minstrelsy's "staging areas"—the place in which the hurly-burly intermingling of African American and Anglo-Celtic cultural experience coalesced on the street and became a phenomenon on the urban stage. But the North Shore of Long Island, the upstate banks of the Hudson, the wharves of Albany and Cincinnati, the Ohio River and the Erie and Pontchartrain Canals, were the conduits of cultural mobility that made that urban synthesis possible. Conversely, those same boundaries and arteries of mobility were also the paths by which minstrelsy could reach out again, more extensively and comprehensively, and at an earlier date, than previous scholarship has supposed. One contribution of this book is to identify the ubiquity of this cultural feedback loop and to demonstrate the degree to which minstrelsy's creole synthesis linked not just diverse ethnicities and musical approaches, but urban, rural, and frontier locations and experiences as well.

It is not coincidental, for example, that the black Long Island fishermen "dancing for eels" to attract trade on the Catharine Slip in 1820 would be found on the Lower East Side; or that they would have used the East River and the Hellgate to enter the city, having speared their eels and crabs on Long Island's North Shore; or that Mount, who lived opposite the Catharine Slip in the early '20s, would also recall and paint the experience of learning from blacks *Eel Spearing at Setauket* (1845) also on the North Shore. It is likewise not coincidental that Long Island slaves or indentured servants who were musicians would be "lent out" by their masters to travel the region supplying music for the white community, or, that, when called upon to depict four dance musicians in the portraits of 1849–56, Mount would carefully endow them with consistent symbols of itinerancy, or the *Banjo Player* with an ornament that signaled his employment as a coachman. Commerce between New York City and both northern (upstate New York), eastern (Long Island), and western (Catskills) rural regions was already extensive by the close of the Revolutionary War, and exploded with the expansion of waterborne internal trade that followed the 1826 opening of the Erie Canal (chapter 3). Indeed, the docks, decks, wharves, warehouses, and streets of the riverine and maritime communities were the very cultural zones that incubated the creole synthesis.

This is why the carnivalesque creole festival called Pinkster celebration could travel downriver from Anglo-Dutch Albany; that William Henry "Juba" Lane and Bobolink Bob and other African American dancers would travel with the Long Island eel sellers into the city; or that Micah Hawkins's ballad opera *The Saw-Mill* (1824–25) should be set on New York State's western frontier, yet should also feature German, Anglo-Celtic, and African American tunes and Manhattan and Long Island accents. Tunes, dances, and other cultural memes traveled by water: into, out of, and through the riverine and maritime communities.[31] This cultural back-and-forth is revealed in Mount's jotted tunes and collated prints, in his sketches of urban as well as rural costume and dancing, and in the bodies, postures, and performance practices he assigns to his dancers.

Historical demographics are important throughout this book to help us recognize the complexity and the uniqueness of wider black-white cultural interaction in rural as well as urban settings, and ways in which that interaction might have shaped the creole synthesis. The cheek-by-jowl involuntary integration of working-class neighborhoods on the Lower East Side of New York, for example, is well-documented and forms an important part of Cockrell and Lhamon's analyses (parallels are found all over the frontier settlements, as well). Not so well-integrated into minstrelsy scholarship is the nature of black-white sociology on Long Island and in other analogous boundary regions. Because of the island's pattern of small, independent farms (dairy, corn, livestock, and so on); the fact that manumission occurred relatively early (most blacks were essentially freed by 1799); and the ongoing contact between blacks and whites, who tended to live in close proximity, in the same communities or even in the same houses, opportunities for musical exchange were ubiquitous and multigenre musical flexibility was an important attribute for a professional musician. We know from period sources and through the evidence of Mount's autobiography and artworks that such musical exchange went on in his own life: for example, both he and his uncle Micah (a leading light of the Lower East Side's musical life, discussed in chapter 3) admired and learned tunes from the freed-slave fiddler Anthony "Toney" Clapp (d. 1816), who after manumission lived with another Mount uncle for the rest of his life. Likewise, William Sidney and his brother Nelson both learned, transcribed, and exchanged tunes from southern and northern black sources, and from the white Long Island fiddlers Shepard Jones (dates unknown) and Nelson Mathewson (dates unknown), and Mount several times depicts black fiddlers playing for white dancing.[32] It is therefore important to this book that we consider the potential impact of rural dance-music practice and the immediacy of access to such practice and resulting musical exchange that Long Island's maritime connection with the city provided.

Given the prerevolutionary roots of Long Island's black-white musical exchange (reaching all the way back to mid-eighteenth-century military bands), it becomes possible to see minstrelsy's earliest roots, not in the 1840s with the Virginia Minstrels, or the '30s with Emmett and Sweeney, or even in the late '20s with Rice and Dixon; but even earlier: at or before the turn of the nineteenth century, or the presence of black musicians in eighteenth-century armies: we can indeed trace the earliest roots of the creole synthesis back to first contact between Africans and Europeans in the New World.[33]

The breadth of at-home music making in the early nineteenth century is widely addressed in existing scholarship; moreover, it lies outside this book's principal focus. However, one crucial aspect of antebellum amateur musical experience is addressed: namely, the unrecognized influence of African American musical aesthetics in that experience. I suggest that in this period such musical influences were reaching, not just into the working-class imagination of apprentices and Bowery Theatre audiences, not just into the Lower East Side, and not just into the repertoire of the borrowed or imitated minstrel tunes. Rather, I argue that subtle but wide-ranging African American aesthetics—elements of dance, rhythm, and inflection—were seeping across social boundaries and reaching musical actors remarkably distant from the Lower East Side: not only New York apprentices and "mechanics," but also Long Island ploughboys, Albany stevedores, Erie and Pontchartrain ditchdiggers, and Catskills dancers and fiddlers, were catching and refracting African American musical elements.

CLASS, RACE, AND GENDER: VISUAL CONSTRUCTIONS

Mount's artworks are full of information regarding period attitudes about class, race, and gender. They reveal complex and sometimes contradictory perspectives on these issues, which contradictions are typical of Mount's background in antebellum Long Island culture and values. As with his political writings, activities, and affiliations, the artworks are consistent for a man of his time and place, and there is extensive commentary on them, especially from Frankenstein, Johnson, and Scott (see the appendix). For the purposes of this study, however, Mount's own personal opinions about class, race, and gender are of secondary significance, because our focus is not on his personal beliefs, but rather on the music cultures he observed and depicted. For example, Mount speaks at considerable length in both prose and pictures about race and his perspectives on the explosive racial debates of the 1840s and '50s, and Kevin Scott's work is especially useful in unpacking the complex allusions to antebellum racial politics in works such as *Dancing the Tavern.*

On the other hand, in both artworks and (especially) autobiographical sketches, Mount is remarkably reticent about issues of class: that is, he expresses outspoken and copious opinions about blacks, whites, and each group's place in the ideal social fabric—but he seemingly avoids discussing parallel tensions between the working class and the middle classes. Scholarly analysis is less forthcoming on this latter issue, but I would volunteer that Mount avoided outspoken expression on the topic of class precisely because he was self-conscious regarding his own. He had been born into the rural gentry, in a socioeconomic environment that was essentially a holdover from the Anglo-Celtic eighteenth century. In his childhood he lived with his uncle, a "tradesman," on the Catherine Wharf, and later returned to the city as an apprentice, yet there is almost no documentation or autobiographical material regarding the period roughly 1824–29. And when Mount does recount his experiences in those years, he quickly glosses over the day-to-day to emphasize the latter years, when he was making a name as a rising young portraitist and member of the upwardly mobile National Academy painters.

Class was a loaded topic for Mount precisely because he, though born into the gentry, had more experience with trade and the working class; in turn, his abandonment of sign painting and commercial illustration in favor of formal training, classical subjects, portraiture, and "fine art" represents a conscious and intentional shift of profession and of its class associations. In this respect, of course, his successful traverse from a working-class adolescence and young manhood into a middle-class maturity almost exactly parallels a contemporaneous traverse of social class by minstrelsy itself—and thus provides another parallel between Mount's life and the transformation of minstrelsy from working-class street practice to middle-class theatrical object.

Various materials in or associated with the Mount biography might be employed in other scholarship on the period: the experience of uncle Micah Hawkins and Hawkins's own artistic output, which spanned a catholic range of genres and classes at a particularly interesting historical moment, versus that of Mount and his brothers in the next generation. Hawkins (1777–1825) was essentially a man of the postrevolutionary period: his ballad opera *The Saw-Mill or, A Yankee Trick* (1824–25) provides a useful tool for understanding how the generation into which Mount was born thought about class and race.

Although not discussed at length in this book, other material that also helps nuance our picture of Mount's perspectives on these issues includes Hawkins's peculiar long comic poem *The Big Red Nose* (1824), which has been read as a complex allegory or classical parody, but which is more accurately understood as a brilliantly detailed comic vignette relating an encounter, in a Five Points market, between a pretentious member of the bourgeois and a foul-mouthed and sarcastic immigrant Irishman.[34] Similarly, a very early work by the young Mount, probably also dating from the same period, presents two Irishmen drinking; this employs all the caricatured physical characteristics with which the nativist press commonly depicted the recent immigrant population. By the 1840s, however, Mount's art, even at its most political-allegorical, abandons such crude racist caricature and argues its subtexts with an aura of middle-class dignity. The transformation of Mount's political vocabulary—not of his beliefs, but of the tools and symbols with which he expressed those beliefs—in the period between 1824 and the 1850s parallels the embourgeoisement of both racial discourse and of the blackface minstrelsy that was the ritualized arena of that discourse. By the '50s, blackface had been commodified, "straightened," "made scientific," and sold to the middle class, as were Mount's art and career.

ANALYTICAL METHODOLOGY

Ethnography and ethnochoreology help us reconstruct the behavioral contexts in which minstrelsy took place. Iconography and biohistorical study of the Mount materials help us reconstruct performance practice and performance function. Performance analysis helps us reconstruct the dancing body and the various movement traditions whose (underreported, oversimplified) synthesis led to the roots of American popular music. Music and dance, their portrayal, and the values and aesthetics expressed about them reveal social and cultural experience of the time period, though such social-anthropological reconstruction is only a component of my principal target, which is rather the sound world of minstrelsy. So music as social activity is explored only insofar as it lets us draw conclusions and inferences about musical practice.

The reconstruction of early minstrelsy's performance practice has been a challenge for notation- or print-based analysis. This is especially true in the case of repertoires that were derogated, caricatured, distorted, or ignored by musical observers of the period. Yet such reimagination is essential if we are to recover how blackface, and the creole synthesis, worked in performance—which in turn is an essential part of recovering their impact and in assessing the scope of their influence. Hence, we must employ a nuanced, rather complex combination of analytical procedures.[35]

It is a truism of social economics that dominant mainstream culture tends to appropriate from subordinate-minority culture, through all ages, societies, and situations, though it is typically at just these margins that new vernacular art emerges. Appropriation yields exploitation, but also sometimes opportunity. And, as with its ambiguous and sometimes equally exploitative cousin "representation," appropriation is at the heart of the process by which popular culture is born, transmitted, and transmuted. In the case of American musics, even in circumstances in which the appropriation has constituted naked opportunism or theft, such boundary-crossing has often yielded, as an unremarked by-product, fertile creole syntheses of languages, religions, cuisines, and musics.[36] New World communicative art forms have often arisen from complicated, ambiguous cross-cultural encounters, especially between Euro-Americans and African Americans.

Previous scholarship has shown the early blackface practitioners to be appropriators and pop-music opportunists, but *also*, arguably, creative artists—and even cultural revolutionaries. Performers like George Washington Dixon and Thomas Dartmouth Rice and their sources ("Bobolink Bob" Rawley/Rowley and Old Corn Meal, for example), like Stephen Foster, Buddy Bolden, Duke Ellington, and Bill Monroe, pioneered techniques of imitation, appropriation, adaptation, and synthesis that recur in later iterations of American pop culture.[37] Musical exchange and synthesis among working-class populations predate the first theatrical performances of the early '40s, even though these creative activities were, at this earlier stage, comparatively invisible to middle-class observation, castigation, or imitation.

In such an interpretation, the success of the Virginia Minstrels in 1843 represents, not a hitherto-unknown yet instantaneously successful commercial synthesis, but rather the theatricalization and commodification of a performance idiom familiar on the streets but previously unavailable on the stage. This is why the street audience so immediately and enthusiastically responded to Dixon, Rice, and the later minstrel troupes; their swift popularity confirms the idiom's powerful attractions and marks the moment of its shift away from synthesis and participation and toward commodification for the middle-class commercial market.

Primary-source information on the creole exchange in this earlier period comes from *litterateurs*, whose essays and traveling writings can sometimes flesh out the picture of minstrelsy's founding contexts. A canonic—though later—example is Charles Dickens's lyrical description of witnessing creole dance virtuosity in *American Notes for General Circulation* (1842). This passage is widely cited in part because of an admiring tone that noticeably contrasts Dickens's general disdain for America (an interesting alternate account is contained in the flash press of the time; see chapter 3); it is often cited because it represents a detailed attempt to describe how an African American dancer moved. A distinguished literary visitor (by 1842 he had already published *Sketches by Boz*, *The Pickwick Papers*, *Oliver Twist*, *Nicholas Nickelby*,

The Old Curiosity Shop, and *Barnaby Rudge*), Dickens made an escorted visit to the Lower East Side mixed-race tavern called Almack's (also discussed in chapter 3). Although the dancer described below is not named, he may have been the Long Island–born William Henry "Juba" Lane (ca. 1825–1852/53), who later starred in competitions and tours in North America and Britain:

> Single shuffle, double shuffle, cut and cross-cut: snapping his fingers, rolling his eyes, turning in his knees, presenting the backs of his legs in front, spinning about on his toes and heels like nothing but the man's fingers on the tambourine; dancing with two left legs, two right legs, two wooden legs, two wire legs, two spring legs—all sorts of legs and no legs—what is this to him? And in what walk of life, or dance of life, does man ever get such stimulating applause as thunders about him, when, having danced his partner off her feet, and himself too, he finishes by leaping gloriously on the bar-counter, and calling for something to drink, with the chuckle of a million of counterfeit Jim Crows, in one inimitable sound![38]

Dickens's is perhaps the best-known literary description of antebellum creole dance, but there are others. An earlier, less well remarked but equally trenchant source is Washington Irving and James Kirke Paulding's ponderously comic epistolary novel *Salmagundi* (1807–8).[39] Irving's description of dancing and music on Long Island in the first decade of the nineteenth century provides useful details of the interactions of white and black dance and music influences in the communities of Mount's childhood, and resonates with Dickens's later account. It thus fleshes out the picture of Afro-Caribbean creole musical influence on Long Island—and, by inference, across a variety of riverine and maritime contexts—in a very early period (see chapter 2). Analogous primary sources, particularly including periodical and oral-history evidence still held in or near the archive of the Long Island Museum, form an important additional resource for this book.

In the secondary literature, Dale Cockrell's *Demons of Disorder: Blackface Minstrels and Their World* provides an important model for the present study through his close scrutiny of descriptions of period performance; for example, his text opens with a detailed exegesis of a dance contest between two prostitutes on a Boston wharf in 1842, reported in the flash paper the *Libertine*.[40] The account—with an illustration by David Claypool Johnson (1799–1865) that includes a left-handed black fiddler somewhat reminiscent of the fiddler in W. S. Mount's 1830 *Rustic Dance after a Sleigh Ride*—also includes details of the dancing, dress, music, and conduct of the mixed-race crowd present, and provides an exemplary instance of his "thick-description" method.[41]

Cockrell recognizes that cultural resistance and solidarity can be identified in minstrelsy's recurrent body vocabularies, asking one of the questions that this book seeks to answer: "Could it be that 'Jump Jim Crow' and kindred songs functioned, during this period, for black people much as they did for common white people, as songs of subversion, about dancing and the body and laughter, and of how the performance of joy and pleasure can remake a less than perfect world?"[42] Cockrell locates a new "rhythmic energy" and "use of syncopation" in "Old Dan Tucker" (1843) that he describes as previously "entirely absent from minstrelsy," but though the prints appear to reveal this new "rhythmic energy," they are a static record.[43] As we discover in chapter 4, the displacement of precomposed or notated rhythm, the "cutting" that Keil calls "participatory discrepancy," was a crucial African influence on European music performance in the Americas.

What Cockrell has identified is a shift in the *representation* of performance in sheet-music form; a kind of appropriation: the straitening and objectification of a sounding improvisational practice into a more fixed and prescriptive form. 1840s sheet music, as sold to a middle-class audience, sought to capture the more accessible, normative, and "scientific" details of the performance practice, being unable to fully capture the more intuitive, imitative, and non-notated elements. And it attempted this capture precisely because a middle-class consumer, distant from the riverine and maritime origin zones of the creole synthesis, could no longer be expected to have heard the sounding performance practice. This pattern of "origination—imitation—objectification—distance" is a recognizable dynamic by which many minority popular-music styles have moved from the periphery toward the cultural mainstream, but its oral and aural focuses also reveal the limitations of a purely semiotic or text-based analysis.[44]

Dena J. Epstein makes a crucial observation about nineteenth-century notations of African American music and their complicated relationship with performance:

> It seems safe to regard all nineteenth-century transcriptions as mere approximations of the music as it was performed. . . . [Such] deficiencies make analysis of these printed notes unsatisfactory, either for evaluating the music as it was performed or for identifying the components that might indicate its origin. . . . But these versions could provide a basis for reconstructing the music as it was performed, utilizing the techniques and knowledge of ethnomusicologists with a broad background of African and European musics and their performance practices. . . . Ethnomusicolo-

gists may [thus] be able to reconstitute provisional transcriptions of what nineteenth-century listeners may have heard.[45]

Minstrelsy's public display implicated complex motives, allusions, subtexts, and issues of cultural power. But to exclusively focus on such display for its symbolic motives and meanings, or to analyze paintings of performance only for such meanings, would be to ignore the physical, participatory pleasure of that performance—the *inward*-directed, "centripetal" rewards and appeal of that participation.[46] Participation was both a fundamental part of Afro-Caribbean and African American performance, powerfully attractive as a target not only of observation but also imitation, and, as a result of this attraction, powerfully subversive. The music and dancing made audiences want to participate; this desire for participatory pleasure is at the root of popular music's appeal.

Middle-class derogation of working-class and minority art forms resulted in part from fear of the threat to order that the "cutting and breaking" techniques of blackface represented. This is why minstrelsy, like Elvis Presley, nightclub transvestism, and early hip-hop, was rightly perceived as threatening to U.S. dominant-culture mores and strictures: because these were participatory, transgressive, illicit, body-integrative, sensual idioms, originating at the margins but powerfully attractive across boundaries of race and class.[47] These factors—the actual performance practice and rhythmic results depicted in Mount's and related artworks (chapters 4 and 5), and the shared, pleasurable physical experience engendered by that performance practice (chapter 6)—are central topics of this book.

William Mahar articulates the "troublesome" racial implications that have made prior generations of scholars reluctant to address the idiom's centrality in American popular music, and the importance of "the application of interdisciplinary methods and interpretive strategies [in order] to understand the content and context."[48] Despite the racist caricature that was and remained minstrelsy's public persona—and source of its condemnation—a more subtle and complex analysis recognizes that several of the blackface initiators, among them Mount, grew up in lower Manhattan among the boys and young men who watched the street dancers during the day and formed the crowds in the theaters at night. There must have been extensive, day-to-day, creative interplay between street performance and stage performance. To dismiss this contact and exchange, as Eileen Southern does for example, as merely "listening and impersonating" both distorts the to-and-fro nature of the exchange and oversimplifies the imitation of the creative synthesis that emerged.[49] It seems more likely that the massive popular response to Dixon and Rice when they first danced on the stages of the Lower Manhattan theaters was a result of the excitement a working-class audience felt at seeing its street culture (what Lhamon calls "the first Atlantic popular culture") depicted on the quasi-legitimate stage for the first time.[50]

Of particular relevance here is the voluminous genealogical, cartographic, and oral-historical material that, while empirical rather than direct, is nevertheless relevant to this book.[51] A second category of underutilized material in the study of minstrelsy's roots is the scholarship on African American music making outside the slave South, especially in the postrevolutionary period. A particularly significant part of scholarship is the work by period specialists on the role of Africans in revolution-era military bands of the Continental, British, and Hessian armies.[52] Robert A. Selig, for example, provides an important and illuminating exegesis of this material, largely unremarked except by specialists in band-music history: the extensive participation by black drummers (and to a lesser extent fifers) of varied geographic origin in this period. Recruited from the British West Indies and from Haitian emigrant populations, as well as the Gaelic-speaking communities associated with Cape Breton exiles of the French and Indian Wars, these black drummers were a point of pride in eighteenth-century New World armies. Indeed, "Black Codes" that circumscribed the rights of Southern blacks made explicit *exceptions* for African Americans to serve in musical roles.[53]

It is important to remember that such activities continued in the postcolonial period, and that militias with "bands of music," often employing both slaves and "free men of color," continued to play a major role in the annual, social, and festive calendars of both southern and northern communities: Butler, for example, confirms the presence of families of black drummers in Charleston by the 1760s.[54] Hence, the bugle mouthpiece of *The Banjo Player*, and the trained drummer's "military" grip of the boy in *Dance of the Haymakers* (both chapter 4) take on added layers of meaning as clues to the rich multi-idiomatic musical interactions of blacks and whites on Long Island and the Lower East Side.

Judith Lynne Hanna provides a path toward a more nuanced understanding of the participatory, transformative, and durable impact of Afro-Caribbean movement sensibilities on American vernacular music, particularly in urbanizing environments:

> The basic contributions African dance makes to [American] society continue . . . as dance adapts to new desires and behaviors, its forms modified,

> its essential stylistic elements persisting. . . . In times of great transience, solace and *tension control* are often sought in traditional dances. . . . For illiterate migrants who regularly dance in urban and suburban areas . . . traditional dance provides a sense of belonging, warmth, and affirmation . . . and a relief from the tensions of the alien, heterogeneous, sometimes hostile urban milieu."[55]

Jacqui Malone describes the recurrence of dances, terms, and body postures in African American idioms since the nineteenth century, providing a detailed analysis of the ubiquity of the dancing body beyond conventional theatrical performance.[56] She also quotes an insightful definition of "the vernacular," by Ralph Ellison, in his *Going for the Territory*:

> I see the vernacular as a dynamic process in which the most refined styles from the past are continually merged with the play-it-by-eye-and-by-ear improvisations which we invent in our efforts to control our environment and entertain ourselves . . . [cites various media]. In it the styles and techniques of the past are adjusted to the needs of the present, and in its integrative action the high styles of the past are democratized. . . . Wherever we find the vernacular process operating we also find individuals who act as transmitters between it and earlier styles, tastes, and techniques. In the United States all social barriers are vulnerable to cultural styles.[57]

Identifying the "implied bodily motion" in static images or objects in turn helps Malone relocate the African roots of minstrelsy's "akimbo" body language, the "knee bone bent" cited in old spirituals.[58]

This book builds on all these sources' insights, to focus on improvisation; performance practice; the Afro-Caribbean as opposed to European performance traditions that were simultaneously minstrelsy's central sources and most powerful attractors for a white audience; iconography; and the actual sound and participatory experience of the creole synthesis: where, when, and why it happened; how it felt; and what it meant.

2 The Creole Synthesis in the New World

Cultures in Contact

THIS CHAPTER ARGUES THAT THE MUSICAL, cultural, and sociological resources for blackface's creole synthesis were in place long before the founding of the Virginia Minstrels in 1843, the event conventionally identified as the watershed "beginnings" of the minstrel show. Indeed, the roots of the creole synthesis predate the first blackface solo performances of George Washington Dixon and Thomas Dartmouth Rice in the late '20s, likewise preceding the "Haytian" dance influences on Long Island, which Washington Irving described in the 'teens, and even the blackface "Mungo" and "Juba" theatrical characters of the colonial and revolutionary periods.

In fact, the conditions for the creole synthesis were present virtually from the first encounters of Anglo-Europeans and Africans in the New World. Few serious musicological investigations of minstrelsy have looked at these earliest roots; more particularly, few have examined in detail the musical, cultural, and sociological elements that gave birth to the performance idioms of the streets, wharves, decks, and canals in the newly minted republic.

Place played a key role in shaping the Anglo-Celtic and African American cultural exchange that made blackface minstrelsy possible.[1] Received musicological history has depicted blackface as a product of northern, urban environments; this book argues instead for its wider geographical origins, including the frontier contexts that both gestated black-white cultural exchange and provided inspiration for the first generation of blackface practitioners. Most specifically, it finds new evidence for the essential role played in minstrelsy's roots by maritime and riverine environments along the Caribbean coasts, the U.S. Atlantic coast, and the U.S. inland waterways.

Tandem examination of these parallel riverine and maritime contexts allows us to unite the disparate communities and locations in which Anglo-Celtic and African American instruments, rhythms, and dance vocabularies met and cohabited: in the urban North (on the wharves of New York, Boston, and Philadelphia, and the lake-and-river routes and new canals of the Northeast and the "old frontier" of Upstate New York, Pennsylvania, and Ohio); on the southern frontiers of the Ohio and Mississippi River towns (Louisville, Cincinnati, Natchez, and Mobile) and in the markets and landings of Charleston, Savannah, New Orleans, and other harbor towns, as well as aboard ship.[2] In these contexts, slaves, free blacks, and poor whites came together in socially mutable, communicatively fluid, working-class performance environments in which tunes and dances, gestural and verbal languages could be borrowed, stolen, imitated, and combined.[3]

Blackface minstrelsy, as pioneered by Thomas Dartmouth Rice and George Washington Dixon in the '30s and codified by Daniel Decatur Emmett and Joel Walker Sweeney (and the blackface troupes they founded) in the early '40s, represents the earliest comparatively accurate and extensive observation, description, and imitation of African American performance in the New World. These early blackface minstrel performers were engaged in what ethnomusicologists might now term "participant observation": that is, they went out to the wharves, docks, canals, and frontier towns; they watched, learned from, and imitated black players; and then they brought those observations back for urban, working- and (eventually) middle-class white audiences.[4]

While imitations of Africans—most famously the comic actor Charles Dibdin's (1745–1814) personification of "Mungo" in the 1768 ballad opera *The Padlock*—had been a staple of Anglo-American popular theater ever since the mid-eighteenth century (or even arguably since *Othello*), these early caricatures seem to have been based verbally and visually on loose evocations of colonial Africans—from Jamaica, Barbados, and Haiti—familiar to British audiences virtually since Shakespeare's day.[5] Inspired by new cultural contacts in the Age of Exploration, and found in Ben Jonson and Henry Purcell with equal ubiquity, such characterizations partake of a generic, exoticized Otherness not much related to the African American experience.[6]

Changes in early-nineteenth-century characterizations seem to reveal a shift of sources: if Dibdin's verbal and visual model for blackface characters was Afro-Caribbean (or Elizabethan, or even Native American), it is evident that, by New Yorker Micah Hawkins's "Backside Albany" in the 1815 production of *The Siege of Plattsburgh* (like his 1825 *The Saw-Mill, or, A Yankee Trick*, set in Upstate New York), the models being imitated have shifted to North America.[7] Dialect, names, costume, and body language all reflect identities rooted in a new, "African American" culture: a black-white creole exchange emerging in U.S. urban and frontier contexts: canals, riverbanks, harbors, and highways.[8]

In short: the immediacy of interplay between blacks and whites in the United States and the Caribbean seems to have yielded enhanced theatrical awareness of a new "creole synthesis" emerging in riverine and maritime contexts. Cockrell and Lott have commented on the transgressive attraction of this "street culture" for working-class whites in the Jacksonian era, but I suggest that the appeal of the creole synthesis was related not only to its irruptive capacities, but also to the participatory bodily pleasures that its music and dancing provided (see chapter 6).[9] Finally, as this chapter will demonstrate, the emergence of this new, "creole" street identity, as it was captured by minstrelsy's architects, was a product of widespread and identifiable historical factors and contexts.

The rightful condemnation of blackface's racist caricature has sometimes led to neglect by historians of the widespread cultural impact of the observation, imitation, and musical exchange that minstrelsy stylized on the stage. Early blackface practices were neither simply incompetent imitation (of southern black folkways) nor mere racist parody, though the racism of the period was unquestionably part of the idiom; rather, they represent a theatricalization of a process of back-and-forth exchange that was present everywhere in the new republic. As Abrahams says:

> One of the realities of American life is that certain features of African American performance style will remain strange and alluring to those outside the culture. Not least among such features is the making of hard social commentary on recurring problems of life, often through cutting and breaking techniques—contentious interactions continually calling for a change of direction, with alterations expressed in rhythmic, tonal, textural, and other kinds of figures. . . . The motives of the Southern white dancers who engaged in the black jig at the end of their formal dances are not that removed from those of the white bluesman, rapper, or break dancer.[10]

There is good evidence that some of the most crucial informants for early blackface practitioners Daniel Decatur Emmet, George Washington Dixon, Thomas Dartmouth Rice, Joel Walker Sweeney, and others based their performances on direct observation of creole environments and behaviors; Howard Sacks describes this historical process as "an informal, interracial musical exchange that *does not neatly fit within a simple scheme of white appropriation of black art*."[11]

In this light, it is no coincidence that virtually all the early exemplars of blackface minstrelsy, the first two generations of Anglo-American musicians who observed and imitated this creolizing street culture and brought it to working-class stages, were products of transracial environments, either raised as children or working as adults in precisely these riverine, maritime, and frontier situations. Thomas "Daddy" Rice, for example, though born in New York City's Seventh Ward the son of a chandler (in 1807 or 1808), had experience as a comic and caricature actor and circus acrobat touring with Noah Ludlow's theatrical company throughout the Ohio and Mississippi Valleys in the late 1820s, before returning to Manhattan, where his 1832 performances of "Jump Jim Crow" at the Bowery and Chatham Theatres marked minstrelsy's first high-profile success.[12] Ludlow, born in New York City in 1795, had toured the frontiers, playing a wide variety of theatrical roles and properties, from 1812. It is likely that elements of the German seasonal tradition of *belsnickel*, the source of the Afro-Dutch "Pinkster" celebrations of colonial-era Upstate New York, traveled with troupes such as Ludlow's, a likelihood that would help explain the wide distribution of Anglo-German-Celtic-African theatrical comedy throughout the frontiers.[13] The Joe Cowell memoirs describe Rice as a touring actor in Cincinnati in 1829, while the earliest extant documentation of him "jumping" Jim Crow date from September 22, 1830, in Louisville.[14] Ludlow confirms that "Jump Jim Crow" in the '30s and early '40s was already perceived as disreputable and socially threatening, exciting middle-class derogation, in both the United States and England.[15]

George Washington Dixon, born in Richmond, Virginia (ca. 1801), and educated at charity schools, toured the frontiers by river with circuses and traveling theatrical troupes from his teens. Like Rice, he found his particular niche as a virtuoso performer of "buffo" roles—which in early-nineteenth-century U.S. theatrical parlance meant singing, dancing, slapstick, and comedic portraits of a wide range of Shakespearian and sub-Shakespearian types: New England Yankees, Kentucky frontiersmen, comic Germans and Italians, as well as black-faced African Americans.[16] Not infrequently, these character roles—rendered in a polyglot, not-readily-identifiable "ethnic" dialect—could be realized as contrasting ethnic "types" according to different actors' specializations, which would in turn favor actors such as Dixon with a wide repertoire of diverse accents and physical vocabularies.

At the same time, some of the sources the blackface architects drew on were creolized individuals: Hans Nathan quotes a claim that the Ohio-born Emmett, founder of the Virginia Minstrels, had learned from "a [Caucasian] banjo player by the name of 'Ferguson,' who was a very ignorant person, and 'negger all over' except in color."[17] Sacks likewise confirms Emmett's extensive tune collecting from the free-black Snowden family of musicians, near whom he retired, in Knox County, Ohio.[18] And J. G. Bennett claimed that Rice, "eat, drank and slept with them, went to their frolics, and [thus] made himself the best white black man in existence."[19]

In the generation after Rice and Dixon, influential blackface figures were likewise raised in cross-cultural environments: Sweeney (b. 1810) grew up near Dixon's own birthplace.[20] There had been an African American banjo tradition in the region since the eighteenth century, but Sweeney (later a noted blackface soloist both with P. T. Barnum circuses in the 1830s and, from 1840, touring New York and eventually to Europe) is widely credited as the "first white man" to play banjo in the North.[21] Emmett (b. 1815), the offspring of Irish American parents, learned music from free blacks on the Ohio and from black drummers in the U.S. Army in the 1830s, eventually publishing a manual on military rudimental drumming, and by age twenty-three was performing as a fiddler, singer, banjoist, and blackface comic dancer in circuses on the riverine frontiers.[22] By 1842 he had reached New York, where the first performances of his seminal Virginia Minstrels (mixing song, comedy, dance, and instrumental music in a full evening's entertainment, and featuring the iconic combination of fiddle, banjo, bones, and tambourine) in January 1843 are conventionally described as the "birth" of both minstrelsy and American popular music. But the idiom begins in the liminal creolizing environments of the southern and western riverine and maritime frontiers.

Though a "frontier" is conventionally understood as a space at the geographical limit of a known world, it is worth remembering that, in the antebellum United States, frontiers also existed at the *social* limit of the middle-class experience that most commonly articulated public consciousness. Reiss, for example, describes frontiers as places of enhanced social fluidity, for black slaves as well as freedmen: "control of the slave was more relaxed. . . . The bondsman could participate in the commercial life of these outlying communities."[23] In fact, such "bondsmen" were essential to the commercial lives of these communities and so both work and leisure situations brought them into, extensive, day-to-day contact with working-class whites.

Hence, the multiethnic, working-class Five Points and Catherine Wharf neighborhoods in New York; the brawling communities of the Ohio and Mississippi River boatmen and longshoremen; the shantytowns of Irish and African American laborers who built and eventually settled the Erie and Pontchartrain Canals and neighborhoods—all qualify as "frontier" zones: that is, all existed in a geographically or culturally distant world of "Otherness"; a liminal space that elicited alternate horror and fascination from middle-class citizens. Both Cockrell and Lhamon have explored the cultural variety and economic opportunity that New York's working-class streets in Five Points and the Lower

East Side made available to those who used public performance as a means of economic advancement and cultural critique; the 1840s flash press and authors Charles Dickens, Lafcadio Hearn, and others confirm there was a substantial and geographically widespread market for both guidebooks and descriptions of those neighborhoods, and of the behaviors imputed to them.[24]

The present study suggests that analogous socioeconomic conditions obtained in locations throughout the United States in the antebellum period, and that the first architects of blackface derived their inspiration for minstrelsy's brilliant synthesis from the cultural collision going on in the streets just outside the theatres' doors. This premise—that blackface music, song, and dance were a new translation to the theatrical stage of a familiar street idiom—would go far to explain minstrelsy's seemingly "instantaneous" popularity immediately upon its appearance: the near riots at the early '30s Bowery and Chatham Theatres performances of Dixon and Rice, and the fame and imitation that followed the first touring minstrel troupes, across the United States and in Western Europe, in the 1840s. Such an interpretation argues that minstrelsy' phenomenal popularity derived not so much from its unfamiliarity or novelty, but rather from the far greater frisson—the shock of recognition—which its working-class audiences derived from seeing "their" performance idiom, the music and dance they knew from the streets, wharves, decks and canals, moved to the legitimate stage.[25] So much has been implied, especially by W. T. Lhamon Jr. and Dale Cockrell.[26] What has not been so widely remarked is that those same mobile boundaries and arteries—rivers and canals, harbors and bays, wharves, highways, and early railroads—were both the earliest incubators and the ongoing conduits by which minstrelsy's urban synthesis could reach out again across the North American continent, more extensively, comprehensively, and far earlier than has been presumed.

The significance of these environments is revealed in aspects of biography shared by minstrelsy's architects: Rice and Dixon, who brought African American song-and-characteristic-dance to northern stages; Sweeney, the first banjo superstar; Emmett, founder of U.S. music's first "pop group." Though of differing geographical origin, these men and others like them shared—as we shall discover—class backgrounds, sociopolitical attitudes and crucial formative experiences. Their working-class, multiethnic natal environments; their touring experience—mostly by water travel—in circuses and theatrical troupes throughout the South and West; their undeniably close and accurate observation of black and white music and dance idioms on the frontiers; finally, their ability to mesh this experience, observation, and imitation in the theatrical contexts of the urban North; all argue that experience on riverine and maritime frontiers, including the South and West, was essential to the blackface architects' eventual artistic and commercial impact. In order, then, to understand why minstrelsy was the way it was, we must understand the riverine, maritime, and frontier social contexts that shaped the music of its African American sources and their Anglo-Celtic imitators.

THE NORTHWEST ATLANTIC

Sometimes neglected in the study of popular music in the Americas has been the sheer ubiquity of Afro-Caribbean cultural influences throughout riverine and maritime environments, which included but were certainly not limited to instruments, dance vocabularies, and conceptions of musical procedure and function. By 1800, black sailors had been a cornerstone of New World maritime culture literally for centuries: borrowing Ira Berlin's term *Atlantic creoles*, Bolster confirms their presence throughout the Caribbean and what became the Atlantic United States from the Age of Exploration, as slaves, freed men, and even buccaneers.[27] They played an essential role in the sugar trade as well, and exerted a powerful cultural influence everywhere that economic engine touched: the Caribbean and the southern U.S. riverine cities, as well as New England, Europe, and West Africa.[28] Jarvis points out that creole sailors occupied "physical and conceptual worlds [that] were among the widest and most cosmopolitan known by any Afro-Caribbean or African American slave."[29]

This creole cosmopolitanism moved inland and across boundaries of class and ethnicity. The Atlantic maritime environment was, for its time, remarkably egalitarian, "precisely because of the specialized nature of seafaring": ships and wharves constituted a unique behavioral zone in which blacks could work alongside, instruct, share with, or even command whites.[30] As Bolster says, the atypical dynamics of the maritime environment were essential in order for a new creole culture to be shared across genetic boundaries: "It is quite appropriate to regard men socialized in those shipboard usages as at least bicultural, as having available simultaneously two or more distinct yet intertwined cultural systems or resources. . . . Nineteenth-century black American seamen daily lived that multiplicity, maneuvering through white and black societies ashore, and maritime society afloat."[31] Moreover, these comparatively integrated and egalitarian shipboard environments migrated, when sailors (who in other seasons of the year might be engaged in "ditchdigging, boot blacking, wood chopping," or other wharf-side labor) came ashore: Bolster for example, cites the remarkable anecdote of an 1812 New York City theatrical performance, when "the crew of an American warship . . . 'marched *together* into the pit, and nearly one half of them were negroes.'"[32] Such solidarity was by no means isolated; indeed, the contact of blacks from different backgrounds with working-class (shipboard or landlocked) whites was a principal factor in the formation of a New World "African American" identity, cultural experience, and musical practice, from a very early date.[33] Wood says:

> The pattern is clear. Black colonists learned from one another and from non-Africans as well. They recalled old songs and sounds and instruments, and they borrowed new ones. Over several generations, they gave birth to a fresh and changing musical tradition. . . . The result was a range of musical expression that was both African and American. . . . It contained unifying threads that became stronger over time. *After 1800 this consolidation would become clearer still*, as access to African roots diminished, communication among black Americans increased, and full entry into the dominant culture remained off limits.[34]

Finally, creolized attitudes, behaviors, and performance idioms that developed aboard ship or at the wharf side also connected sailors with both canal culture (cited below) and the "mechanics and apprentices" who would form urban minstrelsy's first and most avid audience; Bolster describes how, like Irish canallers, black seamen and their white fellow hands exhibited "fierce pride in their technical competence; . . . cultivated a fatalistic stoicism in the face of frequent danger; . . . [and] valued pugilisim and pluck, traits that stood them in good stead both in their rough-and-tumble world and in their routine defiance of ships' officers."[35] Anglo-American sailors learned not only to sing, play, and dance, but even to *fight* like Africans: the notorious head-butt called the Glasgow kiss, a staple of maritime combat, originates in West Africa.[36] Moreover, New Orleans, Savannah, and Charleston experienced extensive immigration and ongoing trade and cultural exchange from the Caribbean, particularly after the Haitian Revolution in 1803; likewise the riverine frontier cities of Cincinnati, St. Louis, Mobile, and Natchez were influenced by Caribbean culture.[37] Charleston, for example, was largely settled by Haitian refugees, who brought their house servants and their servants' Afro-Caribbean culture with them, and New Orleans saw a strong influx from both Haiti and Cuba, as well. Most commonly, the medium for this was the slaves and free blacks who worked the rivers and coasts of the continent and the deepwater trading and whaling ships plying the Atlantic.

Nor was Caribbean influence limited to the maritime South: also extensively engaged were the whaling communities of Long Island Sound (New

Haven, Port Jefferson, and so forth), and the New England ports used by traders bringing and buying sugar in the Caribbean to turn into rum for the European market. In his first, little-remarked book *Salmagundi* (1807–8), for example, Washington Irving (1783–1859) describes a white cotillion on Long Island at which a participant dances in explicitly Haitian style: "He could whistle like a northwester; play on a three-stringed fiddle like Apollo; and as to dancing, no Long Island negro could shuffle you 'double-trouble' or 'hoe corn and dig potatoes' more scientifically."[38] Some scholars have even found Irving's description of Ichabod Crane's terpsichorean skills in "The Legend of Sleepy Hollow" to be likewise African-tinged, while Bolster calls Rhode Island, on the north shore of Long Island Sound, "the blackest province in the region," observing that a black population was a significant part of that state's cultural mix.[39] These northeastern U.S. ports were creolized not only by the sugar triangle (Caribbean, New England, Europe) but also by the whaling trade, whose participants might come from anywhere on the Pacific Rim as well, and that touched Mid-Atlantic and New England areas such as Long Island's South Shore and "East End," Nantucket Island, and the coastal towns of Connecticut, and the Hudson River ports of Poughkeepsie and Hudson, even as far north as Albany.[40]

It is thus no coincidence that, a little later in the period, the first full-length blackface entertainments referenced Atlantic creole zones and the culture-crossing that went on within them: T. D. Rice's 1833 ballad opera *Long Island Juba, or Love by the Bushel* has him playing the blackface character "Gumbo Chaff," and culminates with a slapstick fight in a flour mill that (temporarily) turns the blackface characters white again.[41] William Henry Lane (ca. 1825–1853), also known as Master Juba, a virtuoso exhibition dancer whose skills in New York dance halls were celebrated by Dickens, and which skills took him to Europe to perform for royalty, was born on Long Island.

Afro-Caribbean and Southern frontier musical practices came north, as well: Mount's iconic work *The Bone Player* (1856) employs several factors (dress, features, instrument, and personal ornament, all discussed in chapter 4) that suggest that the original sitter was from the Caribbean, and a number of Mount's sketches of rural Long Island music makers (black and white) show the Afro-Caribbean body percussion known as "patting juba" (from the Dahomeyan word *giouba*).[42] Juba could be applied to any rhythmic music, whether African American or otherwise, and that body percussion directly integrated body vocabularies and rhythmic practices: as Ostendorf observes, "patting juba is a particularly good example of how Afro-Caribbean multiple meters inform black dance in such a way that different body parts follow different meters and drummers."[43] This observation about the "polyrhythmicized body" is essential to our discussion of both *The Bone Player* and *The Banjo Player* (chapter 4), and, more widely, to discussion of the Afro-Caribbean influence visible in Mount's dancers, both black and white (chapter 6).

The Afro-Caribbean influence plays out in material as well as movement culture: the African American banjo (discussed in chapter 4, in the context of Mount's *The Banjo Player*, also 1856) itself derives directly from Caribbean models. The *banza* was well-known in Haiti before a like instrument was ever depicted in North America, and both "banjo" and the West African xylophone called by French explorers *balafon* were employed in the prerevolutionary States.[44] And, despite its relatively late addition to minstrelsy's arsenal, with Sweeney and Emmett in the late '30s, and the continuing dominance of the fiddle as dance music's essential instrument, the banjo (*banger*, *banza*, *banjar*) was played in both the South and the North in the colonial period. Nicholas Cresswell, traveling on the St. Mary's River in Maryland in the 1770s, provides a detailed description of slave music for and dancing to the banjo:

> [I] went to a Negro Ball. Sundays being the only days [they] have to enjoy themselves, they generally meet together and amuse themselves with dancing to the Banjo. This musical instrument (if it may be so called) is made of a Gourd something in the imitation of a Guitar, with only four strings and played with the fingers in the same manner. Some of them sing to it, which is very droll music indeed. In their songs they generally relate the usage they have received from their Masters or Mistresses in a very satirical stile and manner. Their poetry is like the Music—Rude and uncultivated. Their dancing is most violent exercise, but so irregular and grotesque. I am not able to describe it.[45]

Likewise, Wade cites fiddle, tambourine, banjo, drum, fife, and horns as employed in northeastern 'Lection Day festivities prior to 1800, and of course there is the well-known anonymous 1790s South Carolina painting *The Old Plantation*, which depicts dancing to percussion and gourd banjo.[46]

Szwed and Marks confirm the impact of Afro-Caribbean aesthetics on nineteenth-century Euro-American and Anglo-Celtic dance, and the likelihood that there is a three-way connection between them.[47] Both the figures and instrumentation they describe show linkages: in Haiti, the presence of minstrelsy's iconic violin, tambourine, and bones, and of hard-shoe "battering"; in North America, the early-nineteenth-century cotillion, a ubiquitous social dance often accompanied by black fiddlers, borrowed from English country dancing, as had the Irish sets, to include multiple figures in contrasting meters and tempos; parallel variants representing a synthesis of European and African elements were danced throughout the Caribbean.

The music flowed both ways: since the seventeenth century, slave fiddlers had learned the tunes of European court and social dance, and commanded high fees for themselves or their owners, by playing for diverse audiences.[48] Slave musicians, in fact, represented a significant potential source of income for their owners, so both parties' motivation to expand and enhance slave musicians' repertoires was high.[49] As Wood says, in the colonial period "learning to play European instruments allowed a black person to gain status in the community, avoid harsh tasks, and travel widely."[50] Black fiddlers adapted European tunes, "Africanizing" them in form, rhythm, and technique, and then white bodies moved to those Africanized tunes, which were in turn borrowed by the blackface imitators.

Wood identifies this exchange as the site for the late-eighteenth-century development of a unique and new "African American" cultural identity, whose impact on white expressive culture was particularly strong precisely because of its early, large, and essentially involuntary nature.[51] Africans came to the Caribbean and North American continent in large and diverse numbers, and from across a wide spectrum of West and Central African cultures, language groups, and experiences. It was only in the Americas that these persons of diverse ethnic origin were brought into a communal proximity that would lead to the synthesis of an "African American" expressive culture, which could in turn move outward along riverine and maritime channels to fuel the "creole synthesis." When these black fiddlers, banjo players, and uba-patters made music for white dancers, Afro-Caribbean elements were in turn reinjected into the quadrilles and cotillions, and gave birth to the "Virginia reel," "breakdown," and "buck-and-wing" that blacks and whites danced, and that were an essential element in the popularity of the early blackface soloists such as Dixon and Rice.

Roger D. Abraham's study *Singing the Master*, on the ritual aspects of slave corn-shucking parties in the antebellum South, collects numerous examples of whites of all economic classes imitating black dance: Mary Chesnut's undated antebellum diary, for example, describes a "'Senator Semmes of Louisiana [who] danced a hoedown for us: a Negro corn-shucking, heel-and-toe fling with a grapevine twist and all.'"[52] *Singing the Master* emphasizes the long history of such white imitation: "The phenomenon of white Southerners imitating blacks in performance predates even the earliest developments of the blackface entertainments. The earliest reports of whites dancing in slave style . . . come from the period of the American Revolution. And, by the mid-1820s, when such imitations first appeared on the stage . . . the slave owners themselves and their families had been carrying on in a similar manner for their own entertainment for some time."[53] In like fashion, white musicians from Appalachia and the North saw black longshoremen and wharf rats singing, dancing, and playing banjo and fiddle on the wharves of the Mississippi, Ohio, and (eventually) Missouri Rivers, and they imitated, borrowing their tunes. "Old Dan Tucker," attributed to Emmett's authorship in 1843, was probably learned by him on the Ohio in the '30s, and takes its larger-than-life braggadocio from the brawling folklore associated with the river's keelboatmen.[54] Of the minstrel standard "Clare de Kitchen," Hans Nathan comments that is "said to have been [adopted as] a song of 'negro firemen on the Mississippi River,'" though on his own evidence it originates as an English morris tune.[55] "Jump Jim Crow" itself (publ. 1828), Rice's iconic song-and-dance routine, of which hundreds of imitations were spawned in the 1830s, originated in a Georgia Sea Islands children's singing game still extant in the 1960s.[56] The frontier element is recognized—but mischaracterized—in period accounts of minstrelsy's sources: the origin myth for "Jim Crow," promulgated by many nineteenth-century historians and referenced by Nathan, held that Rice had first heard the song in Louisville while on tour in the winter of 1831, from "a very black, clumsy negro used to clean and rub down horses."[57] Though the story of the crippled stable hand is now believed to be a fiction, that Rice might have heard "Jim Crow" in that city is at least plausible: Louisville was a major Ohio River port and the song could easily have made its way upriver via coasting sailors and riverboatmen—which would link it with the Caribbean and the Eastern Seaboard of the United States and Canada, and substantiate the song's origin as predating the 1830s, and probably the nineteenth century altogether. In a similar process of boundary-crossing exchange, many of the shanties sung to coordinate work aboard ships were based in southern black folk and work songs—which shanties were in turn borrowed by the minstrels; for example, "Haul Away, Joe," a shanty borrowed by minstrels in the postwar period, begins as the southern black tune "Jim Along, Josie," which was a staple of the antebellum minstrel tune book.[58] Both reportage and repertoires confirm that the creole synthesis in the Atlantic and Caribbean probably antedated and certainly fueled that same synthesis in blackface minstrelsy.

THE CREOLE SYNTHESIS IN CARIBBEAN CONTEXTS: BARBADOS, BERMUDA, JAMAICA

The "Atlantic creole" cultural exchange found throughout New World riverine and maritime environments was paralleled, and often anticipated, in the islands of the Caribbean; Jarvis actually describes Bermudans of African descent as "Atlantic creoles."[59] In Barbados, for example, which was known to Europeans since the Portuguese landed there around 1510 but settled by the English in the 1620s (and subsequently known as Little England), Irish and Scots came as indentured servants to work tobacco plantations, or were sometimes kidnapped ("Barbadozed") in whole villages from Ireland's West. After the protracted siege of Drogheda in 1649, the scene of a notorious massacre, "the [Irish] officers were knocked on the head, every tenth man of the soldiers killed and the rest shipped to Barbados."[60] The earl of Thurloe argued for the efficacy of this culling, calling it "a measure beneficial to Ireland, which was thus relieved of a population that might trouble the planters, and [be] of great benefit to the sugar planters who desired the men and boys for their bondsmen and women and Irish girls in a country where they had only Maroon women and Negresses to solace them."[61]

Thereafter, the decline of tobacco and rise of the sugar trade on the island in the first half of the seventeenth century brought African slaves who incorporated other dances, percussion, and wind instruments into the cultural mix. Meredith notes that the deciding factor enabling the Afro-Celtic synthesis in Barbados was rhythmic patterning, specifically saying "the fusion of African and European musical elements was a key part of the creolization process that took place wherever European colonial masters employed African slaves."[62]

In the wake of the Cromwellian conquest in Ireland (ca. 1649–53), many who had resisted were sent into exile; to, as Cromwell himself had said, "Hell or Connacht"—or to the Caribbean. In all, it is estimated that around twelve thousand Irish were exiled to Barbados between 1648 and 1655; at the same time, sugar's consolidation as Barbados's principal export displaced white smallholders (mostly tobacco farmers) and led to their emigration, with their slaves, to New England as early as the 1640s.[63] Some ethnic Irish remained, however, and their liaisons with ethnic Africans led eventually to the creole Barbadian community of "Red Legs" who, like Jamaican "Maroons," New Orleans "Creoles," and Florida "Black Creeks" and "Black Seminoles," played a significant role in local history, folkways, and music.[64]

In the case of Barbados, then, Afro-Celtic musical and cultural exchange occurred early, was disseminated widely (including to New England, via the sugar trade), and displayed significant longevity: though slave trading was abolished there in 1807, and emancipation itself came in 1838, the island's twentieth-century *tuk* bands still reflected the influence of an Anglo-Celtic-African synthesis, employing fiddle, flute, or tin whistle; triangle; and drum, in a fairly close parallel to archetypal blackface instrumentation, to accompany dancing.[65] In Barbados, as elsewhere in the Caribbean and in the United States, slave musicians contributed not only dance tunes but also martial music, being prized members of local militias at least as far back as the mid-eighteenth-century wind bands.[66] Meredith points out that this involvement would have provided access to formal musical training, and we will see similar participation and training playing out in the antebellum context as well.[67]

In Bermuda, the maritime occupation itself was the means by which a rich Afro-Anglo-Celtic mélange was created and distributed more widely around the Caribbean.[68] Jarvis calls the island "the crossroads of the Atlantic world in the age of sail," readily accessible and "roughly equidistant" from all the Atlantic colonies.[69] Dependent on a slave-driven tobacco economy since Elizabethan times, Bermuda, like Barbados and Long Island, developed a substantial population of "island-born creoles . . . who were owned in small numbers and integrated into the majority of white households."[70] So important did these slaves become at this "cosmopolitan cultural crossroads" that they were recognized for service as British sailors and soldiers, and made up the majority of the crews on the fast, flexible and durable "Bermuda sloops" that helped masters and merchants undercut New England competitors in the sugar trade.[71]

The island's frontier location "at the unsettled margins of empire" enabled the development of a creole community who were "highly attuned to European ways, having grown up in households . . . where the racial breakdown was more or less even . . . a racially integrated colonial society in which constant daily interracial interaction was the norm."[72] Whites and blacks "grew up in the same households, fished and swam together . . . and in some instances even attended the same grammar schools."[73] As adults, members of these same households often went to sea together; this in turn permitted their contact and cross-cultural exchange with "a plurality of regional maritime cultures . . . within a larger Atlantic world."[74] Finally, although Jarvis does not explicitly say so, it seems inescapable that—in a Bermudan society in which whites and blacks lived in the same houses, "fished and swam," went to school and to sea together, in a maritime environment remarkable for its egalitarian and cross-racial creole character—the sharing of cultural expressions was mutual and multidirectional.

Though it might be anticipated that Jamaica, a major English sugar and coffee colony in the Caribbean from the mid-seventeenth century, would exhibit a similarly strong Anglo-Celtic cultural influence, such does not seem to have been the case: the legacy of Irish indentured workers and free planters on that island is found more in place-names and surnames than in the history or style characteristics of Jamaican music.[75] As had been the case in Barbados, many Irish came to Jamaica, either directly from Ireland or from other Caribbean colonies: the Cromwellian generals Penn and Venables, having failed to take Santo Domingo (Haiti) in 1655, improvised a successful conquest of Jamaica, thereafter importing Irish workers from Barbados and the Leeward Islands (including Montserrat). Coogan and Williams both confirm the analogous movement of indentured Irish between different Caribbean islands, which migration patterns and cross-cultural contacts are strikingly similar to the movement of Africans in the same period, are a product of similar economic pressures, and yielded a parallel "Anglo-Celtic American" cultural synthesis.[76] Even after the consolidation and migration of the seventeenth century, some Irish stayed on in Jamaica, particularly as coopers supplying barrels for the tobacco and maritime trades.[77]

Yet the historical record regarding specifically Irish elements in Jamaican music is quite scanty. Like Trinidad and Grenada, as well as Cuba and Haiti, the ubiquitous Euro-African variants of 18th century quadrilles and later cotillions continue as part of the island's dance music, but a specifically Irish musical influence is not so much in evidence. It seems likely that Anglo-Celtic musical elements were here subsumed into a larger body of country and court dance tunes supplied by creole musicians for the colony. On the other hand, Jamaica still has a rich Afro-Celtic ritual song tradition, as witness the presence of the Jonkonnu festival and various English or English-patois song repertoires.[78] It boasts a rich and complex creole synthesis of its own, traceable in syncretic language, religion, festival behaviors, and musics associated with the island's diverse cultural subgroups. In exploring the January Sixth celebrations of the Accompong Maroons (descendants of Akan slaves released by the defeated Spaniards in the wake of the 1655 English invasion, living in Jamaica's mountainous Cockpit Country), DjeDje describes a process of synthesis "from a variety of African and European traditions" to create an annual celebration "when music, history, religion, politics and economics intersect to create an experience in which all are free and proud to actualize their heritage."[79] This description confirms behavioral details and symbolic parallels between the Jamaica Maroons' January Sixth celebrations and Afro-Dutch Pinkster and Afro-English 'Lection Day (chapter 3). Likewise, the role of music in Baptist and related Protestant traditions was a major factor in the evolution of early Jamaican syncretic religious song.

Later, in Jamaica the twentieth-century acoustic song style called mento displayed clear synthesis (of instruments, language, harmonic language, and so on) between musical approaches typical of the creole Afro-Caribbean: as with the *tuk* bands, mento employs "various combinations of flute, fiddle, harmonica, penny whistle, accordion, clarinets and trumpets . . . guitars, banjos, bass fiddles . . . and rumba boxes . . . and drums, sticks, triangle, tambourine, jawbone . . . and grater" (as percussion).[80] The mento dance, as with the creolized lancers, cotillions, and quadrilles cited above and found throughout the colonial islands, combines African motor behaviors and European choreographic figures.

THE CREOLE SYNTHESIS ACROSS THE WIDER CARIBBEAN

The Afro-Celtic creole synthesis can also be tracked, in brief, beyond the particularly rich sites of Bermuda and Barbados. In Montserrat, for example, marriage between whites and blacks was legal in the eighteenth century, so both formal and informal unions led to a creolized population and culture, most relevantly in the areas of performance.[81] John Messenger includes some astonishing photographs of the social country dances, danced in Irish-style eightsomes to the accompaniment of fiddle, concertina, accordion, fife, triangle, and tambourine—all iconic instruments for minstrelsy—but also including the "jumbie drum" and "babala," each played by the knuckles of the back of the hand in a technique later associated with the Irish *bodhrán*.[82] In Martinique, Gerstin documents the adaptation of the colonial European quadrilles as *kwadril* ("quadrille"), *won* (French *rond*), and *bidjin bele* (*béguine bele*) and so on.[83] On Antigua, a standard dance band consisting of fiddle, banjo, bones, tambourine, and triangle was in place by 1844, and Irish musical retentions are found throughout the Leeward Islands and, for that matter, on the Atlantic coast of South America.[84]

Thus parallels between Anglo, African, and Celtic musical traditions exist throughout the Caribbean.[85] Polyglot riverine and maritime cities such as Charleston, New Orleans, and even Cincinnati are thus not anomalous, but exemplary, of Caribbean cultural creolization. From the British islands of Barbados, Jamaica, Antigua, Virginia, South Carolina, to the French colonies of Martinique, Saint-Domingue, Guadeloupe, and Louisiana itself, indigenous and creolizing ideas about music came to the maritime United States: especially to the Atlantic Southeast, the Caribbean Gulf Coast, the Mississippi Valley, and even farther east and north on the U.S. Atlantic seaboard.[86]

The 1838–51 diary of William Johnson, a "free man of color" in the river port of Natchez, Mississippi, provides an example of the "upstream" impact of Afro-Caribbean creole synthesis. Johnson, the manumitted offspring of mixed parentage, was a reasonably wealthy and very musically engaged member of his community. His diary describes musical events, activities, instruments, purchases, and friendships, and suggests an intriguing synthesis of "American" (i.e., Anglo), "French" (i.e., New Orleanian), black, and Irish traditions in his city.[87] We may note here also that the title of "Natchez Under the Hill," the source for the early minstrel standard "Zip Coon" (and later for the more innocuous fiddle tune "Turkey in the Straw"), references the "Lower Town" of Johnson's time: the brawling working-class waterfront, including a not-insignificant Irish community, where, as theater historian T. Allston Brown describes it, "river pirates, gamblers, and courtesans congregated for the enjoyment of a regular hoe-down, in the old time."[88] African and Afro-Caribbean cultural elements stayed strong well into the nineteenth century: Shane White and Graham White describe a creole synthesis of dress and hairstyle, a combination of African, Caribbean, and European behaviors they have elsewhere termed bricolage, among the city's black population as late as the 1830s.[89] Such circumstances recurred in numerous locations across the Caribbean and the riverine and maritime United States.[90] The cases of two "frontier" cities—New Orleans and Cincinnati, both crucibles for the creole synthesis—serve to demonstrate.

AFRO-CELTIC SYNTHESIS ON THE SOUTHERN AND WESTERN FRONTIERS: NEW ORLEANS

David Gleeson lays out the centrality of both working-class Irish and Africans as cornerstones of the antebellum southern economy:

> Irish immigrants generally dominated the ranks of unskilled urban free men throughout the urban South. In Charleston, fully 60 percent of the free unskilled laboringmen had been born in Ireland. . . . In occupational terms, the nativist slander that an Irishman was a "nigger" turned inside out contained a considerable element of truth in such places. . . . While the structure of the urban laboring class confirmed the degraded status of blacks and identified the Irish with the slave, native-born Southern whites insulated themselves from such imputations.[91]

Black-white exchange was especially rich in river cities through which waterborne commerce passed; in such cities, working-class blacks and whites tended to live in close proximity both to the waterfronts where most worked, and to one another, in a checkerboard street-by-street or even house-by-house pattern: “The whites who lived next door to blacks in all sections of [Cincinnati] . . . generally constituted a fairly homogeneous occupational group among themselves and with their black neighbors. . . . For example, in the East End factory district, blacks (primarily laborers) were most likely to live next door to Irish and German laborers and skilled workers.”[92] Both African and Celtic ethnicities were part of New Orleans society ever since the colonial period: in the 1760s, Irish traders had married into local aristocracy, and Irish soldiers of fortune had served the French and Spanish military governments. By the 1770s, the Catholic Diocese of Bardstown, Kentucky, was extended as far south as the Gulf of Mexico and as far west as the Mississippi River, and in the next decade Irish priests were sent as missionaries into the largely unexplored wilds of Florida and Mississippi, while also maintaining ongoing contact with Haitian émigré communities in Cuba.[93] And, of course, many Irish fought in the 1815 Battle of New Orleans: most notably, the commanding general Andrew Jackson, who exploited his frontier notoriety and “Ulster Scots” public identity, following that conclusive, much-mythologized battle, as fodder for his 1828 presidential campaign.

Irish presence in the Mississippi Valley accelerated with the inauguration of steamboat trade after 1817.[94] The Irish were integrated into every level of New Orleans society, from the respectable arenas cited above, to the ditches, canals, and ships’ forecastles and holds of the Atlantic and Caribbean coasts; later, in the 1840s, Irish escaping the potato famine were the ballast on unladen cotton ships returning from Britain to New Orleans.

Eighteenth-century emigration from Ireland tended to come from Presbyterian populations of Ulster: these were the Ulster Scots who had populated the Appalachian backcountry, served on both sides in the American Revolution, provided Jackson’s public persona, and joined the southern aristocracy.[95] But by the early nineteenth century, immigrants to Charleston, Savannah, Richmond, Norfolk, and Mobile tended to come instead from Ireland’s Gaeltachtai (predominantly Catholic, Gaelic-speaking, typically poor rural regions in Ireland’s west and south); they settled and intermarried throughout the Mississippi Valley (Natchez and Sulphur Springs in Mississippi; Taliaffero and Houston Counties in Georgia; Bienville Parish in Louisiana).[96] The antebellum period also saw extensive recruitment of Irish immigrant laborers for public works: at Nashville (the 1819 bridge across the Cumberland, and subsequent railroad construction), in Georgia (the Ocmulgee & Flint Railroad; the Savannah & Charleston and the Central Georgia Railroads, and attendant canals and bridges in Augusta and Brunswick); and in Charleston and Columbia, South Carolina.

Economic growth in New Orleans in this period revolved around its burgeoning status as the most important terminus and embarkation point in the United States, providing as it did relatively immediate waterborne access to the Caribbean, the Atlantic, and the interior.[97] Because the city was actually located substantially upriver from the sea, the creation and improvement of navigable seaways was an extensive, costly, and lucrative enterprise.[98] Central to this improvement was the project, tying together both new railroad construction and new canals, planned to link the city's downtown on the Mississippi levee and the railroad terminus at Milneburg on Lake Pontchartrain. The largest and highest-impact wave of Irish immigration to the antebellum South was that of the laborers who came to build the New Basin Canal.[99] An 1830 state charter had arranged for the hiring of thousands of Irish laborers, both directly from Ireland and also recruited from earlier construction projects in the North. This recruitment provided another channel for North-South popular-cultural exchange: laborers who had previously worked on the Erie or Ohio Canals, for example, would have brought songs, tunes, dances, slang, and other expressive culture when they relocated south. Though the "New Basin Canal" covered less than four miles, its construction was riddled with unexpected problems, corruption, mismanagement, and exploitation of the Irish workers preferred by the contractors.[100]

Despite several horrific outbreaks of typhoid and yellow fever (the latter sometimes referred to as "the Irish sickness"), the New Basin was completed by 1836, and, as had been the case in canal communities on the northern frontiers, many of the workers who had built it stayed behind to settle.[101] The working-class Irish needed to live within walking distance of their jobs, so, drawn both by the presence of Irish priests at St. Mary's Church, and by the neighborhood's close proximity to the Mississippi wharves, they clustered in the New Orleans *faubourg* (suburb) that came to be known as the Irish Channel.[102] Most found work there as draymen and porters, longshoremen, dredgers and diggers, and "screwmen": a skilled and dangerous position that involved "screwing" bulky cotton cargoes into smaller spaces belowdecks on river barges, and that is cited by name in the shanty "Johnny's Gone to Hilo."[103]

The Irish in New Orleans shared with African Americans both work and leisure experience: Irish Mary Murphy's euphemistically titled "coffeehouse and dancing room" in the Vieux Carré, which trafficked in other activities as well, was frequented by whites, blacks, and Creoles.[104]

Though the Black Codes of the French and Spanish possessions were carried over in New Orleans after 1803, those restrictions did not preclude racial contact.[105] The particular vernacular architecture of the city meant that "backyard houses" (houses sited behind white homes fronting on the street) were often occupied by household slaves, who "lived in close proximity to their owners, in compounds composed of the main house and slave quarters enclosed by walls . . . [and as a result] the interracial housing pattern often led to a disregard of the color line in such activities as drinking, eating, and gambling."[106] In such proximity, New Orleans musicians of diverse ethnic backgrounds crossed class and race boundaries, forming what Fiehrer calls a "marginal, interstitial class" that reflects a close demographic parallel to the musicians, canallers, "Bowery B'hoys," and sailors we investigate in chapter 3.[107]

New Orleanians of Irish extraction moved in all milieus: from the mayoral and gubernatorial mansions; to the counting houses and ship's quarterdecks; to the wharves, docks, and canals; to the streets, taverns, and sporting houses where "northern toughs and gamblers" overwintered and mingled with the locals.[108] Roach describes the city as thus a cognitive frontier, one in which "genealogies of performance" could ritualize competition across demographic groups for cultural space, a kind of "living on the edge of the world—between cultures, between languages, and between races . . . another kind of frontier, or complex of frontiers, in which human difference, like selvage, forms the seams at which separate worlds meet."[109]

As a result, boundary-crossing musical exchange was an essential part of the city's expressive arts: Kmen argues that the legendary Place Congo, a multiracial working-class neighborhood market on the north side of the Vieux Carré, was already a zone of "containment" by the 1810s, wherein local government attempted to confine long-standing festival behaviors formerly practiced throughout the city. The famous New Orleans accounts by French-born architect and traveler Benjamin Latrobe, which describe African-derived singing and dancing at Place Congo, and include sketches of string and percussion instruments, date from this same period.[110] And James R. Creecy's 1834 reports in New Orleans describe the use of the precise combination of protominstrel instruments, "banjos, tom-toms, violins, jawbones, [and] triangles," almost a decade before the first performances by the Virginia Minstrels.[111]

Kmen links the apotheosis of cultural exchange symbolized by Congo Square to the influx of West Indian refugees, and suggests that contact between Afro-Cuban-Haitian immigrants, French Creoles, and Anglo "'Méricains" was a major point of exchange for Caribbean music and dance practices and the source for "American" songs such as "Jim Along Josey," "Yellow Gals," and "Old Virginia Never Tire." As we have seen, many such tunes were also borrowed as shanties (seagoing work songs) in precisely the same period, probably by black sailors working out of New Orleans and the Atlantic ports into the Caribbean and north along the Mississippi, Ohio, and Missouri.[112]

By the 1830s, and despite the contribution made by Irish and African American laborers to the New Basin Canal's completion, newspapers viewed with alarm their public presence, commented at length on their destabilizing behavior, and lamented the social and sexual contact that went on between the two groups.[113] Fischer cites the 1816 public ordinance that forbade "'any white person to occupy any of the places set apart for people of color [the latter of whom were] likewise forbidden to occupy any of those reserved for white persons.'"[114] That the city government felt it necessary to pass legal ordinances prohibiting these behaviors of course confirms that precisely such mingling was going on—and that it specifically entailed whites who, like the readers of the flash press and the architects of minstrelsy elsewhere, sought out culture-crossing contexts, performances, and social contacts:

> While the segregation system prevented Negroes from crossing the color line and participating in white activities and using white facilities, it was virtually powerless to prevent whites who so desired from mixing freely with Negroes in colored taverns, bawdyhouses, and dance halls. In these clandestine pursuits, the color line broke down completely. . . . It was quite common for white men and boys to frequent these Negro saloons "to revel and dance . . . for whole nights with a lot of men and women of saffron color, or quite black, either slave or free."[115]

As was the case on the frontiers, so it was also in New Orleans: those informants imitated by the first blackface practitioners—the men who Rice and Dixon, Sweeney and Emmett observed and copied—honed their performance skills in multiethnic environments. John "Picayune" Butler, a legendary street singer and banjo player, had come to New Orleans in the 1820s from what was then called the French West Indies, held a residency at the St. Charles Theatre in the '30s, was immortalized in the 1857 hit song "Picayune Butler's Come to Town," allegedly taught the blackface circus performer George Nichols to sing and dance "Jump Jim Crow," and was known up and down riverfronts as far north as Cincinnati, dying in 1864.[116] Nichols himself is credited with popularizing "Clare de Kitchen" (another minstrel song derived from English morris dance) after "hearing it sung by negro firemen on the Mississippi River."[117]

An even more direct and extensive inspiration was "Old Corn Meal," a singing-dancing New Orleans street vendor who was so well-known in the early '30s that he eventually appeared on the stage of the St. Charles Theater, with his horse and cart, performing his signature song "Fresh Corn Meal," based on a street call.[118] He sang both African American and Anglo-Celtic songs such as "Long Tail Blue" (an early inspiration for "Zip Coon"), "Sich a Gittin-Up Stairs" (another based in an English morris-dance song, and known up and down the Mississippi Valley), and "Rosin the Beau" (an Anglo-Celtic folk tune, but also documented as appearing in the repertoire of black rivermen), utilizing a huge range of African-derived falsetto and false-bass vocal techniques.[119] For a time, "Old Corn Meal" was something of a visual icon in the *New Orleans Picayune*, occasionally sharing the bill with Caucasian blackface practitioners; both Nichols and Rice had opportunities to catch his act during mid-1830s visits to the city.[120]

URBAN FRONTIERS: CINCINNATI

New Orleans provides a particularly well-documented example of black-white musical exchange, but the dynamics of that exchange are reproduced in a number of other riverine and maritime cities. A series of scalable digital scans of eight daguerreotypes depicting the Cincinnati waterfront taken by Charles Fontayne and William Porter on September 24, 1848, reflecting the remarkable handiwork of the photographic restoration technicians at the George Eastman House Museum in Rochester, New York, and published in *Wired* magazine in early 2011, provide a window on Cincinnati's antebellum communities.[121] In the antebellum period, the city, founded in the wake of the revolution, was a major trading port linking Appalachia and the Ohio River Valley, and formed the very boundary between North and South. The Ohio was thus a frontier for the physical and symbolic confrontation of slaveholding versus abolitionist rhetoric and consciousness, and it is no coincidence, for example, that the climax of Harriet Beecher Stowe's iconic *Uncle Tom's Cabin*, featuring the escape of the slave heroine Eliza, infant in arms, and based on a true historical event, is set on the frozen ice of the Ohio River. In the 1840s, this port city, a major way station on the Underground Railroad, and cited in the coded (though possibly apocryphal) railroad song "Follow the Drinking Gourd," had the largest population of free blacks, over 2,200, anywhere in the North.

At the same time, the construction of the Miami & Erie Canal (1825–27) brought English and Irish canallers to the River, as would the contemporaneous Erie Canal diggings linking the Middle West and New York City. Not surprisingly, considerable competition for jobs existed in Cincinnati between blacks and whites. The Black Codes from 1804 drastically restricted black freedoms, but there were still ongoing racial persecutions, culminating with the riots of 1829, after which a substantial number of free blacks relocated to Canada. The city would eventually play a key role as an embarkation point for Union forces during the war, and the population was actually placed under Union martial law in July 1863 due to fears of pro-South uprisings.

At the time that the Fontayne-Porter images were taken, in the late '40s, Stephen Foster was working on the Cincinnati waterfront as a shipping clerk, the steamboat was entering its brief apotheosis as the heart of U.S. commerce, and, most importantly, the city was an epicenter of black-white musical exchange, particularly along the wharves and docks that were the foundation of its trade.[122] In a much-publicized court case, the "laborer, butcher, barber, and fiddler" Black Bill was nearly kidnapped by slave stealers on the accusation that he was a fugitive from West Virginia, but was defended by locals, not least because "his services were indispensable at dances 'by his ability to play the fiddle and banjo,'" while Dan Emmett was returning from army service just across the river in Covington, Kentucky, to Mount Vernon, Ohio, in part to collect tunes from his African American musical neighbors the Snowdens.[123]

The Fontayne-Porter daguerreotypes, then, capture not only what is claimed as the "first urban photograph ever taken," not only a particular date and time in the 1840s (a little before 2 P.M. on September 24, 1848, as confirmed both by Way and Vitz's painstaking comparison of steamship tables and the clock face visible in one image), but also the first photographs ever taken of free blacks.[124] For the purposes of this book, that serendipity is keenly significant, because it captures for us, at a remarkably early date, precisely the multiracial, frontier, riverine contexts and populations in which blackface minstrelsy—and its inspirations and antecedents—first came into being.

In the 1870s, the journalist Lafcadio Hearn would describe "Negro" singers on the wharves of Cincinnati who could "mimic the Irish accent to a degree of perfection which an American, Englishman, or German could not hope to acquire," and, in a series of essays, a remarkable range of waterfront musical activity in working-class bars and taverns.[125] The lush beauty of Hearn's accounts of life on the waterfront and along "the Row" anticipates the kind of exoticism with which he would likewise depict cultural behavior in New Orleans and Japan, where he settled and eventually died, in 1904. In pieces such as "Black Varieties: The Minstrels of the Row: Picturesque Scenes Without Scenery" from 1875, Hearn provides detailed descriptions of the waterfront tavern called Pickett's Hotel, including setting, décor, time of day, light, costume, the wildness of the entertainments and of the audience response, and dwells lingeringly on the women, who manifested "every conceivable hue possible to the human skin."[126] At the same time, Hearn also describes elements of Afro-Caribbean dress, ornament, and conduct among the "roustabouts and their girls" who make up the crowd. And he portrays a troupe of African American minstrels, including "three professionals from Louisville," providing music, comedy, blackface makeup, and transvestite turns, all in keeping with minstrelsy archetypes.[127] Though Hearn's reports date from the 1870s, demographics and other indirect evidence suggest that the postbellum exchange he describes was equally fertile, and influential on the early roots of minstrelsy, in the prewar period, as well.

These protobohemian subcultures, in which free blacks, working-class whites, and slumming members of the middle-class all collided, are evoked in the editorial content and reader correspondence of the so-called flash press: a relatively short-lived (early 1840s) genre of street literature, peddling mostly scandal, opinion, and eroticism, whose target audience comprised precisely these same groups.[128] Though flash papers, including *The Whip* and blackface practitioner George Washington Dixon's ventures, focused on nightlife in the eastern cities, their correspondents and eager subscribers "map out an impressively wide community of readers, up the Hudson . . . into Connecticut and Massachusetts . . . south through Newark and New Brunswick, to Philadelphia, Baltimore, and even Augusta Georgia, and west to Cleveland and Cincinnati."[129] Moreover, there is contemporaneity and, in some cases, biographical overlap between the flash press and minstrelsy: Dixon himself, as his 1830s career with "Coal Black Rose" faded, became a founding publisher of the flash paper *Polyanthos* (publ. 1838–42)—and the short, colorful career of that scandalous rag reflects, writ large, the transgressive factors Lott finds in Dixon's earlier performance career. In fact, William J. Snelling and several other publishers involved with the flash press shared similar backgrounds with blackface architects: almost all came from multiethnic urban working-class environments, and Dixon himself was reputedly the son of a barber.[130] The roots of Northeast and New York City "bohemianism," in other words, predate the use of that term in Europe to describe boundary-crossing urban arts communities.[131]

The antebellum flash press, including also Lafcadio Hearn's postbellum "ethnographic" reporting, confirms this multiracial and multiclass exchange, focusing around music, dance, and other entertainments, in working-class waterfront urban neighborhoods. Sites such as these, throughout the Atlantic and Caribbean coasts and the inner canal and river towns, played a crucial role in the roots of minstrelsy. In fact, the informants for the first blackface practitioners—the men who T. D. Rice and G. W. Dixon, Joe Sweeney and Dan Emmett observed and imitated—can be demonstrated to have emerged from just such environments. John "Picayune" Butler of New Orleans competed in New York banjo competitions and was known as far north as Cincinnati. The song "Jump Jim Crow" likewise has associations with the city; though the eponymous informant may never have existed, the chance that a mimetic children's song that originated, like Picayune Butler himself, in the Caribbean might have made its way upriver to the Cincinnati waterfront is certainly not beyond the bounds of possibility.[132] Both musicians and tunes themselves crossed boundaries of class, culture, and ethnicity.[133]

Similarly, the ubiquitous eighteenth-century "High Road to Edinburgh" tune, a relative of "Star of the County Down" that was borrowed and distributed widely in Britain, Ireland, and the United States, provides one source for the minstrel melody "Clar de Kitchen." Kuntz quotes a particularly interesting, very early frontier account of that tune's usages and companion pieces, in the context of the cornhuskings that Abrahams has identified as another site for black-white musical exchange.[134] In fact, touring actors and singers were "blacking up" on the frontiers as well as in the East long before Rice, Dixon, or Emmett ever trod the New York boards: Hans Nathan cites the performances of Edwin Forrest as "Cuffee, a Kentucky Negro," in *The Tailor in Distress; or, A Yankee Trick*, which played in Cincinnati in 1823.[135] This sort of blackface theatrics almost exactly coincides with the theatrical ventures of the New York merchant and musician Micah Hawkins (uncle to William Sidney Mount), who includes caricatures of blacks, Irish, Yankees, and Pennsylvania Dutch in his 1825 *The Saw-Mill; or, A Yankee Trick*, set in Upstate New York during the construction of the Erie Canal (chapter 3). African American actors were performing Shakespeare concurrently at the African Grove Theatre in Manhattan, while the English comic actor Charles Mathews had developed an elaborate touring one-man show based on U.S. character types as far back as the 1790s.

Under "The Old Frontiers" in this chapter, we see Lafcadio Hearn's postbellum reportage as a folklorist observing and describing behaviors, ethnicities, songs, and dances in Cincinnati.[136] But the circumstances that made this riverine town—the "boundary" between the North and South—such a rich site for new musical innovation were in place long before the war. We can identify those circumstances in the Ohio River activities of two blackface generations' leading architects: in the first, Thomas Dartmouth Rice, who played the city on numerous occasions with Ludlow's touring theatrical company (in which he specialized in dialect, comic, and "buffo" roles) in the 1820s, and, in the second, Daniel Decatur Emmett, born in integrated Mount Vernon, Ohio, and founder of the Virginia Minstrels, in the 1840s.

Rice was born in 1808 on the Lower East Side of New York, near the Catherine Wharf where W. S. Mount's uncle Micah Hawkins ran a tavern, but by 1827 he was touring as a comic actor with frontier theatrical troupes; by 1829 he is reported performing with Alexander Drake's company. A contemporary describes Rice's extensive experience at playing transgressive, comic, or rebellious characters, including clerks, servants, slapstick Shakespearian fools, and caricatured Irish and Scots.[137] He eventually joined Noah Ludlow's company and performed up and down the Ohio and parts of the Mississippi, playing Cincinnati, Louisville, and Mobile—all river towns with strong elements of cross-cultural exchange, not only between blacks, whites, and Native Americans, but also expat Europeans, and both Atlantic and Caribbean travelers.[138] By summer 1832, when Rice left Ludlow's company in Cincinnati, both he and George Washington Dixon (b. 1801?) were pioneering solo theatrical comic turns in blackface, combining singing, dancing, and banjo or fiddle playing: Dixon with the infectious "Coal Black Rose" and Rice with the archetypal "Jump Jim Crow." An anonymous "Scottish Country Dance Tune," printed in Howe's *Complete Preceptor for the Accordion* (1843), is identified by Nathan as a source for Dixon's signature "Coal Black Rose."[139]

Daniel Decatur Emmett (b. 1815), whose blacksmith father had homesteaded into northeast Ohio from Staunton, Virginia (at the foot of the Appalachian Mountains, not far from Joel Walker Sweeney's birthplace at Appomattox), around 1812, was brought up in Mount Vernon, an area that from its settlement included a free-black population.[140] By 1834 he had enlisted in the army and was learning drumming at either Newport or Jefferson Barracks in Kentucky from the black percussionist John J. "Juba" Clark, who had trained in the War of 1812. He apparently also worked as a printer in Cincinnati in mid-decade and thus, like Mount a decade before (see chapter 3) had a front-row seat to the creole synthesis.[141]

By 1838, Emmett was playing a circus in Cincinnati and supplying new words for the tune "Bill Crowder" to yield "Gumbo Chaff." Two years later, he toured with the Cincinnati Circus Company throughout Ohio, Indiana, Virginia, and Kentucky.[142] Carlin further confirms that integrated audiences were common in antebellum Cincinnati in this period, while it is widely reported that Pinkster, the colonial-era African American syncretic festival that originated in Anglo-Dutch upstate New York and later spread throughout New England, was celebrated on the Cincinnati levees by "jig dancers" performing African-style hard-shoe steps ("Coonjine songs") to the tune of the "Virginia Reel."[143] The "Coonjine" was a repertoire of songs used, in West African style, to coordinate the rhythms of wharf-side work, including "screwing" cotton—and with the specific goal of bouncing the boards of the wharf to add a spring to the workers' steps. The performance practice of these songs thus recalls and foreshadows the hard-shoe dancing depicted in *Dancing for Eels, 1820 Catharine Wharf*.[144]

THE RIVERINE ENVIRONMENT

Riverine and maritime spaces—in the Caribbean, the Atlantic, the Mississippi, and the Ohio—were crucial in providing both the practical conditions and the cultural exchanges that enabled the creole synthesis. Parallel geographical situations provide parallel historical examples: the Hudson River Valley, which linked New York's German-Dutch-African "upstate" and Anglo-African "downstate"; Long Island Sound, which enabled a little-documented but steady, early, and ubiquitous interaction between black and white, rural and urban populations, and the Atlantic sugar, whaling, and trading lines; and the Ohio River Valley, which connected Appalachia, the Mississippi and the Caribbean, formed the boundary of slave versus free states, introduced the Afro-Caribbean banjo to upland whites and to Anglo-Appalachian dance music, and figured prominently in both southern slave and northern abolitionist folklore.[145]

All these locales brought into contact diverse cosmopolitan and transient populations in zones of commerce and mercantile exchange, thus providing both a smorgasbord of culturally diverse modes of expression, but also a degree of urban anonymity. Such anonymity was useful for individuals who, unknown to one another, could assume or attempt new identities: most notoriously, the abolitionist author and activist Frederick Douglass escaped from the slave state of Maryland to Philadelphia in the free state of Pennsylvania simply by donning a merchant seaman's clothes and boarding a train.[146] The northern black dandies who aroused middle-class white anxiety in the colonial period, and were later parodied by Dixon as "Zip Coon" for the same reasons, were able to conduct themselves with comparative social freedom precisely because of this same urban anonymity.[147]

Moreover, because these locations were public "commons" space—that is, physical space whose multifunctionality made formal restriction of their usage difficult—they became home to street cultures that middle-class society viewed as embodying a spectrum of subversive behaviors from "exotic" to "immoral." This in turn elicited and enabled voyeurism, intentional public display, and the ritual working-out of social or cultural resistance, phenomena explored extensively by Lhamon, Lott, and Cockrell in their studies of blackface minstrelsy. Public spaces were conducive to social groups that thrived on transgression of middle-class mores: prostitutes and criminals, yes, but also vendors, singers, dancers, and other public performers. Commerce and display crossed social boundaries and birthed cultural exchange; as Mason points out, public performance "serve[d] both ornamental and *entrepreneurial* purposes."[148]

Third, because riverine and maritime spaces were extensively populated by sailors and other transients, they provided avenues through which mutable social behaviors from the more racially fluid environments of frontiers, shipboard, and the Creole Caribbean could be introduced into the more rigid race-and-class dynamics of the continental United States. They were thus analogous to later New World communities in which creole street culture gave rise to new cultural expressions (the obvious examples being later syncretic musics of the Caribbean: reggae, calypso, samba, and so on).

Thus it is no surprise that Five Points and the Lower East Side in New York, the transient communities of the Ohio and Mississippi Rivers and the Erie and Pontchartrain Canals, the Afro-Caribbean settlements of the Georgia Sea Islands and the Sugar Islands, all should have been favorite subjects of display, description and depiction for the middle-class gaze—in illustrated papers, thunder-and-brimstone sermons, and travelers' tales. As with the later Storyville in New Orleans or Harlem in New York, such zones of intracultural display permitted the virtuous middle class both the opportunity for condemnation and the titillation of transgression.[149] The remainder of this chapter explores examples of the evidence—iconographic, musicological, and biographical—of the riverine and maritime zones' role as incubators of the creole synthesis.

THE RIVERINE FRONTIERS: BEARD'S WESTERN RAFTSMEN

We can now turn to a preliminary example of iconographic analysis that, like minstrelsy itself, reflects the riverine and maritime creole synthesis, and that will serve as a model for our studies of Mount's own works in chapters 4 and 6. The item is a little-known frontier landscape by Mount's contemporary, the Missouri River artist James Henry Beard (1811/1812/1814?–1893).

Analysis of Beard's *Western Raftsmen* (1846), as of minstrelsy's wider melodic, rhythmic, and iconographic record, confirms that some antebellum vernacular painters, as with the blackface architects, were close observers: they watched, learned from, and imitated boundary-crossing individuals of both races. This realization—that the distribution of vernacular iconography parallels the distribution of vernacular musical idioms—expands the map of minstrelsy's geography beyond its presumed northeastern and urban origins, along the cross-cultural highways of the great U.S. rivers and canals: the Hudson, Allegheny, Ohio, Mississippi, Missouri, Erie, and Pontchartrain. It further helps us locate Caribbean, African, English, Scottish, and Irish inspirations in these multiracial polyglot communities; and trace their cultural integration via demographics, description, first-person accounts, reconstruction, and—our present topic—iconography.

The documentation for minstrelsy's creole roots is relatively diffuse but none the less persuasive. The iconographic analyses of W. T. Lhamon Jr., Dale Cockrell's studies of newspaper images and description, Hans Nathan's comparative melodic analysis, Robert Carlin's reconstructions of instruments and their performance practices, can now be supplemented with additional data: statistical and circumstantial evidence, ships' records and census information, and, especially, the work of vernacular painters, both in the U.S. North and the West.[150] In the case of minstrelsy, an idiom whose linkage of music-sound and the visual vocabularies of dance is one of its most directly Afro-Caribbean traits, and whose movement vocabularies are comparatively "conservative," such iconographic study provides a treasure trove of musicological information.[151]

James Henry Beard, the painter of *Western Raftsmen*, was a New York–born, Ohio-raised vernacular artist. Serving an early apprenticeship on the Ohio and Missouri Rivers, Beard joins Bingham (1811–1879) and Mount (1807–1868) in a company whose careers and catalogs reflect the sense of expanded possibilities of the Jacksonian era (roughly 1828–50). Both these painters and the blackface originators were much of an age: painters Beard, Bingham, and Mount were born in 1812, 1811, and 1807, respectively; minstrels Dixon, Rice, Emmett, and Sweeney in 1801, 1808, 1815, and 1810. Their lives share a number of significant influences, which include the expansion of class, economic, and social opportunities that new careers in the arts made feasible; the use of nationalist allegory as a means of selling art and a pragmatic commercial interest in nostalgic, patriotic, historical, or vernacular topics; a close practical contact with and observation of ethnic folkways and the working trades; an interest in presenting these folkways as "true blue Americanisms"; and, finally a remarkable parity in their portrayal of "creolization" in working-class culture.

Of these painters, only the works of Mount have seen much musicological investigation, mostly because his ephemera have long been known to reveal an especially obvious range of musical interests. Even there, however, his musical activities (for example) have been explored primarily as eccentric adjuncts to his paintings or personality; published musicological analysis of his collected manuscripts, much less of his artworks, has not recognized the information he reveals regarding period vernacular practices. Mount is conventionally understood by art historians to occupy a similar artistic context and political moment as Beard (1812–1893) and George Caleb Bingham (1811–1879), the latter of whose paintings of antebellum life on the Missouri were possibly best known in the period.[152] Beard's *Jolly Flatboatmen* (1846) and *Jolly Flatboatmen in Port* (1857) recycle a similar topic and grouping of figures: rivermen in relaxed postures on the afterdeck and cabin roof of their flatboat, while two of their number play instruments (fiddle and a percussive frying-pan) and one dances. This physical strategy of dancing with hard shoes on a resonant wooden surface is a common trope in paintings of vernacular dance and recalls Mount's multiple images of dancers on barn floors: decks, wharves, and barns all provide both acoustical resonance and a quasi-theatrical frame for the dancing depicted therein.

Though Bingham's *Flatboatmen* imagery has been widely reproduced—and was popular in the period as an expression of frontier idealism and optimism—it is not a central topic in my argument.[153] Music making was not widely represented in Bingham's visual vocabulary, and we have little information on Bingham's musical experience or the quality of his observation.[154] Certainly the comparative idealization in his work implies a degree of "fiction" that mitigates against treating it as literal reportage, in the way that we might be able to treat Mount's and Beard's sketches or oils.[155]

Additional reasons for focusing, among this group of vernacular painters, on Mount and Beard have to do with streams of influence: Glese says that Bingham was probably influenced by Mount, having seen his works in New York, and possibly also by James Goodwyn Clonney (ca. 1812–1867).[156] In fact—and ironically, considering that one was celebrated while the other was castigated—Bingham appears to have been influenced by Beard, as well: his *Lighter Relieving a Steamboat Aground* (1847), is topically reminiscent of *Western Raftsmen*, painted the year before, which Bingham could have seen in visits to Philadelphia.[157]

However, one detail in Bingham's *Jolly Flatboatmen* images is particularly noteworthy, as it subtly confirms the presence of the creole synthesis in the riverine environment of the Missouri.[158] The Missouri river landings were a point of contact between Ozark mountaineers and those who worked the rivers, as were Cincinnati and Louisville on the Ohio, and Natchez, Memphis, and New Orleans on the Mississippi. It is thus no surprise that Anglo-Celtic mountain music and Afro-Caribbean river music might meet on the Missouri, and the reality of this meeting is confirmed in this little-remarked detail in *Flatboatmen*.

In the grouping of figures who lounge on the deck and cabin roof of the boat, three are participating in music and dance: a fiddler, a percussionist, and the dancer himself. The fiddler plays with the instrument down on the chest, "choking-up" on the bow, in a fashion associated with Anglo-Celtic folk styles. The dancer, the most idealized figure of the set, is rendered with two different body languages in the two versions of 1846 and 1857. In the earlier *Jolly Flatboatmen*, painted from a slightly more geometric and squared-out perspective, the dancer is up on the right toe, torso straight and pelvis in line with the shoulders, arms extended and the fingers together—all aspects of body vocabulary comparatively consistent with the Anglo-Celtic fling (though the dancer's head is inclined slightly downward).

In the 1857 *Jolly Flatboatmen in Port*, the figures are seen from a more oblique angle, but many of the same factors are in place, including fiddler, percussionist, and dancer. In this later image, the dancer is up on the left toe, right foot turned outward, pelvis squared to the shoulders, the torso erect (even arched), with the arms extended—but, in contrast to the earlier version, the dancer grasps a handkerchief in one hand and a hat in the other. Hence, in most particulars, these Bingham images conform to expectations of Anglo-Celtic dance choreology, posture, and movement vocabulary, though the inclined head of the 1846 image, and the "objects in hands" of the 1857 version both evoke African movement characteristics and thus may reflect elements of Afro-Caribbean influence on the Missouri.

The key detail confirming the presence of the creole synthesis, however, is in the largely-unremarked technique of the percussionist. In both versions, a seated figure to the dancer's right holds aloft a frying pan in the left hand, while banging out a percussive rhythm with the right hand—more specifically, the knuckle of the right forefinger. This is inconsistent with any percussion technique of the sort conventionally expected on the antebellum frontier: it differs for example from the European-derived military sticking depicted in Mount's *Dance of the Haymakers* (1845) or the Afro-Caribbean juba patting appearing in numerous sketches and *Dancing for Eels, 1820 Catharine Market*.

In fact, this technique of using the knuckle of one hand to play on the head of an instrument held vertically in the other is most reminiscent of that associated with the Irish tambourine called the *bodhrán*, originally employed in sung seasonal rituals and only documented as entering into the Irish dance music tradition in the early twentieth century. Yet here, at least eighty years prior to the *bodhrán*'s appearance with dance tunes, and over three thousand miles away from its natural habitat, we find a participant in Anglo-Celtic dance performance employing precisely the *bodhrán*'s technique on an improvised percussion instrument (a frying pan). While this usage may seem anachronistic, inexplicable, or simply fictional—perhaps Bingham simply imagined a frying pan utilized in this fashion?—there is a plausible historical and organological explanation.

We have already established that Afro-Caribbean music and dance practices entered the continental United States via the medium of waterborne transport, and we have seen or will see iconographic evidence of the creole synthesis in images or descriptions from Long Island, the Lower East Side, the Ohio, the Mississippi, and the riverine and maritime zones they created. It is thus reasonable to anticipate elements of the same creole synthesis on the Missouri, whose people and folkways Bingham knew and depicted. So the question becomes whether, and how, this seemingly anachronistic *bodhrán* technique could have entered the riverine and maritime zones. The answer to this question—one that pushes back the presence of the tambourine, played in *bodhrán* fashion, at least eighty years prior to its previous *terminus ante quem*—has to do precisely with riverine-maritime exchange, in this case among the Missouri, Mississippi, and the Caribbean islands: specifically, the British colonies of Montserrat, St. Vincent, and Trinidad.[159] There, Anglo-Celtic elements (especially the morris and English country dances) interacted with Afro-Caribbean musical procedures and aesthetics to yield syncretic dance idioms, much as happened across the Caribbean and in the earliest roots of blackface dance and tunes. In all three of these British colonies, European-style tambourines were played by creole musicians with the bare knuckle, in the fashion captured in Bingham's *Flatboatmen* images; but that same technique was *not* employed in African percussion styles. The tradition of "sheet iron bands" in New Orleans—groups playing "rough music" on improvised instruments for street festivals and holiday—has been documented, but the adoption of Anglo-Celtic percussion techniques has not been previously remarked.[160]

Hence, musicians in English-speaking Caribbean colonies, encountering an imported instrument in the context of European social dancing, adopted and adapted the instrument to play these dance musics, but with an Anglo-Celtic and Afro-Caribbean technique whose hybrid nature, like the dances, the dance rhythms, and the music itself, also reflected the influence of the creole synthesis.[161] Is it possible that Bingham, who was not a musician but knew the riverine communities and activities of the Missouri well, might have observed a musician (of whatever ethnicity) playing improvised percussion on a frying pan with an imported technique migrating to the mainland and up the rivers from the Caribbean? Given the unlikelihood of the coincidental juxtaposition of an eccentric combination of instrument, technique, and dance context, it would seem that our answer must almost unavoidably be "yes."

While Bingham clearly idealized his flatboatmen and keelboatmen, and Mount subtly excised working-class origins and experiences from his personal autobiography in service of upward social mobility, James Henry Beard's stance toward his own working-class background and subjects was more fluid and even contradictory. Born at Buffalo in 1814, he was a product of the same geographic and socioeconomic environments as the first wave of blackface practitioners: his family's emigration from upstate New York to the Ohio frontier, for example, exactly parallels Dan Emmett's family migration from Virginia to the same frontier. Like Mount, Beard's eventual contact with New York's National Academy in the 1840s helped him fashion a later career that brought upper-middle-class respectability, and a gradual change of topics and themes: Beard in fact ended his life as a painter of sentimental portraits of family pets. But in the hungry Jacksonian 1840s, he painted a series of pictures whose topics, critical stance, and allegorical content were far more ambiguous, defiant—and revealing—than his later portraits of cats, dogs, and children.

To understand the indirect but significant musicological evidence Beard and others provide, it is necessary to understand the role of the expressive arts in the mobile, polyglot riverine and maritime frontiers. The presence and boundary-crossing work experience of black and white musicians on these frontiers is attested by biographical, musicological, and archival evidence—as it is by Beard's paintings. Hans Nathan, for example, confirms that the earliest sources of the canonic minstrel tune "Possum Up a Gum Stump" were on the Ohio River as early as 1817.[162] Members of the Virginia Minstrels, later regarded as the "first" blackface minstrel troupes, met and learned from African Americans during Ohio River Valley gigs in 1840; while C. J. Rogers claimed that Dan Emmett, supposed composer of "Dixie" and founder of the Minstrels, got banjo technique from a man "by the name of 'Ferguson,' who was a very ignorant person, and 'negger all over' except in color."[163] Likewise, the teenaged apprenticeship of blackface comic actor Thomas Daddy Rice in Upstate New York on the Hudson River and Erie Canal and thence "on frontier stages in the Gulf States and the Ohio Valley" in the late 1820s.[164]

Contact between blacks and whites in such circumstances was as often contentious as collaborative: throughout the Jacksonian period, as early as the 1820s construction of the Erie Canal in upstate New York, and as late as the 1840s construction of the New Pontchartrain Canal in the South, there was competition for jobs between blacks and whites on the frontiers. But there is no disputing the opportunity and actuality of cultural exchange.[165] While such contacts and the musics that resulted are much better documented in the postwar era (they would lead eventually to the creole genres of ragtime, in the black middle class of St. Louis and Memphis; and jazz, in the working-class communities of New Orleans and other Mississippi towns), their origins lie in the antebellum period. In his study of banjo methods, for example, Robert Winans identifies the sources of the early banjoists in even earlier black stylists, citing the claim that band-leader E. P. Christie learned banjo "with slaves in New Orleans," and identifies steamboat-borne minstrels working on the Ohio and Big Sandy rivers by the 1850s.[166] Goertzen and Jabbour confirm musical exchange in the print and manuscript record.[167]

In fact, black-white musical exchange had been fundamental in U.S. popular culture long before antebellum minstrelsy: Wells traces the "merging" of black-white fiddling as early as the late seventeenth century, and, like Nathan, shows that merger in the adoption and adaptation of tunes across racial boundaries.[168] Jabbour has shown similar exchange and rhythmic synthesis in fiddling techniques still extant in the Upper South (i.e., on the Old Frontier).[169] Iconography supports this same inference: we can confirm that black rhythmic elements (via hand percussion and the body percussion known as "patting Juba"), depicted in the anonymous New York sketch cited by Lhamon, *Dancing for Eels, 1820 Catharine Market*, were there very early. Wells states explicitly that, in the realm of dance music, "acculturation was working in both directions."[170]

These same interactions continued on the western frontiers though they are more sparsely documented: Chevan, for example, describes black string bands working on the Mississippi excursion lines as early as the 1860s. Chevan's sources confirm that these black bands—and, by inference, their predecessors before the war—employed a "feel" (e.g., rhythmic language) that white musicians could not match, but also note that riverboat bands were integrated relatively early.[171] The inescapable conclusion is that white musicians playing in integrated bands would have been able to assimilate this distinctively black "feel," just as the early minstrels did (see Emmett's teacher "Ferguson," above)—and, as this book argues, just as Mount's dancers did.

Like Bingham's better-known *Jolly Flatboatmen* from the same year, Beard's 1846 *Western Raftsmen* depicts vernacular music making on the riverine frontier.[172] Though Bingham was lauded as a kind of "painter laureate" of the West (not least because of the idealized romanticism of his allegory and the appeal of his artistic technique), Beard's very different perspective was grounded in a very different working-class experience. His was a practical education: after relocating to Ohio with his family from upstate New York, Beard married into a flatboat-trader family based in New Orleans and spent his young adulthood working the Mississippi.[173]

Described as something of a bohemian (Husch dismisses his social behavior as "Romantic posturing"), Beard, a working-class Whig and a nativist, initially resisted the eastern arts hierarchy, and the suspicion was mutual: Rash notes that Beard's portrayals of western frontiersmen initially provoked negative receptions from the critical establishment.[174] Husch likewise observes of *Western Raftsmen* that Beard had, controversially, "depicted whites and blacks interacting as equals in a way that, for its time, would have been disturbing. The black dancer and white fiddler are united in pose and gesture as well as by their common activity. The dancer is even slightly elevated, although he is also isolated from his fellows by the diagonal placement of the oar."[175] Husch's precise critical reading of the iconography and allegorical intentions behind *Western Raftsmen* suggests that the anomie, isolation, and decrepitude of the scene were intentional and allegorical: the cabin in ruins, the riverboat beached, the postures of the individuals indolent and ungraceful. I have already mentioned the fascinating, yet previously little-remarked musical information of the Bingham—particularly the portrayal of the fiddler playing Appalachian or Renaissance style down on the chest, and of the man playing percussion, in the fashion of the Irish *bodhrán*, a hundred years before that instrument is conventionally understood to have entered the dance music tradition, and of the likely Caribbean origin of that latter technique. I instead focus here on the layers of allusion in Beard's rendition of the white musician and black dancer. The interaction of fiddle and percussive hard-shoe dance, the location of this impromptu performance on the roof of an idle flatboat, are of course reminiscent of the Bingham, and for that matter also recall imagery of like dancing in the east: most notably the image *Dancing for Eels, 1820 Catherine Wharf* analyzed by Lhamon in his *Raising Cain*, troped extensively, and discussed in chapter 3.

As we have seen, riverine and maritime contexts were both comparatively classless and relatively integrated: demographic information confirms that working-class neighborhoods, crews, and professions in the riverine and harbor cities assimilated black and white, native and immigrant (especially Irish) populations in the shared quest for a living wage. What Beard's 1846 painting confirms is that the conditions that have been documented in biographical, musicological, and archival evidence are *also* to be discovered in art works by period painters with direct, participatory experience of those conditions. Beard had worked those boats and river landings; like the anonymous draftsman of *Dancing for Eels* and, like Mount, whose work is better documented by art history but equally neglected by musicology, his observation can be trusted. A close examination of the image's details reveals much.

In addition to a lounging hunter with two dogs (one curled up sleeping), and a chatting horseman whose steed is attempting to crop the sparse turf, four rivermen are depicted on their beached boat: one lounging, head propped on his arm; another leaning with crossed arms against a ladder, and two others engaged in musical exchange: a white fiddler and a black dancer. As with Bingham's *Jolly Flatboatmen*, both musician and dancer are positioned on the wooden roof of a flatboat's cabin, a resonant surface (like the wooden wharf in *Dancing for Eels*, the barn floors of Mount's rural dancers, or the half doors or rain barrels employed by Irish dance masters for the same purpose) that from the painting's perspective is elevated and angled for a plain view. As was common—and is similarly clearly depicted in works by both Mount and Bingham—the musician holds the fiddle down on his chest, a posture that impedes shifting but enhances both resonance and the ability to play fuller-textured double- or triple-stops, and yields a technique well-suited to executing the simple, narrow-ranged binary dance tunes of the Anglo-Celtic tradition.

Meanwhile, the black dancer, sleeves rolled up and shirt open, dances to the fiddle's strains. As Husch points out, the very interaction, even the comparable elevation, of black dancer versus white fiddler would have been perceived as threatening to East Coast establishments.[176] But more significant for our purposes is the image's implicit cultural exchange. Though we cannot know the specifics of the tune being played, whether it is of Anglo-Celtic or African American derivation or perhaps already reflects the crossover of tunes from one tradition to another, the visual evidence unequivocally depicts white music and black dance interacting. Analogous to Mount's paintings of rural whites dancing to the fiddle, but with elements of African American body language in the physical choreography—and in decided contrast to the idealized Highland fling danced by Bingham's jolly flatboatman—here, with Beard's fiddler and dancer, the bent knee and arms akimbo of "Jump Jim Crow" iconography are translated from the minstrelsy prints; or, more likely, reveal the actual choreographic practices that both the prints, and minstrelsy practitioners, observed and appropriated.

This brief survey of the existing evidence for a broader portrait of minstrelsy's root contexts, one that extends along the riverine and maritime waterways south to the Gulf and west past the Mississippi, situates the works of both Henry Beard and George Caleb Bingham, like those of William Sidney Mount, in a creolizing popular culture, and argues for those works' relevance to musicological investigation. Though Beard's catalog contains far fewer portrayals of music making, and Bingham's fewer and more idealized examples, than does Mount's, the consistency of these painters' biographies, backgrounds, political allegory, and topics; the commonality of their experience with that of the first blackface popularizers; and the precision of their musical reportage, suggest that works of this generation of antebellum vernacular artists, watching and working on the wharves and waterfronts, present a rich, as yet largely untapped, resource for musicological investigation.

THE OLD FRONTIERS: CANALS AND THE RIVERINE IRISH

The federalist and Jacksonian periods—roughly 1792 to circa 1835—saw an explosion of economic, commercial, and infrastructure development in the new republic. The nation's founders, and the businessmen who had bankrolled the Continental Army and often made fortunes doing so, were acutely aware of both the opportunities and the impedimenta presented by the sheer size of the continent. Given that both the colonial victory and the postwar economic boom depended on maritime shipping, and that the majority of domestic commerce was transported by coasting vessels, it is no surprise that water routes were viewed as essential to strategic and economic development.

Even before the revolution, speculators and political leaders had proposed schemes to enhance mobility by dredging, expanding, and linking waterways, typically through the digging of navigable canals. These plans, already in train by 1777, most often drew on the expertise and pioneering texts of those architects who developed the transport network that powered Britain's Industrial Revolution. Canal construction in England had begun as early as 1699, and throughout the 18th century new projects enabled development of the Midlands spinning, weaving, and manufacturing that drove worldwide trade throughout the heyday of the empire. Those employed to actually do the specialized work of digging, blasting, and reinforcing the canals that changed the face of Britain were usually recruited from trades in which related skills were already essential: Yorkshire and Lancashire tin, copper, and chalk miners, and, especially, the immigrant Irish. The Irish would continue to form the cornerstone of the British "navvy" and "sandhog" canal and tunnel work force well into the second half of the twentieth century.

These same workers and their offspring were recruited throughout the antebellum period in the new United States: Robert Fulton, for example, an essential visionary in the development of viable steamboat designs who began his career creating speculative designs for canal locks, was the child of Irish immigrants. By 1792, the Lowell Canals, which connected the mills of northeastern Massachusetts with the wharves of the Atlantic seacoast, had been built by Irish laborers imported from East Boston, and by 1796 Fulton had published his *A Treatise on the Improvement of Canal Navigation*.[177] The successful Hudson voyage of his *North River Steamboat* in 1807, which shortened the duration and lowered the cost of upstream return voyages, proved a further spur to canal development efforts.[178]

Water routes were also crucial on the frontiers that crossed the Alleghenies: the Cumberland, Green, Kanawha, Licking, Ohio, Ohio-Allegheny, Tennessee, and Tennessee-French Broad Canals all reached across the mountains to the Mississippi tributaries and thus provided an inland cross-continental connection between the Atlantic and Caribbean ports. Throughout the 'teens, Irish workers recruited in England worked a myriad of new canals on the old frontiers, in Pennsylvania, in Ohio, and, most visibly and immediately for minstrelsy's Northeast development, on the Erie Canal system that would link the Hudson, Upstate New York, Pennsylvania, and the Great Lakes. The canal's official opening in 1826 was an occasion for enormous civic celebration, with parades and exhibitions in Manhattan. Due to concerns about their public conduct, Irish immigrant laborers, though central to canal construction, were excluded from those celebrations.[179] In later canal dedications, the Irish were more insistent on recognition of their contribution: for the July 4, 1837, opening of the Illinois and Michigan, "[Chicago]'s namesake steamboat was assaulted by Irish quarry workers from a bank above the river. . . . While the laborers' motivation was not clear, it likely resulted from a combination of deviltry and pique at being excluded from festivities initiating a project to be completed by the sweat of their brows."[180]

The 1825 opening of the Erie precipitated a boom in New York City's economic activity and population; the latter would double every decade for the balance of the century.[181] This boom also fueled an explosion in artistic opportunity and "generated an ideal atmosphere for young artists as the new class of merchants and other entrepreneurs became interested in fine arts and culture."[182] Some of these entrepreneurial young artists recognized the fascination of "frontier" culture to their bourgeois customer base. Riverboatmen's transgressive public conduct, their propensity "to fight, challenge each other by crowing like a cock, or neighing like an ass" was the subject of horrified fascination.[183] Irish immigrant canallers, on the Erie and elsewhere, had developed a distinctive community identity that paralleled that of both the brawling, tall-tale-spinning frontier riverboatmen and the Bowery B'hoys of New York's Lower East Side. These same populations formed the core of the populist wave that made Andrew Jackson the "Hero of New Orleans" and in 1829 propelled him into the White House.[184] Way describes them as tough, mobile, insular communities that were "Largely made up of young males . . . sharing a similar ethnic background [and] a rough camaraderie reinforced by male bonding, which manifested itself in the drinking and roughhousing typical of young men . . . a social world of their own [and] an identity that espoused the values of physical prowess, virility, a certain nonchalance to risks, and an equal willingness to live hard outside of work, with drinking and fighting two main measures of a man's worth."[185] In addition to provoking middle-class unease, canaller communities shared other characteristics with the immigrant Irish that in turn became part of the blackface persona. Their attitudes toward sport, gambling (especially horse racing), boxing, alcohol, violence, and political activism recalled both Irish rural precursors such as the Wrenboys and Strawboys, and the liminal behaviors associated with European *carnivale* and Afro-Caribbean festivals such as John Canoe or Junkanoo.[186]

The riverine and maritime cross-cultural synthesis that yielded blackface minstrelsy also yielded the earliest glimmerings of cross-racial working-class solidarity.[187] A quote from a New Orleans stevedore of a later period, cited by David Roediger, epitomizes these first glimmerings:

> I wasn't always a nigger-lover. I fought in every strike to keep Black labor off the dock. I fought until in the white-supremacy strike your white-supremacy governor sent his white-supremacy militia and shot us white-supremacy strikers full of holes. . . . [T]there was a time when I wouldn't even work beside a nigger. . . . You made me work with niggers, eat with niggers, sleep with niggers, drink out of the same water bucket with niggers, and finally got me to the point where if one of them . . . blubbers something about more pay, I say, "Come on, nigger, let's go after the white bastards."[188]

Saxton, for example, invokes Daniel Decatur Emmett to illustrate the shared working-class origins of the early blackface practitioners, who rejected the Protestant ethic and "sought escape into the bohemianism of the entertainment world."[189] In linking the seminal minstrels' background with the new urban working-class archetypes (most notably but incompletely, the Bowery B'hoys and volunteer firemen of the Lower East Side), he references the "sociological congruency between city and frontier" that created a shared "psychological identity between traveling to the city and traveling west."[190] But we should not omit the presence of analogous congruencies between the urban North and the riverine frontiers of the South: both were liminal, fluid, potentially transformative environments, hence especially attractive to those seeking new economic opportunities. Parallel environments gave rise to the populist Jacksonian heroes and antiheroes Mose the Fireman (of the Bowery B'hoys and Lower East Side), Dan Tucker and Mike Fink the keelboatmen (and fictionalized heroes of frontier song and story), and Zip Coon and Jim Crow, the clownish jesters of urban minstrelsy.[191] Though their outward appearances and geographical origins differed, the continuity of experience in all three areas—Northeast, South, and West—centered on African Americans and Anglo-Celts, working ships, rivers, and canals.

The economic downturns of the 1830s, and the competing technology of the railroad in the 1840s, slowed the pace of canal construction, but the laborers who built the Erie, for example, did not disappear after its completion. The Irish communities of Troy, Utica, Cincinnati, Mobile, and New Orleans were first populated by former canal workers, who transferred their skills at demolition and excavation to bridge and highway construction and, often, to the waterfront work (drayage, ship service, and so on) that the canals had brought. African Americans were likewise part of U.S. canal culture since before the American Revolution, as they had been of all three armies, typically as fifers and drummers, involved in the conflict. These occupations continued after the war, and not only in military settings: black drummers were likewise used to beat tattoos, gather crowds, and otherwise "mark" public gatherings.[192] African Americans were part of the river and canal developments that effected a transformation in international trade.

Southern ports such as Charleston, Savannah, and, preeminently, New Orleans gradually supplanted Boston and New York as the continent's overseas trading centers, while the Atlantic and Caribbean coasting trade remained central to domestic commerce.[193] As a result, during the canal-construction era, the immigrant Irish often found themselves working side by side with free blacks. There were frequent disputes between the two communities, typically revolving around economic competition: an 1828 advertisement for "colored" laborers to work the Pennsylvania Canal construction project assures potential hires that "no Irish men" were to be employed, and thus that any potential conflicts would be avoided.[194] In fact, Andrew Jackson, who as an Ulster Scots candidate had been a hero to the immigrants, was forced as president to call out federal troops in 1834 to quell Irish labor riots at the Chesapeake & Ohio Canal.

Of course, numerous examples throughout U.S. history confirm that economic conflict between proximate social groups need not preclude other kinds of cultural exchange—in fact, the evidence suggests that workplace competition was only one component of a complex, ongoing cultural synthesis. Lott's *Love and Theft* confirms the cross-cultural "elbow-rubbing" that was "especially common in frontier towns," and cites Hearn's reference to "Negro" singers who could "mimic the Irish accent to a degree of perfection which an American, Englishman, or German could not hope to acquire."[195] In a biographical sketch, McNeil elaborates on Hearn's postbellum activities as a folklorist observing and describing in Cincinnati and New Orleans both songs ("Liza Jane," the New Orleans brass-band standard, among them) and dances (Hearn provides a detailed description of the Afro-Caribbean *calinda*, ubiquitous throughout U.S. riverine and maritime environments).[196] As we have seen, Hearn's quasi-ethnographic "Black Varieties" newspaper essays in Cincinnati and New Orleans speak to a postbellum appetite for black exotica that has parallels in the prewar period—most notably in the flash press:

> One fact worth mentioning about these negro singers is, that they can mimic the Irish accent to a degree of perfection which an American, Englishman or German could not hope to acquire. . . . A very dark mulatto, named Jim Delaney, sang for us in capital style that famous Irish ditty known as "The hat me fahther wor-re." Yet Jim, notwithstanding his name, has little or no Irish blood in his veins; nor has his companion, Jim Harris, who joined in the rollicking chorus . . . Jim Delaney would certainly make a reputation for Irish specialties in a minstrel troupe; his mimicry of Irish character is absolutely perfect, and he possesses a voice of great flexibility, depth and volume. He "runs" on the river.[197]

STREET REPORTING AND THE NORTHEAST

Washington Irving, who as we see in chapter 3 is a significant reporter on the very early roots of the creole synthesis in the North, also has something to say about "rough music" in Albany in the federalist period. Using the pseudonym "dick Buckram" (a reference to the starched cloth used both for "flash coves'" stovepipe hats, and for binding books), Irving comments sardonically in the New York *Morning Chronicle* (December 30, 1803) on an Albany militia muster: "Our military music consisted of a drum, fife, and two pot lids by way of cymbals, and for want of a trumpeter, the *entrée* of our heroes was announced by a ferry-man with his conk-shell. . . . Our orchestra was in a style equally superb and consisted of three most inveterate fiddlers."[198] In addition to the obvious connection with the "rough music" instrumentation of the *charivari* (see Cockrell, *Demons of Disorder*), Irving's description, dated more than twenty years prior to the earliest performances by Dixon's and Rice's mentors, also documents the creole synthesis in Upstate New York: the percussion instruments associated with military bands (drum, fife, "cymbals") meet the fiddlers of Anglo-African dance music, and the "conk" shell trumpet of the Caribbean.

Other reporters in the 1750s provide descriptions of comic songs performed onstage accompanied by dancing and fiddling, and we have descriptions from the 1790s of the Albany-based circuses whose frontier tours were an early incubator for solo blackface performers.[199] Given the roots of these troupes in the Hudson Valley, it is clear that river traffic between upstate and the city spread Pinkster, 'Lection Day, and related music-and-dance-driven creole idioms swiftly and widely, even before the revolution. This exchange continued and accelerated in the federalist period: Thomas Ashe's *Travels in America Performed in 1806*, for example, cited in Nathan, describes Anglo-Caribbean exchanges in Virginia similar to those Irving relates in the same period in the Northeast.[200]

By the 1820s, the old Hudson River–based distribution networks that had united Upstate New York, Long Island, and Manhattan—and that had given rise to the German-African-English-Caribbean syntheses yielding Pinkster and John Canoe—were overlaid by networks of exchange created by the newer canal culture. As was the case elsewhere, Albany's festivals combined European and African elements borrowed from across the Atlantic and Caribbean worlds. At a minimum, we can count the extensive variety of seasonal holidays celebrated with masking, impromptu, theatrics and mock ceremony, music, and dancing: there are remarkable parallels, for example, between the folk-mumming known on Long Island, Jamaica, and Barbados, all three of which landfalls were touchstones for the Sugar Trade.[201] Reiss cites reports of John Canoe or Jonkonnu as first recorded in Jamaica in 1774, and mentions that the festival "came to the southern [and eventually northern] mainland from the Caribbean."[202]

With roots in the street culture of New York, Boston, and other northeastern cities, but with an audience (revealed through correspondents lists) that reached out along the canals and rivers of the western and southern frontiers, the flash press provides additional empirical evidence for the distribution of creole culture. Though a relatively brief phenomenon, primarily flourishing in the 1840s and largely defunct by the '50s, these cheap street newspapers contain crucial information that is paralleled by other, earlier print sources that are equally revealing. That these overlays exerted and shared influence is confirmed by demographic evidence in Albany, New Orleans, and Cincinnati; by commentary in the popular press (for example, in the reporting on the Erie Canal celebrations of 1825, discussed in chapter 3), and by the musical evidence of works such as Micah Hawkins's "Backside Albany."

THE FLASH PRESS

The flash press publications not only served as guides to the nexus of music-dance-eroticism its readers sought, but also reveal a good deal about both that readership and those entertainments. Subscribers and correspondents were relatively widely distributed in "other larger cities and small villages all over the Northeast and mid-Atlantic states and even to the South, where one communication line stretched deep into Georgia"—a locale that W. S. Mount's brother Nelson would come to know well in the '40s as an itinerant dance master.[203] Cohen likewise confirms avid interest among a far-flung readership in these new entertainments well beyond the Northeast.[204] Particularly notable in this cartographic web is the degree to which the communities of flash readers were found along the same water transport routes—the Hudson, the Connecticut, Long Island Sound, the Ohio, and so forth—that served as the distribution paths of blackface minstrelsy. The flash papers and the blackface troupes of the 1840s found audiences along the rivers and canals precisely because these had been zones of working-class cultural exchange since before the revolution.

This pattern is replicated in later American popular music idioms: an expressive or performance idiom develops "at the margins," whether those margins are social, economic, racial, or geographical (or all of these), and then a precipitating event or set of conditions (often new modes of distribution such as cheap printing, urban theaters, transistor radio, cassette culture, or the internet) makes that idiom more readily visible to a wider demographic. The wider audience, in turn wielding enhanced middle-class buying power, appropriates the genre's externals of dress, language, grooming, personae, music, dance, and so forth. In this sense, minstrelsy's roots, development, apotheosis, and decline are not unique or isolated instances, but rather—and profoundly—early and archetypal examples for the developmental arc of many pop-music idioms throughout U.S. cultural history.

BLACKFACE ARCHITECTS: DIXON, RICE, EMMETT, AND SWEENEY

In order for us to understand the role of individuals in the transmission of the creole synthesis from the multiracial working-class wharves, decks, and streets, it is essential to recognize the contemporaneity and the commonality of their experience: with one another; with George Caleb Bingham, Henry Beard, William Sidney Mount, and other painters; and with the working-class whites and blacks from whom they derived their performance approaches. These were remarkably observant, imaginative, strong-willed, and influential individuals, but their experiences were exemplary—not isolated. In the first blackface generation, the careers of the solo stars Rice and Dixon demonstrate the links between mechanic or apprentice culture, minstrelsy, the flash press, and later proto-Bohemianism. In the second generation, careers of the bandleaders Emmett and Sweeney concretize performance possibilities that had been implicit in the innovations of their soloist predecessors. In this sense, the early, experimental solo turns of Rice and Dixon made possible the more elaborate and fleshed-out new genres of Emmett and Sweeney—and of later American popular musics.

We have earlier traced the career of Rice on the frontiers but to summarize it here: born on New York's Lower East Side in 1808, the son of a rope chandler, by his late teens he was working the Hudson and Ohio River valleys with various theatrical companies, and claiming that he learned "Jump Jim Crow" from a stable hand in Louisville around 1830. As we have seen, even if the eponymous "Jim Crow" himself never existed, it is possible that Rice might indeed have acquired the song, which originates as a mimetic Caribbean children's song, somewhere on the riverine frontiers.

The other of the first-generation blackface soloists, George Washington Dixon (b. 1801?), led a particularly colorful life at the fringes of polite society as actor, blackface singer, flash publisher, competition walker, felon, and possibly pimp.[205] He is described as the "true originator" of the flash press, publishing in Lowell, Boston, and eventually in New York *Polyanthos* (from 1838), in whose pages he carried out scandal reporting, political critique, notorious feuds with rival editors and public figures.[206] But his career begins in the context of working-class theatrics: reputedly the son of a barber, he was born (probably) in Richmond, Virginia, (probably) in 1801. By age fifteen, he was performing in West's circus, specializing in songs and comic recitations, and by 1829 was known as the American Buffo Singer.[207] It is almost certainly on the frontiers that he learned the song "Coal Black Rose," which he would ride to fame in performances at New York's Bowery, Chatham Garden, and Park theaters from 1829 onward.

For the second generation's Joel Walker Sweeney (b. 1810), Carlin has provided an essential and useful career summary. A key contributor in the adoption of the five-string banjo by minstrelsy and in the North, Sweeney was born to Irish American parents near Appomattox, Virginia, on the eastern slope of the Appalachians. His grandfather, a Revolutionary War veteran, had settled in Buckingham County in 1785, and the family homestead and tavern were located "about one mile northeast of Appomattox Courthouse and the Appomattox River, along the Richmond/Lynchburg Stage Road."[208] Though the Appomattox was nowhere near as significant for waterborne traffic as the greater rivers previously discussed, the town's location as a jumping-off point for trans-Appalachian travel nevertheless made it a center for commerce and exchange, as would be confirmed when the last major engagements of the Civil War were later resolved there. Carlin cites references to African American banjo playing in this area dating as early as the mid-eighteenth century, and there are descriptions of slave musicians playing for white dancing by the 'teens.[209] There had been a black banjo tradition in tidewater South Carolina since the revolutionary era at the latest; the seminal watercolor *The Old Plantation* (ca. 1774–94), painted in South Carolina, is both the earliest depiction of the banjo and of slave-era percussion and mimetic dance in the United States.[210]

Sweeney himself seems therefore to have learned banjo from black players in his home region, and as a young man he performed in regional taverns, dance halls, racetracks, and courthouse fairs by 1837.[211] By 1839 he was playing circuses in Charleston, a city with particularly strong Caribbean connections, having been largely populated by refugees in the wake of the Haitian Revolution of 1802–3. Sweeney was employing the banjo for playing solo turns in the Appomattox area by 1840. While he typically performed in duo with singers or dancers, there are also accounts of larger ensemble performances in the round with the Barnum circuses.[212] He worked New York's Bowery Theatre that same summer, popularizing a series of tunes that may well have had their foundation in black banjo repertoires he learned in Virginia: the "Grapevine Twist," "Jumbo Jum," "Tell Me Josey Whar You Bin," and so on.[213] He followed the trail of Emmett's Virginia Minstrels to Great Britain in 1842 and actually surpassed Rice's popularity there; Carlin describes his performances as "less grotesque and stereotypical than [those of] other contemporary minstrels."[214] However, after peaking in the '40s, Sweeney's career gradually contracted in the subsequent decade, and was largely confined to lower-profiled performances in the Appomattox area until his death in 1860.[215]

Though Sweeney's impact is conventionally understood as resulting from his seminal role in popularizing the banjo, and certain iconic minstrel songs, he was neither the first nor the only white banjoist in the North nor necessarily the originator of these songs. But he *is* crucial to our understanding of the creole synthesis: not only because, like Emmett, he was a career musician (unlike Rice and Dixon, who between them seem to have pursued a dozen different professions in their colorful careers). Sweeney is also important because, again like Emmett, we can document his direct exposure to and close study of African American performance idioms much more precisely than those of Rice and Dixon, whose "fieldwork" we must treat more circumstantially and inferentially.

Two examples illustrate the particular direct connections between Sweeney and the black informants he learned from, connections that qualify him to be regarded as a "participant observer" to the creole synthesis (Carlin calls him a "prototypical ethnomusicologist").[216] The first is simply the accident of birthplace: like Rice and Dick Pelham on New York's Lower East Side, and like Emmett or Dixon even closer to home, Sweeney simply had the fortune to be born at the right place at the right time—at least as regards Appomattox's location, where a navigable river met a trans-Appalachian overland route, in a town with a substantial African America and Anglo-Celtic population. This in turn would have enabled nearly as wide and diverse a range of social contacts as those found on the Catherine Wharf by W. S. Mount or on the Cincinnati waterfront by Stephen Foster.

Perhaps even more significant—certainly in terms of the kinesthetic elements of polyrhythmic dance—is Sweeney's early exposure to and special concentration on the banjo. As we see in chapter 4, the banjo itself—like African American culture as a whole—is the product of a collision between diverse cultural influences, both African and European, in the New World. The cross-fertilization of formerly distinctive West and Central African ethnicities led to new linguistic, musical, and polyrhythmic "creole" practices, and both the banjo, and Sweeney's experience of it, reflect that creolization. Of any of the blackface architects we have considered—more than the fiddlers, and perhaps even more than Emmett, another banjoist with experience at percussive dance—Sweeney would necessarily have internalized the kinesthetic, polyrhythmic practices of his instrument, playing the "knocking" or "stroke" style that was a particularly direct connection to West African string technique. He learned from black players in a creole environment; he played (accompanying songs and dancing) on an instrument whose provenance and polyrhythmic mechanics reflected that creole environment; and he situated that tactile, kinesthetic knowledge, of the instrument and the body, at the core of blackface practice. The polyrhythmicization implicit in black fiddlers' approach to monophonic melody, and reflected in the body vocabularies of those dancing to their music, is made direct, physical, and experiential in the body of the banjoist (Sweeney, and the black players he learned from) as he or she plays.[217]

As Carlin's book has done for Sweeney, Hans Nathan's *Dan Emmett and the Rise of Early Negro Minstrelsy* (1962) provides the most detailed summary of the career of Daniel Decatur Emmett, though in Emmett's case, it is important to nuance Nathan's biography with the insights provided by more recent scholarship.[218] We have already spoken of Emmett's upbringing, the child of Irish American parents, in the integrated frontier town of Mount Vernon, Ohio, of his musical contact with the African American musical Snowden family there, of his training as a drummer and a banjoist, and of his frontier employment (like Dixon, Rice, and Sweeney) as a singer, dancer, and musician in touring circuses. A few other details merit additional note, however.

The Irish American Emmett family's origins in Staunton, Virginia, and their emigration to Ohio in 1812, put them among the first groups of settlers in Mount Vernon, the seat of Knox County, where Abraham Emmett was a blacksmith—an occupation that would surely have provided young Daniel maximal opportunity to meet travelers and hear new tunes. Dan himself was trained as a printer, an experience that in the early republic tended to broaden horizons (as it had earlier done for Benjamin Franklin), parallels Dixon's later print notoriety, and would surely have enhanced Emmett's own sense of career mobility.[219] We have previously cited his experience with Anglo-Celtic fiddle repertoires and percussion training at the Newport Kentucky barracks from the black drummer John "Juba" Clark, whom Carroll has suggested was one avatar of a "Western School for Practice" of military drumming that incorporated much more extensive use of syncopation and cross-rhythms.[220]

By 1838, with occasional returns to Mount Vernon during which he seems to have continued his collecting with the Stauntons, Emmett was playing circuses out of Cincinnati, which Sweeney had also done. The touring circus circuit was a crucible for the solo blackface performers, as had been the touring theatrical troupes; not least because both entertainments pioneered early and effective touring networks and logistics.[221] Nathan believes it is in this period that Emmett became interested in "Negro minstrelsy" as a career opportunity, but this suggestion neglects his extensive prior exposure to African American and creole traditions.[222]

Dixon and Rice, Sweeney and Emmett, were not the only blackface originators touring the frontiers in the same era: Nathan describes the teenage dancer Frank Brower (b. 1823) gigging in Philadelphia by 1838, and introducing bones playing in his "Old Tar River" by spring 1841.[223] By late fall 1842, Emmett and Brower were working duo and trio jobs together around New York, including the Chatham Theatre.[224] Within a few months, they would team up with the noted banjoist Billy Whitlock (b. New York 1813), who like Emmett and Dixon had early experience as a printer and compositor, and had worked with Sweeney and Barnum shows in 1838–39 on the frontiers, and the champion dancer John Diamond in the North; Whitlock claimed, as had Rice, to have learned his dance vocabulary on those southern tours.[225] Tambourine-player Dick Pelham, born like Whitlock in New York (1815) but about whose origins little is known, had been performing as a dancer in the City since the mid-1830s and became the fourth participant in the seminal Virginia Minstrels gigs in the winter of 1842–43.

Though Emmett's own mythographic account of the Minstrels' accidental formation is quoted by Nathan to situate those legendary first sessions "in Mrs Brooke's boarding house at 37 Catherine Street," the site is also claimed to have been the "North American Hotel, in the Bowery" (at 30 Bowery).[226] Described in the *New York Clipper* with the old "rough music" term charivari, their first appearances, after a "benefit" for Pelham (a common theatricalism, wherein a given evening's receipts would be dedicated to a specific performer's income), were in January–February of 1843, probably at the Bowery Amphitheatre and the "sporting saloon" (e.g., dance hall or brothel) the Cornucopia, at 28 Park Row.[227] The immediate popularity of the new template—a full ensemble of fiddle, banjo, bones, and tambourine, with songs, recitations, and Pelham and Brower as "end-men" cracking jokes, in a full evening of entertainment—is attested not only by the Minstrels' touring calendar, but also by the host of imitators who sprang up immediately in their wake.[228]

We have already heard that Dan Emmett (b. 1815) learned banjo from an Irish banjoist named Ferguson, who Carlin suggests had in turn learned his own music from slaves working on the western slope of the Alleghenies in Virginia, just across from Ohio: "If Mr Ferguson . . . was indeed from the Kanawha Valley, he could have learned the banjo from Eastern Virginia slaves imported to work for the salt industry at places such as Kanawha Salt Lines on the Kanawha River."[229] Carlin further points out that in this polyglot town, where the mountains met the river, and where the mysterious Ferguson seems to have got his banjo music, there were something like 2,500 slaves in a population of around 10,000 working-class whites; this high (1:4) black-white ratio would certainly suggest a comparably high degree of cultural exchange, of the sort that the blackface architects found in other Ohio and Mississippi River towns where similar musical contact is better documented.

In sum: the Virginia Minstrels' tours, during and after 1843, mark a watershed moment in the history of blackface minstrelsy, but not, as in the conventional mythography, the moment of its "invention." The roots of blackface reach back earlier, at least as far as the '30s (the solo turns by Rice and Dixon that provided the immediate frisson of recognition for Bowery audiences), the '20s (in the frontier performers witnessed by Rice and Dixon), or the 'teens (in the New York theaters such as the African Grove, discussed in chapter 3), or the colonial-period experiments of Mathews and his ilk. Rather, the inception of the Virginia Minstrels marks a different kind of transformation: the professionalization and standardization of an improvised performance idiom—a process—into a reliable, replicable commercial product—an object. Minstrelsy's visibility exploded in the 1842–43 performances of the Virginia Minstrels not because they are the first performances—but because, for the first time, this idiom was being framed for middle-class consumption. As confirmation, Carlin cites the swift codification of the troupe's format, and notes that already, by spring 1843, the Minstrels are describing their shows as "Moral, Chaste and Elegant . . . entirely free from every objectionable feature," and making an explicit claim to the "scientific delineation" of "Sports and Pastimes of the Virginia Colored Race, through the medium of Songs, Refrain and Ditties, as sung by the Southern Slaves, at all their Merry meetings, such as the gathering in of the Cotton and Sugar Crops, Corn Huskings, Slave Weddings, and Junketings."[230] This is essentially a falsehood—none of the blackface architects, with the possible exception of Sweeney, who was not a member of the Virginia Minstrels, is confirmed to have spent time at husking or slave weddings—but it marks precisely the moment when minstrelsy becomes an idiom aiming for both commercial exploitation in the form of iconography and sheet music and for mythologized objectification. While Dixon and Emmett, Rice and Sweeney, along with their working-class informants and audiences, had extensive firsthand experience at watching and participating in cross-cultural creole music and dance, it was only in the 1840s that the creole synthesis became accessible as entertainment for middle-class and overseas audiences who did *not* share that experience. Minstrelsy's boom as a pop-music phenomenon—and its long twilight, with audiences and venues gradually contracting; its performance practice and aesthetic moving into comic theatres and vaudeville; and eventually falling entirely out of public performance but continuing in fraternities, men's clubs, and similar semiprivate environments up to the 1950s—should not blind us to the fact that the winter of 1842–43 marked not only the beginning of the idiom as a commercial idiom, but also the *end* of a period of working-class black-white cultural exchange previously unmatched in U.S. musical history.

CONCLUSIONS

Though there is little direct reportage of proto-minstrelsy behaviors in New Orleans and the urban South—certainly nothing to compare with the relatively extensive northern documentation, from Dickens to the New York illustrated papers to the theatrical reports of Rice and Dixon on the Bowery and Chatham stages—this chapter's survey of the wide range of circumstantial evidence makes several observations essential and inescapable.

First: riverine and maritime environments on the U.S. coasts and southern and western frontiers were precisely the contexts in which African Americans and Irish Americans could come together in close contact and cultural exchange: living, working, and leisure. Second: the degree, dispersal, and intensity of Afro-Caribbean cultural influence in *all* these environments were much wider and deeper than has been understood, and much more fundamental to minstrelsy's creole synthesis. Third: a "creolization" of American popular music was already occurring in these frontier maritime contexts well before the first blackface performances of the 1830s. Fourth: these contexts were available and familiar to the first architects of minstrelsy, because their touring and performing were largely by water to and via the same harbor and frontier cities, and in fact served as a key resource for those performers' observation and imitation.

Fifth: despite claims of some earlier scholarship, the early minstrel performers were not providing an incompetent imitation of an "unadulterated" southern black idiom, but rather a closely observed, remarkably precise, and—arguably—admiring and respectful replication of an already existing creole performance idiom.[231] Sixth: minstrelsy's swift and extensive mass-cultural appeal to working-class audiences resulted not from the idiom's "novelty" (in the sense of "unfamiliarity") but from the pleasurable shock of seeing a beloved street-performance idiom translated to the "legitimate" stage. It was only much later in the idiom's history—in the 1840s and '50s—that it became "novel," because it was only in this later period that minstrelsy's theatricalized realization became visible to middle-class audiences for whom it was unfamiliar and thus exotic.

Finally, minstrelsy can be seen as providing a paradigmatic example for the arc of later American popular music idioms' inception, development, and influence. Beyond the scope of this book, but confirming the plausibility of its theses, is the parallel pre- and post–Civil War frontier synthesis of minstrel songs, other dance musics, fife- and brass-band instrumentation and improvisational techniques that gave birth—in precisely the same communities—to early jazz.[232] By dint of history, geography, transport, demographics, immigration, economics, cultural-linguistic exchange, the riverine or maritime working-class communities of the southern and western frontiers were uniquely positioned to inspire a unique music-and-dance synthesis, whose replication on the blackface stage was one of the first, and is still one of the most influential, of indigenous American popular-music idioms. Understanding the roots of the creole synthesis helps to frame and legitimize W. S. Mount as an observer and reporter, in his own lifetime, upon its flowering on Long Island and the Lower East Side.

3 Long Island and the Lower East Side

Mount's Background, Youth, and Apprenticeships

THIS CHAPTER NARROWS OUR FOCUS from the western Atlantic and Caribbean to examine the creolizing maritime cultures of two islands—Long Island and Manhattan—that directly shaped William Sidney Mount's personal and musical world. It explores the ways in which influences from those islands play out in the life of Mount himself, in that of his uncle and musical mentor Micah Hawkins (1777–1825), and in Hawkins's 1824 ballad opera *The Saw-Mill, or, A Yankee Trick*. This chapter sets the scene for Mount, both chronologically and geographically; it also creates a framing biography for his childhood and cultural contexts, introduces characters who were important musical influences, and investigates Micah Hawkins's major theater piece, which Mount would have known well, and which itself reflects the workings of the creole synthesis. *The Saw-Mill*'s characters, locations, topics, dialects, costume, and musical references directly and essentially prefigure and reinforce the arguments I make about W. S. Mount's own artworks. We frame Micah Hawkins as a role model for Mount himself: after all, Mount knew his uncle, admired him, inherited musical manuscripts from him, and lived with him as a young apprentice on the Lower East Side. Through this exploration, we reconstruct the environments that Mount knew and by which he was shaped, as a child and young adult, in the cauldron of musical exchange that was antebellum America.

Mount's artworks provide extensive, detailed, and reliable reportage on cross-cultural exchange between minstrelsy's source idioms, and a confluence of factors—sociology, history, demographics, biography, and iconography—combined to make his musical experience an unusually enlightening and reliable source. But similar exchanges, though much less precisely documented, were present in riverine and maritime environments across the United States (chapter 2). As a result, it can be argued that the type and range of musical exchange depicted in Mount's visual catalog, even if not so extensively documented elsewhere, were nevertheless widely present. Therefore, while the analysis in this chapter focuses on Mount on Long Island and the Lower

East Side, the cultural-historical dynamics it reveals may be taken as operating elsewhere in parallel.

FESTIVALS: PINKSTER AND NEGRO 'LECTION DAY

Throughout the antebellum period, the U.S. Eastern Seaboard, the Caribbean, and their contiguous rivers saw complex Anglo-Celtic and African American cultural exchange. In these oceangoing maritime and inland riverine communities, African ideas about masking, music, celebration, and dance melded with European seasonal-festival behaviors: the encounter, for example, between English mumming and African festival in the Caribbean yielded John Canoe/Junkanoo in Jamaica and Trinidad, while a parallel encounter between German, Dutch, English, and African American festival behaviors yielded Pinkster and 'Lection Day in the northeastern United States.[1]

The antebellum United States acted out much of its communal identity in public; thus, if the creole synthesis was beginning to shape that identity in the postrevolutionary period, we should expect to find evidence for it in earlier festival performance just as in later blackface theatricals.

Pinkster, which originated in colonial Albany through African American appropriations of German Pentecost celebrations, moved down the Hudson and out along the Atlantic seaboard, and eventually was well-known in New York, Connecticut, Long Island, and beyond, overlapping with Afro-Caribbean festival variants.[2] Originally, as S. White says, "a Dutch and not a black festival . . . by the 19th century . . . [Pinkster] was primarily black and associated most closely with Albany, though it was also observed in other places where there was a strong Dutch presence—along the Hudson Valley, on Long Island, and in East New Jersey."[3] Barnes-Ostrander quotes the memoir of John Durang (b. 1768 in Lancaster, Pennsylvania), a touring actor and dancer who in 1789 published an "Old-Style Hornpipe," which combined European and African American dance instructions:[4]

> The original inhabitants of this place where [were] Hollanders. They speak broken English. . . . There are six churches in this town, a great many taverns without custom except from strangers; about ten stages set out every day from this to other towns . . . I saw no pumps, but a well in the centre, in the crossway of two streets with a roof over it. The streets are paved, and lamps. The square I lived, the lamps where [were] attended by a boy who cried the hour. There is a clock in the English Church. I am informed that no business is done here in the winter.[5]

Despite the strong whiff of derogation in Durang's sardonic description, Albany was a crucial site for cultural exchange between upstate (Dutch), downstate (Anglo-Celtic), and maritime (Afro-Caribbean) influences. The career of Pinkster reveals the spread of the creole synthesis: originating in the late seventeenth century around Albany, documented in New York City by the 1730s, in Massachusetts by the 1740s, and eastern (Dutch) New Jersey by the 1780s, the festival was a "distinctly African American" but also "biracial event" that "whites watched, but [of which] blacks were in control."[6] Both Glass and DeFrantz, for example, cite a detailed 1757 description by James Fenimore Cooper of a Pinkster celebration outside New York City that mentions banjo playing, African-language song, log drumming, and a general aura of festive license, with blacks as instigators and whites as observers and occasional participants.[7] In fact, Pinkster appears to have been primarily an "outsiders'" phenomenon, originating on the outskirts of Anglo-Afro-Dutch communities, and experiencing a relatively late flowering in Manhattan in the 1790s, at approximately the same time that it was fading elsewhere. That this brief urban efflorescence might have served as an inspiration for early blackface, in terms of creolized language, music, dancing, and general conduct, is confirmed by Pinkster's popularity as a spectacle among white audiences; a pamphlet published in Albany, whose language S. White reproduces, advertises:

> *A PINKSTER ODE For the Year 1803. Most Respectfully Dedicated to CAROLUS AFRICANUS, REX; Thus Rendered in English: KING CHARLES, Captain-General and Commander in Chief of the PINKSTER BOYS*, by "Absalom Aimwell."[8]

Further confirmation of Pinkster's likely influence on the New York theatrical scene includes primary source evidence for its literal reproduction on stage: S. White cites an announcement in the *New York Evening Post* in May 1804, touting "PINXTER MONDAY or HARLEQUIN'S FROLICS," to be performed theatrically as a pantomime. In this latter case, it seems most likely that the onstage participants in this urban theatrical setting would have been not African Americans (as in the original festival situations), but whites in blackface, hence providing a possible template for theatrical minstrelsy within a couple of decades.[9]

Similar to Pinkster was Negro 'Lection Day, an annual festival celebrated in May or June shortly after the whites-only General Election Day, which combined elements of European and African behaviors.[10] It is recorded in the Northeast as early as the 1690s, peaking a century later in the immediate aftermath of the revolution.[11] Wade finds records of the festival in Boston, Providence, Portsmouth, New Haven, and fourteen other New England towns, and traces its relatively swift decline to, again, official reservations about black-white contact:[12] "Anxieties focused on the underlife peripheral to the festivals. . . . Some black and white festival-goers attended the rites principally to try their hand at 'shaking pawpaw,' pitching pennies, and tossing quoits. An atmosphere of license was further engendered by the generous supplies [of alcohol] which were sold at the festival grounds, along the main thoroughfares, and in taverns and dance halls."[13] Like the Pinkster festival in upstate New York, John Canoe in the Mid-Atlantic and Long Island, cornhuskings in both North and South, and the evangelical Great Awakening" that swept the colonies in the 1730s, Negro 'Lection Day represented the opportunity to "perform" a syncretic, public, collaborative, participatory, liminal, creolized identity.[14] Similarly, because African Americans played various martial and musical roles (as drummers, fifers, or in their own trainee companies) throughout the colonial and revolutionary periods, at militia training days "blacks would come from miles around, ostensibly to watch the black militia drill."[15] By the revolutionary period, Training Day had become an occasion for slippery cross-cultural behaviors, including dancing, drinking, and music.

Wade argues that such events were major sites for exchange because they "collapsed social boundaries more so than did any other social event in colonial New England, deriving their participants and spectators across lines of race, sex, class, and generation."[16] They provided imitative access, for whites, to behaviors that S. White says "were at the very heart of slave culture in the eighteenth-century North," and that included a strong admixture of recently imported African behaviors, such as the Guinea dance.[17] Thus, like their European and African antecedents, U.S. festivals enabled imitative cultural borrowing and exchange that ran in multiple directions—again foreshadowing blackface. Music and dance played a key role in the transgressive reformulation of identity that such "social performances" entailed; as Mason comments: "The social performer implicitly asserts that the representational aspects—*the gestures, tropes and icons drawn from the sources*—are becoming incorporated into his or her 'own' behavior, that 'this is who I am' . . . the strategy expresses the aspiration to incorporate that aura permanently, to make it inherent or organic rather than borrowed."[18] Just as blacks borrowed and learned tunes and instruments from and for white dancing, and whites borrowed tunes and instruments, antebellum festivals also facilitated a wide range of cultural sharing. At 'Lection Days, for example, "ethnic borrowing by blacks from whites" included formal titles of address, the election of the events' "kings" by balloting, the prohibition of women from such status, the firing of salutes, the use of quasi-military garb and formal dress, and other factors. Conversely, African elements included not only diverse musical instrumentation, extensive "polytonal texture[s] and upbeat rhythms" and an emphasis on percussion, but even parade-style strutting and baton-twirling, which are thought to originate in West African dance practices.[19] These events made African American performance behaviors both attractive for and available to white imitators: "The black communities of colonial and antebellum New England embodied a model of social adaptation based on cultural creolization. . . . The lifestyles of these dominated communities reflected the tangible artifacts of the dominating social system in combination with the subtle mentifacts of the parent culture, the former often apprehended consciously and the latter usually perceived unconsciously." Perhaps most significant for our purposes is the realization that festivals like Pinkster and 'Lection Day were both rooted in and transmitted via the riverine and maritime contexts from which blackface minstrelsy later emerged: Wade notes that "in colonial and antebellum New England, black communication systems were apparently most stable and complex in the black communities of the larger towns along the seacoast and river valleys."[20]

MILITIAS AND MUSICAL DISPLAY

Similarly liminal behaviors, and their attendant cross-cultural musical sharing, occurred not only at creolized calendar events, but also in the case of creolized environments such as waterfronts and ships' decks. Musical exchange also obtained in the case of other events that brought blacks and whites into contact; the influence of black on white musicians is confirmed, for example, by the recruitment of black drummers into eighteenth-century armies, by Benjamin Latrobe's evidence from New Orleans's multiracial Congo Square circa 1820, and by the presence of black fiddlers, dancers and drummers in the sketches and oils of W. S. Mount from the 1850s and '60s.

We examine the impact of black dance in the chapter 6 discussions of Mount's militia sketches, but it is worth mentioning here that, in the antebellum period, any situation of public performance, theater, or spectacle—from Pinkster to 'Lection Day to militia training to corn shuckings to patriotic parades to political demonstrations—might implicate the possibility of black-white cultural exchange, particularly when that situation included dance. We can thus recognize the festival, street, deck, and wharf as performance venues, no less than were the theaters, and as venues displaying a wealth of interrelated models for imitation. When we expand our definition of performance in this way, we can analyze Mount's contribution to our understanding of creole synthesis as a product of remarkable, fortuitous synchronicity of timing, aptitude, and location.

THE CREOLE SYNTHESIS IN THE FEDERALIST PERIOD: MOUNT'S MANHATTAN AND SETAUKET ROOTS

Evidence for these Anglo-African festivals' creole synthesis of behaviors is both direct—that is, via specific reference and description in period sources—and also indirect or inferential: in literature and the demographics of the whaling, sailing, fishing, and trading communities of the Atlantic coast, including the North Shore of Long Island, where Mount was born, and the Lower East Side of Manhattan, where he came to manhood. Using two physical contexts integral to Mount's own biography, cultural experience, and mature catalog of works, and the evidence revealed by close examination of his New York uncle Micah Hawkins's little-remarked ballad opera *The Saw-Mill* (1824–25), we can identify multiple channels by which African American and Caribbean influences entered Anglo-American performance, as well as Mount's own life, art, and music. As on the frontiers, on Long Island and the Lower East Side, black-white interaction was not limited to work or to the siring of children, but extended to social, leisure, and domestic arrangements.

Black slaves, imported both directly from Africa and by way of Caribbean stopovers, had been introduced into the Dutch colonies of the Northeast in 1626, and by the mid-1700s constituted more than 15 percent of the state's population, with the vast majority living and working in close proximity to their masters in small rural households.[21] In the late eighteenth century, New York State slave manumission changed the legal status but not necessarily the material occupations of these now-free blacks: they continued to work in agriculture, farm management, carpentry, weaving, butchering, coopering, whaling, fishing, violin and fife playing, choir directing, sheep shearing, brick making, salt making, and shipbuilding, and to live in close proximity to whites.[22] In these respects, at least, the experience of free blacks on Long Island was consistent with that of those living on the Lower East Side: S. White says many self-employed Manhattan blacks practiced artisanal skills before manumission, as "carpenters, coopers, cabinetmakers, upholsterers, sailmakers, butchers, [and] bakers." In an observation that resonates with *Dancing for Eels, 1820 Catharine Market* and with Dixon's *Love in a Bushel* (of oysters), he points out that many others sold goods in the Manhattan markets, especially in the oyster trade, "which they dominated."[23]

A related result of late colonial manumission in New York was the acknowledgment, by white fathers, of their mixed-race and natural-born children: such acknowledgment, for purposes of confirming these children's rights and independence, was quite common in white landowners' wills and testaments.[24] It is the most tangible demonstration that the social and sexual proximity remarked or restricted across the riverine and maritime United States sometimes led to literal and genetic (as well as cultural) creolization in the early years of the nineteenth century.[25]

There is also more direct confirmation for the Manhattan–Long Island connection. As we have seen, Wells, Goertzen, and Jabbour (among others) have demonstrated the overlap of black and white sources in the repertoires of antebellum fiddlers.[26] And we can see similar overlap in New England: Nathan, for example, says "The "Long Island Negroes,' in particular, were often mentioned as skilled dancers—and that as early as the beginning of the nineteenth century"; while Thomas Rice's early theatrical hit *Long Island Juba, or, Love in a Bushel* (1833) features a comic character named Juba, "a goodhearted chap who plays on his guitar and sings: 'You good to me, dat keepy here, No Mass, dat you never fear.'"[27] A character called "Juba" also appears as early as 1793 in *The Prize, or 2, 5, 3, 8*: both the Afro-Caribbean origins of the word as proper name and rhythmic practice, and its recurrence in the stage name of the Long Island–born dancer William Henry Lane (ca. 1825–1852/53), reinforce its creole connotations and associations.[28] The term seems to originate in Central Africa (*djouba* in Angola) but was common throughout the African Caribbean, as well; while Lane's dancing was the subject of a closely observed description by Charles Dickens in his 1842 *American Notes*.

New England's role in the Atlantic and Caribbean coastal trades and in Pacific whaling meant that Long Island was exposed to a wide variety of outside influences. The triangular sugar trade—raw cane, harvested by slaves and grown in the Caribbean, was shipped to New England for processing into molasses and rum, and then in turn shipped to England and the European continent for sales that funded trading in West African slaves. As a result, Haitian creole language, dress, dance, and music were especially familiar on the Atlantic Seaboard, even as far north as Nova Scotia.[29] Black musicians had performed for white dancing in colonial Haiti at least as early as 1700 (more recent pan-Caribbean dance traditions continued to reflect this early musical sharing) and the resulting syncretic dance music had made its way into both Gulf and Atlantic ports.[30] As Hunt says "trade, the [mercantile] proximity of St. Domingue, the flood of refugees to American seaports, and the cultural links between the slaveholding South and the Caribbean" all enhanced contact between Atlantic and Caribbean coasts.[31] Most significantly for the creole synthesis of blackface, both free mixed-race *gens de couleur* and slaves accompanied their masters in the last Haitian diaspora to North America, while black and mulatto sailors participated in the sailing trade from the seventeenth century.[32]

The French Catholic cities of New Orleans, Savannah, and Charleston, as the three principle destinations for Haitian émigrés, showed this musical influence most strongly and lastingly, but Caribbean influence was not restricted only to them.[33] Historiography and period literature confirm that such influence shaped New England Anglo-European expressive culture, as well. Washington Irving's early epistolary work, *Salmagundi* (1807–8), which far predates his 1820s success as a purveyor of upstate New York folktales such as "The Legend of Sleepy Hollow" and "Rip van Winkle," includes a lengthy account by one character of having attended a ball in "Hayti," and of a Long Island gathering at which both Caribbean dances and Scots fiddle tunes such as "Devil Among the Tailors" are performed.[34] As already mentioned, the ungainly dancing of Irving's iconic character Ichabod Crane ("The Legend of Sleepy Hollow") has been seen as a parody of Haitian "shaking" styles.[35] That story is notable both for the presence of a black fiddler, and for a verbal description of Ichabod's dancing that evokes simultaneously the caricature of later minstrelsy and the literal visual details of W. S. Mount's 1830 *Rustic Dance after a Sleigh Ride*:

> And now the sound of the music from the common room, or hall, summoned to the dance. The musician was an old gray-headed negro, who had been the itinerant orchestra of the neighborhood for more than half a century. His instrument was as old and battered as himself. The greater part of the time he scraped on two or three strings, accompanying every movement of the bow with a motion of the head; bowing almost to the ground, and stamping with his foot whenever a fresh couple were to start. . . . [Ichabod] was the admiration of all the negroes; who, having gathered, of all ages and sizes, from the farm and the neighborhood, stood forming a pyramid of shining black faces at every door and window, gazing with delight at the scene, rolling their white eyeballs, and showing grinning rows of ivory from ear to ear.[36]

For that matter, whistling itself carried associations with creole festivals: S. White confirms that, in New York, "whistling was called 'Negro Pinckster Music' long after the festival itself had died."[37] Virtuoso whistling linked sonic transgression—that is, the making of a loud, unexpected, nearly invisible, intrusive sound in public spaces—and blackface's own irruptive character: Bobolink Bob Rowley (dates unknown), the Long Island dancer whose eponymous sonic association with the bird *Dolichonyx oryzivorus* recalls mimetic connections made between the song "Jump Jim Crow" and the Caribbean turkey vulture *Cathartes aura*, was also a champion whistler.[38] Seeley Simpkins, one of Dan Emmett's major influences, could play fiddle and banjo, call dances, and "outwhistle all creation": Norton (1862) says of Simpkins that, in an underpopulated Ohio where it "took four counties to make a [militia] regiment," Simpkins "gave a challenge to outwhistle any man within them" and was undefeated.[39]

Hunt says flatly that the creole influence in the antebellum United States can be traced to postrevolutionary Haiti: "The distinctiveness of Creole culture in the lower Mississippi Valley (in fact as far north as Illinois), in the Gulf states, and around Charleston and Savannah [and, he adds later, along the Atlantic seaports of Boston, New York, Savannah, and Baltimore] can be traced to those who fled from St. Domingue."[40] Hunt also observes that Haitian émigrés often became leaders in the communities of free blacks in these diasporic cities, founding newspapers, mutual-aid societies, and cultural organizations.[41] Émigré "actors, actresses, singers, dancers, and stage entrepreneurs" were also integral to the explosion of theatrical and musical activity in New Orleans after the Louisiana Purchase (1803) and in turn stimulated both French- and English-language productions and touring networks.[42]

Such touring troupes included not only dramatic and comic actors but also "comedians, pantomimists, rope-dancers, etc."[43] These Haitian-tinged ensembles, touring out of the southern port cities (principally New Orleans) in the early decades of the nineteenth century, would have directly interacted, on waterfronts, ferries, steamboats, docks, hotels, and back stages of theaters, with troupes like Noah Ludlow's from the Northeast (especially New York and Pennsylvania) touring south along the Hudson, Ohio, and Mississippi. Those river towns, where Caribbean or southern and Atlantic or northern performers met, are precisely the time, place, and professional-theatrical environment in which the first solo blackface practitioners—T. D. Rice and G. W. Dixon—experienced the collision of Afro-Caribbean and Anglo-American expressive culture.[44]

During the revolution, Long Island's (both licit and illicit) maritime activities were overlaid with a patriotic tinge: the region was a hotbed of smugglers sympathetic to the rebels and her ports often hid European privateersmen. Water was central to the conflict: maritime tactics were essential to the more famous Battles of Lexington and Concord (1775, when British regulars attempted a secret crossing of Boston's Charles River), Washington's evacuation from Long Island to New York (1776) and crossing of the Delaware before the Battle of Trenton (1776), and the successful French blockade of the British at Yorktown (1781). Similarly, the August 1777 "Battle of Setauket" was fought in the year of Micah Hawkins's birth on the town green between occupying British troops and an invading Continental force that had crossed Long Island Sound by boat from Connecticut.

MOUNT'S FAMILY HERITAGE

The Hawkins and Mount families had been tavern owners and farmers in the Setauket and Stony Brook neighborhood since the mid-seventeenth century, having come from Rhode Island in the 1660s—this emigration probably indicative of their original status as dissenters from Puritan orthodoxy in Massachusetts.[45] Mount's maternal grandfather Major Jonas Hawkins (b. 1752), a militiaman who sat out the revolution, in 1791 took possession of the family home at Stony Brook, where he presided over a large household of relatives and dependents, including African American slaves soon to be manumitted (on Long Island and throughout New England, small-farm practices meant that farmers tended to maintain only a few slaves who lived with and worked alongside family members).

Jonas's son Thomas Shepard Mount (whose birth date Buffet gives, probably erroneously, as 1788) married Julia Ann Hawkins in 1801; they reared five children who lived into adulthood: Henry Smith (b. 1802), Shepard Alonzo (b. 1804), Robert Nelson (b. 1806), William Sidney (b. 1807), and Ruth Hawkins (b. 1808). Jonas also maintained a tavern at Stony Brook, where his son Micah (later William Sidney's mentor and master) was born in 1777 and raised in a postrevolutionary environment in which shared rural and urban, white and black, old and new cultural influences were ubiquitous. Black fiddlers often supplied the soundtrack: Anthony Hannibal "Toney" Clapp (d. 1816), a childhood model for William Sidney and the subject of a heartfelt eulogy from Hawkins on his death, was a member of the Hawkins household both before and after slave manumission.

William's father Thomas ran a store and inn where the New York post road crossed Setauket Green; his clientele included ship chandlers, whalers, distillers, and the local chapter of Masons. After his father Thomas's early death in 1813, William stayed in his grandfather Jonas Hawkins's Stony Brook home, where he most likely learned the fiddle from Anthony Clapp.[46] This period was evidently particularly significant in William's musical development: he later cited "Toney" Clapp and Micah Hawkins as principle musical influences.[47] Clapp was apparently adept at not only the music but also the exhibition dancing associated with minstrelsy, described by Thomas De Voe in his *Market Book*, and depicted in *Dancing for Eels, 1820 Catharine Market*: Buffet recounts an anecdote from Robert Nelson Mount, who claimed that, in addition to playing the fiddle for white and black dancing, Toney Clapp could "place a sixpence on the floor and bend over backwards and take it up with his tongue and rise without any support from his hands."[48]

At age fourteen, Micah Hawkins was bound as apprentice to a coach maker in Morristown, New Jersey, but by 1798 had moved into New York City and gone into business as a grocer, hotelier, and tavern keeper, trades in which he had been raised and in which he would prove to be highly successful. Micah's Manhattan grocery was originally located at 390 Water Street, just across the harbor from Brooklyn, and thus situated to serve the ferry traffic from his former neighbors on Long Island. By 1810 he had moved to the Catherine Slip itself, "where [he] expanded his commercial interests to include the Catherine-Street Ferry House, a hotel and bar."[49] The slip (wharf) was a landing point for ferries from Brooklyn and Long Island and from points farther east (including Connecticut and Rhode Island); Hawkins's hotel-tavern-grocery was thus ideally situated to capture the neighborhood street, dock, and waterborne trade.[50]

In the early federalist period, physical, technological, and economic expansion were matched by an explosion of mobility and intra-ethnic contact, much of it waterborne. Though the percentage of free blacks in overall urban populations actually fell in the period after 1800—due to the vast increase in Caucasian immigration, especially from Ireland—African Americans continued to occupy a position of significant visibility in U.S. cities, including New York.[51] Gradual emancipation in the North "had greater impact in Albany, Brooklyn, and New York than in the other northern cities," in part because so many freed slaves chose not to relocate; sometimes they even went to work as wage earners for their former owners.[52] The expansion of African Americans into the forces of wage earners yielded social and economic pressures, and in response, city governments created ordinances that tightly restricted the trades, neighborhoods, training, or business enterprises open to free blacks—essentially, a kind of protectionism designed to safeguard white working-class jobs. Ironically, but importantly for the development of the creole synthesis, such ordinances tended to concentrate blacks in certain occupations and neighborhoods: often riverine or maritime in nature, and often shared with the newly immigrated Irish.[53] In both South and North, blacks lived in comparative physical proximity to whites, whether in "back-houses" behind their owners' mansions, as in New Orleans, or in mixed-race working-class boardinghouses, as in Cincinnati and New York. The stark separation of black and white populations conventionally presumed on the model of southern plantation culture (cotton, tobacco, rice) was the exception in early nineteenth-century America—not the norm.

As we saw in the case of Frederick Douglass's flight to freedom by rail, the relative anonymity supplied by large, transient, urban populations also made cities especially attractive as targets for escaping slaves: blacks on the busy streets could more effectively avoid identification and thus avoid recapture.[54] This permitted a comparative freedom of conduct—even of defiance—that elicited considerable white middle-class resentment; S. White describes this anxiety, in the short generation between manumission circa 1800 and 1814, as precipitated by free blacks' assertion of a "right to the street [that] almost inevitably involved jostling for space with whites."[55] Caucasian fear of such jostling played out in retaliatory caricatures of "black dandyism" such as Zip Coon.[56]

However, black-white cultural exchange on the urban streets was neither unidirectional nor exclusively fearful: as Curry says "even in the most heavily concentrated black residential area in urban America . . . whites were to be found in considerable numbers."[57] While cities in the lower South offered much more occupational opportunity to African Americans than elsewhere, possibly as a result of southern urbanites being "fully accustomed to the presence of black artisans," such artisanal training, sponsorship, and mentoring was also available, for example, on Long Island.[58] Many ex-slaves had learned trades working side by side in the households of their artisan masters, and upon manumission after 1799 set up in business (or were set up) in those same trades.

Because Micah Hawkins's adult home and occupation were built on his childhood experience in his father's Long Island tavern, when he moved to Manhattan he was well-situated to take advantage of the explosion of riverine and maritime trade in the period between the Revolution and the official opening of the Erie Canal in October 1825. Most significantly, both Hawkins's own experience, and that of the musically and artistically talented nephew who boarded with him in the '20s, were exactly concurrent with, and nearly as polyglot as, those of the first generation of blackface minstrels. Multiple primary sources confirm the Lower East Side's cross-cultural profile. In addition to the folk sketch *Dancing for Eels, 1820 Catharine Market* (a central datum in W. T. Lhamon's *Raising Cain*), the *Market Book* of Thomas De Voe, published in 1867, describes De Voe's experience as a Manhattan butcher before the Civil War. De Voe provides detailed descriptions of the Long Island blacks who were known as exhibition dancers on the Catharine Slip, giving their names (often Dutch in provenance, implying that they were former slaves still attached to older, Dutch families from the island), and details of their dress and dance:

> The first introduction in this city of public "negro dancing" no doubt took place at this market. The negroes who visited here were principally slaves from Long Island who have leave of their master for certain holidays, among which "Pinkster" was the principal one; . . . then, as they usually had three days holiday, they were ever ready, by their "negro sayings and doing," to make a few shillings more. So they would be hired by some joking butcher or individual to engage in a jig or breakdown, as that was one of their favorite pastimes at home on the barn-floor, or in a frolic.[59]

White confirms the liminality of market spaces—the degree to which, in such places, cross-cultural, transgressive public display was essentially expected—and likewise observes that Pinkster was celebrated on the Catharine Slip in the 'teens.[60] Micah Hawkins, in his shop and tavern on the Catherine Market, was adept and imaginative in the use of music to further attract the sailors, apprentices, ostlers, chandlers, longshoremen, and businessmen who crowded its streets: Lawrence describes him as a composer, arranger, violinist, pianist, flutist, comic singer, mimic, poet, playwright, and "conversational wit with the incongruous professions of carriage-builder, grocer, and innkeeper."[61] Having played piano, flute, and violin since childhood, Hawkins was also a respected member, from 1799, of an amateur musical group called the Euterpean Society, much of whose music is preserved in his papers, and he had a piano keyboard built into the shop counter of his store. Micah had begun collecting tunes at age seventeen, while an apprentice, in his *Book of Notes for the German Flute*, which eventually contained 210 pieces, including popular tunes, folk tunes—American, English, Irish, Scottish, French—revolutionary songs, dance tunes, comic ditties, and even such esoterica as "Handel's Water Piece" and a "Comick tune from Orpheus and Euridice." In addition to arrangements for one and two flutes and one for solo violin, the book contains the words but not the music of two popular songs ("The Banks of the Dee" and "The Rambling Boy").[62] Hawkins's musical manuscripts are consistent with late eighteenth-century avocational musical tastes: duets for "German [simple-system] flute" or violin, light-classical arias and Vauxhall Garden songs, transcriptions from Handel and Haydn, and the occasional dance tune or musical exercise all appear. The collection thus reflects the musical language of a talented amateur in the postcolonial period.[63] In addition, some of the material appears to have been sourced from James Everdell, a conductor active 1798–1832, who did a stint at Manhattan's Park Theatre, a central venue in the story of blackface theatricals, and who may thus have facilitated William Sidney's attendance there as a teen.[64]

Hawkins also tried his hand at the composition of both music and poetry: for example, his "Setauket," a paean to his birthplace, is a simple but effective song in the lightly harmonized English Vauxhall Gardens style and employs a charming "La, Sol, Fa" refrain.[65] The papers also contain several odd but amusing doggerel poems, with accompanying comic illustrations, detailing anecdotes and experiences in the streets of New York and employing black, Dutch, and Irish caricatures; these include 1824's "Mynehieur Von Herrick Heimelman, the Dancing-Master: or The Confluence of Nassau-Street and Maiden-Lane, As it was Whilom" and the undated "Big Red Nose, and How to Bleach It . . . where a classic brawl is enacted between the bullying Big Red Nose and his agile little tormentor Pat, 'Hibernia's Son.'"[66] Both recall the doggerel language, comic dialect, and parodic caricatures that recur in Hawkins's ballad opera *The Saw-Mill* (1824–25).

Micah Hawkins is important in William Sidney Mount's story for several reasons: he was an admired mentor to his young nephew, who boarded with Hawkins as a teenager, mourned Micah's early death from typhoid, and lovingly retouched his portrait. Uncle Micah was likewise a musical resource, as William inherited several of his instruments and the vast majority of his eclectic music manuscripts. But additional factors would have shaped Mount's teenage urban musical experience: though he tended to excise these experiences from his own autobiography, lower Manhattan's entertainment culture was changing swiftly in the period of William's apprenticeship.

WATERSHED MOMENT: THE GREAT CANAL

Though river and canal travel would continue to play a role in U.S. commerce and consciousness through the antebellum period, its period of highest visibility and greatest cultural and economic contact was precisely the same period as that of minstrelsy's first development: roughly between 1796, when Robert Fulton (1765–1815) had published his *Treatise on the Improvement of Canal Navigation* (and would shortly go on to well-remarked breakthroughs in designing steamboats that could exploit the new canals), and 1840, when the economic downturns and the expansion in Northeast railways began to dampen new construction.[67] By the 1860s, canal technology was essentially moribund.

But this first third of the nineteenth century was a period when the economic opportunities and the cultural transformations wrought by canal construction and transport seemed almost limitless. As we have seen in chapter 2, canaller culture, combining immigrant Irish, northern English, and free-black populations, yielded new cultural conflicts and combinations, and represented an eruptive, transgressive, working-class consciousness.[68] Cook quotes the interest of the flash press in contests of canallers' "sprinting, sparring, cockfighting, clog dancing, and the like . . . usually with a public wager to heighten the stakes."[69] They would join the first New York audiences for theatrical blackface.

Public discourse on linking the Great Lakes, Upstate New York, and New York City via a canal-and-rivers network dated back to the seventeenth century; in 1699 the Marquis de Vauban, the most famous military engineer of the age, had proposed a canal between Lakes Erie and Ontario as a strategy for maintaining French dominance in the North. Both English and French military, political, and economic strategists recognized the desirability of linking Upstate New York and Quebec with the "Old Frontier." Throughout the colonial and revolutionary periods, there were many suggestions aimed at enhancing trade by developing a canal, locks, and improved navigation on the Mohawk River.

By the 1780s, such improvements were seen as ways of claiming and stabilizing the "frontier settlements" of New York and Pennsylvania, and by 1797, Fulton, ever the promoter, had written to President Washington with proposals for a canal linking New York, via the Hudson, to Lake Erie and the interior. With the immense expansion of U.S. horizons brought by the Louisiana Purchase in 1803, the climate for transport projects of all types continued to improve. In 1816 future governor Henry De Witt Clinton pushed the New York legislature to adopt a canal-building plan, and on July 4, 1817, work began at Rome, New York, 255 miles from New York City. Construction moved relatively swiftly: the middle section (Utica to Salinas) and the Champlain Canal were opened in 1819, and throughout the '20s the opening of new sections, and published reports about its progress, kept the canal very much in New York's public consciousness.[70] Completed on October 25, 1825, the first full passage from Lake Erie to New York City was an occasion for extensive celebration. Thus, the premiere of *The Saw-Mill* in December 1824, and its setting on the frontier and "Grand Canal" near Lake Oneida a few miles away from Rome, represents Hawkins's timely exploitation of a widely recognized technological and commercial watershed. Likewise associated with the canal and intruding on middle-class public consciousness in the 1820s was a sort of horrified fascination regarding new working-class archetypes and behaviors. While there is no question that, as Nathan says, "Zip Coon" was in part "a ludicrous black replica of the white dandy of . . . New York's Broadway," other ludicrous—or ominous—types were being remarked upon on the streets of New York, and such types provided other models for early blackface characterizations.[71] Nathan, for example, says that Zip Coon and Gumbo Chaff "had about them something of the swagger of the real frontiersman and river boatman."[72]

THE FLASH PRESS IN THE NORTHEAST

The flash press of the 1840s captures a later historical moment during which existing multiracial working-class "cellar" entertainments were beginning to obtrude on middle-class consciousness; S. White, for example, describes a subterranean culture of black taverns, restaurants, oyster bars, and dance halls in Manhattan as early as the 1790s; it was the entry of white working-class mechanics and middle-class consumers of the flash press that created the interracial audiences for blackface theatrics.[73] In the wake of the opening of the canal and the radical democratization of the Jacksonian revolution—and the first rise of political organizations intending to organize the working-class vote—middle-class unease was counterbalanced by a certain illicit fascination. Subscription patterns, the topics of reporting, and correspondence submitted to the papers confirms that readers primarily occupied "white-collar jobs as sales clerks, bookkeepers, and secretaries"; in other words, they were of a similar age and marital status to the apprentices and mechanics who were blackface's first audience—but of a higher economic and social status.[74]

The sporting events, saloon halls, brothels, and blackface theaters described in the flash press provided environments in which middle-class young men could mingle with working-class whites *and blacks*, a pattern of interclass exchange that is replicated in later U.S. popular music histories.[75] James Cook unpacks the implications and associations of black-white exchange in Lower Manhattan's Five Points, calling the response of some middle-class white visitors "a voyeurism that routinely included participation and intimate mixing." He adds: "In this way, sporting men put themselves in close proximity to the rougher' social worlds of the emerging urban proletariat, and even identified with some of its causes . . . they overlapped and intersected—temporarily—in particular urban sites: brothels, saloons, boxing arenas, cockpits, gambling dens, theaters, and dance halls." Cook describes, in the period of Micah Hawkins's occupancy and William Sidney Mount's apprenticeship, a Lower Manhattan intersection of Irish immigrants and "newly emancipated slaves" that created, in response to demand and with the "complicity of affluent landlords," a "burgeoning vice trade." And this trade was not small: Cook quotes from E. Z. C. Judson (later author of the "Ned Buntline" dime novels), whose *Mysteries and Miseries of New York* (1848) claims that on a typical night, Almack's Cellar (a dance hall) "held almost two hundred customers of various classes and complexions," and that the (unnamed) star of owner Pete William's floor show, a dancer who may have been William Henry Lane, had a repertoire that included "'flings, reels, hornpipes, double shuffles, and heel-and-toe tappers.'"[76]

The flash papers, then, provided both a practical guide, and (for the timid) a more distant prosodic voyeurism, for "white men of all classes"—but they also confirm the ongoing energy and fascination to outsiders we have located in the creole synthesis. When Dickens came to the United States in 1842, a visit that yielded his iconic description of Master Juba dancing in a Five Points cellar, the fact that he and his guides (including a flash press reporter whose article provides an interesting counterreading of the event) could find Almack's Cellar at all implies that its proprietors intended it to be found.[77] Cook suggests that Dickens's description of Juba dancing in fact "acknowledged the vitality of an interracial dance culture both distinct from blackface minstrelsy and typically invisible beyond poor neighborhoods like the Five Points." The "interracial dance culture" cited by Cook existed decades before Dickens's visit.

The brief apotheosis of the flash papers (1841–43), while concurrent with the launch of Emmett's "first" Virginia Minstrels in 1843, like them postdates the first flowering of blackface performance by at least a decade. Thus the flash presses, like the troupes themselves, represent a later commodification and middle-class theatricalization of a phenomenon occurring in the streets decades before. As an example, we can cite the cartoon *The Pewter Mug on a Saturday Night* (1842), which depicts a group of top-hatted, side-burned young men in a tavern full of cigar smoke: Bowery B'hoys reminiscent of 1820's *Dancing for Eels* sketch.[78] Despite the twenty-two years that separate the two images, they depict the same neighborhood and behaviors: indeed, the 1840s Pewter Mug tavern was located around the corner from Mount's 1827 Nassau Street home, situated just across the East River from Brooklyn and Long Island. The presence on the Catherine Slip of the Manhattan-Brooklyn ferry from 1795—first horse-drawn, and then from 1814 a steam ferry whose lease was held by Robert Fulton himself—meant a huge volume of local and visitor foot traffic; hence, the neighborhood was a perfect location for a tavern and sporting house such as the Pewter Mug, and for Micah Hawkins's more respectable grocery and hotel.

Likewise, a lengthy article in the flash paper the *Whip* (March 12, 1842), describes interracial families in the neighborhood, mentions Almack's at 67 Orange Street, describes "the voice of a gentleman of color calling to the fiddler for 'de Boz Quadrille'" (a sly reference to Dickens's fame as author of *Sketches by Boz*), and notes the dancing of quadrilles and cotillions "to the popular [blackface] airs of 'Sitch a gittin up stairs' and 'Jim along Josey.'"[79] The same article describes African American dancers at "Roache's in Orange street . . . who were compelled to execute Scotch reels and breakdowns," and a multiracial clientele at the Diving Bell tavern and brothel "at the corner of Orange and Leonard Streets," also owned by the Almack's Pete Williams.[80] Almack's was a locus for integrated music-and-dance: the anonymous flash correspondent who accompanied Dickens describes "a large underground room with white-washed walls, wooden benches, and an orchestra platform occupied by fiddle, trumpet, and bass drum," a range of activities including gambling, eating, drinking, chewing and smoking tobacco, and dancing, all reminiscent of Hearn's postbellum descriptions of black Cincinnati. The clientele is virtually a census of the Lower Manhattan street culture depicted in *Dancing for Eels* and (later) *The Pewter Mug*: "Three quarters of the women . . . were negresses, of various shades and colors," while the men present included everyone from "thieves, loafers, Bowery b'hoys, and rowdies to firemen, greenhorns, . . . [to] 'honest, hard working people.'"[81]

The range of multiracial and cross-class venues cited within the pages of the flash press suggest that middle-class voyeurism was big business in 1840s New York.[82] The middle-class white men seeking illicit entertainment in Lower Manhattan (in an elegant historical irony, a foreshadowing of the "slumming" Greenwich Village residents who would visit Harlem, in upper Manhattan, for similar purposes) were notorious in both white and black newspapers of the period: both Dixon's serial *Polyanthos and Fire Department Album* and the African American *Freedom's Journal* (publ. 1827–29) argue that it is not the locals, but the slumming "sporting men," who engage in licentious behavior.[83] Conversely, Cook quotes the middle-class flash press's fearful "litany of complaints about the excessive rowdiness of the east side 'soaplocks' and 'jack tars' with whom white-collar sporting men routinely rubbed elbows."[84]

These contentious, squabbling environments also provided an avenue of alternate experience—indeed the opportunity to occupy a "masked," alternative behavior and identity—that lay at the root of bohemian culture and of theatrical blackface; Cook calls it "an alternative public sphere for white-collar men who rejected the values, tastes, and lifestyles of middle-class moralists."[85]

THE CREOLE SYNTHESIS IN BLACK MANHATTAN: THE AFRICAN GROVE

Another probable inspiration for theatrical minstrelsy already existed in Manhattan's vibrant street and expressive culture, and specifically originated within the black community. This information suggests that the precedent for interpolating street-based material into theatrical productions was already part of African American performance—that in fact, Dixon, Rice, Sweeney, and other blackface architects might have drawn inspiration from observation of black theater as well as black festivals and street dance. The revolution brought about the gradual dismantling of slavery, beginning with manumission for black veterans of the Continental Army in 1781, and accelerating to progressive freedom for those born in New York State after 1799 (the "Law of the Free Womb"), and eventual total abolition in 1827. Gradual manumission throughout the Northeast led to increased black mobility *and* black economic activity. Many ex-slaves relocated from rural to urban settings, seeking increased economic opportunities as well as more flexible social environments. Many more, however, remained in the same general craft trades and geographical locations they had occupied as slaves. Others migrated between locations, either seasonally, as we saw in the case of black sailors and laborers throughout the Atlantic and Caribbean zones, or as part of their regular activities, as we saw in the case of Long Island blacks who spent some time on the Lower East Side as street vendors.

This new social class of freedmen yielded an enhanced sense of community identity, and the creation of institutions that recognized this identity—most notably, in New York, through African American church congregations and free schools. The African Free School (AFS), founded by the New York Manumission Society in 1787, numbered among its patrons the statesmen and abolitionists John Jay and Alexander Hamilton, and enrolled as many as five hundred students at a time; the noted nineteenth-century actor Ira Aldridge, who got his start at the African Grove Theatre but became famous in Europe as a distinguished interpreter of Othello and of other Shakespearian roles (in whiteface), was an alumnus. The AFS was housed at various addresses in lower Manhattan, often in close proximity to the African Methodist, Episcopal, or Baptist churches whose foundation in the same period was another cornerstone of free black New York; it played a central role in the lives of the city's African Americans until it was incorporated into the public school system in 1835.[86]

Beyond the AFS, centers for the black community's public identity also included (briefly) David Ruggles's Bookshop at 67 Lispenard Street, which was burned by a white antiabolitionist mob only a year after its founding in 1834; the African Society for Mutual Relief (at the corner of Orange and Franklin), established by John Teasman of the AFS in 1808; the African American Union Hall, at 101 Anthony Street in the basement of the Broadway Tabernacle; the Philomathean Hall (161 Duane St.), established in 1826 as a "social & literary club for young African American men"; the American Anti-Slavery Society at 143 Nassau (founded 1833); and several black-edited newspapers, including the influential *Freedom's Journal*, with offices at 150 Church Street, founded in 1827 by John Russwurm and Samuel E. Cornish; and its successor *The Colored American* (2 Frankfort St.), established in 1837 by Cornish and Philip Bell.[87] All of these locations were in close proximity to, or at most a few long blocks west from, the epicenter of Irish working-class New York at Five Points (the fabled intersection of Mulberry, Orange, Anthony, Cross, and Little Water Streets), and at only a little slightly greater distance from the East River, the Catherine Slip, and the Long Island ferries. In additional to schools, churches, fellowship organizations, and newspapers, the period also saw a vastly enhanced visibility for African Americans as organizers and community leaders, in the various public activities that promulgated abolitionist ideas, and in general sought to build African American community pride.

The picture then is one of swirling, rapidly evolving geographic and demographic nodes and routes of cultural activity and exchange: into and out of the Long Island and Atlantic ports, and thence to and from the rest of the Atlantic and Caribbean maritime worlds; into and out of the city along the coasts and rivers: Long Island Sound, the East River, and the Hudson; and into, out of, across, and between racial, neighborhood, and economic groups on Manhattan Island itself. In the streets of Manhattan at the turn of the nineteenth century, the general sense must have been one of globalizing cosmopolitanism: diversity of clothing, languages, accents, street food, physical gesture and behavior, and the details of skin color and physiognomy would reinforce this. This diversity played out in the city's expressive cultures, as well, most notably through enhanced visibility for African American performance. The exchange documented in Dickens's rapturous description of Henry "Juba" Lane dancing at Almack's Cellar in the 1840s *American Notes*, which Dixon and Rice acted out on the Bowery stages in the 1830s, is already documented in the streets, cellars, and impromptu venues of postrevolutionary Manhattan.

One such, a central forerunner of minstrelsy, yet mostly unexplored as a source of inspiration for blackface, was a theatrical venture undertaken by a maritime professional seeking better economic opportunities ashore. The "African Grove" Theater, located (originally) in 1816 by a West Indian–born black ship's steward named William Brown in a private home at 38 Thompson Street, seems to have begun as an impromptu performance space but was eventually sufficiently popular to move to a purpose-built wooden theater "on Mercer Street, near Prince, which could seat 300–400."[88]

Both homegrown and touring theatricals had been part of city life since prerevolutionary days: in contrast to the more staid Boston and Philadelphia (which were Puritan and Quaker, respectively). New York and Baltimore, because they were centers for British garrisons and Tory liberalism, offered a wealth of theatrical entertainment. The first U.S. company was founded in New York in 1767, and the first full-length ballad opera on an American topic, *The Disappointment, or, The Force of Credulity* by the pseudonymous "Andrew Barton," a roman à clef set in Baltimore, was composed in 1762, and imported ballad operas were widely popular on colonial touring circuits. New York theaters provided another venue in which diverse classes, races, occupations, and licit versus illicit personalities rubbed elbows. Dewberry notes that, for example, Ira Aldridge could have seen white actors in Shakespearian performances at the Park Theatre's upper gallery, which was "set aside for blacks and white rowdies."[89]

Dewberry provides further period documentation that, by 1820, the company of black actors associated with the African Grove were experimenting with an improvisational, cross-cultural mix of music, song, dance, and both "serious" and comic genres: he mentions "dance and dialogue skits," the interpolation of impromptu comic songs for purposes of parody, entr'actes that consisted of separate, freestanding music and dance numbers, and the use of cross-dressing, racial "whiteface" (i.e., blacks playing white roles), and women as actors in the performances.[90] By 1821, the *National Advocate* could describe the African Grove's "black dandies and dandizettes" as exploiting racial caricatures intended to elicit the middle-class voyeuristic gaze:

> Accordingly, a garden has been opened somewhere back of the hospital called the African Grove . . . at which the ebony lads and lasses could obtain ice cream, ice punch, and hear music from the big drum and clarionet. . . . The gentleman, with his wool nicely combed, and his face shining through a coat of sweet oil, borrowed from the castors; cravat tight to suffocation, having the double faculty of widening the mouth and giving a remarkable

protuberance to the eyes; blue coat, fashionably cut; red ribbon and a bunch of pinch-beck seals; white pantaloons, shining boots, gloves, and a tippy rattan. The lady, with her pink kid slippers; her fine Leghorn, cambric dress with open work; corsets well fitted; reticulate hanging on her arm. Thus accoutered and caparisoned, these black fashionables saunter up and down the garden, in all pride of liberty and unconscious of want. In their dress, salutations, familiar phrases, and compliments, their imitative faculties are best exhibited.[91]

The African Grove's performers, theatricals, and (probably most of all) audience diversity attracted trouble from keepers of the peace: Dewberry says that the company "had to be mobile when they started doing plays because the police were constantly raiding their performances, and pressuring them to stop performing, due to the rowdiness of the white members of the audience."[92] It is possible that it was not only audience conduct but also volatile content that elicited official pressure: for example, the African Theatre Company rewrote the bawdy English ballad opera *Tom and Jerry*, "to include a slave-market scene set in Charleston, with a black cast of slaves and, apparently, a white actor as an auctioneer," and produced other pieces which addressed explosive topics including the 1795 slave uprising in St. Vincent.[93] This politically charged, defiantly oppositional stance would be mirrored in minstrelsy, as well.

Even though the African Grove suffered a relatively peripatetic existence during its few years of operation, its lasting influence can be cited in at least three ways. First, it continued in the memory of New York theatrical historians, both black and white: as late as 1860, the *Anglo-African Magazine* provides a lengthy foundation story on William Brown and his theatre, probably culled from the memories of informants who had attended performances:

> In 1816–17 Mr. Brown, steward of a Liverpool liner, gave up following the sea and hired a house on the north side of Thomas Street . . . and fitted up a tea-garden in the rear of the lot. In the evening he made the garden attractive by vocal and instrumental music. His brother stewards and their wives, and the colored population generally, gave him a full share of patronage. Among his *artistes* were Miss Ann Johnson, since Mrs. Allen . . . and James Hewlett. These evening entertainments were not dry affairs; brandy and gin-toddies, wine-negus, porter and strong all, with cakes and meats, enabled the audience to gratify several senses and appetites at the same time. James Hewlett was quite a character in his line; a very fine singer for the times, he added by degrees, dramatic exhibitions to the

> entertainments. *His off-nights were invariably spent in the gallery of the old Park Theatre*, and spent not in vain, for he soon became celebrated for the talent and versatility which enabled him—anticipating Mathews, we believe—to perform several widely differing characters, very perfectly, at one exhibition.[94]

This passage is significant because it highlights an explicit, three-way connection between the communities and public venues that were important conduits for the creole synthesis in Manhattan (and elsewhere): namely, the black stewards and sailors who plied the transatlantic and pan-Caribbean maritime trades; the burgeoning free-black community and especially the new black entrepreneurs of the city; and the integrated audiences (white, black, working class, middle class, artisans, mechanics, prostitutes, and "flash men") who attended the variety shows and blackface theaters.

Second, the African Grove is important because it was the precise site at which one influential predecessor of the blackface architects researched his stage characterizations. Whites wearing blackface makeup had been part of popular theatrics at least since the Elizabethan period, during which Othello, Shakespeare's Moor of Venice, had been joined by a host of other ethnic characterizations—European, Asian, African, and Native American. This emphasis on ethnic stereotyping, often for comic purposes, was replicated in colonial American theaters and streets in the postcolonial era.[95] In the same period, the English comic actor Charles Mathews (1776–1835) built a London reputation from 1803 as a "monopolylogist"—that is, a specialist in one-man shows that presented panoramas of quick-changing ethnic characterizations and popular song. His theatrical presentation included set-pieces titled "Boston Post Office," "Ode to General Jackson," "Illinois Inventory," and "Militia Muster Folk," all scenes intended to showcase his rapid-fire changes of American characters, dialects, and accents. We may also notice that Mathews used parodic names such as Swigger, Shuffle, Gazeall, and Rattlepot, of the sort common in ballad opera, which in turn anticipate and may well have influenced characterizations in Micah Hawkins's *Saw-Mill*.

Mathews's 1822 U.S. tour brought a wealth of new material. In letters written during the tour, Mathews described seeing an African American coachman in Philadelphia, reins knotted around his neck, controlling his team with the tunes that he simultaneously played on the fiddle.[96] On his return to London, Mathews boasted of the close observation and new inspiration he had derived from watching black performers, saying he would be "rich in black fun": he incorporated into his "monodramatic presentation" *A Trip to America* the character of the "runaway slave Agamemnon," dancing and playing the fiddle, in a recitation called "All Well at Natchitoches," as well as his parodic rendition of a sermon in African American dialect.[97] Mathews in character as Agamemnon is depicted in prototypical Jim Crow bodily posture in the illustrations of cartoonist Daniel Gregory Johnston, who appeared onstage with Mathews in Boston.[98]

That 1822 tour also brought Mathews to the pit of the African Grove, where he claimed to have heard and learned the iconic minstrel tune "Possum Up a Gum Tree," which tune would later form a central element in the finale to Hawkins's 1826 ballad opera.[99] Other period descriptions confirm the musical and improvisational diversity of the Grove's entertainments; Dewberry cites descriptions of an orchestra that "consisted of a violin, clarionet and a bass fiddle, played by two white men and one black," as well as extensive heckling from the crowd (not least from those "White People Who [Did] Not Know How to Behave at Entertainments"), as well as a combination of improvised and interpolated songs and dances of both black and white provenance.[100] In fact, Mathews may have gotten the idea for his parodic dialect sermon from hearing the Grove's actors parody Shakespearian soliloquies.

The brief apotheosis but lasting impact of the African Grove—its notoriety in New York theatrical memory, documentation in the flash press, and influence on Mathews's proto-blackface characterizations—provide a window on the multiethnic contexts of Lower Manhattan. Another clue is the dance hall called Almack's Cellar, located at various addresses along Orange Street, and owned by the extraordinary African American entrepreneur Pete Williams. Cook argues that, in the wake of abolition and the city's booming mercantile activity, "the market revolution [had] pushed the color line in multiple directions"—that this fast expansion of retail activity likely provided new avenues for, and loosened restrictions on, black-white interaction.[101] He describes the east side of Manhattan as "a kind of cultural crossroads" in the 1840s, and links the market revolution explicitly to the parallel revolution in theatrical entertainments, describing "one trail of consumers pointing to the Bowery Theatre to view white men in blackface; another trail leading to the more heterogeneous milieu of Pete Williams's dance hall."[102] Though the flash press and Dickens's Almack's adventure postdates Hawkins's and Mount's lower Manhattan experience by roughly twenty years, the mercantile visibility and expansive scope of creole entertainments in the 1840s suggests roots in the street culture of the '20s—the period of Mount's apprenticeship.

Almack's was listed between 1830 and 1846 at various addresses along Orange Street (in 1830: at number 4; in 1836–37 at 36½, meaning in all likelihood that this was a backhouse, at the rear of a lot behind another street address; from 1843–46, at number 67), and thus as part of a working-class multiracial entertainment zone only a few blocks from the Catherine Slip. More to the point, Cook points out that, as the "in-between" street numbering partially suggests, Williams's venue was "physically connected to at least three white businesses . . . [and to] an interracial shanty colony in the back."[103] Cook also confirms that home and business ownership on this stretch of Orange Street reveals Irish, Jewish, and Italian surnames. On Orange, as in the waterfront neighborhoods of Cincinnati and the Irish Channel of New Orleans, the creole synthesis was already in place, both demographically but also in terms of economy and expressive arts.

The presence and visibility of the African Grove, Almack's, and related venues showcasing creolized performers and properties, confirms that the imitation (and parody, for comic effect, by the blackface architects) went both ways. As Hearn reported in postbellum Cincinnati, and as in the Gilded Age craze for the cakewalk, in antebellum New York black performers imitated and caricatured white comic types no less than whites did blacks.[104] Blackface characters had been part of English stage tradition since the Elizabethans; such characters joined stage Irishmen, Scots, Germans, Welsh, peasants, and many other marginalized ethnic or social groups as targets for comic caricature.[105] This comic tradition continued in the light entertainments and ballad operas of the eighteenth century: not only in the iconic "Mungo" (from *The Padlock*) but in various other works, Dibdin had even included portrayals of singing and banjo-playing African Americans.[106]

However, though "African delineators" had been a part of Anglo-American stage productions at least since the Elizabethans (recall Othello), the first quarter of the nineteenth century heralds a fundamental shift, a watershed moment, in both the characterizations, and the apparent models for those characterizations. Eighteenth-century portrayals of Africans, in Vauxhall Gardens theatricals and London street ballads, had tended to adopt and employ the Enlightenment conventions with which "the Noble Savage" was often portrayed in print and on the stage. Dialogue, costume, and behaviors were in imitation of colonial models, particularly from the English settlements of the Caribbean, and these characterizations were condescending but typically sympathetic, thus in keeping with the Enlightenment model of the noble savage.

It seems possible, however, that the transformation of blackface theatrical characterizations in the United States in the first quarter of the nineteenth century resulted from enhanced contact by authors and actors with a syncretic African American culture—in other words, as a result of practical, direct, and immediate face-to-face contact with the creole synthesis.

This suggests new and different possibilities for observation and reportage. Nathan, for example, points out that the 1799 travel accounts of African explorer Mungo Park (1771–1801) provided a new model for ethnographic reporting that made a virtue of direct contact and precise description.[107] Concurrently, the period between *The Padlock* (1768) and Morton and Bishop's *The Slave* (1816) saw a vogue for black theatrical characters who were comic or heroic, and who appear to be drawn much more concretely from life observation of specific regional dialects.[108] Dibdin's Mungo, for example, is cunning, suggestive, and subversive; all traits associated with servant characterizations at least as far back as commedia dell'arte, but now framed in identifiably creole dialect, costume, and behavior.[109] If the model for blackface characters was evolving to reflect more Afro-Caribbean than Shakespearian characteristics, then by the early nineteenth century, a further shift in the characterizations—in dialect, body language, tunes, texts—also suggests a further shift in their sources, to much more au courant and quasi-ethnographic observations of New World African American culture.[110]

The direct contact implicit in this narrative, and its transformative impact on portrayals of African Americans in the early-nineteenth-century stage, reinforces the demographic and iconographic evidence for exchange between blacks and whites before the advent of blackface minstrelsy. In keeping with Mahar's analysis, my narrative suggests that early blackface theatricals (and before that, blackface solo song) were enriched by new observation and understandings of performance characteristics like timbre, phrasing, and polyrhythm, precisely those that could only be learned accurately by imitation of observed models. If the English-born Mathews could seek to accurately observe and precisely imitate, then Rice and Dixon, Emmett and Sweeney, born and raised in multiethnic working-class U.S. environments, could do likewise. Blackface minstrelsy and its antecedents—on stage, in its precursor street performances in or before the 1820s, and in earlier, analogous music-and-dance exchanges between former Africans and Europeans in the New World—were much different in performance than when captured (incompletely, imperfectly) in notation.[111]

The actor and caricaturist David Claypoole Johnston (1799–1865) provides a direct link between Mathews and Mount: his 1822 comic drawing *Militia*

Muster Folk references Mathews (with whom he had performed in Boston), employs a theatrical frame (the figures illustrated serving as a virtual catalog of comic character types), and also appears to borrow elements of composition and character from the (equally theatrical) sketch *Dancing for Eels*—in both drawings, for example, the artists include downstage-left onlookers who are black.[112] Johnston also supplied the later illustration for the 1837 print of Hawkins's 1815 composition "Backside Albany." That song, arguably the first blackface song composed in America, is traced by Nathan to the Irish melody "The Boyne Water," which has been dated in print as early as 1694, and in manuscript to 1615.[113] Nathan suggests, however, that "The Siege of Plattsburgh" (also known as "Backside Albany"), premiered in 1815 as part of the patriotic pageant *The Battle of Lake Champlain*, and published in the *Columbian Harmonist* that same year, nevertheless represents a watershed in American popular song, though he does not specify precisely what is new about the song, beyond citing the "indigenous flavor of its dialect."[114]

Here, Mahar's work on what he calls black ethnic vernacular (BEV) dialect is useful. As with Raff's study of early renderings of Jamaican patois, Mahar has constructed a subtle, closely argued analysis suggesting that minstrelsy's dialect spellings can be read not only, or even principally, as exaggerated derogatory caricature, but as a much more sincere attempt to render early nineteenth century, African American–inflected, working-class speech as it sounded.[115] Later in this chapter, we explore the complexities of character-through-dialect in Hawkins's own ballad opera *The Saw-Mill, or, A Yankee Trick* (premiered in the winter of 1824–25), but Mahar's study of "Backside Albany" is useful here, as well. Having argued for the comparative ethnographic accuracy in the song's text, Mahar cites the "circumstantial evidence" (including the presence of former slaves like Toney Clapp on the Hawkins-Mount Long Island homestead) as arguing for unremarked accuracy in the song's rendering of dialect: "Hawkins must have had access to speakers who used the dialect. . . . While there is no way of knowing whether Clapp's speech served as a source for Hawkins's work, there is every reason to believe that Hawkins was familiar with other black performers in New York City and rural Long Island."[116]

Such proto-blackface characters continued in the theatrical repertory into the next century: as we have seen, the African Grove actor Ira Aldridge played not only Othello and other Shakespearian characters in America and Europe, but also Mathews's iconic Mungo in a revival of *The Padlock*: a kind of white-faced blackface (e.g., an African American playing a character originated by a white actor in blackface).[117] Hence: by the 1820s, there were resources, venues, models, source idioms, an audience, and a palpable air of innovative theatrical excitement available in Lower Manhattan. In the home of his uncle Micah Hawkins, when he went to work as a seventeen-year-old apprentice for his elder brother Henry, W. S. Mount had a front-row seat to the new performance idioms coalescing on the streets outside the Hawkins' door.

MICAH HAWKINS'S BLACKFACE THEATRICS

Thomas Mount died in 1813, when the boy was six. In the wake of his father's early death, William moved to the Stony Brook home and tavern of his grandfather Jonas Hawkins; it was here that he likely met Toney Clapp and learned the fiddle. At age twelve or thirteen, William was apprenticed to the sign-painting trade, joining elder brother Henry at his shop in the city in 1819 (probably on Chatham Street).[118] Over the next several years he seems to have traveled between New York and Setauket a good deal—as might be expected for the apprenticed teenage son of a widowed mother—but by 1824 he was again in residence in the city. Over the next several years, he periodically boarded at his uncle Hawkins's grocery, tavern, and inn on the Catherine Slip. Buffet suggests that during this period William saw the premiere of Micah's ballad opera *The Saw-Mill* at "Wallack's Chatham Garden Theater" and attended meetings of Hawkins's amateur musical group called The "'Enterprise' [*sic*] Society."[119]

A January 1828 Euterpean Society program provides a hint of the jaunty, comic mood of Hawkins's circle, mandating that "no gentleman will be permitted to wear his hat during the evening, or dance in his boots" and that "standing on the seats [will be] strictly forbidden."[120] In *The Flash Press*, Cohen, Gilfoyle, and Horowitz describe a similar audience demographic more directly, identifying both occupations and leisure activities, and providing a link between urbanizing immigrants and the blackface audience:

> New York City and other urban centers in the 1830s were rapidly expanding in numbers of single white men and women aged 15 to 30. Some among the young men were native New Yorkers, from artisan and working-class families of the city's lower wards, well described by one scholar as an urban "bachelor subculture" of unattached men expressing male camaraderie around sporting events and saloon-hall drinking [and attendance at blackface theaters]. But *probably as many flash press readers were newcomers drawn to the city by the promise of entry-level jobs in a rapidly commercializing economy.*[121]

Hawkins's second essay in blackface composition, after 1815's "Backside Albany," was "Massa Georgie Washington and General Lafayette" (1824), which was printed with a cover illustrated by Johnston, who had earlier parodied Mathews. Edward Riley, whose music store was located close by on Chatham Street, published an eight-page version in October 1825 that included not only the song but also eight pages of comic dialect; "Massa Georgie Washington" was likewise included in some performances of *The Saw-Mill* (it is not clear whether the print preceded or, more likely, followed the stage premiere).[122] Johnston's image includes markers closely associated with blackface caricature: it depicts a black man in military uniform, with a wide toothy grin, standing with head inclined, his left arm akimbo, and the iconic "knee-bone bent." This image for "Massa Georgie Washington," like *Dancing for Eels* itself, confirms that body vocabularies associated with blackface predated the iconography specifically associated with Dixon and Rice: in 1824, the "bent knee and arm akimbo" already signaled creole influences.[123]

As part of *The Saw-Mill*, "Massa Georgie Washington" was not just a song interpolated within the play. Rather, it was the centerpiece of a whole, free-standing scene complex; Nathan describes James Roberts as "singing, speaking, laughing, cheering 'heartily,' dancing, and rattling off a historical account with many confusing details and in a broken English patterned after the speech of the American Negro."[124] The parallels to descriptions of the African Grove performances and the theatrics of later minstrelsy are unmistakable.

THE SAW-MILL, OR, A YANKEE TRICK

Micah Hawkins's full-length ballad opera *The Saw-Mill* was premiered at Manhattan's Chatham Theatre in early December 1824; it is thus one of the first full-length ballad operas written by an American.[125] With the exception of the Vauxhall Gardens–style song "The Boys and Girls Must Love Each Other" (song 14 in the playscript), found elsewhere in the Hawkins papers as a separate piece of notated music, only the libretto is preserved.[126] Hence, any linkage of specific texts within *The Saw-Mill* to specific melodies or formal genres, absent specific tune titles, is tentative. Nevertheless, *The Saw-Mill* is a valuable source of information regarding Micah Hawkins and his likely influence on his nephew, but also about the range of musical styles and character types we have identified as available, employed, combined, and familiar in theatrical New York of the 1820s. Internal evidence regarding characterizations, dialogue, and (especially) stage directions is useful and illuminating.

And there is one specifically musical stage direction in the finale that is highly significant, and links the worlds of rural Long Island, the Manhattan stage, the Erie Canal diggings, the upstate festivals of Pinkster and 'Lection Day, riverine and maritime southern and western frontiers, and the prototypical blackface repertoire.

The Saw-Mill played at the Chatham Theatre, a cornerstone of popular entertainment (and, shortly thereafter, of blackface minstrelsy) during William Sidney Mount's Manhattan apprenticeship to his brother Henry in the early '20s. Given that he was living off and on in the Hawkins home on the Catherine Slip, his already-strong interest in music, and the fact that a playbill announcing the performances is to be found in his papers, it seems likely that William might have attended his uncle's premiere; it is certain that his brother and master Henry Smith Mount did so.[127] Oscar Wegelin quotes a Micah Hawkins letter that describes the show's run and the indisposition of one of the female leads: Micah says that it "went off tolerably well. It has been played four nights, with increased approbation. . . . The manager wishes to continue it before the Public, but until Mrs. Waring recovers . . . I shall not permit it, having in my possession both words and music."[128]

The Saw-Mill's plot is based on an anecdote Hawkins allegedly got from Richard Smith of Setauket, based on actual events on the Genessee River in the 1780s. Hawkins's fictionalization transplants the setting to Lake Oneida; in the early '20s, this area of western New York State was a part of the exotic "frontier" that the construction of the Erie Canal kept much in the news. The convoluted plot, which plays on tropes of class, identity, comedy, and deception common to other period comedy, revolves around an offer by a cartoon "Old Dutchman," Baron Scafferdwal, of one hundred acres of Oneida Creek land to anyone who will agree to build a mill on it; the implication is that the baron wishes a mill built in order to serve a growing frontier community and perhaps lower his costs as a wheat farmer.[129] The two male leads, Bloom and Herman, wishing to win both the land and the hands in marriage of the Baron's daughter and her friend Louisa, hit upon the idea of disguising themselves as two "Yankees." In the stock characterizations of the day, this makes the disguised Bloom and Herman laconic, tight-fisted, drawling, "sharp practitioners."

Plot, setting, dramatis personae, and dramatic arc all fall within the expectations of the genre. However, several factors are particularly relevant as they reflect the musical idiom of the time and Mount's youthful experience. First is the mise-en-scène "in northwestern New York State during the building of the Great Western [i.e., Erie] Canal."[130] Second, Micah's dialogue and musical settings evoke both the working-class characters and the musical behaviors Manhattanites would have associated with the Erie Canal works and communities. More broadly, the *Saw-Mill* libretto depends in significant measure on musical illustrations, demonstrations, and puns: for example, in act 1, the third musical number, "What joy breaks forth when friends do meet," employs "fa-so-la" *solfege* syllables as text for its "folderol" refrain, and is framed with stage directions that specifically call on the characters to provide musical demonstrations:

> "SONG—Jacob—(Music No. 3)
> "What joy breaks forth when friends do meet—
> (Long absence whetting their thinking)
> On retrospection O how sweet
> They dwell, while o'er the bottle clinking.
> 'Tis then old tales and sayings wise,—
> Their hearts grow'ng light as,. Even straw-coal—
> Such harmony between them rise,
> As comes from singing Fa mi la sol.
> Sol la mi fa sol—la mi fa sol.
> [continues with above as refrain]
> (Sings the common chords, &c. with their relative minors,
> or otherwise, of many keys.)[131]

The cast includes an assortment of city and country characters: "Servants, Canal Lockmen, Workmen on the Saw-Mill, Ladies and Gentlemen, Rustics, &c.," many of them stock comic types whose speech Hawkins renders in convincing—if caricatured—dialect. More central characters include Bloom's rival for the Baron's daughter, the elderly German Count Stoduff, a "stuffy aristocrat" (Moffat). The disguise as "Yankee" that Bloom and Herman assume evokes a comic type iconicized in period theater as "Brother Jonathan," the archetypal stage version of the character was created by James Kirke Paulding (1778–1860), in his 1812 *Diverting History of John Bull and Brother Jonathan*.[132] Building on this trope, the actor Royall Tyler (1757–1826), a specialist in comic caricature, played stage Yankees at the Chatham Garden Theatre from the early '20s.[133] Elizabeth Johns provides a useful summary of some of the "Brother Jonathan" characteristics that play out in *The Saw-Mill*'s Yankee characters:

> A farmer, Jonathan was a model agrarian: he owned his own land, worked hard, and had pure manners. But he was also simple on occasion, to the

> point of seeming doltish, and at these times his behavior was hilariously comic. Yet underneath this façade, Jonathan was shrewd, and he usually obtained precisely what he wanted. . . . Coupled to his agrarian virtues were the city audience's disdain for the farmer's remoteness and their half-admiration half-contempt for his reputation as a sharp bargainer. . . . It was in this rich combination of virtue and slyness that Jonathan triumphed on stage over the representative of the Old World.[134]

We thus find in the "virtue and slyness" of Brother Jonathan another archetype that, like the festivals of Pinkster and 'Lection Day, provided opportunity for overlapping cultural resonances. Trickster characters such as Elegua and Anansi-the-Spider parallel Brother Jonathan and are equally significant in West African and Afro-Caribbean folklore, under various names and guises.[135] Murphy calls the masking and disguise of such characters, as in the case of blackface minstrelsy, "secret sources of creativity for transcending the ordinary boundaries of movement, expression, and even allowable social behavior."[136] The Yankee archetype is again linked to William Sidney Mount in a comment on his "Cradle of Harmony" violin design: Mount's friend Charles Lanman called it a fiddle "suitable for Brother Jonathan to play upon."[137]

In *The Saw-Mill*, Hawkins captures Manhattan street dialect in the speeches of Norchee, a servant woman from the city whose attraction to servingman Jacob forms a comic counterpoint to the leads' romance: "Odrot [O drat] de Grand Conol [Canal], for all me . . . Weze [Louise] Clark, I wont trape [traipse] one step furder wid you—Wont . . . I was'nt never any ting else but A weak, tick-headed, ignorant, dumb Dutch woman" (act 1, scene 4). The details of Norchee's and Jacob's shared comic dialect, in the absence of a specific statement that she is "Dutch," might well have been read as stereotyped African American speech. A similar confusion is present in the comic character "Raccoon" from Barton's 1762 *The Disappointment*: is Raccoon African American, or German, or does his accent, as Mahar implies, suggest a creolized dialect and cultural identity?[138] The physical characteristics of ethnicity, like those of age, foolishness, or physical infirmity, were stock targets for nineteenth-century humor, but it seems likely that what Hawkins is capturing in Norchee's speeches, with much greater precision than has been presumed, is another example of BEV. Study of Hawkins's version of a related dialect, as reproduced in the *Saw-Mill*'s speeches of the self-described "ignorant Dutch woman" Norchee, further nuances Mahar's interpretation of period dialect in chapter 2: what Hawkins is reproducing, at least in these speeches, is not exclusively a Black Ethnic Vernacular because Hawkins has

Norchee proclaim herself to be Dutch. Found in other New York theater of the period, these dialogue characteristics, far from being simply the racist caricature that superficial examination of blackface texts has sometimes presumed, may well represent attempts to capture a creole dialect shared across ethnic groups, in sometimes unexpected ways.

S. White confirms this in a characteristically exhaustive examination that demonstrates the impact of the Northeast's polyglot linguistic landscape on what he calls black language. Citing newspaper advertisements and travelers' accounts, he confirms that, in New York and New Jersey, it was common well into the 19th century to find ex-slaves and free blacks who spoke Dutch, French, English, remnants of West African languages, or some combination of these.[139] And he reproduces a wonderful excerpt by Alexander Hamilton, a colonial doctor (not the revolutionary hero) who while traveling with his black servant Dromo in 1744 Long Island, describes a conversation between Dromo and a local: "'Dis de way to York?' asks Dromo. 'Yaw, dat is Yarikee,' said the wench, pointing to the steeples. 'What devil you say?' replies Dromo. 'Yaw, mynheer,' said the wench. 'Damne you, what you say?' said Dromo again. 'Yaw, yaw,' said the girl. 'You a damn black bitch,' said Dromo, and so rid on."[140] Though Norchee is caricatured as a "thick-headed, ignorant, dumb Dutch woman," many of the details in which her speech is rendered recur in the stage speeches of blackface characters throughout the decade after *The Saw-Mill*. While it has traditionally been assumed that this is simply generic and sloppily inaccurate "comic ethnic" dialect, Mahar and Rath convince us to trust Micah Hawkins's linguistic precision, as William Sidney's musical autobiography persuades us to trust his visual precision. Though "Dutch" (e.g., New York German) in ethnicity, Norchee "sounds like" a blackface character precisely because New York street English in 1824, like New York street performance, was already a creole dialect. Confirmation of Norchee's speech as Lower Manhattan street English is in her own autobiographical statement to Bloom, which gives as her natal point of origin the Bowery itself, just a few blocks from the Catherine Wharf.[141]

Stage directions and references to both character types and song types confirm that the tropes of minstrelsy, and of the *Dancing for Eels* street culture that gave rise to it, were associated not only with Manhattan, found not only in saltwater ports in the North, but also in upstate New York, the Finger Lakes, and Erie Canal contexts. When Bloom and Herman do adopt "Yankee" disguise for the titular "Trick," they enter costumed in full-blown Lower East Side manner: "Enter BLOOM and HERMAN, from the house, dressed humorously odd—their hair being cued with eel-skins, &c. &c. having in their hands broad-axes, addices, chisels, various mechanical implements, besides each one a handkerchief of wearing apparel."[142] Though the concealed-identity aspect of the plot depends on Bloom's and Herman's "humorously odd" disguise in the character of stage Yankees, the visual details of the protagonists' dress closely recall the creole costuming of New York mechanics and street dancers. S. White, for example, quotes De Voe's *Market Book* to the effect that Long Island blacks clubbed their hair in a queue wrapped with a dried eelskin.[143] Likewise, the stage direction of "handkerchief of wearing apparel" directly recalls the neckerchiefs associated with minstrelsy's maritime contexts (see *Dancing for Eels* and the cover of *Backside Albany*), Mount's own paintings (see *Haymakers*, *The Bone Player*, *The Banjo Player*), and the "Haitian" elements of dress Hearn described in postbellum Cincinnati.[144] Moreover, Bloom and Herman hold in their hands "various mechanical implements"; they may be called "Yankees" in the title, but they carry implements that signify that they are (in antebellum parlance) "mechanics."

In short, Micah Hawkins dresses and equips his disguised heroes in a fashion that directly imitates the Erie canallers and Bowery apprentices who were minstrelsy's first audience, and Mount's contemporaries and friends, and who were flooding onto the streets of the Lower East Side, just outside the doors of the theater, in December 1824. The confirmation that the employment working-class street characters as disguise for heroic male leads was potentially revolutionary is found in reviews of the show, which found the more traditional stock characters (Simpson's "Count Stoduff," for example) "irresistibly droll" but called Bloom's and Herman's dress "improper," and Robert's "Jacob" a "flagrant attempt to please the vulgar at the expense of refinement and delicacy."[145] Why should more traditional comic caricatures be judged "irresistibly droll" but more au courant caricatures of "Yankees" and blackface minstrels (remember, Roberts premiered "Massa Georgie Washington," and sang it again during *The Saw-Mill* as an entr'acte) be deemed "improper" and "vulgar"? What we are seeing, in a short run of performances at the Chatham Theatre at the end of 1824, in a ballad opera written by one of the city's most active musical amateurs, is the introduction—the "legitimization"—of new character types, new dialects, and new modes of musical expression, as they moved from Manhattan's streets onto the New York stage.

The *Saw-Mill* is essential to our understanding of Mount, and of the musical genres he knew, because its characters, setting, and dialogue reflect the creole synthesis, and its musical information does, as well. The producers obviously regarded James Roberts as a strong audience draw and a direct link between *The Saw-Mill* and blackface theatrics: to him was assigned not only the entr'acte "Massa Georgie Washington," but also the play's closing air and chorus (no. 16):

> Closing air sung by Jacob (#16): "And long may this saw-mill saw;
> Yet never saw asunder
> THE tale of its origin—
> A YANKEE TRICK—and BLUNDER.
> And long may, &c. [Chorus by all the characters]

The class-subverting implications of the lyric, as well as the audience's prior associations with Roberts as a character actor specializing in blackface and other working-class comic types, would not have been lost on those critics who found his role "vulgar."

A particularly amusing and semiotically rich set of connections can be derived from Count Stoduff's version of "Yankee Doodle." Though Hawkins does not specifically identify the song's melody, internal textual evidence for once brooks little ambiguity. "Yankee Doodle," a tune that already been the subject of contested semiotics as far back as the prerevolutionary era, carried a particularly potent, and patriotic, message when sung as a comic tribute to the Brother Jonathan–style characters of Bloom's and Herman's disguise, and to the frontier sensibilities that were associated with working-class Jacksonian democracy.[146] Moreover, in Hawkins's text, the song mentions molasses and ginger, two essential components of the sugar triangle that, we have argued, helped bring Afro-Caribbean culture to New England and fuel the creole synthesis there:

> Yenkeetutels come to down
> For to puy molashes—Make Bungkin Bies
> An' Shingerpred
> Sweet as sugar-candy—
> Yenkeetutelstantee.

Dance was also a crucial part of the show: in addition to the textual allusions in some of the sung musical numbers, other numbers without specific tunes are explicitly identified in stage directions as dances (no. 13 as a waltz, for instance), while the closing scene finale requires a dance for the full company. Just as operatic verities would expect, that closing finale knits together all the disparate plot threads and theatrical elements: it includes the full cast, reveals all disguises, reconciles all conflicts, unites the lovers, and employs the full range of expressive tools. In addition, it includes a quartet on the topic of love for couples—Jacob and Norchee, Herman and Louisa—but also employs a familiar, accessible and homegrown musical form, "a kind of Catch, or Round, the piece ending when each character has sung all the lines."[147]

Hawkins's stage directions make clear that he expected his set designer to pull out all stops for this finale: they call for a near-full-size sawmill in motion, and a replica of the Grand Canal, then often in the news as it neared the final stages of construction. This is how the stage directions set the final scene:

> SCENE LAST.
>
> Night.—A mountainous, and extremely romantic situation.—On the right a mill-dam, over part of which the water from the mill-pond tumbles in great luxury.—The part of the dam, farthest from the audience, has attached to it a Saw-Mill, with every necessary appurtenance, tail-race, &c.—A bridge crossing both the tailrace and the sheet of water which rolls over the dam, connects the back with the fore-ground. On the left, through the trees, appear many buildings, &c. &c. seemingly of a direct relation with the improvements immediately in view.—The extreme distance is bounded by a section of the Grand Canal, with a Lock, &c. The fore-ground represents a kind of rude alcove, brilliantly lit up—having tables sumptuously stored with a profusion of every thing—Seats arranged alongside of them, on which is discovered many well-dressed persons of both sexes.—The Baron (now very richly dressed, having on his orders, &c.) is seen busily showing the excellent qualities of the mill, and its contiguous beauties of art and nature to a number of ladies and gentlemen, among them being Count Phlegm, who, with his usual characteristic coldness and indifference to every thing around him, merely nods to all of the old gentleman's infatuation.—Louisa, Jacob, and Norchee appear to have formed an acquaintance with a few rustics, with who they are strolling,—amusing themselves about the mill, &c.—all, however, seating themselves together in front, soon after the scene opens.—Stoduff is very officious among all of the roe-ground, addresses them most pompously.

This beautiful, elaborate stage design (act 2, scene 2 is another extended example) may have represented Hawkins's ideal production values, or a bid to promote attendance through their publication in advance. But such rich physical detail also makes a literal and an allegorical contribution to framing and telling the story, just as it would be in the genre paintings—many of which employ visual conventions borrowed from the theatrical stage—that William Sidney would create just a few years later. In this sense, we could make the claim that the designs Mount saw on the stage, including those for *The Saw-Mill* (and the description in the script), were an influence on the framing and "staging" of his own genre paintings.[148]

We have sampled the complexity of the musical, cultural, demographic, and perspectival information implicated in Hawkins's *Saw-Mill*, and can imagine the powerful impression the show would have made on his admiring, seventeen-year-old nephew when (we infer) William saw it in December 1824. But perhaps the most significant, revealing, and revolutionary elements appear, fittingly enough, in this same finale. Framed by the elaborate stage design, including the eponymous sawmill, Count Stoduff finds his suit rejected, but in the magnanimous buffa tradition celebrates his rival's victory, and announces that he will dance with the lovers to the tunes of the fiddle:

> Sc. V:
> Sto. I like tish [this] saw-mill supper vot te Parren [that the Baron]
> Gives to te Yenkeetutels [the Yankee Doodles].—Yes, I tu, [do]
>
> For, py mine zeal [by my zeal], tow I pe [though I be] eighty-one
> Year old, I'll tish night tance [dance] long mit a kall [?],
> Howteffer notmitstantin' tet te vitlers [however notwithstanding that the fiddlers]
> Am tem boor hipzinzawyer blayers [Are those poor ? players].—(dances)

Though it is difficult, through the obscurity of the comic dialect, to identify the adjectival "hipzinsawyer" players, there is no question that the magnanimous Stoduff is proposing that all should dance in celebration to the music of the "fiddlers" (surely onstage). And then Stoduff "sounds his trumpet," and cries "Come! Moosick liekise / tanking 'mong te whole. / Come, hipzinzawyers,—Possum up te gum-tree" and at "Appropriate music," the mill "is set going," and there is "a general dance" to close the play.

The tune that the comic German aristocrat calls for is "Possum Up a Gum-Tree" (music fig. 1), the ubiquitous minstrelsy melody, which appears throughout early blackface both on the frontiers and in cities, and also in Mount's own manuscript collection, partially inherited from his uncle; it is likewise cited in correspondence between William Sidney and his brother Robert Nelson.[149] The tune is claimed by Scott to have been borrowed by Charles Mathews from Ira Aldridge's African Grove performances, though Buckley has Mathews learning it in Philadelphia in 1824.[150] Dickens's *American Notes* (1842) has it being played in the integrated performance at Almack's where he saw Master Juba dance. It is likewise the "tune" being whistled in Mount's late

Music Figure 1. "Possum Up a Gum-Tree."

painting *Catching the Tune* (1866), four decades after *The Saw-Mill*.[151] "Possum" also appears in a bound manuscript book belonging to Micah Hawkins that Otto Kinkeldy calls "not impossibl[y]" the part-book for *The Saw-Mill*.[152] A derivative of the earlier tune "Cooney in de Holler" (the phrase appears in the "Possum" refrain), it is also documented in the 1830s in Philadelphia and New York's Five Points.[153]

Yet, although Hawkins's usage in the *Saw-Mill*'s finale confirms "Possum" as common melodic currency in New York as early as 1824—that is, at least a half decade before Dixon danced "Coal Black Rose" in New York—it can be traced back still further, in a citation that confirms melodic exchange between the riverine frontiers and the two islands of Manhattan and Long Island. Nathan quotes "Possum" in a frontier anecdote from James Kirke Paulding (Irving's collaborator in *Salmagundi*, previously cited in the discussion of Haitian influence on Long Island) in his *Letters from the South*. Writing in 1817 from the vicinity of Lexington, Virginia, on the eastern slope of the

Appalachians, within thirty miles both of the Emmett family homestead in Staunton and of Sweeney's birthplace in Appomattox, Paulding describes a "batteauxman" [boatman] who at the end of a day's river travel "fastened his boat to the stump of a tree . . . and began to sing that famous song of 'The 'possum up the gum-tree.'"[154] The tune thus displays wide geographic distribution, early ubiquity, proximity to southern sources of minstrelsy's repertoire, and substantial longevity—and serves as the finale of the genre-bending, class-crossing ballad opera that Micah Hawkins authored and that his teenage apprentice nephew saw.

In December of 1824, at the Chatham Theatre in New York City, a few blocks from the streets and docks of the Catherine Slip where Long Island blacks, their hair tied up in eel skins, were "dancing for eels" to attract trade; where he maintained a grocery store and tavern with a piano built into the shop counter; where his sensitive, artistic, and musical teenage nephew boarded as he learned the craft of sign painting and dreamed of success as a portraitist, Micah Hawkins took the swirl of ethnicities, accents, linguistic and musical dialects he saw out the front of his shop, and put that creole gumbo on the stage. And his nephew took note.

FIRST WORKS, AND A NEW CAREER PATH

Micah Hawkins died unexpectedly of typhus in July 1825.[155] The loss of this mentor inaugurated a season of significant changes in William's circumstances, location, and ambitions. Indirect evidence (e.g., annotated souvenir programs) suggest that he was, with brother Henry, by the following spring already attending the early shows of the upstart National Academy, which had been founded in 1825 by a board that included Samuel F. B. Morse to provide enhanced opportunities for young, native-born artists shut out by the American Academy. And in an autobiographical sketch, tentatively dated 1854, Mount claims that by the age of eighteen (1825), while still an apprentice, he had "commenced drawing with lead pencil and sometimes with white chalk in my brother's paint shop, No. 104 Cherry Street, New York."[156]

In 1827, perhaps in response to circumstances resulting from Micah Hawkins's death, William Sidney returned to Stony Brook—having, seemingly, permanently abandoned his sign-painting apprenticeship. By spring 1828 he succeeded in placing a work for showing at the National Academy, the allegorical *Christ Raising the Daughter of Jairus*.[157] His first oils, including this one, betray incomplete control of technique and a certain flatness of perspective and affect that recalls other vernacular painters of the period.[158] Yet even at this early date, a contemporaneous self-portrait makes his commitment to music explicit: he holds a simple-system, six-hole wooden flute (in boxwood, with ivory bands).[159]

Over the next several years, though often staying at the family homestead in Stony Brook, William was a regular and frequent visitor to the city, and lived off and on at a variety of addresses all within a few blocks of the familiar Lower East Side and Catherine Wharf neighborhood.[160] In the same period, he was quickly expanding his list of clients in the field of portraiture—where the money was to be made—and showing works regularly, a rising young star in the annual exhibitions of the National Academy.

MOUNT'S RUSTIC DANCE: AN APPRENTICE COMES OF AGE

Mount's third scenic painting, 1830's *Rustic Dance after a Sleigh Ride* (see plate 4), was completed only two years after he began formal art studies and represents both his earliest surviving genre painting, his first in a "rustic" vein, and his first on the theme of vernacular music and dance. It also offers an opportunity for us to assess the impact of earlier vernacular painters, and of his Lower East Side experiences, on his developing artistic sensibility. In a letter from the 1850s, written from Stony Brook in response to a request for biographical information (and in which Mount betrays his own reticence, saying "It is hard for a man to skin himself"), he annotates the *Rustic Dance* as follows: "I used a chair for an easel [when painting it] . . . while the carpenter was making [me] one."[161] Mount was proud of the work, telling brother Nelson that "My Contra Dance attracts great attention" and quoting an anonymous newspaper critic's qualified and versified praise.[162] Likewise, he later contacted the secretary of the National Academy, of which he had been a leading light in the '40s, asking for the medal recognizing the work that he had won but not received in 1830.[163]

The *Rustic Dance* was seen as adhering to a tradition of genre paintings of rustic dance, but exerted its own influence on subsequent works: Durand's *The Pedlar Displaying His Wares* (1836), for example, seems to borrow the black coachman from Mount's painting.[164] At this early stage of development, Mount—aged only twenty-three, and only a few years away from the sign-painter's workshop—is not yet a technical master: he still struggles with some issues of anatomy, physiognomy, and perspective. Nevertheless, the narrative, musical, and choreological information contained in the image is already essential to our investigation of the creole synthesis on Long Island.

Buffet, whose serialized 1923–24 Mount biography in the *Port Jefferson Times* is both the earliest and, possibly, the closest to a primary source, suggests, in his chapter, "Colored Fiddlers and Micah Hawkins," that the setting of *Rustic Dance* may have been "the big middle room of Maj. Jonas Hawkins' tavern at Stony Brook."[165] If Buffet is correct, this would further confirm the accuracy and reliability of Mount's visual reportage, and of the impact of childhood music-and-dance experiences on his artistic vocabulary and repertoire. Buffet also mentions the presence at the Hawkins tavern, in Mount's childhood, of a black fiddler from Huntington named "'Lige," and relates a funny story about 'Lige hiding under a bed when a puritanical parson appears at a dance—though whether this fiddler is a palimpsest of Mount's fiddle teacher Anthony "Toney" Clapp, or the player depicted in the painting, is unknown.[166]

The art historian and musicologist Kevin Scott has suggested that *The Rustic Dance* may reference political currents of the period; that the picture was understood in allegorical terms is confirmed by the fact that in October 1830 it was requested for and hung at the Third Annual Trade Fair, at New York's Masonic Hall.[167] The fair was sponsored by the American Institute, a protectionist organization that, judging from its extant literature, explicitly evokes the rhetoric of the period's nativist groups.[168] In such environs, the *Rustic Dance*'s celebration of seasonal merrymaking was surely seen as exemplifying "true-blue American" values.

Understanding the parallels between Mount's work and various nativist-protectionist concerns is useful for two reasons: first, because such rhetoric situates Mount's own experience in the 1830s, when working-class and merchant whites were at odds over the merits, potential, and threat of internal migration (free blacks) and external immigration (especially Irish and Germans) to trade and employment. Working-class whites feared competition from both these outsider groups for jobs, while middle-class merchant whites welcomed the growth of new target clienteles.

It was from precisely this fluid and contested context that blackface would emerge. Down the street from the Masonic Hall that housed the American Institute exhibition were located the Bowery and Chatham Theatres, where the mechanics, apprentices, volunteer firemen, and other Bowery B'hoys who swelled the street cadres of the nativists would, in the evenings, rush the stage to dance "Zip Coon" with Dixon and jump "Jim Crow" with Rice. Though the scene depicted in the *Rustic Dance* is rural, nostalgic, and idealized, its inception and reception—and aspects of its composition and implicit narrative—were understood as referencing urban, contemporary, and hotly political concerns.

But a more significant second reading yields information of sufficient precision as to demand more extended attention. Alan Buechner has noted, though not analyzed, the painting's relevance to musicological studies, seeking "a fuller understanding of the paintings and the music and choreographic traditions which underlie them."[169] Likewise, although Buechner interprets certain of the choreographic specifics, or "preparation" for same, his bicentennial essay does not provide detailed or concrete exegesis.[170] There is more to be seen here.

In the painting, Mount's fiddler, playing with the instrument down on his collarbone, is well-dressed, wearing a green jacket, soft collar, red cravat, and dancing shoes. He is seated on a stool in the chimney corner, next to a participant who looks a bit the worse for drink, both conveniently close to a whiskey jug. A black house servant holding a set of bellows is visible in the chimney corner, and, peeking in through the door, a third black man wearing a stocking cap and holding a whip—perhaps the sleigh's driver? The convivial, familial, and modest setting, a simply furnished room with a garland of Christmas greenery strung around the walls, the indicated hour of three on the grandfather clock, and the relative ease of black-white contact, are an apt depiction of the musical interaction that we have reconstructed in the Anglo-Afro-Dutch family farming communities of Long Island after manumission. The technical composition of this early work confirms not only Mount's ongoing interest in a kind of "theatricalized" painting—that is, painting that employs visual composition reminiscent of the theatrical proscenium (see, in chapter 6, his extensive employment of barns and storefronts for such framing)—but also his awareness of earlier vernacular conventions: there is a long tradition of "rustic" scenes featuring fiddlers, pipers, or dancers.[171]

Not remarked, however, is the possibility of a third layer of influence on the work, beyond Mount's idealization of rural Long Island and the conventions of vernacular painting: both the composition and the physical behavior of the bodies involved also evoke elements of the African Caribbean; namely, the ring dance called the *bamboula*, most famously depicted in E. W. Kemble's 1880s *Century Magazine* illustration of Congo Square, the multiethnic market of antebellum New Orleans.[172]

Of course it is completely possible that Mount's use of the visual cliché of the circular dance, and of the central couple who will initiate partnering, is a result of vernacular conventions, rather than observation of such dancing on Long Island. On the other hand, there is at least the possibility that Mount's *Rustic Dance* is portraying a choreographic behavior present in "rustic" Long Island that was both Afro-Caribbean in origin and a result of his direct, accurate observation. Could it be that Mount's *Rustic Dance* implicates hints of the *bamboula*?

First we must understand that Kemble's 1886 illustration, which accompanied antebellum reminiscences authored by George Washington Cable (1844–1925), cannot be based in direct observation: though recognized as a thoughtful and accurate observer of African American subjects, Kemble was born only in 1861. In the absence of his direct observation, we might presume that Kemble was therefore working from Cable's verbal descriptions—and admit the possibility that his visual rendering of such descriptions may reflect little ethnographic accuracy. Indeed, his use of the circle, and of the male dancer advancing and offering his hand to a potential partner, may reflect rather Kemble's own debt to conventional illustration rather than to observation: the conventions that shaped *The Rustic Dance* may antedate and indeed influence the 1880s *Century* illustration.

On the other hand, reliable antebellum sources documented the *bamboula* circle dance in Congo Square, and throughout the Caribbean, from at least as early as 1800.[173] It is cited in sources from Martinique, Haiti, Guadeloupe, and the Virgin Islands as well as New Orleans, often in multiethnic situations implicating creolizing dance exchange: Epstein quotes a period description, for example, of a Mardi Gras celebration, March 3, 1808, in which "the Negroes danced a *bamboula*. . . . Or rather, there were two groups, side by side, one dancing a *bamboula*, and the other a *contredanse*."[174] That the *bamboula* was ubiquitous (and thus available for observation) throughout the century and the hemisphere, and associated with both drumming and body percussion, and that it had the opportunity to interact with European dances, is confirmed by numerous sources.[175] That it was equally available for observation, imitation, and illustration in antebellum Long Island is certainly quite possible: certainly the lanky, red-cheeked, somewhat disheveled young man advancing into the circle of the *Rustic Dance* is an apt visual analog to Irving's comic textual versions of similar characters performing "Haytian" dances on the island. Thus, Mount's 1830 *Rustic Dance* may possibly be read as a depiction of actual dance practices, which practices were in fact already exhibiting creolized elements. The interplay between black and white, rural and urban demographics, across the Atlantic and Caribbean maritime and continental riverine contexts, was much more extensive than has been realized. In the next chapter, we see those creolized experiences and influences play out, both globally and precisely, in the portrait works of Mount's artistic maturity.

4 Minstrelsy's Material Culture
The Evidence of Mount's Portraiture

THIS CHAPTER CONCENTRATES ON INSIGHTS provided by examination of the paintings from Mount's maturity into the material culture of instrumental dance music in the "creole synthesis." Principal evidence is drawn from four portraits of dance musicians that he painted in 1849 (*Just in Tune*), 1850 (*Right and Left*) and 1856 (*The Banjo Player* and *The Bone Player*), works of technical and expressive virtuosity but that, more importantly, provide confirmation of his expertise in and admiration for the details of African American vernacular music (see plates 5–8).[1] Mount was fascinated by instrumental music: his collection and design of, experiments with, and patents for instruments, as well as the sketches, paintings, and the manuscripts, all bear this out. He was knowledgeable, as player and observer, about Anglo-Celtic and African American dance traditions, and was equipped by aptitude, skills, and profession to identify and depict their contrast and synthesis.

Three of the four images in the portraits discussed in this chapter are most likely of dance musicians (both fiddlers and the bones player), while the fourth (the banjo player) could be imagined to accompany singing but equally likely completes the dance-band instrumentation—fiddle, banjo, and bones representing three-fourths of the iconic ensemble of minstrelsy. Though the earliest of the four portraits was modeled by a white musician (identity unknown, though formerly believed to be Mount's brother Nelson), the other three subjects are all African Americans. The sitters' ethnicity had been recommended by Schaus, Mount's commercial publisher, in an attempt to exploit the European craze for "exotic" images of blackface minstrels.[2] Yet despite the ubiquity of racist caricature at midcentury, as it appears widely in blackface iconography, Mount omitted denigration in these works. Instead, he employs the conventions of heroic portraiture: stance, expression, and composition.

As an aspiring fine artist, Mount borrowed and imitated classical models; but, as a painter for hire, he specifically employed such borrowed elements to frame and position the life models depicted in the portraits and some of the genre paintings.[3] The classicizing impulse need not be seen as contradicting the verisimilitude of his musical observation: it is clear that Mount sought to ennoble his subjects—which, in the case of the musicians' portraits, may put paid to the accusation that he was a simple antiabolitionist or nativist.[4] Much more significant is the accurate observation and the unmistakable air of command with which Mount renders these musicians. Mount intends his African American "Banjo Player" and "Bone Player," and the anonymous fiddler of *Right and Left*, to be seen as skilled professionals, confident instrumentalists, and proud artists. These musicians are portrayed, not as passive subjects, but as active shapers of the dance music experience that Mount prized, and idealized, above all others.

On the other hand, Mount was not interested in ennobling African Americans purely because of their ethnicity or historical mistreatment in the Americas—in fact he would probably have despised such idealization as abolitionist twaddle. The nobility that he finds in these subjects is rather a direct reflection of the respect with which Mount observed, admired, imitated, and painted musicians. Musicians, especially dance musicians—and, in his masterpieces, African American dance musicians—were the individuals he specifically wished to "ennoble" and those to whom he assigned commanding agency. These portraits contain valuable biographical and allegorical information, and these are the commonest perspectives from which scholarship has approached Mount's works. But I seek something else from them: to derive evidence by which aspects of the subjects' class, communities, musical experiences, and musical practice can be reconstructed.

A comparative absence of supplemental evidence is precisely why George Freeman, an African American indentured servant to one of Mount's uncles, who sat for *The Banjo Player*, is important: because combining such information with the carefully observed detail in Mount's portrait can help us reconstruct otherwise-lost aspects of Freeman's life, experience, and music. Direct information on the antebellum African American musical experience that birthed minstrelsy is so sparse that *The Banjo Player*, *The Bone Player* and *Right and Left* provide an invaluable source of otherwise-unavailable data about the influence of that experience on U.S. vernacular music. Investigated more deeply and interpretatively, and with an awareness of both Mount's reliable reportage and the details of African American experience on Long Island, these portraits precisely depict essential insights about the creole synthesis.

PENCIL VERSUS OIL: OBSERVATION VERSUS IMAGINATION

However, in order to employ Mount's visual reportage accurately and effectively, it is important to understand the relationship between his inveterate, extensive, preliminary, and "private" pencil sketching, and his much more selective, considered, finalized, and "public" oil painting. Both were fundamental tools in his artistic arsenal and essential to his artistic vision, extensive sketching almost always preceding and typically informing eventual work in oils. But there are also crucial and categorical distinctions: the musicological relevance of the two media can only be understood through a clarification of their complementary roles in Mount's artistic process.

Mount sketched throughout his entire life, in a much wider range of situations, contexts, and topics than in his oil painting, and—also in contrast to his work in oils—he continued to sketch after his eyesight deteriorated in the early '60s. His pencil sketches are sometimes annotated with color codes, presumably so that he could recall the original subject's color palette when he referenced these sketches as sources for paintings. But the sketches do not just function as preliminaries to the oils: they represent, much more comprehensively, Mount's day-to-day visual experience. Because they are based in direct professional observation, the sketches thus are a particularly important source for understanding what Mount saw, the roles music played in his daily experience, and how he modified, adapted, abstracted, or "fictionalized" observed music in the paintings. Even more significantly, analysis of the sketches' content, and the ways in which Mount employed that content as sources for paintings, reveals precisely the same blurring of class, ethnic, and musical boundaries that I have suggested was an essential component in minstrelsy's creole synthesis, and that helped ensure the carriage of African American performance's infectious influence into mainstream Anglo-American popular music.

Before close analysis of the portraits, it is useful to touch upon a few examples of the visual borrowing and the blurring of class, race, and genre boundaries that appear throughout Mount's corpus of sketches and paintings. Such examples argue quite persuasively for the palimpsest-like overlap of these elements, not only in his visual vocabulary, but also in his cultural and musical imagination—and in the antebellum experience as a whole.

As we saw in chapter 1, Mount often transforms characters from white-to-black and vice versa, particularly notably in the pencil studies for which *Power of Music* and *Dance of the Haymakers* are the final results. Observed situations

PLATE 1. William Sidney Mount (1807–1868), *Dancing on the Barn Floor*, 1831, oil on canvas, 25 × 30 in., 0.1.3. Credit: The Long Island Museum of American Art, History & Carriages, Gift of Mr. and Mrs. Ward Melville, 1955.

PLATE 2. William Sidney Mount (1807–1868), *Study for Dance of the Haymakers*, n.d., oil on paper, 2010.00.561. Credit: The Long Island Museum of American Art, History & Carriages.

PLATE 3. William Sidney Mount (1807–1868), *Dance of the Haymakers*, 1845, oil on canvas, 24 × 29.75 in., 0.1.19. Credit: The Long Island Museum of American Art, History & Carriages, Gift of Mr. and Mrs. Ward Melville, 1950.

PLATE 4. William Sidney Mount (1807–1868), *Rustic Dance after a Sleigh Ride*, 1830, oil on canvas, 56.2 × 68.9 cm. Credit: Museum of Fine Arts, Boston, Massachusetts. Bequest of Martha C. Karolik for the M. and M. Karolik Collection of American Paintings, 1815–65, the Bridgman Art Library.

PLATE 5. William Sidney Mount (1807–1868), *Just in Tune*, 1849, oil on canvas, 29.25 × 25 in., 0.1.10. Credit: The Long Island Museum of American Art, History & Carriages, Gift of Mr. and Mrs. Ward Melville, 1955.

PLATE 6. William Sidney Mount (1807–1868), *Right and Left*, 1850, oil on canvas, 30 × 25 in., 0.1.2726. Credit: The Long Island Museum of American Art, History & Carriages, Museum Purchase, 1956.

PLATE 7. William Sidney Mount (1807–1868), *The Banjo Player*, 1856, oil on canvas, 35.75 × 28.75 in., 0.1.11. Credit: The Long Island Museum of American Art, History & Carriages, Gift of Mr. and Mrs. Ward Melville, 1955.

PLATE 8. William Sidney Mount (1807–1868), *The Bone Player*, 1856, oil on canvas, 91.76 × 73.98 cm. Credit: Museum of Fine Arts, Boston, Massachusetts. Bequest of Martha C. Karolik for the M. and M. Karolik Collection of American Paintings, 1815–65, the Bridgman Art Library.

sketched in pencil could be adopted and modified, or "fictionalized," in the paintings. In a blurring of racial boundaries similar to that found in *Power* and *Haymakers*, an adolescent itinerant black fiddler sketched playing in a tavern (*Comb and Brush*) was transformed into a white fiddler playing for *Dancing on the Barn Floor*.

Creolizing musical exchange likewise appears in Mount's sketches of ensemble music making, particularly those of the Long Island militia musters, which show white brass-band musicians, with black drummers and dancers as essential peripherals in militia situations. There is a strong tradition of such black "peripheralization" in other vernacular painters, and Kevin Scott has provided a close reading of the antiabolitionist symbolism specific to Mount's militia sketches.[5] It is possible to read the proximity of black and white musicians to be merely allegorical, representative, as Scott would argue, of Mount's beliefs about race and class. However, it is also possible to read these sketches, from life, as recording black and white musical exchange and situations that Mount literally observed. The suggestion that Mount's representations of black-white interaction may be more accurate, more reportial, than has been presumed would be consistent with the linguistic reevaluations of "Black Ethnic Vernacular" proposed by Rath and Mahar.[6] Given Mount's penchant for sketching under wide circumstances, and his attested insistence on sketching from life, it is certainly worth examining his sketches for the concrete musicological detail they may contain.

SYMBOLISM

The complex layers of racial, economic, and political symbolism in Mount's work have already been extensively explored in the art-historical literature.[7] I am not seeking to recover Mount's symbolism—music's meaning to him personally or politically—except insofar as it reveals the era; it is sufficient to say that his symbolic vocabulary is consistent with other painters of his class, time period, and background. Rather, I am interested in Mount's reportage on musical behavior: improvisation, dance, performance practice, melody, and rhythm. His depiction of the music of the creole synthesis is as close as we can get in the period before documentary photography or phonography.

THE GALLERY

The four portraits of solo instrumentalists, and the sketches and ephemera that frame them and help us understand their musicological significance, form the focus of attention in this chapter, and a kind of gallery of classical portraiture. Although the rather bedraggled subject fiddler in *Just in Tune* (1849; see plate 5) is not a likeness of him, Mount's feckless dance-master brother Robert Nelson Mount (1806–1883) may have modeled for it.[8] The first of Mount's oils to be lithographed, *Just in Tune* was widely popular in European and U.S. print versions, both legally issued by the Paris- and New York–based Goupil and Company, and in pirated copies that appear in newspapers and advertisements of the period.[9] The heroic *Right and Left* (1850; see plate 6), depicting now a left-handed fiddler, employs an unidentified model whose clothing, instrument, ethnicity, facial features, and vernacular technique strongly suggest a "creole" musical identity. The work's punning title—a reference both to the player's left-handedness, and to the square dance call "Right and left"—and its allusion to dance music, were obscured when the Paris lithographers, thinking to correct a mistake, reversed the image to render the fiddler right-handed.

The remaining two works probably represent Mount's masterpieces in the realm of vernacular portraiture, and certainly the apotheosis of his musicological reportage. The first is *The Banjo Player* (1856; see plate 7), whose model, garb, precisely rendered instrument and playing technique, facial features, and ethnicity present a remarkably photographic detailing of a contemporaneous black dance musician—even if his accoutrements were selected and combined at Mount's request. This painting has been studied and reproduced widely by art historians, publishers, and banjo experts, but its full musicological significance has not previously been recognized. Its companion is *The Bone Player* (1856; see plate 8), whose topic is equally emblematic of minstrelsy and of black dance music: an unidentified player of the percussive bones, whose clothing, precisely detailed instrument and meticulously accurate playing technique, facial features, and body choreography provide a detailed source of data on performance practice, improvisation, and rhythm. As with *The Banjo Player*, this painting has never been analyzed for its musicological import.

GENERAL COMMENTS, SHARED ELEMENTS, AND THEIR MUSICOLOGICAL IMPLICATIONS

In these four portraits, Mount featured three of minstrelsy's four canonic instruments—fiddle, banjo, and bones (omitting tambourine)—apparently in response to his agent William Schaus's suggestion that African American subjects might be especially salable.[10] By the 1850s, minstrelsy had become a worldwide commercial phenomenon in the wake of the Virginia Minstrels, and Schaus was sufficiently canny to realize that renderings of blackface minstrels might appeal to both domestic and overseas markets for exotica. Mount, however, politely declined to caricature.[11] Kevin Scott has provided tools for analyzing the layers of irony and signification that Mount's personal symbolic language represents, but leaving aside their sociopolitical narratives, we may ask of these paintings more fundamental music-historical questions.[12]

Mount typically painted in the studio; biographical anecdotes confirm his reliance on the technique of meticulous sketching, watercolors, and oil painting from sitting models. This suggests that the three portraits of African American musicians were painted from life rather than from pure imagination. Mount was an inveterate pencil sketcher, refusing to sketch except from life, and we have cited numerous examples of figures, topics, or activities initially captured in pencil, from life, which recur in more "fictional" paintings.

Many painters employ sitting subjects primarily in order to capture physiognomy, anatomy, and similar draftsmanship issues accurately, "dressing" those subjects arbitrarily with instruments, ornaments, or clothing; this may account for Buffet's claim that Robert Nelson supplied the stance and posture, but not the facial features, for *Just in Tune*.[13] On the other hand, Mount's detailed and accurate depiction of instruments and playing technique, coupled with his preference for sketching from life, argues for a more direct and literal replication of performance practice. I suggest that, in this gallery of four, Mount painted sitters whose instruments and physical technique reflected the reality of those subjects' professional lives. And, even allowing for the omission of Nelson's features in one of these four, I suggest that these models were in fact dance musicians he knew, admired, recruited to sit for him, and painted from life.

This raises another round of investigative questions. There are no reported instances of African American minstrel troupes in the antebellum period—those would come after the war. The template set by the Virginia and Christy Minstrels, and hundreds of other touring groups, called for four Caucasian musicians, attired in ragged costume and burned-cork masks, playing the canonic instruments of banjo, fiddle, tambourine, and bones, in a full evening's entertainment. Schaus's suggestion of African American rather than Caucasian musicians would seem to have been merely a smart piece of marketing. Yet while Mount employs the instrumentation and techniques of minstrelsy, he steers away from period caricature, choosing instead to depict actual African American musicians in a manner that idealizes their skill, confidence, and artistry. This heroic realism did not erode their salability: lithographs of *Right and Left*, *The Banjo Player*, and *The Bone Player* were immediately and continued to be popular in both Europe and the United States. Who were these subject musicians, where did they come from, what communities did they serve, how did Mount know them, and, most importantly, what about their music did he reveal in these portraits?

At last two contrasting interpretations seem possible. First, the gallery visually confirms the presence of African American dance ensembles—or, at least, solo musicians: that is, black fiddlers and banjo players, and bones players to accompany them—on Long Island as well as elsewhere in New York, in rural as well as urban contexts, during the antebellum period. Given the known data, this is certainly a plausible inference: black musicians in both slave and free states were widely recruited to play for white dancing, and their dance-music repertoires reflected both African American and Anglo-Celtic tune sources. Moreover, given the relative intimacy and diversity of black-white interactions on Long Island throughout the nineteenth century, and the evidence of his expressed admiration for "Toney" Clapp and that contained within his music manuscripts, it is certainly reasonable to assume that Mount might have maintained acquaintance with African American musicians who could be recruited as subjects, as well as sources of repertoire. However, there is almost no documentation for Long Island's Anglo-African music culture, or of the presence of prototypical minstrel-band instrumentation among African Americans until after the Civil War. Yet, African American music making in the North was much more extensive, much more diverse, much more influential, and (crucially) much more integrated, than has been supposed.[14] So the presence of all-black ensembles playing for dancing on Long Island is a distinct possibility.

It might be argued that the fiddle-banjo-bones ensemble implicit in our gallery could merely be Mount's construction, an imagined assemblage created solely for purposes of symbolic narrative or programmatic fiction, or because the combination would recall the minstrel troupes' instrumentation. However, if this is true: if the sitting subjects were not musicians, then Mount's observational expertise and accurate depiction of subtle fiddle, banjo, and bones techniques is particularly impressive. Either his subjects knew how to hold and play the banjo, fiddle, and bones—and to do so with an air of commanding authority that argues for lengthy and skillful professional experience as dance musicians—or the artist himself did, to such an extent that he could instruct his nonmusician sitters in how to model actual players' technique and posture.

Thus, regardless of whether Mount knew these individuals as musicians (as I believe), or did not, his visual data are still uniquely valuable. Either

Mount was observing and accurately rendering African American musicians and their techniques as subjects at a time when musicologically useful documentation of such players is otherwise absent—or he was visualizing and precisely depicting imagined musicians using accurate techniques. It is even possible that Mount was observing the technique of white musicians and transmuting them, as he did with the black fiddler who was the sketch source for the white player in *Dancing on the Barn Floor*, back across the color line. If that is so, his white sitters were employing African American performance practices—hence confirming the wider ubiquity of the creole synthesis.

In the end, regardless of whether Mount saw African American musicians playing these instruments and accurately depicted them, or saw white musicians playing them and transmuted those observed subjects into African Americans, or simply drew on his own precise knowledge of instruments and performance practice, the "creole synthesis" of African American and Anglo-Celtic music making is here made visible: rendered accurately, extensively, and informatively. The presence, breadth, and accuracy of musical detail—and its comparative absence anywhere else in period evidence—make Mount's paintings of Long Island African American musicians essential to our understanding of the roots of minstrelsy.

ANALYSIS

All four portraits share certain symbolic and representational elements. Although allegorical interpretation is not the focus of this book, it is worth noting some of the symbolic elements that Mount employs in these particular portraits. He used these elements in consistent and conscious ways in order to provide practical information about his musician subjects; as a result, they merit our attention.

Mount employs symbols of itinerancy: of the mobility or unpredictability of the music professional's lifestyle; these include ragged or jaunty hats, worn or draped greatcoats, and various background elements common to liminal, commercial, or shifting contexts: a horseshoe, tavern signs, furniture, and settings. He likewise employs symbols of musical professionalism: a fiddle case, a bugle mouthpiece, an unidentifiable but intriguing fiddle ornament, meticulously rendered *and decorated* instruments, and active body postures and choreographed movement that project vitality, familiarity, comfort, and confidence. All suggest expert players for whom making music is a constant and probably remunerative activity—not a hobby.

Similarly, Mount is meticulous in the precise delineation of instruments and of their performance practice, so much so that aspects of the *Banjo Player*'s instrument, for example, have been used by builders of historic replicas. He is equally meticulous in details of physical posture, body mechanics, and the performance practice of each instrument. He employs instruments for their complementarity: as mentioned above, although these works were painted over a span of almost eight years, it is likely not a coincidence that the instrumentalists make up three fourths of the iconic blackface instrumentation.

Finally, Mount carefully combines fine details to yield detailed and unique portraits of individuals of contrasting ethnicity. These are not generic or anonymous (much less caricatured) portraits, but rather represent individuals of unique facial features, ages, creole ethnicities, and body types. The distinctive portrayal of specific individuals is strongest in the later *Bone Player* and *Banjo Player*, less strong in *Right and Left*, and (paradoxically, considering Mount's brother Nelson's possible service as sitter) least distinctive in *Just in Tune*. The facial features, hair, and skin tone of the young fiddler in *Right and Left* and the *Bone Player* certainly evoke creole ethnicity, while the West African features and hair and darker skin tone of the *Banjo Player* imply yet a third ethnic mixture. Such multiracial genetic diversity mimics the demographic and expressive creole synthesis found throughout the western Atlantic, multicultural Long Island, and Mount's own depictions of music, as throughout minstrelsy's performance practice.

DISCUSSION OF THE PORTRAITS

Just in Tune

This 1849 image (see plate 5), which was painted on speculation but which became Mount's first successful lithographed print, is an affectionate, lighthearted portrait, formerly thought to have been modeled by William's elder brother Nelson, an itinerant dance teacher and musician.[15] The facts that the fiddler is in the act of tuning rather than playing and that he is Caucasian make *Just in Tune* marginally less relevant for the current study; it does, however, contain elements that recur in later images and that illuminate the roots of minstrelsy. These details, some biographical and some allegorical, include symbols of itinerancy: specifically, a rakish and worn hat, a loose and unpressed white shirt, a loosely knotted cravat, and a greatcoat; also symbols of ethnicity, behavior, and class: a wispy beard and mustache, uncombed hair, and rumpled clothes—but also a wedding band.

Musicological observation is less extensive but no less precise. Mount accurately depicts the fiddler's tuning technique of propping the instrument end pin on the knee and turning the belly toward the ear; grasping the bow's frog with the last fingers of the right hand while using the same hand's thumb and forefinger both to seat and turn the high E-string's peg, and the left thumb to pluck single strings, with the left-hand fingers steadying the body. He shows inlaid decoration on the bow's frog and pegs, a fiddler's carefully trimmed left-hand nails, an extra string looped through the peghead and projecting past the scroll (probably employed for hanging the instrument on the wall when not in use), and, in a particularly appealing and subtle touch, the painter's initials "W.S.M." below the button.

Right and Left

This work (see plate 6), from 1850, was the first of those African American "heads" suggested by Mount's agent and publisher William Schaus: on Mount's query regarding the ethnicity of the sitter for a companion to the previous year's *Just in Tune*, Schaus had proposed "a Negro."[16] Mount responded with a painting that partakes of both portrait and genre characters, being likely modeled from life, but containing a narrative element reminiscent of his extensive catalog of genre works.

The programmaticism begins with the work's title, a pun combining a reference to the player's left-handedness and to square-dance calls of the period. This in turn implies a genre narrative, namely, that this player himself might both fiddle for, and call the steps of, a social country dance, a not-uncommon combination of services among dance musicians (and possibly undertaken by the black fiddler in 1830's *Rustic Dance*). Given Mount's propensity for modeling from life, and his immersion in Long Island's social dance culture, it is a clear reminder of the ubiquity of black fiddlers supplying music for—and calling—white dances. Though the sitter is unidentified, there is no internal evidence to dispute the possibility that he was a black fiddler and dance caller of Mount's acquaintance.

Mount again deploys his stock signifiers of parallel itinerancy and musical professionalism: the fiddler wears a ragged but rakish slouch hat reminiscent of that in *Just in Tune* (and in the later *Bone Player*), but also of that worn by the African American fiddler sketched in *Comb and Brush* (undated), who in the interim had been transformed into the similarly garbed Caucasian fiddler of *Dancing on the Barn Floor* (1831). He also renders the rumpled loose shirt, fancy waistcoat, loose cravat, and greatcoat (over the back of his chair) of the fiddler's colleagues in the gallery. Likewise, the painting again incorporates symbols of dance music's liminal and itinerant performance contexts: a horseshoe, emblematic of both travel and unpredictable luck, and a battered fiddle case.

The genre characteristics of *Right and Left* might lead us to infer that it is a staged image—that Mount assembled model, instrument, clothing, ornament, and other props in the studio. Even if that is so, as with *Just in Tune*, the accuracy of musical detail yields a kind of visual ethnomusicology. The fiddler uses the eponymous technique, with right hand assuming the left's usual role (fingering), and the left hand taking the right's (bowing). Consistent with folk fiddling technique, he plays without a chin rest, and seemingly down on the chest (though this is somewhat obscured by the angle of the player's body). This position permits a looseness, relaxation, and variety of grips that in turn facilitates dance fiddling's diverse bowings, but in contrast to "classical" technique requires that the palm of the fingering hand (in this case, the right) must support the instrument's neck. This in turn precludes ready shifting of the hand on the fingerboard, and tends to mandate playing primarily in first position, using the "fiddle-friendly" sharp keys (fundamentals of G, D, A, and selectively E, B, and C). Such keys also emphasize the natural resonance of the unaccompanied instrument, making them especially suitable for (and ubiquitous within) a wide variety of vernacular fiddle styles, both Anglo-Celtic and African American.

Observation and decoration of the fiddle, like that in *Just in Tune*, and even more in the banjo and bones of the later paintings, more specifically identify the model as an actual musician. Though there is some peculiarity of perspective or proportion in the size and height of the fiddle bridge—it seems excessive, and would in reality result in an unplayably high string action—Mount renders the bridge's profile with the relatively flat string-to-string angle preferred by folk fiddlers; such an angle lowers individual strings' amplitude, but facilitates bowing of double- and triple-stops, in keeping with the unaccompanied fiddler's desire for enhanced resonance and sonority. Moreover, there is a cord strung through the f-holes into and again out of the soundboard of the instrument. Though there is no way of knowing the specific purpose of this cord, it is likely there in order to facilitate setting the instrument's sound post properly, though it is a little unusual for the cord to be left within the instrument once the sound post is set.[17]

On the other hand, it is at least possible that strung onto the cord and inserted within the instrument is a set of rattlesnake rattles—a widespread southern folk-fiddle tradition, alleged to ward off spiders, and, more practically, helping to control humidity within the instrument.[18] If this deduction is correct, it would certainly tend to support the inference that this musician was a visitor rather than a Long Island native (though *Crotalus*—the rattlesnake—did occur on the island in the nineteenth century).

Though he is quite young, the fiddler's posture, and particularly the way in which Mount poses him, looking sidelong over his left shoulder as he plays, is intentionally reminiscent of eighteenth-century European heroic portraiture.[19] At the same time, his facial features (aquiline nose, full lips, and curly hair), and olive skin coloring mark him as being of mixed, "creole" ethnicity. Of all the portraits in the gallery, it is arguably *Right and Left* that most explicitly seeks the romantic appeal of exoticism; in any event, that appeal was successful, as the print was massively popular and sold widely in the European market.

The Banjo Player

Of the four portraits we examine, *The Banjo Player* (see plate 7) has become the best-known and most widely distributed. An iconic image for both African American art historians and banjo scholars, it depicts a young man playing a minstrel-style Boucher banjo, and displays a degree of accuracy and specificity that has made the painting an attractive resource for both book designers and luthiers. Mount again deploys symbols of musicianship and itinerancy, including beautiful detail and careful dressing of clothing and ornament. Despite the absence of a programmatic title, close observation of these details, and selective investigation and reconstruction (in this special case) of the sitter's background and community, yield a complex and compelling history.

Though historiography of the banjo in North America has been prone to a good deal of inaccuracy and misinformation, more recently Carlin, Winans, Conway, Pestcoe, and Jagfors (among others) have traced the instrument's earlier manifestations, in the Caribbean, and its earliest roots, in Africa, in a much more complete and nuanced fashion.[20] As Carlin has made clear, and a wide range of the material evidence confirms, the banjo's development occurs much earlier than minstrelsy, and results from the first contact of diverse West and Central African ethnicities in the African Caribbean.[21] In particular among these authors, Carlin's *Joel Walker Sweeney* includes a detailed discussion of the Afro-Caribbean roots of the instrument, focusing in part on the rich evidence contained in what seems to be the earliest extant iconography of the banjo in North America: an anonymous painting titled *The Old Plantation*.[22]

That image's connotations for the interpretation of creole dance are discussed at length in chapter 6, but here, in the context of the banjo's early provenance, Pestcoe's is an illuminating complementary interpretation.[23] He mentions Melville Herskovits's acute—but insufficiently informed—analysis in an exchange with the Gullah specialist Lorenzo Turner, who identified both stringed instrument and drum as Yoruba or Hausa, which émigré populations were known in Brazil as well.[24] This would confirm relatively direct West African music and dance behaviors in tidewater South Carolina in the prerevolutionary period. This Yoruba-Hausa cultural influence grew in the wake of the 1739 Stono Rebellion, whose instigation slave owners associated with slaves directly imported from Angola and Kongo.[25]

Pestcoe provides a useful corrective to this early scholarship, however, and finds a number of arguments that legitimate calling the instrument in *The Old Plantation* not a Yoruba or Hausa *molo* but, authentically and persuasively, an early example of a New World adaptation: that is, "an African American instrument [gourd banjo] of West African heritage."[26] Further, Pestcoe suggests that this instrument's Afro-Caribbean origins, and the creole collisions of European and West African musical heritages there, are directly responsible for the transformation of the *molo* into the early *banza* or banjo: he identifies, for example, the *Old Plantation*'s banjo's "flat fingerboard, wooden tuning pegs, and string nut" as adoptions from European lutes (*vihuela*, *cavaco*, *tiple*, *cavaquinho*). He also reminds us that some of the first citations of the instrument by name actually come from the U.S. East Coast: New York City (banger, 1736), Maryland (bonja, 1748), and South Carolina (bangio, 1749), this in turn confirming the ubiquity of the instrument family among Atlantic creoles.[27] As Pestcoe says, the gourd banjo was "originally created in the Caribbean, sometime in the 17th century, by enslaved Africans and their African American offspring."[28]

The presence of the Afro-Caribbean *bangio/bangar/banza/banjo* in the colonial-era United States leads to several inferences with significant implications for the present study. First, it serves as further evidence confirming that Afro-Caribbean musical influences were distributed widely throughout the eastern United States, on both coasts and rivers. Second, it confirms that the instrument was associated with African American communities—including those communities that originated festivals such as Pinkster, and disseminated them along the riverine and maritime routes that carried minstrel song repertoires. Third, it suggests that white players in the North could have found opportunity to observe and imitate Afro-Caribbean banjo music, as they did creolized songs and dance tunes. Finally, the presence of the banjo as an explicitly Afro-Caribbean instrument, played mostly within African American communities until taken up by white minstrel players, confirms the intentional effort by those players to engage in observation and imitation—what we have earlier termed "participant observation" among these "prototypical ethnomusicologists."[29]

The historical biographies confirm this: in addition to the stories of Dan Emmett learning banjo from an Irishman named Ferguson and from the free-black Staunton family, and Sweeney from black banjo players in the eastern Alleghenies riverhead of Appomattox, we have stories of the Haitian creole banjoist John "Picayune" Butler playing as far north as Elmira, New York, in the 1850s, and of Billy Whitlock, the white virtuoso who was first banjo player for the Virginia Minstrels, "steal[ing] off to some negro hut to hear the darkies sing and see them dance . . . [where] he got his accurate knowledge of the peculiarities of plantation and cornfield negroes."[30] Though the last quotation repeats inaccurate generalizations about the geographical origins of the creole synthesis, the suggestion that early minstrel banjo players learned from black teachers holds true.

That the instrument was well-known and in demand, not only among the African American population in its hand-built, gourd version, but also among Euro-Americans in a much more standardized version, is confirmed by the production of high-quality instruments by the Boucher Company of Baltimore from the early 1840s, that is, roughly contemporaneously with Sweeney's popularization of the instrument on the minstrel stage.[31] Boucher, a well-established instrument maker, is the first builder known to have adopted the use of snare-drum lugs to hold a skin head onto the face of the instrument; in the earlier, handmade "tackhead" models, the skin of the head had been permanently fastened onto the wooden rim, and thus difficult to tighten or replace. Boucher's incorporation of lugs not only made repair much simpler (with interchangeable parts) but also permitted heads that were under higher tension and thus louder.[32]

So to George Freeman, and the Boucher banjo, and *The Banjo Player*, and what this image can tell us about the creole synthesis. As with *Right and Left*, the sheer physical beauty of the model and of the painting's techniques and formal composition directly reference the classical tradition's idealism and similarly seek to portray a sense of heroic command. As with the other members of the gallery, the model wears a rumpled white shirt and loosely knotted cravat, with a fancy waistcoat (this time with a handkerchief tucked into its watch pocket), and is depicted with a greatcoat draped over the back of his chair. In contrast to the rakish slouch hats of *Just in Tune*, *Right and Left*, and the later *Bone Player*, the *Banjo Player* wears a striped stocking-cap—a headgear choice that elsewhere in Mount's work has tended to symbolize working-class or itinerant status.[33] The beardless teenage model both recalls and contrasts musicians depicted elsewhere in the gallery: his hair texture, facial features, and skin tone signal African ethnicity particularly strongly, and one contemporary dance scholar has pointed out his physical resemblance to Fulani peoples of sub-Saharan West Africa.[34]

This image is particularly useful in seeking to recover the music of Long Island's African American community, despite that community being undocumented and unremarked by musicological scholarship; it is thus key to understanding Mount's assimilation of the creole synthesis, through the medium of fiddlers Toney Clapp and the anonymous " 'Lige," and of banjoist George Freeman. Mount's diaries for May 1858 diary offer tantalizing clues about the painting's genesis; he says "I painted the Banjo player in eight days (16 sittings), two sittings a day," but provides no other information about the sitter's identity or musical experience.[35] According to the first Mount biography, a collection of newspaper columns authored by Edward Buffet, based in oral and family history, and serialized in the *Port Jefferson Times* in the late 1920s—when the children of Mount's 1840s and '50s sitters could still provide comparatively direct oral history information—the sitter for *The Banjo Player* was an indentured servant named George Freeman:

> He was bound out to R.N. Mount's father-in-law, John Brewster, in whose home . . . William Mount was a frequent visitor. Mr John B. Mount [John Brewster's grandson] well remembers that his Uncle William arranged with his grandfather to let George go to Stony Brook a certain number of times to sit for the picture. The artist had taken quite a fancy to the colored boy. George's parents lived in that section of the Island called The Ridge, and his articles of indenture, which still exist, were drawn up by Gen. John R. Satterly of Setauket . . . Mount completed The Bone Player in the same year (in fourteen sittings) and it was sent to Paris.[36]

Buffet's columns provide the most immediate biographical information and by far the most copious first-person accounting of the people, contexts, and communities in which Mount's sketches and paintings originated. In the absence of contradictory evidence, and in light of certain visual confirmations within the painting, it is reasonable to trust Buffet's biographical sketch of George Freeman.[37]

So who was this *Banjo Player*, George Freeman? What was his experience; what was the sound of his musical world, and how did it impact on and reflect the roots of minstrelsy? We can draw on the sociohistorical information presented in the chapter 3 discussion of minstrelsy's rural and urban staging areas to begin addressing these questions. In addition, Mount's precise visual evidence includes details illuminating the diversity, complexity, and impact of music in African American Long Island, and, by historical analogy, in many other creolizing contexts throughout the young Republic.

Freeman plays a precisely rendered banjo as manufactured by the William Boucher Banjo Company, a principal source for instruments, and innovators in banjo design, in the antebellum period.[38] In all details the depicted instrument conforms to extant examples: its deep and large-diameter "pot" (resonator), calfskin head, and sparse lugs (clamps used to position and tighten the skin head) betray the influence of military snare drum technologies; its gut strings and fretless fingerboard link it to the African and Afro-Caribbean gourd *banjar* and *banza* as described in colonial-era sources; the short drone string, played by the right thumb in opposition to the fingernail in an interlocking polyrhythm, replicates the multipart ensemble aesthetics of African solo instrumentalists; the sensuous curves of the chanterelle's fingerboard extension and of the peghead on the other hand imitate the design of European stringed instruments, most notably the fiddle.

Yet this precise detail, while confirming Mount's accuracy as an artist committed to sketching from life models, raises additional questions, most notably regarding the *source* of this instrument. No banjos were found in Mount's collection, and his diaries make no reference to the same. Indeed, the banjo, in 1856 New York, was most commonly associated with the white blackface minstrels who made up Boucher's principal clientele, rather than with black servants. Did Mount borrow this first-class instrument from a Long Island acquaintance, family member, or neighbor, in order to dress this model, or did he own it?

On the other hand, did this instrument perhaps belong to George Freeman? While there is no reference in Buffet or in the diaries to Freeman as a musician, and comparatively little documentation of banjos among Long Island blacks (the fiddle was the ubiquitous dance-music instrument in both communities during this period, as we have seen in the previously cited experience of Mount's childhood mentor, the fiddler Toney Clapp and in Mount's own *Rustic Dance*), we do know that gourd banjos were played by African Americans in the North as early as the 1730s.[39] Moreover, there is no question that Mount was painting from an actual Boucher model—the details of the instrument are nearly photographically precise. Finally, aspects of the playing technique, of which we have established Mount in other cases to be a precise and knowledgeable observer, are equally revealing.

As always in the iconographic analysis of music and dance techniques, the two-dimensional static representation of a three-dimensional action risks conflicting or ambiguous interpretation. Nevertheless, Mount's specific reconstruction of one particular performance technique is supported by the full range of visual and contextual evidence. The left-hand technique is relatively unambiguous: Freeman fingers notes with the second and third digits (possibly the first, as well). Because of the diversity, nonstandardization, and sparse documentation for African American banjo tunings in the period, it is probably impossible to identify the specific sonority being sounded: though the fingering is relatively unambiguous, in the absence of a known tuning, the notes sounding cannot be determined. Nevertheless, it is clear that multiple strings are being fingered and sounded, whether simultaneously or in arpeggiated fashion, against the unfingered high drone of the chanterelle. The implicit texture is of some combination of independent voices or polyphony. The dynamic, with the instrument's gut strings and low-tension head, would be relatively quiet and the timbre of the instrument relatively dark. But, at the same time, the sound would be relatively full, plunky, and percussive.

The right-hand technique is both more ambiguous and more important, because the range of diverse picking techniques available in the period would drastically alter the rhythmic, textural, and percussive character of the sound, and the ratio of "African" versus "Anglo-Celtic" influence on the instrumental conception. If the player is plucking the strings downward with the thumb, and upward independently with alternating fingers (the arpeggiated technique borrowed from Renaissance cittern and early guitar, that, transferred to steel-string guitar, became known as fingerpicking), then he is depicted as employing the Europeanized accompanimental method that came in the 1850s and '60s to be associated with later blackface minstrels. Conversely, if he is striking the strings downward with the nail of the first finger, and striking the short chanterelle string with the thumb as an offbeat drone, then he is employing the earlier percussive, polyrhythmic stroke style or knocking (later called frailing or clawhammer).[40] This technique is the instrument's most direct link to the performance practice of the Afro-Caribbean Haitian *banza* and, further back, to the memory of West African plucked lutes such as the *akonting* from Senegambia.[41]

In music image 2 is an example of the fingering techniques and resultant musical texture in the African-derived knocking style.

As with the instrument's tuning, the static and silent nature of the medium precludes uncontested identification of the right hand's motion. On an older or less well-cared-for instrument, the pattern of the fingers' wear as

Music Figure 2. Example of banjo "knocking" style.

revealed by discolorations on the calf-skin head might clarify whether the technique involves the (Europeanized) up-picking, or the older (African) down-picking or knocking: up-picking would leave relatively little wear below the treble strings, while in contrast, the down-picking style would yield an oblong discolored patch from the follow-through of the fingernail against the head. The absence of such discoloration restricts conclusions about technique based on wear.

Very subtle anatomical details, and the play of light and shadow, may resolve this question of right-hand technique, and thus of the likely African versus European sources (and aesthetics) of that technique—given that the instrument itself is already African in conception, Afro-Caribbean in realization, and is here played by an African American musician. We may note that the right-hand index finger is held outward, and separate, from the second, third, and fourth fingers, which are curled together. In contrast to these, the index is extended and opened, while the thumb rests on the drone string. That is, the player's hand is poised, in the shape of the eponymous claw, in the striking position: the nail of the index finger about to strike the melody note or notes percussively downward, knocking on the downbeat, while the trailing thumb supplies the polyrhythmic following upbeat. Such cross-rhythm is a marker of African American dance, and on the banjo, knocking on the downbeat combined with the upbeat droning thumb replicates the interlocking multi-rhythmic ensemble parts of African tradition.[42]

Further confirmation of the right hand's essentially "African" performance practice lies in Mount's expert depiction of the play of light and shadow on the calfskin head: the shadow of the thumb is separated from the digit itself by precisely the height of the chanterelle string above the head—which would be expected were the thumb at rest against the chanterelle, in the African style. Conversely, the relatively greater distance of the forefinger's shadow from the digit—its greater distance from the skin head—and the fact that the melody string (second from highest-pitched) is depicted as below the finger, with the nail about to strike downward against the string, further suggest that George Freeman is knocking in the African style on the Boucher banjo.

But the instrument itself tells us more about George Freeman and his experience of community music. As with *Right and Left* and *The Bone Player*, the carefully personalized decorations of this instrument, in addition to the high quality of its manufacture, suggest a musician confident in his skills and proud of his trade. Perhaps George Freeman, a teenage indentured servant in the house of Mount's uncle, was not the owner of this particular instrument. But there is little question that he was intimately familiar with this banjo, knew how to play it, and possessed a skilled approach to its technique. Likewise, the essentially African nature of that technique would have a polyrhythmic effect on the sound of the banjo music that he created, and in turn on the sound of any ensemble in which he participated or the bodily sensation of any dancer for whom he played.

While the unaccompanied banjo is depicted in the antebellum slave South, in the North and also on the frontiers, it was more commonly paired with, or replaced by, the fiddle for dancing, not only in the repertoire of blackface minstrelsy but also in the gradually Africanizing repertoire of Anglo-Celtic tunes. Whether George Freeman was playing, for example, "Possum Up a Gum Stump" (one of the most venerable and ubiquitous of minstrelsy's borrowings from the southern black repertoires) or the very different "Such a Gettin' Up Stairs" (another popular minstrel tune, derived from the English morris tune "Getting Up Stairs"), the polyrhythmic, syncopated, droning, and percussive nature of his banjo accompaniment would have unavoidably skewed the resulting musical result, regardless of the original melodic source, toward Africa.

What is the import of this? The inescapable conclusion is that, by 1856 *at the latest*, the black musician who Mount saw or imagined was playing for dancing in rural Long Island using an African-derived banjo technique and rhythmic language. It is impossible that this Afro-Caribbean rhythmic language, in performance, would not have profoundly shifted Anglo-Celtic fiddle melodies—and Anglo-American bodies dancing to those melodies—toward Africa, or at least toward the creole synthesis this book hypothesizes.

One final visual element is relevant but has not been previously observed or discussed: the ornament that hangs against Freeman's waistcoat, suspended by a cord around his neck. This ornament has not been remarked by any extant scholarship, yet it provides significant musicological insight as we seek to reconstruct the nature of George Freeman's musical world. Close examination of this suggests that the "ornament" is in fact a musical tool: namely, the brass mouthpiece of a coachman's bugle.[43]

This simple organological identification vastly enriches our picture of George Freeman's musical identity. As both a symbol of his profession, and as a practical tool used for signaling, the presence of a bugle mouthpiece in Mount's painting means that George Freeman was (or at the very least is depicted as) not only a banjo player but also a coachman, and not only a dance musician at night but also a trained practitioner of a respected, mobile profession during the day. A coachman would enjoy both a secure income and a place in the household employing him—and, especially in prerailroad-era Long Island, a valued and essential expertise.[44] Even more importantly, a coachman would enjoy an unusual level of mobility and range of geographical contacts, both of which would have been invaluable to a professional musician.

Identifying Freeman as a musician-coachman links him to earlier accounts of similarly mobile musical individuals: recall those admiring observations from Charles Mathews, who described seeing a black coachman, reins knotted around his neck, controlling his team with tunes played on the fiddle.[45] The intentionality and specificity of *The Banjo Player*'s symbolic evocation of dance music and highway music, of nighttime music for entertainment and daytime music for travel, is also confirmed by another, earlier appearance of the stocking cap in Mount's own catalog: that is, in the headgear of the black coachman depicted in Mount's first successful painting of black-white music-dance interaction, the 1830 *Rustic Dance*. Whether the stocking cap worn in 1856 by model George Freeman was his own or was supplied by Mount in recollection of that earlier painting of 1830, there is no arguing the two images' linkages of music and travel, and of the symbolism of that linkage. Likewise the bugle mouthpiece: whether it belonged to George Freeman or was supplied by Mount as part of "dressing" his subject (more likely the former), its presence in *The Banjo Player* links George Freeman not only to the coachman in *Rustic Dance*, but also to more ancient African traditions of music as a ubiquitous, essential, practical tool in accomplishing the myriad skilled tasks of day-to-day life, and of musicians as mobile, mutable, empowered, and "slippery" purveyors of liminality. Identifying George Freeman as a banjo-playing coachman also links him directly with the mobile, ambitious, skillful, transgressive, culturally and ethnically creolized performers of the highways, canals, waterfronts, theatres, frontiers and other liminal spaces (the Catherine Wharf, the Virginia High Road, the Ohio and Hudson Rivers, the Erie Canal) that we have identified as the original incubators of minstrelsy's cultural synthesis.

The Bone Player

The Bone Player (see plate 8) was painted in the same year (1856) as *The Banjo Player*, and shares with it elements of composition, color palette, symbolism, and portraiture. Likewise commissioned by William Schaus with an eye to the overseas market for lithographed prints, it depicts a player of another of minstrelsy's consort of fiddle, banjo, tambourine, and bones. As with the other three images in our gallery, art historians have convincingly argued that, in *The Bone Player*, Mount intentionally imitates the postures and compositional of heroic classical portraiture. But this work transcends genre: as in *Right and Left* and *The Banjo Player*, Mount here captures an African American musician in the act of performance in a rendering that rejects the caricature of blackface, the passivity associated with the still life, and the voyeurism of the genre painting. Instead, he creates an admiring portrait of an individual who is musically confident, proud of his skills and his craft, and in the act of commanding the most fundamental parameter in any dance music—that is, the rhythm. Although we lack the sorts of biographical clues about the sitter's identity that Edward Buffet was able to provide in the case of George Freeman, such a lack need not invalidate the musicological information that *The Bone Player* can still supply.

In contrast to *Just in Tune*—or, for that matter, the early genre paintings such as *Rustic Dance* (1830) or *Dancing on the Barn Floor* (1831)—*The Bone Player* does not imply a narrative backstory; in that sense, it avoids the anecdotal obligations associated with vernacular painting, and with most of Mount's catalog. Rather, as in *The Banjo Player*, Mount provides the painting a simple professional title, and depicts its titular musician in the act of performance.

Even more than the *Banjo Player*, the *Bone Player*'s posture captures the beautiful, full-body physical choreography required to play percussive dance music. This allusion to dance is significant: of the three canonic minstrelsy instruments that Mount included in the four works in our gallery, it is the bones' physical technique that most closely approaches—indeed, erases, in a fashion consistent with Afro-Caribbean aesthetics—the boundary between playing and dancing. Mount's *Banjo Player* is both a musician and a dancer, playing for dancers, driving and commenting on the rhythm of the accompanying ensemble and the syncopated polyrhythms of the dancers' feet. Whether he is (as seems a reasonable inference) accompanying a fiddle or banjo tune, or something more obscure, or even—as in so many of the Mount sketches depicting solo accompanists "patting juba" on the body—providing the lone percussive rhythm for dancing, *The Bone Player* is a carrier of the creole synthesis. Any music-and-dance event in which he participates tilts toward Afro-Caribbean sound, sensation, and rhythmic experience, and literally embodies the contribution of the creole synthesis to American vernacular culture.

As with *Right and Left* and *The Banjo Player*, Mount employs visual references that symbolize itinerancy, including the loosely tied cravat, rumpled white shirt, fancy waistcoat, and greatcoat; but also those that for Mount convey independence: notably the jaunty though ragged slouch hat, and, in an ornamental touch that most explicitly evokes the Afro-Caribbean creole culture, a swashbuckling ring in the left ear.[46] Mount also repeats symbols of the itinerant musician's transitory and liminal contexts—the highway and the public house—by including both a fiddle case and a pitcher with drinking glasses. This is not a wealthy or middle-class respectable musician, for he is too ragged and marginal a figure (he has not even doffed his coat to play, and his waistcoat is visibly missing a button), but there is no question that he is in command of the musical rhythm, of the musical situation, and of his profession.

Physical characteristics such as facial hair and features, skin tone, and body type, while distinguished from those of both *Right and Left* and *The Banjo Player*, like them suggest a creole ethnicity mirroring that of the implicit music. Of the four portraits, the *Bone Player* provides the most direct reminder of the direct contact between Long Island Sound communities (including those on the island, as well as those across the sound on the coasts of Connecticut, Rhode Island, and Massachusetts) and worldwide maritime culture.[47] It is well to remember that Afro-Caribbean musical aesthetics (and even repertoire—recall that "Jump Jim Crow" developed from a Georgia Sea Island children's song, and probably before that from Haiti or West Africa) and Afro-Caribbean musicians, such as the Bone Player, could equally likely have arrived directly into Long Island from around the Black Atlantic—and from Long Island thence into the Lower East Side.[48]

As with *Right and Left* and *The Banjo Player*, the sheer compositional and visual beauty of technique and subject make the painting not only appealing but heroically monumental. Even more than in those images, however, the *Banjo Player* is kinesthetic, displaying what is for a static medium a remarkable sense of graceful rhythmic motion and bodily agency. Dance scholars have suggested that such imagery, as with the Jim Crow iconography, can tell us about the music that accompanied such movement. This is particularly the case if we understand the depiction to represent a body *moving* through space, rather than in a static pose; such a perspective helps us recover the springy kinetic rebounding of Jim Crow's leaps and twists—its "wheels and turns" perceived through the image's "fleeting moment in dance":

> Some moments in a dance—when a dancer changes from rising to falling, from compressing to expanding, from reaching to contracting or from stretching to contracting—have in common a moment of zero velocity with a non-zero acceleration. *This gives the visual appearance of both stillness and motion at the same time.* . . . [Such] moments linger visually because of the zero velocity and linger mentally because of the paradoxical perception. These are moments of maximum and minimum breath, the peak of a rise, the moment of recovery.[49]

As with the earlier images of *Dancing for Eels*, of G. W. Dixon and T. D. Rice dancing "Zip Coon" and "Jim Crow," and the thousands of sketches and prints that appropriated the signifying body language of those archetypes, *The Bone Player* captures powerfully, in a "fleeting moment," a dancing body's motion through space.[50] And Mount's reliability as a source of kinesthetic, iconographic, and musicological information suggests that earlier blackface images, noxious racist caricature though they are, may likewise represent (as Mahar discovered in his BEV analysis of blackface texts) an attempt, in part, to capture the vital, transgressive bodily appeal of blackface dance. The genius of Mount's extrapolation, considering its period and Mount's own racial politics, is that while *The Bone Player* retains the bodily energy, flow, and visualized kinesthetics of earlier blackface images, it is purged of their racist caricature. He has not just observed this musician—Mount has admired him. And he integrates this idealism with a rigorous visual honesty that, while memorializing the *Bone Player* through the conventions of European heroic portraiture, also captures the participatory, sound-and-motion-integrating creole synthesis of the portrait's (silent, but not absent) music.

While, as with other portraits in the gallery, it is possible that Mount recruited a nonmusician to sit as a model whom he subsequently "dressed" as a percussionist, his documented dependence on sketching from life, the demonstrable presence of African American musicians in Long Island dance contexts, and the precision with which accurate playing technique is rendered, all make it equally likely that this (sadly anonymous) Bone Player was a musician who Mount knew and whose music he admired. The details of instrument and technique confirm *The Bone Player*'s relevance in reconstructing the creole roots of minstrelsy's musical synthesis. Like the banjo itself, the African American percussive bones are a New World recollection and reconstruction of an ancient organological archetype. Though documented around the globe for five millennia, including medieval and (occasionally) Renaissance European sources, and likely imported into the Caribbean and U.S. colonies with Anglo-Celtic settlers, in the antebellum United States the bones were already associated with creole culture and music.[51]

Linked to Mount's depiction of the banjo and fiddles in the earlier portraits is his rendering of the bones in this one: not only is the instrument's specific physical and bodily technique (discussed ahead) accurately portrayed, but equally important is the ornamentation of the bones themselves. A closer look reveals that they have been carved with decorations on their outer surfaces (i.e., opposite to the inner striking surfaces). The symbolism of this decoration is as consistent and as significant as the ivory inlays on the fiddles of *Just in Tune* and *Right and Left* and the painted decorations and dangling ornaments in *The Banjo Player* and *Right and Left*. As in those images, in *The Bone Player*, Mount depicts a musician who is sufficiently proud and confident, and sufficiently commanding in the execution of his trade, that he decorates his professional tools. This is not an amateur or a musical illiterate, not a shuffling or grinning primitive of the sort caricatured by antebellum middle-class representation or by sheet-music illustrators, or as castigated by abolitionist rhetoric. Rather, a more precise analysis of the complex evidence in this painting reveals this sitter as a confident, competent, skillful, commanding, even "heroic" musical sophisticate, the sonic impact of whose instrument, like the droning, percussive, polyrhythmic texture of the banjo, would skew *every* musical situation in which he participated toward the creole synthesis.

The anatomical and kinesthetic expertise in this painting can be recognized through analysis of Mount's observational accuracy, but it is enhanced, and its relevance to musical reconstruction further revealed, through consideration of the physical technique the instrument requires. The bones were traditionally made from polished pieces of cow or sheep rib, which produce high-density, resonant striking surfaces with the requisite backward curve. Precisely as is depicted in the painting, in performance a pair of such dried, carved and polished bones would be held in each hand, with the convex striking surfaces inward, one of the pair between the index and middle fingers, and the other between the ring and fourth fingers. The thumb would be allowed to rest against the penultimate joint of the index finger but does not play a crucial role in the technique. The overall grip is relatively loose, allowing the two bones to pivot between the anchoring pairs of fingers, while relying on the skin's surface oil to prevent slippage. With such a loose and flexible grip, a twisting snap of the wrist, similar to the motion of flicking water from the fingers, permits the pivoting bones to strike against one another.

In performance, the right and left hand, each holding a pair of bones in precisely the loose-but-secure grip Mount depicts, are flicked back and forth, along a variety of axes between the horizontal and vertical, either in tandem or in rhythmic counterpoint to one another. The bones player can simply echo a melody's rhythmic groove, but can also superimpose melo-rhythmic or polyrhythmic commentary, or both, on that basic groove. Mastery of technique and of the accompanied music's rhythmic language permits a complex variety of rhythmic ornaments, up to and including complex tuplets and syncopations. As with so many "folk" percussion instruments of relatively simple physical design from around the world, the bones—like the frame drum, goblet drum, tambourine, and so on—are, through the development of a diverse and virtuosic set of playing techniques, capable of remarkably sophisticated musical results, particularly in an ensemble situation. Moreover, the kinesthetic and choreographic result of the required technique links the bones particularly directly to the African tradition's integration of music and dance, an integration that demonstrates a reluctance to separate these into disjunct idioms. In performance, the bones player's body—not just hands, but wrists, arms, and shoulders, and thus upper body to the pelvis (at the very least)—is directly implicated in the necessary instrumental technique. The act of realizing the music's polyrhythms on the instrument requires that the player's body itself become part of the dance.[52] As with any dance-music instrument, but particularly with the polyrhythmic percussion instruments of the African tradition, performance requires expertise in—indeed, performance is—both playing and dancing.

To play or dance to the bones—like dancing and singing "Jim Crow" along with and in imitation of G. W. Dixon or T. D. Rice, or playing or dancing to the polyrhythmic percussive stroke style of the *Banjo Player*, or to the cross-rhythmed Afro-Caribbean jigs and reels of Mount's fiddling idol Toney Clapp, the "Negro-touched" fiddle of Nelson Mount or the simultaneous fiddle music and square-dance-calling of *Right and Left*—or even simply to imagine the sound of *The Banjo Player* and *The Bone Player*, was itself to participate in the creole synthesis. For Mount's contemporaries and neighbors and admired musical mentors and for Mount himself, and for thousands of other impressionable young working-class whites—whether on the Catherine Wharf or the floor of a rural barn, the pit of the Bowery Theatre or a Liverpool music hall, and whether celebrating fried eels, the successful harvest, or the return from a winter sleigh ride—to play or dance to the music of the creole synthesis was, for the duration of the dance, to become creole oneself.

That is the meaning and the lasting resonance of minstrelsy's creole synthesis, whose semiotic complexity and cultural resilience Cockrell, Lott, and Lhamon have identified. Minstrelsy's transgressive, transformative, opportunistic, shameless, and admiring magpie appropriation and integration of diverse and marginalized styles provided both the inspiration and the mechanism by which a uniquely U.S. popular music practice emerged: that of Lhamon's "First Atlantic Street Culture." Mount's ability to help us recover the sound of that culture—in the fields and barns, as well as the wharves and theaters, in rural and urban, working-class and middle-class, dancing and singing, even approving and disapproving contexts—is the focus of this book, precisely because it helped precipitate the poly-ethnic artistic collaboration that has fueled American popular music ever since. His paintings reveal this; in the next chapter, we discover that Mount's music manuscript collections reveal it, as well.

5 Melody's Polyrhythmic Polysemic Possibilities

The Bodily Evidence of Mount's Music

Body knowledge . . . is not "conceptual" or "verbal," it is not inhibited by contradictions but can recognize many meanings at once—its intelligence is polysemic. . . . It does not need to identify by name and so is a more direct way of knowing the thing in itself.
—Rebecca Sachs Norris, "Embodiment and Community"

OF ANY MUSICAL PARAMETER—texture, instrumentation, tempo, timbre, and other—rhythm is the most essential component to understanding dance music, in any cultural tradition, in any sacred or secular context. More than any other parameter, what defines dance, or a dance, or a dance melody, or a dance performance, is rhythm—the interaction of rhythmic sound and rhythmic motion. That interplay is at the heart of human body knowledge: "Music is the keeper of all the rhythms whose complex manifestations distinguish each personality from every other. . . . The instrument of dance is the human body, remarkable in its expressiveness, but always carrying with it, however implicitly, the undertones of musical rhythm."[1] The fundamental transformation of borrowed tunes (many but not all of Anglo-Celtic origin) into minstrelsy's core repertoire cannot be explained simply as a result of melodic borrowing, variation or recomposition, or of retextualization, or even of reinstrumentation, with the iconic blackface ensemble of banjo, bones, and tambourine joining the fiddle.[2] Despite comparatively little prior analysis of minstrelsy's rhythmic performance practice, it is precisely this parameter, precisely this unique and new creolized approach to rhythm, that accounts for both the transformation of Anglo-Celtic tunes into blackface songs and for the latter idiom's lightning-fast public adoption and enduring musical influence. Through rhythmic transformation, the "Africanization" (or "Afro-Caribbeanization") of Anglo-Celtic tunes, and of dancing to those tunes, created minstrelsy's musical creole and accounts for its participatory appeal—and that Anglo-African creole musical language became the foundation of American popular music.

The end of the eighteenth century saw a transformation in U.S. melodic vocabularies via the infusion of new tune types; the new nineteenth century would bring a parallel transformation of its rhythmic languages. In the Jacksonian period, a dance-tune repertoire that had been dominated since colonization by Anglo-Celtic and other North European imports was deeply and swiftly enriched by diverse sources: European court dance (the quadrille, minuet, and eventually cotillion, mazurka, and waltz) and country dance (especially English morris and Scots highland tunes), and even more by a wealth of dance tunes deriving from the impact of Afro-Caribbean rhythms, steps, body vocabularies, and instrumental techniques. On the North American continent, including Atlantic Canada, and all across the United States and the western territories to the Mississippi, and extending up the western rivers as they were explored, mapped, and populated, this Afro-Caribbean repertoire mixed and mingled with German, Scots, English, Irish, and other tunes on the riverine and maritime frontiers, ensuring that by the early 1800s, U.S. melodic vocabularies had become richer, larger, more diverse, and far more rhythmically polyglot than ever before.

The same creole cosmopolitanism is reflected in the tune collections, consisting of both manuscript and loose printed sheets, owned by William Sidney Mount. It is thus possible to situate Mount's own melodic repertoire within the wider context of the era's dance music. Indeed, the transformation of U.S. tune repertoires can be traced in the evolution of sources between Micah Hawkins's extensive collection—which Mount inherited—and those of his nephew William Sidney. As we have seen in chapter 1, scholarly monographs focusing on the contents of specific tune collections or regional tune repertoires have confirmed the presence of a new synthesis and recombination of tune types, mostly oriented toward the fiddle, in the early nineteenth century.[3] This chapter builds on the implications of these individual studies, to suggest that the black-white exchange of the creole synthesis can be traced in movement vocabularies, just as Goertzen, Jabbour, Wells, and others have traced it in tune vocabularies.

This chapter further suggests that the creole synthesis was as present a factor in dance musicians' tune repertoires as it was in dance rhythms. The data reinforces the argument that the early sources of minstrelsy, and particularly Afro-Caribbean rhythmic practices, represent a transformation of American musical consciousness. The contents of Mount's own musical collection and recollections, as preserved (primarily) in his papers at the Long Island Museum of American Art, History, and Carriages in Setauket, New York, constitute the focal evidence in support of this argument.[4] Mount operated not only as an observer and consumer of social dance music, but also as its provider and documentarian. A major consideration, of course, is the demonstrable accuracy of his visual observation and reportage, but other sources independently confirm his involvement in vernacular music making. Even without the indirect evidence of his paintings, in which black musicians feature prominently and sympathetically, we would know that Mount was an admirer of their music through the direct testimony of his own extensive letters and sketchbooks.

Mount's brother Robert Nelson (1804–1883) was for a time an itinerant dance teacher, and their sibling correspondence is full of descriptions, sketches, and notations of music. From Jasper County Georgia in January 1841, Robert writes to his brother that he has opened a dance school but is experiencing difficulty attracting sufficient students.[5] He offers to send his brother seeds of Georgia's Scupernong grape, alludes to politics and Texas independence, expresses the desire for further dance training in New York City, and implores William, "If you have any thing new in the way of Cotillions, send them to me."[6] Robert offers William other music in return: "While in Hillsboro I heard a short Reel played which I was so well pleased with that I took the notes of it. If you wish to give it the Negro-touch, you must raise the bass string one note. I will endeavor to collect something better if a favorable opportunity should occur, until then you may saw away on" and here Robert's handwritten musical notation is interpolated within the manuscript; see music figure 3.[7]

It is a simple, diatonic, binary tune, of a type and degree of anonymity ubiquitous throughout New England and the South. But the degree to which music of various sorts was part of the brothers' ongoing epistolary conversation, the precision of Robert's transcription, and, in this case, his notes about performance practice, testify to a particular sensitivity to African American music. His reference to "rais[ing] the bass string one note" means to retune to ADAE, a drone-oriented *scordatura* common in Anglo-Celtic (especially

Music Figure 3. "Possum Hunt."

Scots) fiddle music but also borrowed by black fiddlers who played for white dancing. This means that Robert not only acquired the tunes but noted the performance practice of black musicians he encountered—and that such performance practice (the use of a Scots fiddle tuning that Robert describes as giving "the authentic Negro touch") blurred ethnic boundaries.

This chapter addresses Mount the musician. From his Long Island childhood, he had played dance music —with one of his principle musical mentors being the fiddler and ex-slave Toney Clapp.[8] In his adolescence and early manhood, he was an avid attendee and observer of popular music entertainments: a fact attested both by the backstage watercolors among his artworks, by the previously remarked theatrical framing that appears most notably in the various "Barn" paintings (and which echoes that of *Dancing for Eels*), and by the presence in his music collection of loose sheets from the music saloons of the period.

After returning to Setauket in the late 1820s, William Sidney became an in-demand participant in social and dance music making: the collections still retain various billets-doux from admirers inviting his services for balls and cotillions; there are also letters in which he and friends discreetly or desperately seek to enlist one another to "cover" for various musical obligations.[9] At this juncture, the role of another character in Mount's musical world sheds insight: the widely admired but notoriously unreliable Shepard Jones (dates unknown). Jones was a close friend and musical companion, who lent his name to a road in Setauket, played dances and other social events widely throughout central Long Island, and is both captured in portrait as the fiddler in *Dance of the Haymakers* and receives the painting's informal dedication; he also supplied a number of the tunes in Mount's manuscript collection.[10] Jones fiddled for dancing; so did Mount—particularly when Jones, like Nelson Mathewson, was deemed too unreliable to hire.[11] Thus, William Sidney Mount's music collections, and the way they reveal his perspective as a thinking, working dance musician, provide uniquely valuable resources for understanding early minstrelsy's melodic imagination and rhythmic transformation.

MINSTRELSY'S MELODIC RESOURCES

Mount's lifetime—and especially the period of his childhood, adolescence, and young manhood (ca. 1814–30), when he moved from one relative's Long Island farmstead to another, shifted to the Manhattan homes of his uncle and older brother, and finally moved more or less permanently back to the island—is a particularly salient one in the history of American popular music. Chapter 4 has prefaced and framed Mount's period through the musical experience of his uncle, Micah Hawkins (1777–1825). In the federalist era (1789–1801) of Micah's majority, the U.S. dance-tune repertoire was still dominated by the legacies of the prerevolutionary period: English, Scottish, Irish, German, and (occasionally) homegrown tunes that had been fifed, fiddled, whistled and sung by civilians and soldiers on both sides of the independence question. On Long Island, where consciousness of the immediate revolutionary past was still present, the dance tunes and songs of the colonial era—"Yankee Doodle," "Washington's March," and the like—still formed the musical lingua franca. In postrevolutionary Manhattan, a rapid expanse of immigrant (especially Afro-Caribbean) populations was beginning to transform the musical language and the communities of musicians employing it, yet the tunes in Micah Hawkins's collection are still largely Dutch, German, English, and Anglo-American in origin.

This changed rapidly in the first two decades of the new century. The social mobility and boom in transport options that followed the war; the French and Irish Revolutions of the 1790s; the long Haitian revolutionary war of attrition that culminated in Toussaint's 1802 imprisonment and the subsequent colonial diaspora to the United States (especially New Orleans, Charleston, and Savannah, but also Mobile, Natchez, and the Eastern Seaboard); the exploration of new territory and of "national" consciousness that followed the Louisiana Purchase (1803); the increase in the Atlantic, Gulf, coastal, and worldwide shipping trades; and the War of 1812: all these factors accelerated social, cultural, and musical transformation.

Across the new nation, and particularly in riverine and maritime contexts, new cultural resources, experiences, and musical languages met and melded at a fast pace. Whether welcome, in the medium of new middle-class dance crazes such as the quadrille and cotillion, for example; or unwelcome—in the medium of involuntary working-class neighborhood integration driven by economic restrictions—new cultural trends reflected the reality that more and more Americans were living in diversifying, urbanizing, and modernizing contexts. The overlapping music collections of Micah Hawkins (b. 1777) and his nephew William Sidney (b. 1807), because of their owners' particular occupations, interests, and locations, reveal the diversification of the melodic vernacular with great clarity. Though both were surely more curious about and receptive to new and different music than their nonmusician contemporaries might have been, the contrasting content of their respective collections accurately maps the shifting melodic landscape of the early antebellum period:

not only of rural Long Island, but also of the Lower East Side of Manhattan, and beyond, to streets, docks, wharves, and decks across the riverine and maritime United States. These are the contexts, and the tune repertoires, from which originated minstrelsy's melodic language.

But more can be gleaned from the Mount-Hawkins manuscript collection than just lists of tunes. When coupled with analysis of ethnographic contexts, physical techniques, and iconography, the material in these manuscripts can also reveal rhythmic practices. To do this, however, we must understand not only melodic taxonomies, not only the social and semiotic connotations of dance iconography and public spectacle, not only the performance practice and pedagogical traditions of period instrumental music, but, most crucially, the ways these diverse sources illuminate one another, and the breadth, complexity, and chronology of minstrelsy's bodily exchange.

Many aspects of W. S. Mount's biography, chronology, and location are by no means unique: his family background, apprenticeship in the trades as an adolescent, gradual and intentional movement up the economic ladder into the middle class as a young man, and adulthood as a respected professional, were all consistent with the experience of thousands of others in the period, and, as we have seen, with the careers of other vernacular painters, James Henry Beard in particular. In fact, the commonality of Mount's experiences in these areas helps legitimize him as an informed observer, even a participant-observer, in minstrelsy's social-cultural contexts: he lived where and as the prototypical minstrels and their audiences did. However, as we have already seen, minstrelsy's sources were not confined to New York, or the urban North, or even exclusively to either urban or frontier contexts. We can therefore extrapolate from Mount's experience on Long Island and the Lower East Side, as we can from the experiences of Dixon and Rice (in the urban North and on the frontiers) and Emmett and Sweeney (in the South, on the frontiers, and in the urban North). The leisure activities in which Mount engaged, the street performances and shows he saw, and most especially the tunes and songs he played and sang, can be reconstructed from the available evidence, and in turn shown to reflect those of other upwardly mobile young men across the entire eastern United States.

There was melodic as well as cultural exchange between the Eastern Seaboard and the Caribbean, along U.S. rivers and canals, and between the upland South and the frontier and urban North. Extensive overlap between southern and northern (really, "northeastern") tune families has been revealed by Wells, by Goertzen and Jabbour, and by Carlin, and an informal comparison of Mount's tune repertoire with that of Sweeney, for example, confirms the currency, mobility, and ubiquity of certain popular tunes, across geographic and other boundaries.[12]

On the other hand, the more unique aspects of Mount's life—his combination of musical aptitude; acute observation; artistic talent; experience as transcriber and participant; family background and musical inheritance—are significant precisely because they are comparatively unique among music-themed illustrators of the period. Though contemporaries such as Beard and Bingham in their respective geographic locations were well placed to witness the creole synthesis, they were nowhere near as musically literate and are thus less reliable observers of musical practice. Similarly, the period sources that provide observation and reportage on creole music, notably the illustrated newspapers (in the North) and occasional travelers' tales and letters (Benjamin Latrobe in the South, for example) do not originate with practitioners, and are not written from a musically informed standpoint.[13] Mount uniquely combines both a shared experience (as apprentice and young bachelor) and maritime and riverine contexts (on Long Island and the Lower East Side) with tools suiting him for musical reportage.

The fundamental task of this chapter, then, is to reexamine the melodic corpus revealed in the Mount papers and to situate that corpus relative to contemporaneous dance repertoires: principally, the ongoing resources represented by Anglo-Celtic tunes; the newer dance-types of the polka, quadrille, and cotillion; and the already-creolized tunes explicitly associated with blackface minstrelsy and New York comic theatricals. Our hypothesis is that the creole synthesis confirmed in Mount's circumstances, and revealed in this and the next chapter in his artworks, should also be present in his tune collections; evidence for its presence in the archival materials will be powerful confirmation of his value as a source.

However, in order to recover the sound of these tunes, we must understand the rhythmic conventions with which they would have been played and danced, which may or may not be obvious on the page. When we reconstruct the performance practices and the realizations that would have resulted, we discover that most of the tunes in the Mount repertoire were Anglo-American in melodic origin but creolized in performance. This realization transforms our understanding of the rhythmic sound and kinesthetic nature of antebellum vernacular music.

The dance tune types represented in Mount's manuscript and print collection occupy three categories: first, imported Anglo-Celtic tunes (e.g., morris tunes; Playford tunes; various Scots or Irish reels, hornpipes, marches; and their derivations and relations) that had been the standard New England country-dance repertoire since before the revolution, and which repertoire is well-represented in the Hawkins materials, as well; second, relatively "newfangled" and au courant imported dances coming into vogue among both rural and urban middle classes (polkas, quadrilles, cotillions, and the like); and, finally, tunes associated with blackface minstrelsy, a few of which appear not only in print but also in manuscript among the Mount materials. In this third category, several of the most ubiquitous (especially "Possum Up a Gum Tree") were clearly part of Mount's melodic soundscape by his midteens at the latest.

In comparing tunes and tune types from the Mount-Hawkins materials against a wider sampling of contemporaneous tunes across the Continent, we begin to see how closely Mount's melodic repertoire mirrors those in other geographic locations. This confirms the fertile exchange of tunes between the Northeast and the rest of the nation, but that is only a first step, the first layer of insight that examination of the collection reveals. More challenging and rewarding is the reconstruction of the rhythmic idiom through which these tunes would have been realized in performance.

To understand just how fundamentally the creole synthesis made possible new popular music idioms in the colonial Americas, it is necessary to understand the uniqueness of its rhythmic language: not only via melodic taxonomies à la Nathan; not only through the transgressive akimbo of the body's semiotic representation à la Lhamon and Lott; not only in the European festival behaviors of carnivalesque "rough music" recognized by Cockrell. Our task is to frame the analysis through reference to the prior scholarship, while employing the detailed precision with which Rath's and Mahar's microhistorical examinations have revealed the creole synthesis in transcriptions of period dialect, and the theoretical constructs of ethnochoreological kinesthetics. And finally, we must bring to this discussion historical performance's acuity regarding the use of iconographic analysis as a tool for reconstructing performance practice. In short, if we look at Mount's sketches and paintings of dancers, fiddlers, juba-patters, and drummers; reconstruct their performance in light of the creole rhythmic practices implied in those images; and "hear" the tunes in his and his uncle's collections with this reconstruction in mind, we begin to "hear" the Anglo-African creole synthesis as it was heard and danced in the period.

To do this, we must revisit a canonic work—Hans Nathan's 1962 *Dan Emmett and the Rise of Early Negro Minstrelsy*, still the standard reference work on minstrelsy's European tune sources—in order to complicate Nathan's conclusions about the sound of blackface in performance.[14] His book, though published decades earlier than the more recent scholarship of Lott, Cockrell, Lhamon, and Mahar, is still commonly referenced for specific musical details on the blackface tune repertoire.[15] Nathan's comparative taxonomy of tunes, tune families, and relations confirms that, with a few significant exceptions, the original melodic sources for the tunes of blackface songs were in the same Anglo-Celtic traditions as the fiddle repertoires of the federalist period. However, Nathan's presumption that minstrelsy's melodic repertoire "is" essentially Anglo-Celtic obscures the complexity of vernacular musics' rhythmic interplay in the U.S. context and mistakenly equates extant notational evidence with the sound of performance. Robert Winans's brief commentaries have provided a corrective to Nathan's presumptions about the sound of the blackface quartet, but there has been little study of iconographic evidence.[16] Mount (and, to a lesser extent, Bingham and Beard) thus fills a crucial gap, because in his works we can see blacks and whites interacting musically and observe the appropriation of physical vocabularies and performance practices from one group to the other; in turn, we are able to reconstruct aspects of musical sound.

This is why the study of dance iconography in any era (see chapter 6), is an essential element of understanding that era's dance musics and rhythmic languages—particularly when those musics are swiftly evolving. Such reconstruction is doubly important when those synthesizing musics involve a percussive "sounding" element to their dancing, and it is triply important when those percussive dance vocabularies are both proximate and receptive to one another. As we have seen, black cloggers, character actors, and Jim Crow dancers lived and worked in close proximity, in rural and urban contexts, to white hard-shoe dancers, folk dancers, and musicians. Nathan makes it clear that there was exchange of tunes; in addition, there was exchange of body vocabularies.[17] This book focuses precisely on the nexus at which black and white tunes and rhythm, sounds and bodies, met—and on the musical sound that emerged at that nexus.

But a notation-dependent analytical method provides unsatisfactory results in reconstructing the sound, intent, and impact of a dance repertoire, most notably in the area of rhythm and, more generally, in the myriad aspects of performance practice including phrasing, dynamics, articulation, and timbre. Notation is ill-suited to precisely those expressive aspects that make vernacular-tradition musics sound the way they do; not coincidentally, those aspects that would have struck minstrelsy's original audiences as most unique and intriguing, and that were lost in the migration from working-class performance to middle-class sheet music. Nathan himself acknowledges his own difficulty in rendering into notated rhythm "the Negroid complexities of banjo-fiddle music.[18] Transcription omits precisely those "Negroid complexities" (timbre, phrasing, articulation, etc.) cited above, thereby distorting the resulting picture.[19]

And yet, it is possible to "work backward" toward a reconstruction of minstrelsy's sound—to integrate insights based on both musical taxonomy and dance iconography with those dependent on notation. Carlin has shown, essentially by identifying "banjo characteristics" in period methods that employed fiddle notation, that the music's sound was nothing like the "thin etc" timbre described by Nathan.[20] Nathan's dating of minstrelsy's "origins" to the 1840s with the birth of the Virginia Minstrels results in part from his failing to understand when or how widely African American musical characteristics began to shape the American tune repertoire, precisely because those characteristics, namely timbre and rhythm, are not readily captured in his notation-oriented method. Mount's evidence confirms that the nearly instantaneous appeal of theatrical minstrelsy resulted from the recognition onstage of the creole synthesis, of "European melody subjected to African American rhythm," already happening in the street culture.[21]

RECONSTRUCTING CREOLE RHYTHM

Detailed examination of tunes appearing in both the early repertoires of minstrelsy and Mount's manuscripts confirms those collections' shared melodic sources, and it confirms Mount's own exposure to and awareness of those tune repertoires; so much was established by Nathan a half century ago. Reconstruction of the sound of the instruments, by Winans on the banjo most notably, conveys something of the sound of the prototypical blackface ensembles.[22] But reconstruction of the performance practice of the street musics that provided the blackface archetypes—particularly recognition of the impact of Afro-Caribbean dance rhythms on the mixed bag of antebellum American tune repertoires—transforms our understanding of how the music worked—and provides clues regarding its remarkable capacity for participatory, boundary-crossing, danced community.

The balance of this chapter explicates the information afforded by a rhythmic reconsideration of the melodic resources, specifically in those tunes in the Mount collection come from the core blackface repertoire. Viewing Nathan's melodic taxonomies in terms of Mount's collection, and through the lens of African American performance practice, iconography and ethnography reveal, in aspects of both transmission and performance practice, a process of "creolization" that closely parallels a similar process in the dance languages.

Nathan's taxonomy confirms the tangled complexity of these tunes' provenance.[23] Though he cites their frontier locations and (frequently) African American transmission, he most often roots them in "the idiom of the English stage music of the eighteenth century."[24]

But minstrelsy and its source idioms were dance musics that achieved their first, most remarkable popularity long before they were ever transcribed or printed. In the hands of the first generation of theatrical practitioners such as Rice and Dixon, the music and dancing in performance, not through publication or description, elicited popular response. It was likewise in performance that the strongest influence from African American musical practice—movement, polyrhythm, timbral specifics, and collective improvisation—would have been most evident. Such interethnic musical exchange is confirmed in allusions from period sources, including antebellum slave narratives from Appomattox County (Mrs. Fannie Berry), Southampton County (Mrs. Marriah Hines), Suffolk (M. H. Perry), Charlotte County (L. Pollard), Lynchburg (R. Williams); by travelers' reports (the French-born architect Benjamin Latrobe, 1764–1820, provides particularly vivid accounts of music in New Orleans); and, as we have seen, by a host of demographic, mercantile, geographic, and iconographic evidence.[25] A few scholars have addressed this exchange in parallel studies—especially notably, in Abrahams's magisterial analysis of the southern plantation cornhusking ritual—but the scope and distribution of the creole synthesis has been largely absent from musicological studies of minstrelsy.[26]

The next chapter explores in greater detail the rhythmic information that can be derived through iconography, but for the melodic analysis here, it is worth citing Lydia Parrish's early, naive—but important—fieldwork collection *Slave Songs of the Georgia Sea Islands*.[27] Parrish (1871–1953), the wife of artist Maxfield Parrish, went to the Georgia Sea Islands first in 1909 and spent many years living on St. Simons. Her work began in the early '20s, decades before her book's 1942 publication, and is especially valuable because her informants, many quite elderly, were a comparatively direct conduit to pre–Civil War practices, while the Sea Islands location makes the connection to the African Caribbean likewise immediate.[28] Especially valuable are the book's musical transcriptions, by Creighton Churchill and Robert MacGimsey, which render not only melodies but also the rhythmic and percussive accompaniments to which the songs were sung. In several cases, the songs themselves previously appear in the minstrelsy repertoire—and in a few tantalizing instances, Parrish provides photographs of dances (to "The Buzzard Lope" and "Juba Dis, Juba Dat") that went with those blackface-associated songs.[29]

Of course, we must be cautious about presuming that 1920s–30s photographs can be read as a direct reflection of creole performance practice a hundred years earlier.[30] However, we can infer an ongoing tradition, into the twentieth century seemingly unbroken since the eighteenth, of a particularly strongly "African" version of the creole synthesis in those islands, as elsewhere in the Caribbean.[31] Aspects of rhythmic dance that Parrish's data provide from the 1920s may legitimately be argued to shed light on creolizing musical practices in the century before, even as far back as the antebellum period. The Churchill and MacGimsey transcriptions show rhythmic accompaniments that strongly suggest Afro-Caribbean percussion patterns. If "juba" accompanied rowing songs in the Sea Islands in the 1920s, and "dancing for eels" on the Catherine Wharf in the 1820s, then it is reasonable to infer similar distribution and lasting rhythmic impact on Anglo-Celtic dance tunes elsewhere.

Churchill's transcription of the Sea Islands rowing song "Knee-Bone" provides an example of the polyrhythmic complexity that these accompaniments could create around the simplest monophonic melodies; see music figure 4.[32]

This simple, symmetrical, call-and-response melody, whose solo line covers the range of only a fifth, is typical of hundreds of work songs, both maritime and landlocked, in the Afro-Caribbean and African American traditions; similar songs have been widely reproduced by collectors at least since 1867's *Slave Songs of the United States* (an inspiration for Parrish's collection), and recur in the large body of Afro-Caribbean sea shanties.[33] However, Churchill's approach is the exception in one important particular: transcriptions of slave-era melodies—like Nathan's collection of blackface tunes—almost always omitted the information most central to the creole genres' Africanization: the use of polyrhythmic "cutting" and percussive accompaniment; the "interactional rhythms" that link sound and movement.[34] The following represents a sampling of the blackface-associated tunes found in Mount's manuscripts, and an analysis of the insights provided when they are rendered with an Afro-Caribbean rhythmic sensibility derived from sourced like Parrish.[35]

The presence of the creole synthesis in Afro-Caribbean and Anglo-Celtic dance musics, and the continuity between southern and northern practices, is confirmed by both indirect and parallel evidence. For our purposes, it is not so important to determine whether "Juba," for example, "originated" in the Georgia Sea Islands or in the minstrelsy repertoires: the larger and more significant point is the demonstrable ongoing exchange between repertoires throughout the antebellum period and, indeed, down to the early twentieth century. Likewise, as Evans has pointed out, it is likely that "Jump Jim Crow," the iconic minstrel song and dance popularized by T. D. Rice, also derives

Music Figure 4. Transcription of "Knee Bone." Transcription after Parrish, Lydia Parrish, comp., *Slave Songs of the Georgia Sea Islands* (Athens: University of Georgia, 1992), 81.

from an Afro-Caribbean dance: "John Crow" is a common Jamaican patois name for both the turkey buzzard and for a mimetic dance, as for that matter is the Buzzard Lope—the latter also found in Parrish's collection.[36]

An essay in rhythmic reconstruction applied to Mount's version of the minstrel tune "Old Molly Hare" provides evidence of the surprising transformations that Afro-Caribbean rhythmic sensibilities wrought upon Anglo-Celtic dance tunes in performance. Kuntz suggests that the tune derives directly from a composition by Scots fiddler Nathanial Gow (1763–1831), composed for the Fife Hunt Ball in 1802 (though, as so often with dance tunes, it is possibly based in turn on older, unknown tunes).[37] It recurs as "The Fisher Laddie" in northern England, where it was later collected as a sword dance tune by Cecil Sharp

Music Figure 4. *Continued*

(1859–1921), and also appears as "Old Molly Hare" in blackface, Civil War, and southern black repertoires. As a song, the title and text seem to be indigenous to the United States; in fact, the relatively swift transformation of the earlier tune illustrates the speedy dispersal and popular ubiquity that prototypical minstrel tunes enjoyed as they were carried along the waterways by players, singers, and dancers. Like the tune itself (music figure 5), the simplicity of the text supports a percussive, syllabic, declamatory—and participatory—singing style:

> Old Molly Hare, what you doin' there,
> Running down the road as hard as I can tear.
> Old Molly Hare, what you doin' there?
> Running through the briarpatch as hard as I can tear.[38]

In the version notated by Mount (music fig. 5), it is a simple, four-square binary melody, not dissimilar to the "Possum Hunt" that Robert Nelson Mount had sent to his brother from Georgia. But the tune's scansion, contour, and dance character are fundamentally transformed by our hypothesized addition of

Music Figure 5. "Old Molly Hare" with polyrhythmic accents added. Transcription after W. S. Mount, Sheet Music Box 1, KSA032110, Hawkins-Mount Family Papers, Long Island Museum of American Art, History, and Carriages.

Afro-Caribbean polyrhythmic accent: this cross-accent is a common strategy among Anglo-Celtic dance players as well as African American ones.

The polyrhythmic cutting supplied by adding the relatively simple and ubiquitous backbeat emphasis fundamentally alters how we hear, and how period dancers would have experienced, "Old Molly Hare." With the addition of this cutting, it is the *rising* foot—at the moment of the "bending knee-bone"—that experiences the cross-accents on the "and" of the second beat and the "and" of the fourth.[39] Such cross-accents are equally ubiquitous in Anglo-Celtic and African American dance-tune practice: the feet hit the floor on the downbeats, the accent "lifts" the feet on the "ands" of the upbeat, and the bodily experience is one of rising, upward, expansive, rebounding motion.

Moreover, the melody, as rerhythmicized in Mount's instrumental version, even leaves space within the bar: the displacement of the sixteenth-note anticipation allows an interlocking percussive accent on the "and" of beat 2—an elegant demonstration of Keil's "participatory discrepancies."[40] Such rhythmicization yields a kinesic response; the rhythmic cutting elicits, in the dancer, a polyrhythmic bodily experience that is visible in period iconography.[41] With this in mind, we can see polyrhythmic cutting in the bodies of T. D. Rice and G. W. Dixon in minstrel prints; in Mount's "Haymakers" and militia dancers, in Bingham's "Jolly Flatboatmen" and Beard's *Western Raftsmen*. We have read about such polyrhythmic movement in descriptions both comic—Irving speaking of Ichabod Crane's outlandish Albany capers—and virtuously outraged—the various travelers' descriptions of slave dance.[42]

We can therefore reimagine the polyrhythmic experience in the bodies of dancers rushing the stage of the Bowery Theatre in 1828, clapping along to the juba-patters on the Catherine Wharf in 1820, and dancing in the pit to "Possum Up a Gum Stump" at the finale of Hawkins's 1824 *The Saw-Mill*: an experience of full-body engagement, of polyrhythmic motion to infectious sound, of communion with others likewise moving in responsive improvisational freedom. Finally, we can discover the creole experience, below the Anglo-Celtic surface, and settling in the African American tilted pelvis, twisted spine, and "knee-bone bent" of Mount's *Dance of the Haymakers* (1845)—and of thousands of other Caucasian dancers in whose bodies the physical transformations of the creole synthesis took root and spread.

Analogous rhythmicizations of other iconic minstrel tunes contained in the Mount manuscripts, especially those sourced in Anglo-Celtic repertoires, yield a similarly rhythmically complex and engaging Afro-Celtic synthesis. For example, an anonymous "Scottish Country Dance Tune," printed in Howe's *Complete Preceptor for the Accordion* (1843) and identified by Nathan as a source for Dixon's signature "Coal Black Rose" (music fig. 6), yields an infectious polyrhythmic interplay between tune, text, and accents.[43]

In the A strain, the percussive accent on "Lub-ly Ro-sa Sam-bo . . . hear de ban-jo tum, tum, tum" is countered by the expansive longer-note values on the B strain's opening syllables "Oh, Rose," and in turn by the staccato "wish I may be cortch'd" ["catched"]. Both lines of text display a wonderful "in-the-pocket" interaction of space on accented words ("Oh," "Rose," and "Coal," for example) and percussive accents to propel sixteenth-note anticipations ("de," "if I," etc) that move the rhythmic line forward. As with "Old Molly Hare," the text of "Coal Black Rose" is arranged as simple call-and-response, while the melody is symmetrical, of narrow compass, and mostly employs stepwise motion: all these characteristics maximized its accessibility and appeal in the participatory, communal environments of the 1820s blackface solo shows. And, as with "Jump Jim Crow," or the later "Old Dan Tucker," the simplicity, symmetry, and repetitive nature of the melody all facilitate the creation of new and unique contrafact texts, precomposed or perhaps even spontaneously improvised, to the same tune.[44]

Music Figure 6. "Coal Black Rose" with polyrhythmic accents added. Transcription after Nathan, *Dan Emmett and the Rise of Early Negro Minstrelsy*, 160.

Another particularly immediate example of the process of rhythmicization that led to the Afro-Celtic creole synthesis is "Sich a Gittin Up Stairs," which borrows particularly literally from the morris dance tune "Getting Upstairs." The melody has been related to the tune "Indian Et a Woodchuck" under which title it appears in Knauff, and collected in both white and black repertoires.[45] It is cited in the repertoires of both T. D. Rice and P. T. Barnum, in the latter's early blackface days, and has also been associated by Nathan with "Mr Bob Farrell, the Original Zip Coon" (it also betrays a close relation to the Anglo-American children's song "This Old Man").[46] Once again, a treatment that takes into account Afro-Caribbean polyrhythmicization yields a rich palette of cross-accents, cutting, and melodic-rhythmic interaction; see music figure 7.

In the case of the minstrel song "Clare de Kitchen," Kuntz identifies a relative in the ubiquitous eighteenth-century "High Road to Edinburgh" melody, in turn related to "The Star of the County Down," which was borrowed and distributed widely both in Britain, Ireland, and the United States. He quotes Paul Tyler's particularly interesting, very early frontier account of the tune's usages and companion pieces, in the context of the cornhuskings

Music Figure 7. Melodic comparison of "Sich a Gittin' Up Stars" to "Getting Upstairs" (Sharp) and "Getting Upstairs" (Virginia). Transcription after Nathan, *Dan Emmett and the Rise of Early Negro Minstrelsy*, 169.

that Abrahams has identified as a key site for black-white musical exchange (see *Singing the Master*); see music figure 8.

> One Joseph Hayes, born in 1786 in Pennsylvania, who moved from that state down the same Ohio river to settle in Lawrenceburg, Indiana. Late in his life he dictated memories of fronteir life from c. 1810, including an account of dancing after cornhuskings. Hayes writes that at these events "in one corner would be seated the fiddler delving away with fingers, elbow, cat-gut and horse-hair, to the joy of all around. The pieces mostly called for were 'The gray cat kittened in Charley's wig,' 'Captain Johnston,' 'Buncomb,' and the whole ending in a jigg called 'Clear the Kitchen.'"

Kuntz adds, "The minstrel dialect 'Clare de Kitchen' appears in Howe's Musician's Companion, Part 2, published in 1843."

The Hayes account is particularly interesting because it shares some attributes with Mount's: it is place-specific; it is contemporaneous with the

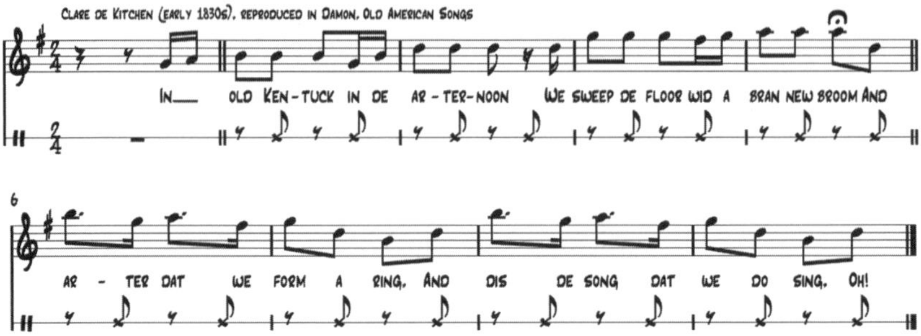

Music Figure 8. “Clare de Kitchen” with polyrhythmic accents. Transcription after Nathan, *Dan Emmett and the Rise of Early Negro Minstrelsy*, 164.

roots of the creole synthesis (Hayes would have been a rough contemporary of Mount’s musical uncle Micah Hawkins); it identifies specific tunes by specific titles; and it relates these to the experience of an individual born in an existing northeastern colony who moved downriver (the Ohio) to the frontiers, and there encountered precisely the mélange of Scots, Irish, and creole tunes that we find in the Hawkins and Mount manuscripts and the early blackface repertoires.

Of course, Anglo-Celtic song tunes and dance melodies were not the sole source for minstrel music, though their ubiquity as part of the (white or black) dance fiddler’s trade, from the seventeenth century, certainly made them a primary resource. Parallel contributions came from other lingua francas on the riverine and maritime frontiers, particularly Anglo-Celtic and Afro-Caribbean work songs (shanties, preeminently), and tunes that were, seemingly, more purely African. Examples of the former include “Bow Wow Wow,” a fragment of which is published in Aird’s *Selections of Scotch, English, Irish and Foreign Airs*, is employed for a number of late-eighteenth-century London music-hall songs, and is also associated with a range of Irish- and English-language texts.[47] It was collected in Northumberland in the nineteenth century (see Robson’s list ca. 1800) and continued in usage into the twentieth century as a sea-shanty, but it appears in early minstrelsy as the iconic “Gumbo Chaff”; see music figure 9.

“Jim Along Josey,” on the other hand, was premiered around 1838 by Ned Harper as part of his “The Free Nigger of New York”; in that (comparatively later) theatrical context, the song was clearly intended, not as delineation of a southern plantation slave, but of a northern freeman à la Zip Coon.[48] Carlin, however, suggests the possibility of a much earlier Cincinnati provenance, once again evoking the migration and exchange of tunes from the riverine

Music Figure 9. Melodic comparison of "Gumbo Chaff" to "Bow Wow Wow" (Sharp), with polyrhythmic accents added. Transcription after Nathan, *Dan Emmett and the Rise of Early Negro Minstrelsy*, 173.

and maritime frontiers.[49] When rendered with the implicit Afro-Caribbean accent, "Jim Along Josey" reveals the same characteristics of Parrish's Sea Island songs: an interplay between text and rhythm, the presence of "empty" beats in the melody that are "filled" by the percussive interlock of the rhythm, eighth-note anticipations to the downbeat that are in turn "sprung" by the backbeat 4, and so on; see music figure 10.[50]

Of the seemingly more African-inspired tunes in the minstrelsy corpus, several of them duplicated in Mount's collection, exemplary is the triple-meter "Pompey Ran Away" (Pompey, like Caesar and Brutus, was a classically inspired name commonly assigned to male slaves), which appears, like "Bow Wow Wow," as a bit of "foreign" exotica, in Aird's *Selection of Scotch, English, Irish and Foreign Airs*. However, despite that early European publication and the classical reference in the title, the melody suggests an Afro-Caribbean provenance: African traits include the use of short, repetitive cellular motives, the descending-then-rising shape to the phrases, and the triple meter, which is relatively uncommon in the early blackface repertoire compared to the commoner duples. Keeping in mind the early date and English locale of this published version, rhythmicization of "Pompey" yields particularly interesting results, as an Afro-Caribbean rhythmic treatment creates particularly complex participatory discrepancies. Typically, in African music situations in which simultaneous 6/8 and 3/4 time signatures are implied, the second

Music Figure 10. "Jim Along Josey" with polyrhythmic accents added. Transcription after Nathan, *Dan Emmett and the Rise of Early Negro Minstrelsy*, 177.

quarter note of the 3/4 is heard as a kind of accented anticipation, "kicking" the rhythm forward in the same way that the fourth-beat accent does in the commoner 2/4 and 3/4; see music figure 11.

Mount's music collection also contains handwritten transcriptions—or, more frequently, loose printed sheets—that reflect the later commercialized output of blackface minstrelsy: "Old Dan Tucker," the "Pea-Patch Jig," "Ole Tare River," and so on; evidently his interest in urban pop music did not cease with his move to Long Island in the early 1830s. But more telling is the simultaneous appearance, on the same manuscript page, of hand-copied tunes

Music Figure 11. "Pompey Ran Away" with polyrhythmic accents added. Transcription after Nathan, *Dan Emmett and the Rise of Early Negro Minstrelsy*, 187.

from the morris, Scots, Vauxhall, and Afro-Caribbean traditions. They are in Mount's writing; ergo, they were part of his internalized musical imagination.

In addition to the chronological diversity the prints' presence reveals in the collection, these later items also reveal Mount's continuing interest in blackface minstrelsy, well after his return to Setauket from Manhattan and his ascension to status as a respectable middle-class painter. Though he is conventionally understood to have been a "homebody" (and a bit of a hypochondriac) in middle age, seldom stirring far from the family environs in Smithtown and Setauket with the exception of comfortable expeditions by train into the city on professional business, his possession of these items suggests that he continued to frequent minstrelsy's urban performance venues into the 1850s.

The music collection contains manuscript notations of blackface-associated tunes, including these few examples:[51]

1. "Mississippi Sawyer" no. 2D; "Mississippi Sawyer" No. 1A; "Ki-i-I Jig" D; "Negro Jig" G.
2. "Keemo Kimo," inscribed "written by Philo Pfeiffer" "as played by Wm. S. Mount Oct 15th 1855" D (also includes version in B♭).

3. "Old Dan Tucker," inscribed "Dec 29th 1843."
4. On the same page as "Old Molly Hare, what are you doing there?": "Indian Whoop" (inscribed "From the brothers Pfeiffer" "As sung & played, by some of the musical Southern Negroes"), "From Mr H Pfeiffers Collection of Music—Jan 1st 1859."[52]
5. "Arkansas Traveller," inscribed "As Played by H.J. Cook" "Stony Brook August 22 52."
6. "Old Sussanna don't you cry for me," inscribed "From Mr. Titus—in the spring of 1848" "108 Madison St."

In addition to these manuscript tunes, the collection also contains loose printed sheets for songs sung in New York theaters or music saloons, or printed by New York publishers. These single sheets, probably from *Howe's Collection* (edition unknown), include a single printed sheet number containing "Miss Lucy Long. Such a Getting Up Stairs. Old Zip Coon. Old Dan Tucker. Jim Along Josy" (p. 43) and "Independent Sett" (p. 44, including Mount's own penciled-in sixteenth-note rhythmic subdivisions for violin).[53] Other related materials include a four-by-five-inch printed sheet of "De Banks of de Ohio," imprinted "Flute or Violin. Birch. Baack 81 Fulton. St." (probably a giveaway from a concert saloon, attested by the inclusion of underscored words for the refrain alone, not the verse), and with a similar inscription, "Julie is de Hansum Gal." "Flute or Violin. Birch. Baack 81 Fulton St.," and "Mary Lee." "Flute or violin. Birch Baack 81 Fulton St."[54]

Fewer in number but also present in the collection are folios of the sort published for home consumption by the expanding music printing business; a late and archetypal example is "I Wish I Was in Dixie's Land" "Written and composed expressly for Bryant's Minstrels by Dan. D. Emmett. Arranged for the Pianoforte by W. L. Hobbs." "New-York: Published by Firth, Pond & Co., No. 547 Broadway," and dated 1860.[55]

Beyond this, the Mount collection includes a range of other genres, particularly those associated with the parlor. The presence of these more middle-class genres provides useful parallel evidence, because it means that Mount had interest in a class-disparate body of repertoires—and probably occasion to employ them in the Long Island setting. He was much sought-after as a dinner companion and cotillion guest—the papers in both the Long Island Museum of American Art, History, and Carriages and the New-York Historical Society contain many examples of his carefully preserved invitations, tickets, and dance cards—but also as a practical provider of music within his middle-class community.[56] A particularly charming, though undated, example of his community music activities, in Mount's own handwriting, is obviously notes for a musical "at-home" evening. The notes' light-hearted tone, and his gallant acknowledgment of the after-concert ice cream to be "performed" by "the ladies of Smithtown and Setauket," help to explain Mount's welcome as a social and musical companion:

> Part I.
> 1. March from Norma. by. The Band.
> 2. ~~Song~~ Solo for the Flute. Mr. S.A. Mount.
> 3. Song (Italien). Mrs. Smith ~~Mrs. Wells~~
> 4. Solo for the Piano. Mrs. Wells
> 5. Mobile Serenade Polka. The Band
> 6. Song. a Lady
> 7. Pas Styrienne. Mr. H. Liebner
> 8. Song. [xx] C. Mount.
> 8. Solo for the Violin. Mr. Henry J. Mount.
> 9. Song. Mrs. Mortimer
> 10. Mobile Serenading Polka. the Band
>
> Part II . . .
> 1. Warrior's Joy (or Monte Christo) March. by. the Band.
> 2. Solo for Violin. I.L. Pfeiffer.
> 3. Song. a lady.
> 4. Solo for Violoncello. F. A. Pfeiffer
> 5. ~~Aria~~ Song. Mr. M Kearney
> 6. Solo for Flute. Mr. Mortimer.. ~~[xxx]~~ a Song. a Lady
> 7. *Pleasures of Matrimony*—Galopp. Messieurs Pfeiffer & &
> 8. Chorus. by all the Performers. .
> 9. Solo Medley. . Mr. W.S. Mount.
> 10. Hail Columbia. the Band.
> 11. Railroad gallop. the Band.
> 12. *Ice Cream*—performed by the ladys of Smithtown & Setauket, &, &[57]

Though the above repertoire, in both tone and content, clearly skews toward the gentility of the middle-class parlor, the wider diversity of Mount's full collection confirms the range of his musical interests. The tunes in his own repertoire, if not identical to those of the black musicians who played a creole repertoire for both black and white dancers, certainly exhibit analogous diversity of sources, especially in the case of the notations transcribed in his own hand. Moreover, as a working fiddle player, a collaborator and comusician with his dance-master brother, his black fiddle teacher Toney Clapp, and his feckless but admired musical associate Shep Jones, Mount's own playing on the flute and fiddle must have likewise reflected the creole polyrhythmic sensibility identified in the musical examples he transcribed and the musicians and dancers he painted. It was precisely in such performance—that could not be transcribed but may be reconstructed—that Afro-Caribbean's "cutting" and cross-accents would have most extensively, and revolutionarily, impacted the Anglo-Celtic sense of polyrhythm and bodily experience.

This is the musicological explanation for theatrical minstrelsy's seemingly instantaneous popularity. Semiotically, the idiom was a transgressive and rebellious acting-out, on the theatrical stage, of those conflicts and renegotiations of class and race that swirled through the streets and wharves of an urbanizing United States.[58] But blackface was also a communal, improvisatory experience, an engrossment of the senses, in which the call to kinesthetic active participation created a transformative popular entertainment. This creolizing musical process—the Afro-Caribbean polyrhythmicization of predominantly Anglo-Celtic melody—yielded accents and anticipations that created the dance rhythms, the "lifting foot" and "knee-bone bent," the kinesic experiences that minstrelsy audiences—themselves thereby sucked into participatory dancing—found so engrossing. As the dance anthropologist Jane Cowan says: "To be a participant in the dance is to be in (and with) the group; it is also to be in the thick of the meanings created."[59] Afro-Caribbean rhythm made the creole synthesis possible, and dancing to the rhythmic music of the creole synthesis made possible the transformation of Americans' bodily experience.

6 Akimbo Culture
Dance and the Participatory Pleasures of the Body

The . . . affective axis of the [African American dance] apparatus involves its celebration of the body as the site of pleasure—in its transformation of identity into style, in the centrality of rhythm and dance, and in its courting of sexuality and sexual practices. The musical practice itself is inserted into the apparatus at the site of the body: it is a music of bodily desire. There is an immediate material relation to the music and its movements. . . . The body becomes the site at which pleasure is restructured and desire potentially redirected.
—Lawrence Grossberg, "Another Boring Day in Paradise"

THIS CHAPTER EXPLORES THE MUSICAL information that can be derived from visual depictions of blackface dance (particularly those by Mount himself), and works backward from that evidence to further reconstruct performance practice and the impact of performance practice on minstrelsy's sound and experience. Historically, this chapter links theatrical blackface with the street performance idioms that were its predecessors, by locating prototypical blackface dance vocabularies and rhythmic practices in vernacular art works of the earlier nineteenth century. I argue that it was precisely the interplay of music and motion—rhythm and dance—between performers and audience, that accounts for minstrelsy's remarkably immediate yet enduring popularity and influence. The sight of dancing evokes a physical response in the viewer, whether that viewer is "passive" observer or active participant; in dance, the body provides the vehicle for participatory, interpersonal connection via the sharing of "liminal" (boundary) experiences. Smyth says "Something happens as normal perceptual information comes in which relates it to the movement system of the observer. . . . The perceptual input links to the motor command system, which becomes active and somehow gives rise to sensations which actually are from the observer's body."[1]

Music and dance, especially in tandem and especially in groups, have the capacity to create *communitas*, a cognitive phenomenon that cultural anthropologist Victor Turner describes as "a strong, total communal experience of oneness in which an individual senses . . . a merging of awareness. . . . In group performance, where members are competent, the concept of *communitas* can overtake the group and, in these circumstances, an orchestra [or other ensemble of performers] may seem to be a living organism . . . this is a sensation which every group performer knows . . . In such a moment, each performer can become acutely aware of everything happening around him/her, while s/he automatically performs her/his part."[2]

Communitas has been identified by Allen, for example, in gospel quartet performance; she calls communitas "a moment of spiritual communication," and says that "analogous parallels can be found in many other African American popular music idioms."[3] This interconnection, a physiological and cognitive link between observers and participants, was the source of blackface's remarkable popularity and longevity. The music-and-dance of the creole synthesis, both on the boards of the blackface stages where it became famous and on the streets and wharves from which it originated, became the first American popular music craze precisely because it was capable of creating participatory communitas: because, like the Afro-Caribbean dance musics that were among its most vital sources, it made possible a body-driven, syncopated experience of shared spiritual communion. This chapter demonstrates the presence, and thus the influence, of Afro-Caribbean bodily vocabularies in visual depictions of African American and blackface dance, and thereby shows the "creolization" of North American bodily vocabularies.[4]

This hypothesis is not without surface challenges: the attempt to reconstruct a sounding rhythmic and musical language from the "silent," static, two-dimensional medium of painting and drawing may seem perverse or impossible. However, both pragmatism and philosophy necessitate the undertaking: pragmatically, because any attempt to recover details of historical dance music benefits from study of iconography and period descriptions of performance practice, along with study of intent, reception, and related dance traditions. In any dance music, the relationship between rhythm and the body is essential: a musicological investigation of dance music that neglects the body, or the iconography of the body, therefore omits relevant rhythmic information. However, philosophically, to ignore participants' own linkage between music and movement would be to fundamentally disregard those participants' own agency and intent.

Minstrelsy's movement languages were perceived as transgressive.[5] Both its presence in public spaces and its specific physical vocabulary embodied resistance: resistance to middle-class control, to bourgeois strictures regarding "graceful" motion, even to definitions of "music" versus "noise." While Lott and Lhamon have demonstrated to us the transgressive semiotic implications of archetypal Jim Crow iconography's bent knee and twisted spine, our analysis of minstrelsy's visual body language need not end with sociological analysis. As Mahar and Raff did with renderings of creole language, we can here read those images as a more literal representation of how minstrelsy's bodies moved, and of what frozen motion might tell us about musical sound.[6]

The fact is that, in addition to the symbolic transgression of bourgeois grace implicit in Jim Crow's akimbo representation, the images' anatomical distortions also capture movement, not stasis: the archetypal Jim Crow posture of "heel and toe" represents the dancer's body as it wheels and turns through space. We can reanimate such an image by melding iconographic analysis of the body's orthopedic and muscular mechanisms with performance analysis of reconstructed musical sound. For example, the "bent knee" of the iconography (and of period song texts) is not likely a crouch, but rather the springy action of absorbing the aftermath of a leap—of "jumping" Jim Crow. A jump requires not only an ascent but also a descent, not only a leaving-of-the-earth but also a resilient return to that earth. Such springing-and-absorbing in turn carries rhythmic implications: we can ask ourselves where, within minstrelsy's duple melodies, the body might rise and fall in the dance, and how that rise-and-fall might accent, and reflect the accents of, the accompanying music. We can visualize a springy, expanding-and-contracting, rising-and-falling motion of the body, falling on beats one and three, rising on two and four, a bending and straightening of the spine, and an overall impression of polyrhythmic verticality—of "jumping," in short.[7]

Yet at the same time: this up-and-down, head-bobbing, vertical-axis orientation differs from both West African dance, which supplies Jim Crow's bent spine, waving arms, and akimbo legs, but in contrast to blackface maintains a "cool" head; and also from Anglo-Celtic dance, which counters with a vertically aligned trunk and spine but supplies the percussive feet. "Jump Jim Crow," as iconography, as sound, and as reconstructed motion, is thus neither simply Afro-Caribbean nor Anglo-Celtic, but uniquely African American. The "dancing for eels" combination of a mimetic Afro-Caribbean "bobbing" akimbo motion with the Anglo-Celtic tradition's clattering feet is direct evidence of a synthesis: indebted to both its immigrant parents, but at the same time an authentically "new thing."

At the same time, recognizing that blackface iconography reveals information about participants' bodily experience of the music has philosophical implications, because it reassigns agency to the dancers and to the artists who depicted them. If our analysis can reconstruct participants' kinesic experience, we begin to recover the emotional and psychological rewards of the communitas they experienced. This is important because it helps us grapple particularly directly with the difficult issue of blackface racism. Racist caricature played a central, even defining role in shaping blackface performance. But to presume that all blackface iconography is caricature and no more—that it has nothing to tell us about black and white participants' own experience and the emotional and psychological rewards of that experience—would be to rob those participants of consciousness, identity, and agency.

People make choices. More specifically: in the expressive experience of music and dance, participants make choices that yield pleasurable bodily sensations. If we accept that blackface iconography provides insight into participants' musical and physical experience, we have begun to recover those participants' conscious, creative, intentional choices. Seeing Mount's, Beard's, Clonney's, and Bingham's figures as choosing to participate in the dancing's psychological and emotional communitas permits them agency. They become, not passive symbols of racist buffoonery or postmodern exploitation, but individual humans, making intentional expressive, creative, and pleasurable choices. Reading against blackface's racist surface narrative in this fashion opens the possibility of ascribing more complex motives to the painters as well: it allows us to imagine that the works of Bingham, Beard, and preeminently William Sidney Mount contain and depict not only racism, but also reportage; not only caricature, but also precise observation. We begin to recover—even to see for the first time—something of the excitement, engagement, innovation, and sense of participation its first audiences found in the new idiom.

Finally, recovering the visual, kinesthetic (and hence rhythmic) vocabularies of blackface movement helps us recognize those vocabularies' most relevant musicological import: the fact that dance, the watching of dance performance, and even the iconography of dance, elicit a physical as well as psychological response.[8] Hanna calls this response "kinesthetic empathy,"

Allen "intense human interrelatedness," and Hast "peak moments," but all are describing a psychological and physical experience when the dancer and the viewer are communicatively joined. Jordan-Smith provides a particularly detailed and comprehensive explanation of the phenomenon, which he calls cathexis:

> The overall result of the tension/release dynamic is *cathexis*, a raising of energy that occurs not only physically, but emotionally and mentally. The demand that raises physical energy need not be aerobic, but it is often "merely" a matter of coordination and timing. The mental demand occurs in the need to remember the sequence of figures. The demand that raises emotional energy has much to do with feelings of self-enjoyment, the spirit of play, and the satisfaction of belonging to a community. It has been speculated that the cathectic contour of a dance event involves the production of endorphins, chemical messages resulting in "the dancer's high," an experience of self that leaves dancers in a state of euphoria.[9]

In blackface performance, and even in the iconography of such performance, the dancer leaps, and the viewer responds: the muscles twitch; the pelvis tips, the spine twists, the "knee-bone" bends—and the viewer, either in the pit of the Bowery Theatre or across centuries of iconographic distance, experiences the physical "cutting" of the rhythm that was the most profound and long-lasting musical bequest by the creole synthesis to the New World.[10]

RESOURCES FOR RECOVERING THE KINESICS OF MINSTRELSY

Mount may be the best or most copious source for my analysis, yet—as I hope previous chapters have made clear—he is by no means an isolated one. This chapter works backward from the information contained within the static, two-dimensional medium of artworks (both preliminary sketches and final oils) by Mount and one or two contemporaries, to reconstruct from that iconographic data a model of early minstrelsy's movement languages, and to discover within those movement languages the cross-cultural Afro-Anglo-Celtic synthesis we have elsewhere located in minstrelsy's contexts, material culture, and tune repertoires.

Of course, dancing had been an essential and popular element of New World Anglo-Celtic leisure ever since the Age of Exploration: even the Puritans, emblematic of conservative distrust of the body, believed dance to be acceptable in a surprisingly wide range of contexts.[11] In the new republic, local musicians and itinerant dancing masters frequented the river landings, waterfront dance halls, and highway taverns that were the eventual incubators of the creole synthesis.[12] However, certain elements enter Anglo-American choreology specifically through the medium of contact with African American and (specifically) Afro-Caribbean dance, and transformed working- and middle-class movement vocabularies in the years after 1800.[13]

Stephen Johnson has suggested that contradictory statements about minstrel dance, far from confusing the issue, can actually enrich and usefully complicate our understanding of its sources.[14] He makes the point that Master Juba's "exhibition" of "the dances of his own simple people" was probably not an arbitrary or indiscriminate mishmash of styles but rather a relatively accurate replication of specific dances, including "the highland fling, sword dance, Lancashire clog, hornpipe, minuet, polka, as well as whirling dervishes, and the 'willies.'"[15] This diversity both parallels that of the late-colonial theatrical stage—and thus is in keeping with the descriptions of the African Grove, of Charles Mathews's character dances, and of the range expected of theatrical "buffo" performers such as the young Rice and Dixon—and as in those other cases represents the pragmatic response of a canny professional entertainer to diverse audience tastes. Not so widely examined, however, is the realization that command of diverse idioms would also have led to the option of stylistic mixing. It is obvious, based on the descriptions alone, that Juba was capable not only of dancing each style—but also of combining style. This is the creole synthesis at work. Prose and visual representations of Juba in performance evoke blackface iconography's bending and twisting but also reach back to Afro-Caribbean aesthetics of balancing a "cool" (smooth, erect, steady, stationary) upper torso and head versus "hot" (bending, flexing, twisting, quick-moving) pelvis and limbs. Robert Farris Thompson's work, when applied to this evidence, locates a series of African-rooted dance characteristics, including a percussive character (e.g., hard soles on a resonant surface), the polyrhythmic "simultaneous execution of several time signatures," the use of the body as instrument, and a participatory "call and response" between limbs, music and movement, and performer and audience.[16]

Before 1843, when the explosive popularity of the Virginia Minstrels and then the Christy Minstrels expanded the market for commercial prints, there is a comparative paucity of early iconography. Yet even those early, caricatured illustrations of "Zip Coon" (ca. 1829) and "Jump Jim Crow" (ca. 1832), "Gumbo Chaff" (undated, but probably early 1830s) and "Coal Black Rose" (ca. 1830), such as those employed previously for Hawkins's "Backside Albany" (1815) and "Massa Georgie Washington and General Lafayette" (1824), already depict a distinctive body vocabulary that anticipates the prints of the 1840s and '50s.[17] There are clear parallels between the body vocabularies of later blackface iconography and earlier depictions of African Americans; if we "read past" their racist caricature, we can find, as we did in elements of creole dialect, accent, and polyrhythm, the attempt to capture in print actual movement vocabularies.[18]

BODILY KINESICS AND THE VISIBLE EVIDENCE OF AFRO-CARIBBEAN INFLUENCE

In the antebellum Northeast, black and white dance styles, like black and white fiddle musics, influenced one another and had probably done so, as in the Caribbean, since first contact between Europeans and Africans.[19] Ostendorf has identified the kinesthetic creolization, in a later period, in a particular element of transgressive bodily contortion that can also be located in both Jim Crow iconography and Mount's own works: "'Gimme the knee bone bent' is the invitation to assume a 'black' posture in jazz dance. . . . Bent knees, lowering the body, and galvanizing the pelvis all seemed singularly obscene to early white observers. . . . [And as a result] this crossing of purposes and of desires gave rise to an endless series of parody, travesty, and imitation. Since the early days, both groups copied and imitated each other on- and offstage in a two-sided ritual of antagonistic acculturation."[20]

As we saw in chapters 2 and 3, certain conditions had led to extensive music-and-dance exchange between blacks and whites in riverine and maritime contexts throughout the New World, all the way back to the seventeenth century. Looking at the historical record's accounts of performance, and employing analytical approaches derived from iconography and the anthropology of dance, makes it possible to use images to recover the sound and the participatory experience of blackface minstrelsy. Thomas DeFrantz articulates an important nuance in recognizing the creolizing bodily effect of African American dance in integrated contexts; he observes that, in the Americas, "the centuries-old use of 'blackness' as a metaphor for Otherness . . . became transformed by the daily proximity to black bodies and African-derived performance practice."[21] In other words, the Otherness that

Lott, Lhamon, and Cockrell identify as key to blackface's semiotic appeal does not completely explain the idiom's appeal; "proximity" also led to creolization of *movement vocabularies*. In addition to transgressive allure, the creole synthesis in participatory contexts yielded a kinesthetic communal exchange. A surprisingly large percentage of minstrelsy's iconographic representations can be interpreted as intending to portray a body language that artists, like audiences, musicians, and dancers themselves, recognized to be a new synthesis of parent vocabularies. They could not have known the scope or long-term historical impact of the creole synthesis—indeed, they may not have been conscious of its processes—but there is no question that, as participant observers, they recognized something new to be happening in American popular entertainments.

Now, the attempt to recover a dance music's sound from its visual iconography is speculative, hypothetical, and open to challenge; this should not, however, justify its neglect.[22] Seebass offers a useful distinction between two contrasting approaches to dance iconography: those that treat the topics "as [either] a subdiscipline of choreology or as a subdiscipline of art history."[23] In the field of musicology, an art-historical approach—the analysis of dance symbolism—has predominated, but it is the former, "choreological" approach that is most relevant to us.[24] Seebass argues that this body-centered approach usefully shifts the focus from concept to act; from idea to performance; suggesting that "if we try to return [analytically] from the image to the dance itself, we take a methodologically different road, redirecting our scholarly attention from the conceptualization of dance in the mind of the artist to dance itself . . . *to the moment when it was performed*."[25] In other words, study of dance iconography from a choreological (rather than art-historical) perspective helps us recover the experience of participatory performance. This kind of reproduction is least problematic when we can confirm the artist's own cultural and choreographic expertise; in this respect, Mount's portrayals of country dancers, juba patters, and fiddle players, and his own status as dancer and dance musician, surely qualify him as an expert witness.[26]

We may find it particularly useful to recall the consistent appearance, across all of blackface iconography, of an Afro-Caribbean practice that may be identified both visually and rhythmically: namely, the interruption of regular line. In this central trope, the iconography of the creole synthesis displays postural lines as bent, twisted, interrupted, rendered "with the kneebone bent and the arms akimbo." Similar interruption appears as syncopation and cross-rhythm in blackface melody. This cutting—represented in visual terms by the bent spine, raised leg, tipped pelvis, and tilted head, hat-brim, or upraised hand, and in sounding terms by syncopation, hemiola, and polyrhythm—is a core element of the creole synthesis.[27]

Dozens of period accounts attest to viewers' fascination with Afro-Caribbean dancing's exotic otherness.[28] Very often, that otherness is crystallized for viewers in the bending and twisting that so controverted European notions of bodily grace. We have already confirmed, for example, that "Jump Jim Crow," despite Rice's creation myth of the crippled stable hand, had earlier roots in the polyrhythms implicit in Sea Islands and Caribbean mimetic dance.[29] Minstrelsy's akimbo "knee-bone bent" appears in the Parrish collection version of the rowing-song "Knee-Bone," which body vocabulary is worth citing here: "In the shout song, Knee-Bone, curious twists and exotic tones are employed . . . that must be heard to be appreciated. None of our musical symbols is capable of suggesting the strange turns used in this. . . . The shouter, in this musical chant, obeys instructions and bends the knee far down *with the rhythm of the words* 'Bend my knee-bone to the ground.' The full sung text of the rowing version calls for 'knee-bone bend to the elbow bend.'"[30]

In "Knee-Bone," then, the resultant complexity of rendering meter in the rowing version connects us to Afro-Caribbean rhythmic practices. The percussive parts that surround this simple monophonic tune yield a web of polyrhythmic possibilities, readily accessible by the limbs of the dancing creole body.

Of particular interest in the excerpt from Parrish's transcriptions (music fig. 4)—aside from the eponymous "Kneebone Bend"—is the syncopation on the third beat of the "oars" part, forming a "cutting" cross-rhythm with the voice and the hand-clapping part. It is of course no coincidence that we would find rhythmic cutting similar to that found in blackface dance in a song for rowing a boat—another full-body physical activity that demands the bending and flexing of the trunk, arms, and legs.

Likewise, the still-extant "Buzzard Lope," an explicitly mimetic dance that is probably a close relative of the Jim Crow choreography: the turkey buzzard (turkey vulture) of the West Indies is described as "John Crow," and in Jamaica inspires another mimetic dance, "Jancrow."[31] Parrish's action series of still photographs of the Buzzard Lope is quite well-known and once again employs the bent-knee, arms akimbo, and twisted spine we know from blackface iconography of a century before.[32] We see similar longevity in not only the "knee-bone bent" of the Jim Crow/Jancrow/Buzzard Lope dance complex—which is dated by name as far back as the 1820s, and as recently as the 1950s—but also in the ubiquity of the Afro-Caribbean body percussion that Parrish links, in the Sea Islands, to "Ham Bone Ham Bone" and the dance she calls "Rusty Butt." She transcribes a song called "Juba Dis an' Juba Dat," providing indications of the song's foot and hand percussion, and includes a series of photographs of the young musician "Snooks" dancing, singing, and patting Juba.[33] "Snooks" could as easily appear in the rough sketch *Dancing for Eels, 1820 Catharine Market* as he does in Parrish's photographs from a hundred years later.[34]

THE MULTIVALENT ETERNALITY OF JUBA

"Juba," as a song, dance, body percussion, and dance character, appears widely throughout the historical as well as the ethnographic record: the earliest known reference, found in the account of the free black Henry Bibb (publ. 1849), details his Methodist distaste for the encouragement by slave holders, in his childhood, of secular amusements such as dancing, patting "juber," singing, and playing the banjo.[35] Dena J. Epstein, in her lengthy discussion of the practice, quotes 1835 correspondence from a friend of Edgar Allen Poe's, T. H. Chivers, who describes juba as a "jig which must be accompanied by a measured clapping of the thighs and alternately on each other," while in his 1880 *The Science of English Verse*, Sidney Lanier says, "I have heard a Southern plantation 'hand,' in 'patting juba' for a comrade to dance by, venture upon quite complex successions of rhythm, not hesitating to syncopate, to change the rhythmic accent for a moment, or to indulge in other highly specialized variations of the current rhythmus. Here music . . . is in its rudest form, consisting of rhythm alone; for the patting is done with hands and feet, and of course no change of pitch or of tone-color is possible."[36] In 1838, in the *Farmer's Register*, William B. Smith describes a persimmon beer dance from Virginia, and "two athletic blacks . . . clapping Juber to the notes of the banjor . . . I have never seen Juber clapped to the banjor before. . . . The clappers rested the right foot on the heel, and its clap on the floor was in perfect unison with the notes of the banjor, and palms of the hands on the corresponding extremities."[37] Smith also specifies that the song being sung and played began "Juber up and juber down, Juber all around the town"—clearly the same song Parrish recorded and photographed in the Sea Islands eighty years later.[38]

Thomas Washington Talley's *Negro Folk Rhymes: Wise and Otherwise*, published in 1922 and thus almost exactly contemporaneous with Parrish's Sea Islands collecting, contains a particularly rich "Juba" description and commentary:

> There are Negro Folk Rhyme Dance Songs and Negro Folk Dance Rhymes. An example of the former is found in "The Banjo Picking," and of the latter, "Juba," both found in this collection. . . . The procedure was as follows: Usually one or two individuals "star" danced at time. The others of the crowd (which was usually large) formed a circle about this one or two who were to take their prominent turn at dancing. . . . Those forming the circle, for most of the time, repeated the Rhyme, clapping their hands together, and patting their feet in rhythmic time with the words of the Rhyme being repeated. It was the task of the dancers in the middle of the circle to execute some graceful dance in such a manner that their feet would beat a tattoo upon the ground answering to every word, and sometimes to every syllable of the Rhyme being repeated by those in the circle. There were many such Rhymes. "'Possum up the Gum Stump," and "Jawbone" are good examples. . . . As there came variation in the words from stanza to stanza, the skill of the dancers was taxed to its utmost, in order to keep up the graceful dance and to beat a changed tattoo upon the ground corresponding to the changed words.[39]

We should recall Samuel Floyd's observation that patting juba is best described, not merely as accompaniment to dance, but as actual dance itself.[40] In the context of antebellum Anglo-Celtic movement vocabularies, this integration of music and dance, song and movement, participants and observers; this visual violation of straight and flowing lines—this bending and twisting: of the trunk, of the extended arms, of the pelvis and legs, of the head and the hat-brim—was understood as defiant, eruptive, and transgressive.[41] To "violate" the smooth and flowing line of the body was, metaphorically, to "violate" middle-class social statutes that idealized such smoothness. Bending and twisting, rising and falling, the akimbo posture itself thus became a rebellious expression, and a central marker of blackface defiance.[42] Yet precisely such disequilibrium and recovery, beyond the semiotics of transgression, are the source of Keil's participatory discrepancies—and thus a marker of Afro-Caribbean influence.[43]

To "cut" the rhythm is a central tenant of Afro-Caribbean musical aesthetics: that is, to interrupt, trope, comment on, subvert, even "rebel against" the predominant line of regular pulses in such a fashion that both the added rhythm and the original rhythm are heard anew, as two or more interlocking parts of a greater whole.[44] To cut the rhythm, in such a context, is to create interest in the field of rhythmic pulses—to find a way of entering and then coexisting in polyrhythmic counterpoint with those predominating pulses. The phenomenon has been recognized to obtain both within and beyond African musical sensibilities: Henry Louis Gates Jr. finds it in prose and oral literature as "signifyin,'" and Robert Walser has applied the same concept to analysis of more contemporary African American musics as disparate as Miles Davis and Public Enemy.[45]

Participatory discrepancies are essential to completeness and musical satisfaction in an Afro-Caribbean or African American context. Such "sublime dissonances" are also closely analogous to that counter-pulse (the backbeat on beats 2 and 4) that Irish and Anglo-Appalachian fiddlers employed in an unaccompanied melodic line to create polyrhythmic interest.[46] Cross-accenting of pulse, as with the sound of hard shoes on a resonating surface, represented a crucial sonic commonality, a shared sensibility, in which African American and Anglo-Celtic dance and music aesthetics could meet. It likewise represented the avenue by which blackface audiences (white mechanics, sailors, and slumming middle-class "flash men") discovered the sense of connective communitas that group dance makes possible.[47] And this "taking on of another's experience," across boundaries of race, cultural background, and class, was made possible precisely because the medium of communication was the body: "We recognize a particular state in another because we share the potential for certain experiences. I learn a gesture because my body is constructed in the same way as another human's. A feeling is communicated to me through the posture and/or words of another because that feeling is an authentic product of body experience and culture. Sometimes we intentionally copy others in order to take on their experience."[48]

AFRICAN MOVEMENT AESTHETICS

Barbara S. Glass has provided a useful taxonomy of African movement aesthetics.[49] Among them are those recognizable from blackface iconography, including "angular bending of arms, legs, and torso; shoulder and hip movement; scuffing, stamping, and hopping steps; asymmetrical use of the body; and fluid movement," pantomime or the "imitat[ion of] animal behavior," as well as a "wide, solid stance, [which] flexes the knees," and dancers who could "dance to more than one beat at once . . . [and] move their shoulders to one beat, hips to another, and knees to yet another" (to these may be added, from Meredith, "movement concentrated in the pelvic region").[50] All of these characteristics—angularity, stamping and hopping, asymmetry, flexed limbs, and a pelvic emphasis—are ubiquitous in blackface iconography.[51]

The cross-cultural synthesis between Anglo-Celtic and Afro-Caribbean dance styles is documented, in fact, as early as seventeenth-century Jamaica, and indeed across the Atlantic: Glass quotes an 1842 source from Liberia (which had been recolonized by members of New York's African American community) containing a description of "jig-type" dancing by "Kroomen."[52] In the African Caribbean, and particularly in the English-speaking, Celtic-inflected colonies of Barbados, Jamaica, and Trinidad, the creole synthesis included not only language, and music, but also dancing. Meredith also confirms the centrality of movement vocabularies, saying "the fusion of African and European musical elements was a key part of the creolization process that took place *wherever European colonial masters employed African slaves*."[53]

Glass herself provides an analysis of one of the first North American depictions of the creole synthesis in a watercolor, probably painted in South Carolina sometime in the 1790s, called *The Old Plantation*. This piece of folk art depicts a group of slaves, with slave quarters in the background, dancing to the accompaniment of banjo and percussion. Details of dress suggest the dating; as we have seen other details suggest particularly strong West African cultural retentions.[54] The image usefully demonstrates a number of African or Afro-Caribbean movement characteristics: the pelvis sinking, knees bent, an earthward orientation and an interest in footwork (revealed both by body posture and by the direction of the dancers' gaze), the carrying of sticks or objects, and so forth. The image also evokes certain of W. S. Mount's later conventions, as captured in *Rustic Dance* (1830) and his "barn-door" series (*Dancing on the Barn Floor*, *Dance of the Haymakers*, *The Power of Music*, etc.). Finally, in the middle background, between the foregrounded dancers and the distant "big house" and slave cabins, the artist has depicted a river, with oared canoes or rowing boats in evidence. This bit of iconographic symbolism is a reminder that such scenes were observed and painted by vernacular artists within riverine and maritime contexts. Those painters—and the blackface architects, from Mathews to Emmett, who were their contemporaries and (often) friends—reveal both the movement languages and the sounding performance practice of the creole synthesis.

Glass also identifies movement characteristics shared between Afro-Caribbean and Anglo-American dance traditions in period iconography; these include "pride in footwork"; "public competition"; "dancing on resonant surfaces"; and, less significantly perhaps, holding objects and balancing containers on the head.[55] Such commonalities support the suggestion that the synthesis occurred precisely because participants of multiple (and multiplying) ethnicities recognized common aesthetics, artistic procedures, and social functions for the expressive arts. We find examples of all in W. S. Mount's depictions of both Anglo-Celtic and African American dance.

It was common for black musicians to play Euro-American tunes for dancing; Winans says that, though African-sourced tunes were not so well-documented (because carried in the aural tradition), black fiddlers' repertoires also included the "contradance, square dance, cotillion, waltz, quadrille." Winans adds that these European dances were often decorated, by white dancers, with fancy steps of African origin, including "cutting the pigeon wing, buck dancing, knocking the back step, jubas, shuffles," and so on.[56] Events such as Pinkster, 'Lection Day, John Canoe, and southern cornhuskings were sites for musical exchange whose role playing, ritual behavior, and social function mirrored both Afro-Caribbean and northern Black festival behaviors.[57] Finally, and especially crucially, Winans makes explicit the back-and-forth mutual influence between black and white dancers and players, describing:

> Blacks listening to white music and . . . whites listening to black music. One can also find a few references to whites teachings blacks how to play an instrument, mostly the fiddle. . . . Black musicians are noted as playing for white dances as well as their own. Much less expected are the references to whites playing for black dances, which apparently was not all that rare. The usual situation involved a plantation owner who loved to play the fiddle and who regularly played it for his own slaves' dancing. All of these interactions, plus the instruments the black musicians most often played, the kinds of dances for which they played, and the repertoire . . . indicate that in the mid-nineteenth century . . . black instrumental music traditions represented a considerable amalgamation of white and black elements.[58]

In addition to period reports of black fiddlers playing for white dancing, black drummers playing for white marching, and the implications of period iconography showing both, there is direct evidence for whites' imitation of black vernacular dance. The journal of a U.S. medical student interned in Britain during the War of 1812 contains an account that echoes both West African festival and West Atlantic festival practices. Benjamin Waterhouse of Massachusetts (1754–1846), commissioned as surgeon aboard a U.S. privateer, was captured and confined with other black and white prisoners of war at Dartmoor Prison in Devon. In this first-person account, he recalls:

> There are about four hundred and fifty negroes in prison No. 4; and this assemblage of blacks affords many curious anecdotes, and much matter for speculation. These blacks have a ruler among them whom they call king DICK. He is by far the largest, and I suspect the strongest man in the prison. He is six feet three inches in height, and proportionably large. This black Hercules commands respect, and his subjects tremble in his presence. . . . King Dick keeps a boxing-school, where the white men are sometimes admitted. No. 4 is noted, also, for fencing, dancing and music; and, however extraordinary it may appear, *they teach these accomplishments to the white men*. A person, entering the cock-loft of No. 4, would be highly amused with the droll scenery which it exhibited. . . . Here he may see boxing, fencing, dancing, raffling, and other modes of gambling; and to this, we may add, drawing with chalk and charcoal; and tricks of slight-of-hand; and all this to gratify the eye; and for the sense of hearing, he may be regaled with the sound of clarionets, flutes, violins, flagelets, fifes, tambarines, together with the whooping and singing of the negroes.[59]

Micah Hawkins's prototypical blackface song "Backside Albany" (published 1815) appeared in the immediate wake of the war. In its rendering of dialect and representation of dance vocabularies, "Backside Albany" should be understood not simply as racial caricature but as an attempt by Hawkins, like Mount after him, to render a relatively accurate version of an actual street vernacular—in this case, of dialect:

> Back side Albany dar Lake Shamplain,
> One leetle Pon half full a water,
> Platsburg dar too close upon de main,
> Town small he grow bigger doe here arter,
> On Lake Shamplain
> Uncle Sam set he boat,
> And Massa Macdonough he sail em,

While Gen'ral Maccomb,
Make Plattburgh he home,
Wid he army whose courage nebber fail 'em.[60]

This is the same period in which Hawkins ran his store and tavern in Lower Manhattan, and (from 1820), provided a home to the fatherless William Sidney Mount, and during which the remarkable sketch *Dancing for Eels, 1820 Catharine Market* was created, on the same wharf in which Hawkins had his business. Previous chapters have confirmed the contemporaneous existence of creole exchange in riverine and maritime contexts across the eastern half of the Continent. I would like now, however, to return to the Catherine Wharf, to Hawkins's shop and tavern there, and to Mount's experience as a teenage apprentice there. What *Dancing for Eels* reveals, on the planks of the wharf, is precisely the cultural exchange that would subsequently be reframed and theatricalized by Rice and Dixon and other blackface architects. The black dancer, dressed in maritime garb that echoes garb portrayed by Johnston in his illustration for Hawkins's "Backside Albany" (published 1837)—and did Johnston perhaps see the *Dancing for Eels* sketch, or was he perhaps simply an observer of like scenes?—the juba-patters, clapping along as they gaze at the dancer's footwork; the top-hatted, side-burned, cigar-smoking Bowery B'hoys laughing and clapping as well: these are the inhabitants of the Catherine Wharf, and of all those other wharves, ships' decks, and river landings, who both vernacular painters (Mount, Bingham, and Beard) and blackface architects (Rice and Dixon, Sweeney and Emmett), saw, knew, and imitated, in oils and on the stage.

In addition to "Backside Albany/The Siege of Plattsburgh," Hawkins made a second essay in what Mahar calls Black Ethnic Vernacular (BEV): the celebratory "Massa Georgie Washington and General Lafayette," introduced at the Park Theatre during the 1824 run of *The Saw-Mill*. Kevin Scott links the song unequivocally to Mount and the dancers of the Catharine Market, saying that there "Mount witnessed Bob, Jack, Ned, or other dancers doing versions of the jigs and breakdowns he had probably seen performed most often—and very differently—back on Long Island by whites in groups."[61] If "Bob, Jack, Ned, or other dancers" on the Catherine Wharf were performing "versions of jigs and breakdowns" they had seen in the homesteads of rural Long Island, where they lived and worked side by side with white families, and if black fiddlers were providing music for and teaching music to young white dancers, then surely those white dancers were assimilating elements of black rhythm and bodily inflection as well. Hawkins's early "Backside Albany," moreover, provides an additional clue to the black-white synthesis: its title, topic, and setting—as with those of Hawkins's ballad opera *The Saw-Mill, or, A Yankee Trick*—locate the black-white synthesis not only in Lower Manhattan, where the song and show were composed and performed, but also within the upstate communities of Albany and the Erie Canal, where Irish, Germans, and blacks at Pinkster and Negro 'Lection Day were observing, exchanging, and synthesizing music, language, dance, and festival behaviors.

Rath, with seventeenth- and eighteenth-century transcriptions of Afro-Caribbean music and language, and Mahar, with Hawkins's nineteenth-century transcriptions of BEV, have shown us a way to approach period transcriptions from a more optimistic, yet more rigorous, critical perspective.[62] Mahar demonstrates that "Backside Albany" borrows extensively, and surprisingly accurately, from Black English; we have likewise argued for Hawkins's linguistic and ethnographic accuracy in his ballad opera *The Saw-Mill*.[63] When the ex-slave fiddler Anthony Clapp (1749–1816) died, Hawkins composed a touching, if patronizing, epitaph revealing his respect for his "brother musician."[64] Toney Clapp's speech, and his fiddling, and the folkways of other Long Island African Americans, could in fact have served as inspiration for both Micah Hawkins's theatrical dialogue and W. S. Mount's fiddle repertoire. Observations by Hawkins's contemporary Thomas De Voe, in his *Market Book*, show that interracial street entertainment was far more common than conventional blackface history has recognized.[65]

We can find Glass's "angular bending of arms, legs, and torso; shoulder and hip movement; scuffing, stamping, and hopping steps; asymmetrical use of the body; and fluid movement" in depictions of Dixon, Rice, Juba, and in *Dancing for Eels*.[66] Glass also cites an "Orientation to the Earth": that is, bodily movement that, especially in contrast to vertical and upright European stances, "often bends slightly toward the earth, flattens the feet against it in a wide, solid stance, and flexes the knees"; Johnston's cover for "Massa Georgie Washington" provides a particularly clear example.[67] Glass recognizes practitioners' freedom to modify dance vocabularies, either moment by moment within the course of a single performance, or as a more gradual and permanent evolution within a given community's style over years. This evolution and comparative fluidity is cited repeatedly in prose descriptions of dance solos and competitions: we see a particularly clear example of this in the newspaper articles that form the central anecdote in Cockrell's introduction to his *Demons of Disorder*.[68]

Glass also contrasts an Afro-Caribbean preference for "Circle and Line Formations" (as in the *bamboula* or ring shout) to European court-dances that emphasized the pairing of male-female couples.[69] She says, "Africans could dance to more than one beat at once. . . . Dancers could move their shoulders to one beat, hips to another, and knees to yet another."[70] Such polyrhythmicization of the body is surely one source for the angularity, asymmetry, and hyperextension visible in much blackface iconography: the images seek to convey not only the "akimbo" nature of blackface body posture, but also the multi-rhythmic and contrasting nature of its motion.[71] As a result, the "polyrhythmic body" may have been the single strongest signifier of the transgressive defiance that Lott, Cockrell, and Lhamon have all identified as focal to minstrelsy's carnivalesque working-class appeal.

Mimesis of all sorts was a hugely important part of minstrelsy and subsequent U.S. vernacular dance: it was in fact the raison d'être of the Buzzard Lope, Jump Jim Crow, and (later) of the notorious Cakewalk, which though perceived by postbellum observers as a comic and incompetent imitation of white society dancing, has subsequently (and more subtly) been analyzed as an inventive parody by blacks of white pretense.[72] She also cites among Afro-Caribbean dancers the use of "something in Hand": that is, while dancing, holding in the hand an object (a handkerchief, musical instrument, implement, or—in a noted parallelism between West African and African American usages—an umbrella). The object may become part of the dance's choreography (as in the handkerchiefs employed in a wide variety of Afro-Cuban dances) or simply a means of extending the lines and curves of the choreography (as in English morris dancing). This is another area in which certain characteristic dances in the Anglo-Celtic tradition (particularly those Irish and English group and solo exhibition dances that involved a broom, stick, handkerchief, or other implement) would have been seen as aesthetically familiar and appealing to African stylists. And, of course, the waving hands, hats, and caps found in works such as Mount's *Dance of the Haymakers* and Bingham's *Jolly Flatboatmen* (in some versions) continue this parallelism.

Creole street and theatrical performance provided an environment in which two cultures' expectations about dance aesthetics and techniques could meet and mutually modify each other. They provided the channel for exchange of contrasting dance philosophies: for example, in democratizing European cultures, dance provided a tactic for social advancement impossible in West Africa, where specific dances were far more firmly restricted to specific age, gender, or social groups.[73] In this respect, we may view the semiotic associations of body movement vocabularies within the creole synthesis as a place wherein a new intercultural identity was being invented and performed on the streets and wharves—where defiantly democratic working-class whites could meet newly manumitted ex-slaves and work out together, through dance, a new world of new social identities. Such overlap is especially evident in the body vocabularies associated with immigrant labor, including the percussive, syncopated hard-shoe clogging of North England and the flexible, improvisational *sean-nós* dance of western Ireland's *Gaeltachtai*—the regions from which early nineteenth-century rural emigrants would have come to the Caribbean and the southern United States.[74] Both indirect and direct evidence—the latter exemplified by the shoes-on-wharf-planks of *Dancing for Eels, 1820*, as by Beard's and Mount's later sketches and paintings—suggest appreciation of percussive dance that moved flexibly across ethnic and social boundaries.

The historical evidence shows that African Americans and Anglo-Celts would have experienced as compatible a considerable range of dance characteristics and aesthetics. We then seek to locate in the "gesture language" of Mount's artworks, and the performance practice implicit in these images, the capacity for Keil's "little discrepancies . . . that create 'swing' and invite us to participate"; that is, the frozen representation of polyrhythmic motion that we find in the banjo's technique, the fiddle's backbeat, the juba-patter's body, and the tunes that all accompanied.[75]

The riotous, interactive, participatory pleasure provided to blackface audiences by African American dance is directly confirmed by period descriptions and iconography, most powerfully in an image of Thomas Dartmouth Rice dancing "Jump Jim Crow" onstage during his unprecedented fifty-seven-night run at the Bowery Theatre in 1833.[76] The image employs the theatrical proscenium as framing device, which thus invites the viewer in as if a member of the audience. It emphasizes the hurly-burly action of the pit's standees, who, depicted in Bowery B'hoy costume (top hats, cigars, sideburns), have crowded onstage on either side of Rice's blackface-masked, akimbo-armed, grinning figure, and its literal accuracy is confirmed by period reviews of his performances: "When Mr Rice came on the stage to sing his celebrated song of Jim Crow, they not only made him repeat it some twenty times, but hemmed him in so that he actually had no room to perform the little dancing or turning about appertaining to the song."[77]

Viewed through the lens that locates the dancing body in the tune and text of "Jump Jim Crow" and the percussive choreography of Mount's *The*

Bone Player, Rice's performance on the Bowery stage is a visual and visceral depiction of the physical pleasure found in sharing improvisational dance. It portrays precisely the participatory bodily engagement that the creole synthesis made attractive and possible. Dancing becomes a tool for the construction and reconstruction of identity: "The *meaning* of participation in dance and music groups goes beyond the satisfactory performance of physical movements. Participants often see their dancing as a component of their personal identity, philosophy, and lifestyle choices."[78] Blackface dance creolized its piebald audiences. No matter whether those audiences (youth or adult, white and black, rural or urban, working- or middle-class, North American or Western European) were conscious or unconscious of the phenomenon, such creolization—specifically, the participatory bodily experience of polyrhythmic dance—was the source of minstrelsy's appeal. When we unpack the actions and implications captured in blackface iconography, we recover something of the sound and physical sensation of these performances.

Such analysis likewise helps us explain the accounts of young whites dancing, singing, and picking up instruments immediately on being exposed to those performances; see especially here Carlin on the Virginia Minstrels' 1843 tour of Britain, which, in an ironic foreshadowing of the 1950s skiffle movement and the 1960s blues revival, inspired hundreds of banjo-plunking imitators.[79] There is no question that lower Manhattan was one particularly visible and thus influential staging area for the transformation of creole street performance into blackface theatrics, but, contra previous scholarship, it was by no means the only one. The close proximity of whites and blacks in the special circumstances of riverine and maritime contexts meant that participation in African American polyrhythmic dance and dance music in this period was unusually and immediately available to whites, across the urban and frontier United States and throughout the African Caribbean.

MOUNT'S CHOREOLOGICAL EVIDENCE

That William Sidney Mount, like his brother and uncle, was familiar with social and vernacular dance is confirmed not only by the archival evidence of his biography and tune collections but also by the iconographic evidence of his pictures, including his relatively early (1831) *Dancing on the Barn Floor*. In this image, on a theme and topic to which he would profitably return several times, Mount depicts a couple dancing to music supplied by a folk fiddler.

Though idealized and romanticized—and possibly depicting an imagined scene—the painting still provides a surprising quantity of precise musical detail. Dancing in hard shoes on the raised and resonant floor of a barn—or a rain barrel, or a half door laid on the ground—was a long-established folk practice, one common throughout the English and Irish as well as the New England countryside.[80]

Likewise, the fiddle player holds the instrument down on his collarbone, without chin rest, fingers in first position, and chokes up on the stick, using a two-finger grip, in a fashion consistent with documented Anglo-Celtic folk styles. *Dancing on the Barn Floor* is indebted to other, earlier works: the pencil sketch *Comb and Brush*, depicting a teenage African American fiddler, provides the model for its musician, while both Johnston's *Backside Albany* illustration and (possibly) *Dancing for Eels, 1820 Catharine Market* provide models for the male dancer. Additional iconographic evidence, particularly the copious pencil sketches in the Mount collection at the Long Island Museum of American Art, History, and Carriages, includes additional examples of cross-cultural visual borrowing (black to white and white to black): he obviously loved to sketch fiddlers, tin whistlers, dancers, and juba-patters. Of course recurrence of a literal image from an earlier sketch in a later oil (such as *Comb and Brush* vis-à-vis *Dancing on the Barn Floor*) is only one way in which observed musical practices may be expected to have influenced Mount's visual language, but such appearances do provide particularly direct confirmation of the breadth and detail of his musical observation.

I now return to 1845's *Dance of the Haymakers* (plate 3), in order to focus on the movement vocabularies attributable to the central figures. Two adult males, these dancers are clad in modest, rumpled clothes suggesting their working-class status. One is wearing a stocking cap, which for Mount is a recurrent symbol of itinerancy; the other is waving his slouch hat, recalling Glass's "object in hand" taxonomy.[81] Both employ a posture—one hand raised, body erect, poised on the toes—that simultaneously suggests the Highland fling, or possibly a hornpipe, but is also comparatively consistent with that of the central African American figure in *Dancing for Eels.*

As with *The Banjo Player*, we have some tentative biographical information about *Haymakers* from Buffet's 1920s serial biography, identifying the "young man playing the fiddle" as Mount's admired fiddle mentor Shepard Jones—an identification indirectly confirmed by Mount's having placed a handwritten transcription of "Shep Jones's Hornpipe" between canvas and matte in the back of the frame. Buffet says that the dancer at the left, "with the tenuous fringe of black beard, on his throat, may be Tom Bigs and the other dancer Wesley Ruland."[82] With the exception of the (unidentified) drummer standing outside the barn and looking in, participants are thus drawn from Mount's autobiographical experience; if the figures were sketched from life and then rendered in oils, as was his wont, then it depicts an observed scene roughly contemporaneous with or predating its 1845 date of completion.

At the same time, other visual factors also evoke the creole synthesis; for example, the dancers in *Haymakers* employ a movement vocabulary similar to that of the anonymous black man drumming up business in *Dancing for Eels, 1820*: up on the toes, one hand waving and the other on or near the hip, the torso crooked. Both Johnston's illustration for "Backside Albany" and Mount's 1831 *Dancing on the Barn Floor* (plate 1) seem to echo in 1845's *Haymakers*. "Tom Bigs" and "Wesley Ruland" employ the same body posture as in Mount's earlier images, but also wear the open shirt, low-crowned hat, or baggy, high-waisted trousers of the dancers in *Eels* and in Johnston's illustration. In light of both the creole synthesis, and the various constituent works that preceded and probably informed it, *Haymakers* represents a complex intermingling of cultural and artistic influences. In fact, the dancers in this image probably *are* dancing what they believe to be a "highland fling" (or perhaps Shep Jones's eponymous "Hornpipe"). At the same time, whether Mount was aware of the physical impact of the creole synthesis or whether he consciously intended its visual depiction, already—by 1845?—we are seeing in *Haymakers* the influence on an Anglo-Celtic rural population of movement vocabularies from Afro-Caribbean dance.

The story becomes even more complex when we examine the related painting called variously *Music Hath Charms* and *The Power of Music* (ca. 1845?). In this image, the outside observer is not a young percussionist but an adult black male who is participating not by playing but by listening. The complexity of these images' interrelations increases yet again; in an untitled watercolor cartoon (undated) that is an obvious study for *Haymakers* (plate 2), Mount's outside observer is a teenage African American, who is dancing (using the stereotyped crooked-legged posture of "dancing for eels" and "Jump Jim Crow") as he imitates the steps of the dancers within, who in a very different posture to *Haymakers* are flirting the skirts of their laborer's smocks like Highland lassies.

More complex again: in a pencil sketch, almost certainly from life—and thus possibly the earliest of this whole complex of related works—the African

American participants are inside the barn, one dancing and flirting his skirts while the other pats Juba. In a precise reverse from the final oils, the outside observer is an adult Caucasian male, while Mount's own chosen title (*Two Men Jigging at Barn Door*) employs ambiguous terminology: *jigging* may reference either the Anglo-Celtic dance type or minstrelsy's more generic connotations for a characteristic dance—or perhaps he intends both.

And if we remain with the cluster of images associated with *Haymakers*, and a particular concentration on the dancing body, even more visual insights become available. It would appear, as we have stated, that the undated *Jigging at the Barn Door* (see image 6) may be the earliest of the extant images: it seems to inform both *Music Hath Charms*—though, as we have said, Mount flips the ethnicities of dancers and observer—and also the watercolor study for *Haymakers*. Caucasian versions of the dancers in both *Charms* and *Haymakers* link to those in *Barn Floor* (the girl flirting her skirts in that latter), but the watercolor featuring the "Jim Crow" dancer adds another, significant, characteristic element. The original pencil sketch showed dance crossing the color line: specifically, white observation and enjoyment of black dance, in the fashion of *Dancing for Eels, 1820*. "Jigging" supplies the quasi-theatrical frame of the barn door—and, perhaps, a hint of minstrelsy's voyeuristic pleasure. The watercolor transforms the white passive observer of the sketch into a black dancing participant. Although the three dancers in the watercolor are separated by ethnicity (white versus black), by physical location (inside versus outside), and even by relative elevations—a factor that, we have seen, carried class associations in Beard's *Western Raftsmen*—the proximities of the creole synthesis are explicit: both Anglo-Celtic fling and quasi-blackface movement vocabularies are being danced to Shep Jones's fiddling. This is both a literal and a metaphorical depiction of the kinds of cultural exchange on which the creole synthesis depended.[83]

One additional example of Mount's precise observation of musical technique further supports the cross-cultural nature of the music being depicted. In the final version of *Haymakers*, another instrument is depicted, in addition to Shep Jones's fiddle and the sound of the dancers' own leather soles on the barn floor. The anonymous African American youth standing outside the barn, which is outside the theatrical (and, metaphorically, political) frame, and looking in at the music, is not just an observer. He is tapping on the barn wall with what appears to be a pair of hand-hewn drumsticks.[84] Thus, the soundtrack of fiddle and stamping feet also includes improvised drumming.

If we look even more closely at the drummer—and if we remember Mount's confirmed and meticulous attention to the visual details of instruments and performance practice—we can observe that the young man is holding the sticks, not with the double-overhand grip we might expect of an untutored player, but with the matched, palm-up and palm-down usage that percussionists call a traditional, or, more accurately, military-snare grip. Moreover, he appears to be cross-sticking: that is, bracing the tip of one stick against the resonating surface, and striking the braced stick with the other, in what in modern parlance would be called a rim shot, typically employed on snare drum or side drum.

These are not amateur or untutored techniques. On the contrary: they are consistent with formal percussion training, most likely in a military-band setting. We have noted the underremarked presence of African Americans in colonial-era militias (chapter 3) and the impact of military drumming on the early blackface architects, most notably Dan Emmett (chapter 2). Military drumming was a trade passed along in black families as early as the prerevolutionary period.[85] It is thus absolutely plausible that the young drummer in Mount's painting could have been drawn from life, or from closely recalled observation; that he could have received training in drumming in multiethnic military-band contexts; and that his precisely depicted, expert drumming technique is therefore completely historically possible. The track record of Mount's precise reliability as a musical reporter suggests that he witnessed scenes like this.

Beyond the addition in *Haymakers* of the black drummer, and the interesting progression of agency assigned to African American participants in this scene—from listener in *Power of Music* to Jim Crow dancer in the watercolor to the active, sounding, contributing musician of *Haymakers*—aspects of the Anglo-Celtic dancers' body vocabularies clearly recall Glass's African movement characteristics: the dancers in *Haymakers* betray a definite "earthward" orientation: the knees are deeply bent, and the pelvis sinks; in contrast, for example, to the earlier *Barn Floor*, wherein both (especially the young man) dance erect, with shoulders back. In *Haymakers* the head is tilted, especially in the right-hand figure of "Wesley Ruland," but with the same tendency visible in both; this again forms a contrast to *Barn Floor*. There is a sense of increased relaxation and "flow" in the bodies depicted in both *Barn Floor* and *Haymakers*, but in *Barn Floor*, arms are held straighter, especially by the young woman, and exhibit a clearer sense of line or curve—an echo of Anglo-Celtic practice. In contrast, in

Haymakers, though legs are relatively extended and heels are lifted, both knees and elbows are bent akimbo: the limbs thus display both European and African American vocabularies.

In *Haymakers* we likewise see some bend or twist to the torso (especially in the left-hand dancer, identified as "Tom Bigs"); for example, the shoulders are twisted farther to the left than are the hips; this yields Kealiinohomoku's "irregular alignment of the torso."[86] In contrast, *Barn Floor*'s dancers hold their shoulders essentially in line with the hips, even though each has turned the head to look over the shoulder—their body torsion is thus more in keeping with European dance aesthetics.

In *Haymakers* there is substantial foot flexion and pronation—that is, lifting of the heel, and turning-out of the toes—which again recalls Kealiinohomoku and earlier, blackface-associated kinesics: see, for example, the "Backside Albany" and "Massa Georgie Washington" illustrations. We can contrast these to the feet of the dancers in *Barn Floor*; though we may note that, in this as in several other aspects discussed above, the male dancer displays a bit more of Kealiinohomoku's African American body tendencies.

In *Haymakers*, the dancer on the right ("Wesley Ruland") holds his cap, "which extend[s] . . . the range of movements" of his right arm.[87] We can identify similar usage, this time with a handkerchief, from the dancer depicted in Beard's *Jolly Flatboatmen*. A particularly obvious African American element in *Haymakers*, displayed by both dancers, is Kealiinohomoku's "torsos [that] are flexed forward and exhibit[ing] some form of sway-back"; this crook-backed bending and twisting is integral in African, African American, and Jim Crow dance languages.[88] We may note also bodily parallels between the *Haymakers* dancers and some of the studies for the black dancer in Clonney's 1841 *Militia Training*, who is likewise up on the balls of the feet in European fashion. The depiction of such behaviors in both black and white dancers, both within and beyond Mount's corpus, and in the iconography of blackface, is further evidence for the ubiquitous creolization of bodies in early-nineteenth-century expressive culture. It suggests, in fact, that black dancers *learned* this ball-of-the-foot stance, so different from the pronation and "rootedness" of Afro-Caribbean footwork, from Anglo-Celtic models.[89]

Finally, the variations between the versions of this image certainly suggest that Mount is mixing and manipulating the cultural associations of body vocabularies consciously and intentionally. That is, he explicitly evokes Jim Crow caricature in the body of the watercolor study's dancer, but then excises it from

Haymakers; moreover, in the final oil he enhances the African American's agency by making him a sounding contributor to the music, and renders him much more naturalistically than in the preliminary watercolor. Conversely, he moves the Jump Jim Crow gestures into the white bodies of "Tom Bigs" and "Wesley Ruland." Of course, we cannot—and need not—deny the various European elements that remain in the *Haymakers* figures: for example, both dance on the ball of the foot (though, as we have seen, that is a posture also depicted in black dance in the same period, and thus consistent with the creole synthesis); each dances with a hand raised as in the fling (though "extension" with a hat or other object adds an African element).

At the same time, the multiethnic implications of *Haymakers* contrasts with Mount's own *Rustic Dance after a Sleigh Ride* (1830, plate 4). That earlier image, which depicts a similar dance event, reveals several revealing contrasts with the later and technically more skillful *Haymakers*: in *Rustic Dance*, the dancing has not yet begun: the girls are just lifting their skirts to advance on the dance floor. The one man already on the floor exhibits qualities of caricature and comedy (red cheeks, slightly disheveled clothing, and grin) not dissimilar to Irving's much early prose description of Ichabod Crane dancing Upstate, or to Johnson's illustration for "Backside Albany," and he holds one hand in his pocket, a violation of middle-class bodily etiquette that conveys either his "rustic" working-class origins or his state of inebriation—or both. He is poised on the balls of his feet like the dancers in *Haymakers*, but the fact that he is dancing already, prior to others entering onto the floor, conveys a bit of a sense that he is "dancing an invitation": that he may have begun "battering" the floor before the formal figure, or even that this is part of the intended comedy. Yet at the same time, such an entry or invitation into a circle of dancers also evokes the Afro-Caribbean *bamboula* depicted in Kemball's rendering of Congo Square.

We may remember that the framing of *Rustic Dance* is theatrical, the walls and ceiling of the room itself forming a kind of proscenium, with the viewer as audience, and that it exploits a generally geometric composition that recalls both theatrical images of the early 1830s (note particularly the close parallels to the image of Rice dancing "Jump Jim Crow" on the Bowery Theatre stage) and the earlier *Dancing for Eels, 1820*. In *Eels 1820* we note Kealiinohomoku's African characteristics, but we should also remember that it represents a creolized body vocabulary: aside from the presence of the white onlookers, and the maritime garb (à la *Backside Albany*), one hand is held on the African

American dancer's hip in the style of an Anglo-Celtic hornpipe. He combines Afro-Caribbean pronation and bent knees, and arms akimbo, but dances in Anglo-Celtic style on the balls of the feet, to the accompaniment of African American body percussion.

Brief examination of a selection of other images of music making from the Mount collection reveals the consistency with which he records and manipulates the cultural associations of body vocabularies: a late sketch from 1867, in pencil on a piece of lined notebook or copybook paper, depicts a single dancer, in appearance probably African American, observed in a chance encounter by five others, including several children and a man wearing military cap and jacket (*Fun by the Way Side*, image 3). The dancer displays the crossing step of African American dance styles; he sinks the pelvis and dips the head. The crossed ankles even imply the poised moment before a dance movement: possibly the clockwise spin of the "wheel about and turn about" in "Jump Jim Crow."

Group of Men Fiddling and Dancing in Front of Jayne Store (image 4), which bears, in his own handwriting, the inscription "W.S.M. Oct. 22 '67" (a sketch late in life—he died only thirteen months later), recalls the previous image.

Image 3. William Sidney Mount (1807–1868), *Fun by the Way Side*, December 23, 1864, pencil on paper, 7.875 × 12.125 in., 77.22.227. Credit: The Long Island Museum of American Art, History & Carriages, Bequest of Ward Melville, 1977.

Image 4. William Sidney Mount (1807–1868), *Group of Men Fiddling and Dancing in Front of Jayne Store*, 1867, pencil on paper, 4 × 6.5 in., 77.22.229. Credit: The Long Island Museum of American Art, History & Carriages, Bequest of Ward Melville, 1977.

Mount once again employs quasi-theatrical framing, depicting a group of loungers outside a store bearing the sign " . . . TON JAYNE"), and includes a slouching, capped soldier downstage left he has employed elsewhere.[90] This time, however, the focus of the loungers' attention is two African American performers: a fiddler seated on an upturned barrel, his gaze fixed on the feet of a jig dancer, whose body language closely recalls that of "Tom Bigs" and "Wesley Ruland" in the earlier *Haymakers*: bent knees, low pelvis, some twisting of the shoulders in relation to the hips, and a tangible sense of "sinking" and bodily relaxation—once again evocative of a moment of impact and rebound: that is, for example, "Jump Jim Crow."

A very late, untitled item from 1866 contains one small, quick sketch, somewhat the worse for wear, which again depicts African American performance for an informal happenstance audience: a black juba-patter is watched by two boys, and a man holding the hand of a child (image 5).

The musician, dressed informally in smock and trousers, sinks deeply, with bent knees and feet flat to the ground, as he slaps out the rhythm, probably as accompaniment to his own singing. He is closely reminiscent of the

Image 5. William Sidney Mount (1807–1868), Untitled (Sheet of Eleven Drawings), n.d., pencil on paper, 10.5 × 13.5 in., 77.22.322. Credit: The Long Island Museum of American Art, History & Carriages, Bequest of Ward Melville, 1977.

Image 6. William Sidney Mount (1807–1868), *Dancing in the Barn or Two Men Jigging at Barn Door*, n.d., pencil on paper, 4 × 6.25 in., 77.22.130. Credit: The Long Island Museum of American Art, History & Carriages, Bequest of Ward Melville, 1977.

juba-patters in *Dancing for Eels, 1820*, from almost fifty years before—and his presence in this life sketch confirms the ongoing presence of such African American music-and-dance practices as Juba, observed by Mount at a postbellum date and in a rural Long Island context.

Dancing in the Barn or Two Men Jigging at Barn Door (image 6) is the pencil study for *Power of Music*, which reverses ethnicities to depict a white listener and black performers—and renders the focal performance as a dancer and juba-patter. It is a particularly elegant, if swift, representation of this trope: the dancer in Afro-Caribbean fashion bends the knees, rises on the toes, twists the shoulders, sinks the pelvis, and holds the arms akimbo—yet also forms a close parallel to the Anglo-Celtic "Tom Bigs" in *Haymakers*; while the percussionist leans against the barn's interior wall and crosses the right ankle on the left shin, thus providing additional striking surfaces for executing "juba."

An untitled sketch (see image 5), again on lined copybook paper and unnumbered, but carefully signed "W.S. Mount," is even more evidently a constituent of *Haymakers* and thus likely predates that painting: employing

Mount's favored framing of barn door as theatrical proscenium, it provides, in the left foreground, the small dog (watching the dancers in the sketch, but a cat under the barn floor in *Haymakers*), and a female figure at an open door in the background. The central figures are, again, a dancer—this time facing the viewer, rather than in profile, as in *Haymakers*—who again is executing the bent-knee, arms-akimbo body mechanics we have associated with the creole synthesis.

Although the quality of *Dancing in the Barn* (image 6) somewhat obscures this factor, this teenage dancer appears to be African American, which makes the identity of his accompanist, who is standing but occupies roughly the same basic location as "Shep Jones" in *Haymakers*, even more interesting: that accompanist is a *Caucasian* juba-patter! The sketch predates *Haymakers*, because it clearly employs elements of that later painting, and, like *Barn Floor*, borrows the posture and activity of a sketched accompanist (the white juba-patter from this sketch; the black fiddler from *Comb and Brush*), but transmutes that accompanist's ethnicity. As we have earlier and extensively seen black fiddlers executing Anglo-Celtic tunes, here we see a white percussionist executing Afro-Caribbean accompaniment. Moreover, both visual composition, and the activities of black dancer and white, hatted and frock-coated white accompanist, closely recall *Dancing for Eels*, and suggest Mount's familiarity with that 1820 image.

MOUNT'S INTEGRATION OF THE CREOLE SYNTHESIS

We move now to a more extended discussion of a more elaborate and carefully observed series of life sketches in which dancing is a constituent element, and to a consideration of what these reveal in juxtaposition with both Mount's own works and those of contemporaneous vernacular artists. *Setauket Military Band* (undated) is a quick but good-sized pencil sketch of the musicians in a volunteer militia unit at a moment of ease (see image 7). Mount's militia sketches are relevant to the discussion of blackface dance for a number of reasons. We have established his insistence on sketching only from life (see the anecdote of his sketching a pet dog, and refusing to complete the sketch after the animal had moved, in chapter 1), and it is reasonable to presume that this militia sketch was no exception to that rule. We can infer that Mount was present at such events, an inference confirmed by his own statements regarding band music as a tool for creating political comity, and we can further infer that he saw African Americans dancing to militia wind-band music.[91]

The militia topic itself was not uncommon among vernacular artists; of particular note are similarly themed works by David Claypoole Johnston (1798–1865) and James Goodwyn Clonney (1812–1867).[92] These two vernacular artists, one born in 1798 and the other 1812, neatly bracket the "blackface generation" of William Sidney Mount (b. 1807)—that is, those painters and performers born between 1801 (George Washington Dixon) and 1815 (Daniel Decatur Emmett) who we have identified as collectively capturing a peak moment in the blackface synthesis. Johnston's and Clonney's observation and experiences readily paralleled those of Mount, Bingham, Beard, and Dixon, Rice, and Emmett. Like these other painters and musicians, Johnston and Clonney were close observers of working-class and vernacular public culture, and often sketched scenes from life for later reworking in commercial artworks.

As we have seen, militia gatherings and musters were festival events, creating liminal spaces in which whites and blacks could engage in participatory, culture-crossing activities: such activities were precisely the roots and the attractions of events such as Pinkster and Negro 'Lection Day. We have likewise established that militia bands, from the prerevolutionary period, were contexts enabling ethnic and musical exchange, noting the presence of black drummers in British, Continental American, and Hessian armies. Black drummers, like black fiddlers, continued to play significant roles in postrevolutionary musical and festival contexts. We have also confirmed something of the wide musical experience of "free men of color" Mount would have known on Long Island and the Lower East Side, from Anthony "Toney" Clapp the ex-slave fiddler to George Freeman the teenaged banjoist and bugler. I thus suggest that we should see this militia band sketch as both a metaphor and a literal representation of the interracial dynamics and musical situations that Mount observed on Long Island and the Lower East Side. First, however, it will be helpful to frame Mount's sketch as part of a longer tradition of militia-themed vernacular artwork.

The 1792 Militia Acts had mandated the formation of state militias, but by the 1820s two kinds of unit profiles had developed. These included the "enrolled" (i.e., mandatory) militia, which "had too often degenerated into displays of ineptitude, or, worse still, spectacles of public drunkenness," but that did provide ample fodder for theatrical or iconographic comic farce.[93] Such groups were understood to be quite different from the newer "volunteer" militia unit, which typically "adopted a distinctive dress uniform, equipped itself with arms of a consistent type and style, and often supplied itself with a marching band, commissioning and publishing marches and dances for it."[94] Johnston's 1828 *Militia Muster*, no doubt of an "enrolled" unit, contains a level of caricature not present in Mount's (probably later) sketch, but strongly evokes the comic conventions of the ballad opera, and of later blackface: as Tatham points out, "the militia was a subject of fun in the 1820s."[95] And Johnston's own career reflected experiences shared with the blackface originators': a Boston native, he was active not only as a caricaturist (his work was banned in Boston as too controversial in 1821) but also in theater.[96]

Also relevant to our discussion of Mount's musical milieu on Long Island is Tatham's observation that volunteer militias were social and cultural organizations, of the sort for which Mount was both an appreciator and, often, a volunteer musician.[97] As with his illustration for Micah Hawkins's "Backside Albany," Johnston's *Militia Muster* is a virtual catalog of comic theater's martial characters, including rumpled yokels, obese shopkeepers, top-hatted "Bowery B'hoys," and posturing "officers."[98] This art, though comic and parodic, also has links with the early Jacksonian period's fierce (if selective, because extended only to white males) "democratic egalitarianism": no matter the comic unsuitability or ineptitude of the various recruits, the "enrolled" militia situated diverse classes and character types in the ranks together.[99] Such egalitarianism provided for topical comedy, and Johnston's biography confirms that he had, like Mount, not only a visual but also a personal experience of popular theater: he was a member of Boston's Chestnut Street Theatre company from 1821 to 1826, and in fact had appeared in the chorus during Charles Mathews's blackface performances of 1822–23.[100]

James Goodwyn Clonney's 1841 *Militia Training*, on the other hand, remains aware of militia's comic associations, but like Mount's sketches establishes a different expressive field than do Johnston's illustrations. There is little or no caricature in Clonney's preliminary studies or in the final oil. Their precise observation is also reminiscent of Mount's own, and probably for similar reasons: sketched from life, they provided Clonney a means for working out technical and compositional issues, but also as jogs to his visual memory. Clonney's mode of "direct translation" of pencil sketches into final oils is close to what we have inferred Mount's to be.[101] Giese confirms the link between Clonney and Mount, providing a detailed comparison of *Militia Training* to various Mount works—and suggests that Clonney more than once literally imitated Mount (see his trope on Mount's *Farmers*

Nooning).[102] Giese also finds links between this image and George Caleb Bingham's *Jolly Flatboatmen* (1857): the Clonney sketch *Dances on a Stone Boat* may have served as an inspiration for Bingham's later, more idealized image.[103] But Clonney, like Mount, is a more naturalistic and accurately informed observer than Bingham, as well as a fine and precise draftsman and hence a more useful reporter on the militia muster and the blackface synthesis.

Giese does not discuss the two studies, of a black youth dancing on a half door, playing to the music of a young white fiddler, or the second, beautifully executed sketch of the dancer himself—yet they provide historical and interpretive information relevant to our discussion of Mount and the creole synthesis. Clonney's rendition of the dancer's body language is as apt and accurate as is Mount's, and the body language in the second study is reminiscent of that in *The Bone Player*. Certainly, if there is any remaining question regarding the choreological inks between *The Bone Player*; the "dancing body" depicted in *Haymakers*, *Western Raftsmen*, and *Dancing for Eels*; the arms akimbo and knee-bone bent of blackface iconography (illustrations of "Backside Albany," "Massa Washington," "Jump Jim Crow," "Jim Along Josey," Rice at the Bowery Theatre); and Dickens's and Irving's lyrical descriptions of black dancers, it is erased by Clonney's beautiful, sympathetic, and naturalistic studies for *Stone Boat*. Whether or not they are holding instruments or standing on a dance floor, all participants in African American music-making, as the precise observation of Beard, Clonney, and Mount makes clear, were, at least implicitly, dancers.

We may now consider Mount's *Setauket Military Band* (image 7) in light of Johnston, his predecessor, and Clonney, his contemporary and imitator. Notable for the ease and economy of Mount's line and for the informality and naturalism of the musicians' postures—they are variously rendered sitting on drums, tuning drumheads, or practicing techniques—it almost certainly depicts a group of volunteer militia of the sort described by Tatham above. The consistency and good order of their uniform, the casual dignity with which Mount sketches them, and the likely date (and, in turn, the likelihood that Mount was sketching in or around the Long Island home of his young manhood) all tend to confirm this.

Most significant of all, for our purposes, is the presence of two additional figures: at a short distance from the bandsmen are two African Americans, dressed in the same quasi-military uniform (tapered trousers, short-tailed frock coat, top hats) as the musicians. As Kevin Scott has commented, and as is common in iconography of the period, the African Americans are depicted

Image 7. William Sidney Mount (1807–1868), *Setauket Military Band*, n.d., pencil on paper, 10.5 × 13.5 in., 77.22.113. Credit: The Long Island Museum of American Art, History & Carriages, Bequest of Ward Melville, 1977.

as present with, but separate (by physical distance or type of activity) from, Anglo-Americans in the image: we have seen the same "present-but-separate" status in other Mount works, from the *Rustic Dance* to *Dance of the Haymakers*.[104] Yet the inclusion of these two figures, and most significantly the nature of their activity, is important for the present investigation—precisely because they are dancing. More specifically, one is dancing, using the bent-knee and arms akimbo we can now associate with Jump Jim Crow and related African American dance, and the other—just as in *Dancing for Eels*, in various other Mount life sketches (cited above), and in Clonney's study for *Stone Boat*—is patting Juba.

This is hugely significant. We know from his own and others' reportage that Mount insisted on sketching only from life subjects. His finished oils, painted for a commercial market, might imagine, transform, or otherwise fictionalize the scenes depicted, but his sketch work, which he continued avidly long after failing eyesight had caused him to abandon oils, was extensive and it was from life. It is thus reasonable to infer that, though the figures and composition of this dancer and juba-patter may or may not recur in a later painting, *Setauket Military Band* represents a scene Mount actually observed.[105]

The presence of these two participants in this scene of informal Anglo-American music making literally and symbolically reveals the black-white working-class cultural interaction we have discovered elsewhere. Mount's visual evidence is persuasive confirmation of the presence of Afro-Caribbean rhythmic languages in the Long Island context—and by extension throughout all Atlantic and Caribbean riverine and maritime contexts. Just as the top-hatted Bowery B'hoys of *Dancing for Eels* are seen experiencing Afro-Caribbean dance and juba-patting on the wharves of 1820s Manhattan, so here the top-hatted militia-men playing drums and winds in *Setauket Military Band* are seen experiencing Afro-Caribbean dance and juba-patting in rural 1840s Long Island.

And the significant revelations go further. The presence of the dancer and juba-patter, coupled with Mount's insistence on accurate observation and representation in his sketches—no less than his eschewal of the period's presumptive racial caricatures—confirms the presence of what has formerly been understood as exaggerated theatrical dance in a nontheatrical, participatory, cross-racial environment. Of course, racist caricature exaggerating body and movement characteristics was part of minstrelsy's visual and sonic languages. But to presume that period renderings of African Americans (either visual, dialogical, or theatrical) were always or only racist caricature is to miss entirely the rich musicological information those renderings contain. In fact, these African American dancers, knee-bones bent and arms akimbo, dancing to the music of the Anglo-Celtic volunteer militia, at a general muster or other public event, *show* us the creole synthesis in action.

It is worth remembering that the occasion for such exchange is a festival music situation; the juxtaposition of Afro-Caribbean dance and military wind-band drumming thus parallels concurrent Anglo-African contexts enabling cross-cultural experiment and exchange: Pinkster, 'Lection Day, and General Training Day in the North; Carnival, John Canoe, and related Afro-Anglo festivals in the English-speaking Caribbean. Proximity to a riverine or maritime environment facilitated musical contact across disparate culture groups—northern and southern, black and white, rural and urban, Caribbean and Atlantic, Long Island and the Lower East Side, and so on—and vastly accelerated musical exchange and creole synthesis.[106] The African American dancer and juba-patter of *Setauket Military Band*—like the African American musicians depicted in *The Bone Player*, *The Banjo Player*, and *Rustic Dance*, and equally, as this book has shown, the Anglo-American musicians in *Dancing on the Barn Floor*, *Haymakers*, and *Banjo Player in the Barn*—are active participants, indeed carriers, of the creole synthesis. Mount, like Beard and

Clonney, documents the contexts, participants, and practices that injected Afro-Caribbean rhythmic languages, the "cutting," syncopation, and "participatory discrepancies" we have found to have transformed the Anglo-Celtic melodic repertoires, into the larger repertory of U.S. and Caribbean body vocabularies; in short, to have transformed how Americans moved, thought about, and experienced their own bodies.

Conclusion

The Creole Synthesis in American Culture

THE GOAL OF THIS BOOK HAS BEEN to use primary sources—demographics, tune repertoires, archival materials, and most especially iconography—as tools to construct a portrait of the multiethnic nineteenth-century world that gave birth to blackface minstrelsy; to recover the sounds of that world; and to understand how the sound and movement vocabularies of this synthesis accelerated the creolization of North American culture. Though my examination has culminated with the biographical experience and visual reporting of William Sidney Mount, the book has also sought to "open out" this analysis, in order to encompass deeper roots and a more expansive history than blackface scholarship has formerly recognized. I have argued that the resources and conditions for the creole synthesis existed across the riverine and maritime zones of the continent, and—equally significantly—that not only inference but also empirical evidence support the claim that these conditions birthed the creole street-performance idioms that were the sources of blackface theatrics.

I have sought to counter essentialist presumptions about what blackface "was" and "did," though not so much in order to rehabilitate minstrelsy, as the foundations for such rehabilitation have already been laid by Lott and Lhamon, Cockrell, Carlin, and Mahar. Rather, I built on these foundations in order to rediscover a sense of creative agency manifested by the Anglo-African musicians who were the blackface minstrels' inspiration. Modern analyses of blackface have tended to focus on the signification intended by white performers and understood by white theatrical audiences; the result has sometimes been a lack of attention to the ways earlier street musicians and creative artists, Anglo- and African American alike, responded to social or economic restrictions. I wanted to investigate what it "felt like" to be a creole street musician, dancer, or audience member, because recognizing the intentionality and creativity of those early informants is essential in our quest to recover their performance practice. The musicians of the creole synthesis were marginalized, discriminated against, and denied power. But it would be a mistake to presume that they were therefore unable to recognize, analyze, respond to, and symbolically contest dominating strictures through creative action. Building on the earlier scholarship, this book has demonstrated that such contestation, in the ferment of the Jacksonian period, was a significant component of theatrical blackface's popular appeal.

But beyond symbolism, I have more centrally sought to recover the sound of the minstrels' music, and the conceptual, semiotic, organological, and kinesthetic tools they used to create that sound. Recovering blackface performance practice, and the intentions that underlay it, is crucial to understanding the impact of the creole synthesis on the Anglo-American audiences who I have argued internalized its rhythmic and bodily sensibilities. That appeal, as embodied by the blackface avatars who first translated African American street idioms to the stage, was not only symbolic, but also physical, participatory, and transformative. The music made people want to dance, and to dance in a creole fashion. In turn, hearing the music, internalizing its sonic and aesthetic intentions, and responding bodily to those intentions, creolized its dancing listeners.

The first stage of minstrelsy's rehabilitation cited above—the attempt to construct a rigorous scholarly analysis of the idiom's impact on North American musical history—is exemplified by Nathan's magisterial taxonomy of its melodic repertoires.[1] The second stage is represented by another wave of scholars—Cockrell, Lott, Lhamon, Mahar, and Carlin—who extensively reevaluated fundamental presumptions about the music's semiotic meaning (Cockrell, Lott, and Lhamon) and, less extensively but with considerable acuity, diagrammed its textual and instrumental sound and sources (Mahar and Carlin).[2] Lott and Cockrell, in particular, identified the liminal spaces of transformation that minstrelsy's transgressive strategies created, and demonstrated the semiotic appeal of that liminality to the mechanics and apprentices who were its first theatrical audiences. On the stages of the blackface theaters, the early soloists Dixon and Rice, and Emmett and Sweeney, created an experiential space in which existing social pressures could be mitigated or oppositional social behaviors could be explored. Thus, in the Jacksonian period's squabbling, contentious reevaluations of race and class, blackface was a powerful tool for questioning existing power structures: Lott and Lhamon have shown this quite clearly.

This book provides a third stage in the reconsideration of blackface minstrelsy: to continue the recovery of its sound *as performed* (versus the sound implied or dictated by sheet music), to understand the impact of that sound on the dancing body, to demonstrate the bodily pleasure that participation in blackface dance made possible, and to understand the cultural transformations resulting from such participation. It has been possible, as well, to show the ubiquity of the necessary conditions and historical evidence for the creole synthesis across the Caribbean and the riverine and maritime United States, and thus to better account for minstrelsy's wide and immediate appeal. In this construction, blackface becomes, not a phenomenon "invented" and achieving quick popularity, seemingly by chance, in 1830s–40s New York City—not, in other words, the spontaneous beginning of something new—but rather a coalescing and commodification of idioms that were already familiar to audiences from the streets and wharves outside the theater doors. This helps to explain the idiom's nearly-instantaneous vogue with working-class audiences, and the speed at which it was adopted and disseminated as one of the first American pop music crazes.

This investigation locates the widely distributed idioms and geographical locations that preceded the blackface revolution; it demonstrates the routes by which these synthesizing idioms traveled and the locations wherein they were exchanged; it shows the presence of creole music and movement vocabularies in those situations, and it enhances our ability to see elements of such music and movement in contexts not formerly understood as creole. In addition, the book provides a methodological model for thinking about the role of history, geography, and demography in a music's evolution and dissemination, as well as for reconstructing a historical vernacular dance idiom using a combination of organology, iconography, and contextual analysis. Finally, the book explains not only what blackface was, but also where it came from; how it sounded, looked, and felt; why it became a remarkable, virtually worldwide popular music phenomenon; and, most fundamentally, what blackface meant, and means, in the history of American popular culture.

The book provides a model for reconstructing the sound, and thus the cognitive impact, of non-notated vernacular dance musics in North America. Situating the earliest roots of blackface in the historical collision of African and European movement and sound vocabularies, and in the ongoing attempts by each culture group to borrow from or otherwise appropriate the other's idioms, significantly shifts our picture of the "roots" of minstrelsy. This semiotic reevaluation concretizes the linkage not only between minstrelsy and European carnivalesque transgressive behaviors, but also parallel links between blackface and a wealth of creole festival performance behaviors found throughout the African Caribbean and the Eastern Seaboard of the United States. The book demonstrates that the conditions for the creole synthesis predate the Jacksonian period and were already in place by the period of the American Revolution.

Demographic and primary-source analysis of a wider geographic context and longer historical time span helps us see antebellum minstrelsy as one more cycle of cross-cultural contact, imitation, and synthesis: not the first and most definitely not the last such example in American musical history. The "creolization" of my title has been part of African and European interaction since the Age of Exploration; similar ethnohistorical studies of other zones of New World multicultural contact may be expected to reveal similar cases of creole exchange.

By the same token, framing the specific Northeast cultural contexts in which Micah Hawkins came of age and into which William Sidney Mount was born as part of wider patterns of creolization legitimates the use of Mount's artworks as case studies for analysis of those wider phenomena. We have situated the Hawkins-Mount biographical experience within a particular ethnocultural mélange that yielded Afro-Dutch Pinkster, Anglo-African 'Lection Day, the Lower East Side's Catherine Wharf, and the creole character types, linguistic dialects, and musical syntheses in Micah Hawkins's 1824–25 ballad opera *The Saw-Mill.* Such indirect evidence—notably iconography, prose fiction, and documentarian literary accounts—for the strong presence of Afro-Caribbean musical behaviors in the Northeast as well as in the South and the Caribbean further legitimates Mount's artistic biography as a source on the process of creolization within his own social and ethnohistorical contexts.

This wider contextualization likewise helps us recognize the historical insights available via technical analysis of key paintings and ancillary materials from Mount's artistic maturity between roughly 1830 and 1865. We have confirmed both the accuracy of his musicological reportage and that ethnochoreological analysis of those artworks reveals the creole synthesis operating in rural Long Island as well as urban Manhattan, in the bodies of white dancers as well as black musicians. Iconographic analysis of visual evidence, including details of clothing, physiognomy, instrument construction, playing technique, and dance vocabularies, makes it possible to recover the sound of the creole synthesis beyond the printed music. Archival materials, especially those that help us reconstruct the experience, intentions, and performance practice of the musicians Mount depicted, are likewise important here.

At the same time, analysis of the contemporaneous evidence of Mount's manuscripts and primary-source materials reveals the ways in which these tunes, if "realized" with an awareness of creole performance practice, might yield a sounding rhythmic-melodic idiom quite different than the surface details of notation otherwise suggest. Such analysis, which borrows from the reconstructive techniques associated with historical performance practice, provides a corrective to some prior scholarship's implicit presumption that the "sound" of blackface music in performance could be fully represented in the conventions of standard notation. It suggests instead that realization of blackface melodies within the frame of Afro-Caribbean rhythmic practices probably provides a much more nuanced picture. A central insight derived from such realization is that blackface melody's "polyrhythmic polysemic" characteristics in performance were a key factor in creating minstrelsy's experience of cross-cultural working-class *communitas*.

Chapter 6 applies the iconographic analysis techniques of chapter 4 and the melodic and rhythmic reconstructions of chapter 5 to close examination of several images of vernacular, Anglo-American, African American, and blackface dance; it suggests that the creole synthesis is expressed in the kinesthetic movement vocabularies depicted in the akimbo bodies of the dancers. We found "creolized" gestures, postures, and movement in images that both accept or reject racist caricature (e.g., Johnson's "Backside Albany" versus Clonney's "Stone Boat" dancers); or that depict these creole vocabularies in black or white bodies (Mount's numerous images of dancers of both ethnicities, versus those by Bingham or Beard, for example). Finally, most importantly, and most revolutionarily for our understanding of where blackface came from, and where it went, such analysis identifies Afro-Caribbean movement vocabularies in the bodies of dancers previously assumed to represent idealized Anglo-American rural archetypes. This key insight—that antebellum Anglo-Celtic bodies could move in Afro-Caribbean ways—confirms that the creole synthesis was far more widely disseminated, in much more diverse rural and urban populations, and in ways which those populations experienced both consciously (say, dancing on the stage of the Bowery Theatre) and less consciously (e.g., dancing to the tunes of a fiddler influenced by Afro-Caribbean rhythm). Through this lens, we see the creole synthesis reaching far beyond the theater stages and urban contexts conventionally understood to be blackface's original sites, and pervading North American music and movement far more extensively than previously understood.

The musical repertoires and professional biographies of the first blackface architects—George Washington Dixon, Thomas Dartmouth Rice, Joel Walker Sweeney, and Daniel Decatur Emmett—further confirm the particular confluences of geography, theatrical experience, riverine and maritime contexts, and black-white exchange and appropriation that gave birth to blackface theatrics. Cultural exchange in a wide variety of demographic, primary-source, and musical or archival data is mirrored in the musical repertoires, personal histories, and family records of the Mount and Hawkins clans on Long Island and the Lower East Side.

Mount was a uniquely situated and demonstrably precise visual reporter, but he is by no means the only period illustrator whose work is receptive to these analytical methods. Ancillary examinations have proven artworks by George Caleb Bingham, James Henry Beard, David Claypoole Johnston, and James Goodwyn Clonney to be rich sources for visual evidence of the creole synthesis. Close analysis of Mount's own papers has found parallel evidence for the creole synthesis in the biographies (real or imagined), tools, and repertoires of the musicians he knew, worked with, and depicted. Analysis of the polyrhythmic sound and participatory movement vocabularies of the creole synthesis in the bodies of Mount's, Beard's, and Bingham's dancers, as well as of the blackface architects and their audiences, points the way toward a reevaluation of analogous cultural exchange in other case studies from American popular music history.

Particularly useful topics for investigation that are relevant to understanding other periods of creole synthesis in American popular music include performance practices, especially movement and rhythmic improvisation; qualities of experience, especially bodily pleasure and dance *communitas*; and processes of exchange, especially the complex, contradictory simultaneity of imitation, appropriation, adaptation, and creative synthesis. While it is for other books and other authors to say, it seems quite likely that analogous imitations and adaptations of performance practice, qualities of bodily experience, and processes of boundary-crossing cultural exchange have played a central role in many American vernacular musics, and that recovery and analysis of these factors can enrich our musicological understanding of both those musics' histories and of the cultural contexts from which they emerged.

We have observed that the channels and contexts of working-class travel and exchange (in this period, riverine and maritime environments) yielded fluid, rich, and transformative cultural synthesis, between and across regions, ethnic or immigrant groups, and social classes. We have identified the opportunities and mechanisms that white, often Anglo-Celtic musicians exploited in a kind of imitative apprenticeship with admired or disparaged African American and Afro-Caribbean models, and the degree to which such "participant observation" was essential in the adoption of musical performance practices not available via notated transmission; we have further identified the degree to which this adoption or adaptation yielded new and different popular music evolutions. Finally, we have recognized the degree to which such borrowing, appropriation, and imitation, and the creole synthesis itself, involved musical influences traveling from and between ethnic and economic groups, and the degree to which the roots of blackface lie, not solely in Euro-American or African traditions (or racist imitations thereof), but rather, like African American culture itself, in the collision, conflation, and endless creativity of the creole synthesis in the New World.

This book addresses a lacuna in the historical analysis and reinterprets that omission—specifically as regards the extent, chronology, and complexity of black-white exchange in American musical history. This exchange was older, more polyvalent, more extensive, more influential on, and far more integral to, American popular culture than some previous scholarship has believed: the creole synthesis, from the early colonial period, has been an ongoing process by which black and white, immigrant and "native," marginal and mainstream, working-class and bourgeois peoples have struggled to make sense of a contested American identity. It has helped shape our national, musical, and cultural sense of self: the creole synthesis in part defines who we have been. We are Americans precisely because of the messy, conflicted character and emergent, never-ending nature of this synthesis.

Of course U.S. popular culture is not solely the product of encounters between Anglo-Celtic and African American music-and-dance expression; of course, every immigrant and indigenous community has added to the gumbo of our expressive arts. But, just as the life, music, and works of William Sidney Mount provide an unusually clear and detailed snapshot of the particular moment and processes through which colliding cultural groups created one new expressive art-form, so the riverine and maritime, geographic, demographic, ethnic, and musical roots of blackface minstrelsy provide an unusually early, clear, and detailed example of the processes of cross-cultural encounter, collision, and piebald synthesis by which American popular culture has always been and is still defined. Minstrelsy—like ragtime, blues, jazz, R&B, hip-hop, polka, soul, gospel, Norteno, Tejano, Appalachian, country, go-go, house, rock 'n' roll, funk, and so many more American popular music idioms—could *only* have happened here, on this continent, as a direct, intimate result of our complicated, contested, painful, extraordinary colonial history. It is through these musics—and their imitation, appropriation, contamination, exchange, dissemination, and sheer human vitality; their vision of "what a fantastic monument to all the best instincts of the human race" this country *could be*—that Americans have imagined and invented who we are.[3]

And what we hope and aspire to become.

Appendix

Blackface Scholarship

GENERAL COMMENTS: OBSERVATION, APPROPRIATION, AND SYNTHESIS

The scholarly literature informing the present study occupies several overlapping areas of investigation, both within and beyond that of musicology. The modern "rehabilitation" of blackface minstrelsy as a topic for serious scholarly investigation dates roughly from Hans Nathan's 1962 *Dan Emmett and the Rise of Early Negro Minstrelsy*.[1] Since that publication—which still forms a cornerstone of the repertoire's musicological analysis—subsequent texts by Dale Cockrell, Eric Lott, William Mahar, and W. T. Lhamon Jr., among others, have deepened our understanding of minstrelsy's theatrical, semiotic, economic, and sociological implications.[2] This book takes a crucial next step by arguing that, for all the noxious racist stereotypes that blackface no doubt manifested—and that recent scholarship has successfully nuanced and complicated—the blackface minstrels not only were opportunist appropriators but were also engaged in a kind of quasi-ethnographic "participant observation."[3] At least as far back as Charles Dibdin (1745–1814) in his 1768 ballad opera *The Padlock*, and probably since first African immigration to the New World, close observation and imitation of expressive arts, crossing the color line or lines in both directions, had been prototypical components in the creole synthesis.

Unquestionably the minstrels' activities involved racism, exploitation, appropriation, and opportunism.[4] Yet despite these tendencies, which in some scholarly eras have delegitimized minstrelsy as a topic for research, the African American sources' creativity and the Anglo-Celtic imitators' close observation, and their willingness to blur certain racial boundaries, made possible the first American popular-music craze. The racial bias and economic exploitation inherent in the blackface innovators' conduct need not—any more than in other epochs of popular music and indeed of ethnographic scholarship itself—blind us to the potential insights available in their observational data.[5]

The following texts, which represent all eras of blackface scholarship, have played a significant role in developing the thesis of this book. In the discussion, the assignment of various texts as representative of certain categories of scholarship should not be taken as limiting those texts' relevance only to those single categories.

PRIMARY SOURCES

The fundamental primary sources in any study focusing on Mount as a reporter on minstrelsy's creole synthesis are his own artworks, ephemera, and physical heirlooms, the vast majority of which are held in the archive and collection of the Long Island Museum of American Art, History, and Carriages, in Mount's birthplace of Setauket, New York.[6] The museum collection includes both material objects (Mount's flutes, tin whistles, self-designed violin and music-stand prototypes—even his kazoo and tuning fork); thousands of letters (of interest especially for the correspondence between himself and his musical colleagues, including brother Robert Nelson Mount, an itinerant dancing master); diaries and other autobiographical material; a vast collection of printed and manuscript music both collected by Mount and inherited from his uncle Micah Hawkins; hundreds of pages of pencil sketches and watercolors; and over three fourths of his total catalog of oil paintings. Additional primary source materials are held by the New-York Historical Society on Central Park, the New York Historical Association in Cooperstown, and, in small numbers, at various museums elsewhere in the United States.[7] This book is heavily dependent on extensive investigation in these archives, and is particularly indebted to the assistance of the staff, historians, archivists, and friends of the Long Island Museum of American Art, History, and Carriages.

Other types of primary-source documents also make essential contributions. Although the illustrated newspapers cited widely by Cockrell, Lhamon, and Lott are an important resource for understanding minstrelsy in the 1830s and '40s, their reportage on earlier multiethnic contacts and music in New York is relatively indirect—and their print runs largely postdate the street roots of minstrelsy.[8] On the other hand, the *Market Book*, a set of antebellum reminiscences by Lower East Side butcher Thomas De Voe, is frequently cited, in part because of its relatively unique character—few contemporaneous sources match it.[9] Analogous primary material is also available in the reminiscences of period actors and singers: for example, most of the information available on the preminstrelsy theatrical career of "Jump Jim Crow" originator Thomas Dartmouth Rice (1808–1860) comes from the autobiography of his first employer, the Albany-born impresario Noah Ludlow (1795–1886).[10] Ludlow's prolix memoirs are a useful primary resource on the experience of early nineteenth century touring theatrical troupes and the degrees to which their members' practical combination of comic, acrobatic, and dance abilities shaped the skill sets of the early blackface performers. Ludlow's narrative also confirms the practical importance and the creative centrality of marginal, liminal, maritime, riverine, and frontier spaces, recounting tales of Rice's exploits in Montgomery, Mobile, Louisville, Cincinnati, Philadelphia, and only eventually in New York City. At the same time, an important corrective to the picture derived from Ludlow is a reconstruction of the early musical history of Long Island, whose maritime trade made it as much of a cultural crossroads and creolizing space as were those other locales.[11]

MUSICOLOGICAL SCHOLARSHIP

Modern scholarship on nineteenth-century blackface minstrelsy rests on a relatively small corpus of highly influential works, only a few of which are primarily musicological in perspective and analytical methodology. In *Dan Emmett and the Rise of Early Negro Minstrelsy*, still in many ways the most detailed technical study of the blackface repertoire, Nathan brings to his investigation strengths in both archival and analytical areas, and a remarkable command of minstrelsy's melodic materials. Nathan, like William J. Mahar, is also valuable in helping us understand the theatrical forerunners of blackface—the eighteenth-century touring theatrical idioms that both provided training for the first generation of blackface minstrels and prepared audiences for minstrelsy's creole synthesis as it moved from the street to the stage in the 1820s.[12] Later studies have built on Nathan and added a focus on contextual studies of the idiom's meaning, utilizing critical approaches taken especially from theater history, folklore, semiotics, and American studies.

Dale Cockrell's 1997 *Demons of Disorder: Early Blackface Minstrels and Their World* is the most effective musicological investigation of blackface since Nathan and compensates for some limitations in that earlier text. Cockrell constructs an incisive, readable, and effective study of the links between nineteenth-century minstrelsy's masking and riotous character and the earlier European traditions of *charivari*, carnivale, and "rough music."[13] He approaches primary sources (newspapers, imagery, and musical specifics) with a combined analytical and interpretive approach, informed by musical analysis and cultural history, which strongly influences this book.

Grounding his work in "economics, politics, status, and music," Cockrell argues for the validity of a "thick-description" cultural-anthropological approach, arguing that "anecdotal evidence," because it reflects historical attitudes, can be "a form of social myth . . . at least as powerful [and thus revealing] as fact."[14] He quotes Prague School literary critics, Bakhtin principal among them, to link blackface in the masking and liminal disruption of minstrelsy to European traditions of carnival and charivari that had continued in the New World as, for example, Pinkster (in Upstate New York), mumming (in Pennsylvania), and John Canoe (in the Tidewater South).[15] And he extends this culture-studies approach into the realm of the musicological, linking specific songs and dance on the minstrel stage—most notably the archetypal "Jump Jim Crow"—to folkloric sources.

Cockrell's *Demons of Disorder* thus yields useful perspectives and practical evidence for debunking the simplistic presumption that blackface was merely an incompetent northern white caricature of southern black folkways; instead, he situates blackface in the history of transgressive, boundary-crossing festival as public or social protest. He confirms the degree to which blackface in the years *prior* to the 1843 launch of the Virginia Minstrels—that is, in the same "early" period that forms a central topic of this book—existed in a complex cultural environment, full of collisions between wildly divergent performance idioms and sociopolitical trends. In Cockrell's interpretation, blackface may thus be seen as a staging of carnivalesque liminality and Jacksonian social-political mobility, and a dramatization of conflicts between period definitions of public versus private space and working- versus middle-class values.

Cockrell makes another important contribution to the present study—if only in passing—when he suggests that one way to undercut simplistic accusations about "racism" in minstrelsy is simply "to imagine a performance of a minstrel show . . . [and thus] to envision something else" than "mere" parody.[16] He recognizes that the 1840s context was a specific and idiosyncratic space for performance and reception, and that modern scholarship that ignores contextual and historical considerations is liable to error. Cockrell's sensitivity to minstrelsy's contexts of performance, and the sounds that resulted, provide an important justification for analysis of performance practice as one part of the present study.

However, Cockrell's ability to reconnect blackface with the European branch of its roots (e.g., through the Upstate New York celebration called *Pfingster* or Pinkster) means of necessity that he places less emphasis on the original African American informants; it also indicates the possibility of an expressive exchange that went both ways.[17] As a result, *Demons of Disorder* is comparatively devoid of attention to Afro-Caribbean performance aesthetics.[18] Cockrell is masterful at recognizing the role of liminality, dichotomy, boundaries, borders, and "in-between" places in minstrelsy's core appeal. But a text-focused approach tends to deemphasize the idiom's central appeal via performance and participation, and it does not focally address the ubiquity of the creole synthesis across a wide range of riverine and maritime geographic contexts.[19]

Cockrell does a particularly effective job of locating behavioral archetypes in the careers of three antebellum performers. He situates the song and character of "Jump Jim Crow"—the ragged, slow-talking, tongue-twisting dancer and leaper whose character traits recur in Topsy of *Uncle Tom's Cabin* and Alfalfa of the *Our Gang* movie serial—in the life, career, and artistic choices of Thomas Dartmouth "Daddy" Rice.[20] He finds "Zip Coon"—the flash-dressing, fast-talking, foppish dandy or pimp who emerges again in archetypal African American trickster characters as diverse as Staggerlee and Snoop Dogg—in the singer, actor, dancer, publisher, and social outlaw George Washington Dixon (1801?–1861). Third and latest in Cockrell's semiotic lineage of blackface archetypes is the song and character "Old Dan Tucker"—the tall-tale-telling, giant-brag-spouting frontiersman—who Cockrell locates in the prototypical urban ethnomusicology of banjo virtuoso and blackface troupe leader Joel Walker Sweeney (1810–1860).[21] Cockrell's strategy is borrowed in W. T. Lhamon Jr.'s later *Raising Cain* (1998), which articulates cultural tropes as "lore cycles" and identifies the dance steps of *Dancing for Eels, 1820 Catharine Market* in the buck-and-wing steps of Bill "Bojangles" Robinson (1878–1949) and MC Hammer's videotaped autobiography (ca. 1982).[22]

Cockrell also describes the gradual codification and co-optation of blackface in the 1840s and '50s: the way that, in the symbolic contestation of public space and appropriation of public idioms by working- versus middle-class forces, the expanding bourgeois was essentially victorious. He links this semiotic victory to a gradual standardization and codification in notation of what in earlier minstrelsy had been an improvisational performance practice. Such objectification—part of a larger pattern of expanding middle-class markets also revealed by the nineteenth-century explosion in sheet music publishing—confirms blackface's cross-class shift in this period. As minstrel songs entered the respectable middle-class parlor, the musical and improvisational elements—particularly those having to do with polyrhythms and the moving body—that had made those songs' performances transgressive were carefully pruned away.

Robert Carlin's *The Birth of the Banjo: Joel Walker Sweeney and Early Minstrelsy* is that rare example of a musicological analysis enriched by a practitioner's perspective. The fruit of decades of work on Sweeney and the banjo, Carlin's book confirms that, by dint of background, geographical origin, and aptitudes, Sweeney was, like Dixon, Rice, and Emmett, a "prototypical ethnomusicologist."[23] He learned the banjo directly from black informants, and, like them, had extensive experience in cosmopolitan, multiethnic, boundary communities (the Ohio River Valley, Tidewater Virginia, and South Carolina) in which to experience the roots of the creole synthesis. His emphasis on performance practice, dance iconography, contemporaneous musical vernaculars, "player's knowledge," and sociocultural context provides important perspectives for this book.

In the edited volume *Inside the Minstrel Mask* and in his own *Behind the Burnt Cork Mask*, William J. Mahar provides pilot studies whose methodological approaches and detailed analysis are also models for this book. His "'Backside Albany' and Early Blackface Minstrelsy: A Contextual Study of America's First Blackface Song" is relevant here because of its recognition of the importance of reception in understanding the intentions and specificity of minstrelsy, and because of his insistence upon analyzing primary texts not only for their symbolic intent but also for their actual performative content.[24] Like many blackface scholars, Mahar is indebted to the primary-source recollections contained in De Voe's *Market Book*, but he also provides an important corrective to some earlier scholarship through his recovery of African American spoken and musical dialects as a source illuminating performance practice.[25]

Dena J. Epstein's *Sinful Tunes and Spirituals: Black Folk Music to the Civil War* is a standard reference work, based in primary source study (newspapers, plantation records, printers' bills, street literature), on African American musical contributions prior to 1861, and it remains useful because of its detail and comprehensiveness.[26] Epstein provides particularly useful information on pre-1800 African American music makers in the slave South, but also includes northerners, dancers, and banjo players, and thus directly informs the present study.

Robert Winans's essay, "Early Minstrel Show Music 1843–1852," with its topical focus on banjo history and performance practice, like Carlin's Sweeney book brings the perspective of a player to the analysis of performance practice.[27] He makes good observations about the centrality of musical sound—not just texts—to minstrelsy, and provides useful evidence on instruments and instrumental technique. His concrete tabulations from minstrel show programs reveal stylistic and topical shifts in song topics and types in two periods (1843–47 and 1848–52) during which minstrelsy was gradually codified, these in turn confirming the changing patterns of marketing and consumption already remarked by Cockrell. Winans also links to Cockrell's and Lott's analyses of minstrelsy as transgressive burlesque, and to the postbellum period's "blacks in blackface" and later African American dance idioms.[28]

RECEPTION STUDIES

In contrast to the literature on minstrelsy's musical components and antebellum black-white interaction, the vast majority of scholarship focusing specifically on the life and work of W. S. Mount is art-historical in nature. Mount is widely recognized as one of the first great American vernacular painters, and an artist whose biography, subjects, and symbolic language are useful sources on the expressive and political culture of his time. In contrast, very few studies address musical themes in Mount's works; art history's perspectives on Mount the musician, mostly dating to the mid-1970s, are exemplified by Alfred Frankenstein's statement that "William Sidney Mount is not a milestone in American musical creativity."[29] It is unsurprising that art historians might miss the significance of the musical evidence, and it is true that Mount's talents as an artist evidently outweighed his talents as a musician. Nevertheless, it is surprising that so rich a source of period musical data should not have been the focus of extended musicological monographs.[30]

Most blackface scholarship, like most art-historical commentary, recognizes that minstrelsy's public display implicated complex motives, allusions, subtexts, and issues of cultural power. But to presume that such display was only focused on outward-directed symbolic motives and meanings, as does much of the musicological scholarship, or to analyze paintings of performance only for such meanings, as does most art-history scholarship on Mount, is to ignore the physical, participatory pleasure of that performance. Symbolic analysis of this sort fails to recognize the *inward*-directed, "centripetal" rewards and appeal of that participation, which I argue are a fundamental source of its immediate and resilient popularity.[31]

Participation was a fundamental part of Afro-Caribbean and African American performance, powerfully attractive as a focus not only of observation but also imitation, and, precisely, as a result of this attraction, powerfully subversive. As Cockrell, Lhamon, and Lott show, middle-class derogation of working-class and minority art forms was an implicitly political response to the liminality and threat to order that these art forms represented. Blackface minstrelsy was (accurately) perceived as threatening to dominant-culture mores and strictures: because early minstrelsy was a participatory, transgressive, illicit, body-integrative, sexual idiom, originating at the margins but powerfully attractive across boundaries of race and class. The factors that made the experience of minstrelsy both transgressive and attractive—the actual performance practice and rhythmic results depicted in Mount's and related artworks, and the communal, participatory experience engendered by that performance practice—are central topics of this book.

Satire and mockery were integral to European carnival, but blackface imitation à la "Zip Coon" and the later cakewalk was equally influenced by Afro-Caribbean and African American models. The early blackface practitioners, who I have suggested may usefully be regarded as practitioners of participant observation, would have internalized the African American traditions of caricature as surely as they did elements of movement and music.[32] Art history of the antebellum period locates the internal contradictions in middle-class elitist attitudes about minstrelsy but has sometimes failed to recognize the single most significant factor subverting that elitism: the powerful and seductive attraction of the performance itself. Not only working-class but also bourgeois audiences were intrigued by minstrelsy: hearing it, seeing it, singing the songs, learning the dances.

Antebellum cultural arbiters denigrated minstrelsy's working-class performance because its attraction had to be delegitimized. This is why composers, conductors, critics, and political leaders denied a vernacular music's aesthetic quality and asserted its immorality, why they claimed that bodily pleasure was unacceptable, why a canon of "great" (e.g., middle-class-legitimated) works, intended for contemplation and not participation, was created in the first place. In the face of the demonstrable, pleasurable bodily and participatory experience of African American performance, those who profited through the maintenance of hierarchized aesthetic categories had to find rationales for dismissing blackface.

Some more localized sources, less widely known or employed, provide useful bits of information, particularly about Mount's experience, biography, and subjects. For example, the exhibit catalog *William Sidney Mount: Works in the Collection of the Museums at Stony Brook*, prepared by the then-curator at the museum holding the vast majority of Mount materials, provides a useful synthesis of art-historical and biographical-contextual perspectives.[33] Several of its analyses, of works both focal (*Dance of the Haymakers*, *The Banjo Player*) and peripheral (*The Sportsman's Last Visit*) to the present study, can be argued to support a crucial claim: that Mount's earlier urban experience on the multiethnic Lower East Side continued to inform (and appear in) his paintings during the later, post-1830 middle-class and rural period of his life. I have argued that the "creole synthesis" was witnessed by Mount; that it appears (sometimes explicitly, but also implicitly, and quite widely) in his paintings; and finally, that those paintings can be "read" for the musicological information they provide regarding minstrelsy's earliest improvisational and participatory creole roots. The catalog's synthesis of art criticism and local biography provides effective evidence in support of these arguments.

SEMIOTICS AND CULTURE STUDIES SCHOLARSHIP

Some of the most influential and far-reaching recent scholarship, that which has gone the farthest to "rehabilitate" blackface as a legitimate topic for research, has occurred in the field of semiotics and culture studies. Prior to these works, which commenced with Lott's *Love and Theft* (1993), most scholarship on minstrelsy predated the 1970s, and took the analytical and comparative approach of Nathan's 1962 *Dan Emmett and the Rise of Early Negro Minstrelsy*. The William Mahar–edited *Inside the Minstrel Mask* (1996) presents a useful summary of 1990s scholars' approaches to the topic. It is a concise and diverse collection of contemporary scholarship on blackface minstrelsy, and the most influential authors—Lott, Lhamon, Mahar, Cockrell, Nathan, and Robert Carlin—are all represented. W. T. Lhamon Jr.'s "Every Time I Wheel About I Jump Jim Crow: Cycles of Minstrel Transgression from Cool White to Vanilla Ice," is a good summary of Lhamon's perspectives and methodology as worked out in more expansive form in his *Raising Cain* and *Jump Jim Crow*. As a literary scholar, he is able to link manifestations of minstrelsy, its "structural indeterminacy and improvisation," and its creole synthesis, to contemporaneous street culture, to Melville, Twain, and later performance idioms, including the entire history of "white mimicry of the black carnivalesque." Lhamon argues that the actual sound of blackface, and its relation to Afro-Caribbean sources, is unknowable, saying "we can debate how much or little minstrels were trying to copy black culture until the cows come home." But with the right analytical tools—and the right sources, W. S. Mount being exemplary—we can confirm the complexity, the vitality, and the specific musical content of the blackface synthesis.[34]

Also in *Inside the Minstrel Mask*, Barbara Lewis's "Daddy Blues: The Evolution of the Dark Dandy" provides useful information regarding the African American theatrical roots for minstrelsy in New York City, and the interplay between minstrelsy and other forms of traveling and vernacular theater.[35] Like Lhamon's, Lewis's is a literary critical and culture studies analysis, in this case of the caricature of the black "dandy," which originates as a racist parody of African American pretenses toward upward economic mobility, in the song "Zip Coon." Her information about New York's African Grove Theater, founded in 1821 by the Caribbean-born William Henry Brown, which staged all-black performances of Shakespeare in competition with white houses in the 1820s, provides valuable documentation of the underreported agency of African Americans in the antebellum New York City theater world.

Marian Winter's article "Juba and American Minstrelsy" from 1947 on the 1830s African American character dancer William Henry Lane ("Master Juba") (ca. 1825–ca. 1852/53) remains the analysis that most effectively recognizes the role of the body and of improvisation in the blackface synthesis.[36] She provides an essential perspective on the actual history of African experience in North America, and, presaging later scholars, she identifies in West African idioms the roots of the participatory song-and-dance worship form called the ring shout. At the same time, she articulates the crucial recognition that, by the nineteenth century, African source idioms had *already* been synthesized into a pan–African American dance consciousness.[37] Winter identifies the African roots of the dance and body percussion called Juba (*giouba*) and the presence of both black and white renditions of Caribbean dance in eighteenth-century theatres, and situates Master Juba as both the inheritor and the transmitter of a specifically African American improvisational performance synthesis. Finally, she notes the sparse visual evidence and the challenges—but significance—inherent in using these sources as iconography. Winter's analysis is a crucial foundation and inspiration for this book's identification of Afro-Caribbean elements in Mount's dance paintings.

William Mahar's "Ethiopian Skits and Sketches: Contents and Contexts of Blackface Minstrelsy, 1840–1890" in many ways presents *Inside the Minstrel Mask*'s most sophisticated integration of musicological and culture-studies approaches. Mahar clearly articulates the "troublesome" racial implications that have made some scholars reluctant to address the idiom's role in U.S. popular music, and the importance of "the application of interdisciplinary methods and interpretive strategies [in order] to understand the content and context." He describes a range of analytical methods *and* of source materials that facilitate better cultural and historical understanding, but in practice largely limits himself to considerations of late (post-1840) minstrelsy as theatrical text.[38] His analysis of the race and class semiotics of early American theatre is a useful, more scholarly complement to Lhamon's more impressionistic treatment.

Eileen Southern brings a matchless command of primary sources to the question of minstrelsy. Her *Inside the Minstrel Mask* essay provides important commentary on the contribution of African American source musicians to early minstrelsy: John Picayune Butler, the marvelously monickered "Old Corn Meal" and "Pot Pie" Herbert, and William Henry "Juba" Lane, as well as their white imitators: Bob Farrell, Joe Blackburn, John Diamond, and of course Dixon and Rice. Southern recognizes the relationship between African American street sources and whites-in-blackface stage transformations but does not address the processes of exchange that connected them. Southern's trademark bibliographic research usefully unearths a long and detailed essay by J. K. Kennard in the *Knickerbocker* magazine, ethnographic descriptions of performances in the slave South that are strongly reminiscent of Anglo-Celtic mumming, and good commentary on the interplay between northern white minstrel songs and southern black folkloric sources.[39]

Several of these blackface initiators, like Mount, grew up in lower Manhattan and might well have been among the crowds of boys and young men who watched the street dancers during the day and formed the crowds in the theaters at night. To subsume, as Southern does, this year-after-year and day-after-day contact and cultural exchange under the simplistic description "listening and impersonating" distorts the to-and-fro nature of the exchange.[40] To the contrary, this book argues that the massive popular response to Dixon and Rice when they first danced on the stages of Lower Manhattan theatres resulted from the excitement working-class audiences felt at seeing their street culture (what Lhamon calls "the first Atlantic Street culture") on the quasi-legitimate stage for the first time.[41]

Eric Lott's 1993 *Love and Theft: Blackface Minstrelsy and the American Working Class* inaugurated a fundamental shift in studies of minstrelsy, drawing as it did on semiotics, cultural anthropology, and post-Marxist critique (notably Adorno, Gramsci, and Bourdieu) to show how minstrelsy embodied and enabled a white, male, working-class response to economic and psychosexual realities in the Jacksonian United States. Lott reaches well beyond the traditional arenas of music history but primarily occupies himself with blackface's symbolic meanings rather than its participatory experience. He does identify the transgressive and liminal capacities of minstrelsy's ritualized performance as the source of its appeal across ethnic boundaries in an era of sociopolitical contestation and transformation, and provides an "analysis of cultural forms, [and] the various sorts of textuality and subjectivity."[42]

Lott's study is, with Guralnick's *Sweet Soul Music: Rhythm and Blues and the Southern Dream of Freedom*, possibly the best, most insightful, and most useful articulation of the complexities of black-white racial borrowing throughout U.S. popular music history, and in its understanding of the layers of attraction-repulsion that drove white responses to black expressive culture.[43] Lott identifies the multisemiotic communities and performance idioms that "intersected" in the world of early minstrelsy, provides an effective link between Cockrell's location of minstrelsy within the heritage of European carnival and the scholarly literature on folklore and festival, and shows that minstrelsy—like later black-white syntheses—embodied complex signifiers of sex, gender, and class. He also provides particularly effective evidence that early minstrelsy was more directly observed and more accurately replicated than has previously been presumed, but he is not equipped to analyze sound, dance, or improvised performance.[44]

Lott's *Love and Theft* was a watershed work in rehabilitating scholarly approaches to minstrelsy, paralleling Cockrell's insights about blackface's European carnivalesque social and critical lineage, and bringing perspectives from literary, semiotic and gender studies analysis. Such perspectives permit Lott to identify in minstrelsy semiotic dichotomies that lie deep in the U.S. cultural psyche: insider/outsider, black/white, male/female, obedience/transgression, and so on. Lott's "Blackface and Blackness: The Minstrel Show in American Culture" provides a useful summary of that larger argument.[45] Lott's key points are that minstrelsy was powerfully attractive at least in part because it provided a "mask" that let working-class whites position themselves as socially superior to the poorest blacks and thus seek upward mobility, but also mock the middle class they were seeking to join, as well as create the performed semblance of defiance. However, as with *Love and Theft*, in this essay Lott does not address the participatory bodily experience of African American performance. His Prague School–informed, Gramscian analysis is thus effective for unpacking semiotic layers in the reception of blackface but continues to treat its audience's enjoyment as contemplative, rather than participatory.

Robert G. Allen's *Horrible Prettiness: Burlesque and American Culture*, which predates and would seem to have influenced Eric Lott's *Love and Theft*, is a fascinating, well-informed semiotic analysis of the social, class, and gender implications of theatrical burlesque, a slightly later idiom but one whose marginalization, gender play, and transgressive liminality exhibit useful parallels with minstrelsy's symbolic and political meaning. Allen himself makes these explicit:

> The link between burlesque and minstrelsy is considerably stronger than that suggested by [their] formal similarities. Both forms worked upon principles of transgression and inversion. Both were constructed around ironic, low-other characters, whose speech, costume, behavior, and demeanor helped to structure different but homologous ideological problematics: gender and race, respectively. As low-other constructions, both the bur-

> lesque performer and the blackface minstrel were subject to simultaneous contrary interpretations by their audiences.[46]

Allen's study enriches Mahar's, illuminating the linear progression from the earliest U.S. touring theatrical idioms (notably, English ballad opera) through circuses, minstrelsy, and Italian opera, into the postbellum idioms of burlesque and vaudeville. His analysis of burlesque's webs of signification, which implicated sex, gender, morality, and social power, presages Lott's on minstrelsy, and he has a marvelous turn of phrase about the exchange of vernacular art forms.[47] In addition, Allen's insights regarding the influence of eighteenth-century masking and carnival (especially the northeastern African American festival called Pinkster) and of nineteenth-century festival, street, and mob actions, directly illuminate minstrelsy's creole social roots. And his clearly articulated analysis, based in Foucault and Bakhtin, of the "pleasure principle" and bodily anxiety that participatory theatrical performances enabled—the degree to which idioms like blackface and burlesque elicited physical and kinesthetic responses—is central to the present study.

William J. Mahar's *Behind the Burnt Cork Mask: Early Blackface Minstrelsy and Antebellum American Popular Culture* is one of the standard contemporary texts on minstrelsy and represents solid and detailed musicological scholarship.[48] Mahar deals primarily with the antebellum minstrel troupes, and less with the soloists Rice and Dixon (and their inspirations) who preceded them. Mahar's demonstration of the parodic light-classical sources of many minstrel texts and theatrical entertainments, and consequently of minstrelsy's shared roots in European music-theatrical idioms already extant circa 1800, thus parallels Cockrell's situation of blackface's shared roots in European carnival.

W. T. Lhamon Jr.'s *Raising Cain: Blackface Performance from Jim Crow to Hip Hop* is the most far-reaching, if idiosyncratic, exploration of minstrelsy since Lott's *Love and Theft*, and Lhamon's background in literary criticism and culture studies equips him well to address its semiotic implications. His key intuition is that there are aspects of African American performance aesthetics (garb, body vocabularies especially dance, and terminology especially as regards expressive taste) that have been remarkably consistent and resilient—forming what Lhamon calls elsewhere lore cycles—through all the epochs of African American culture.[49] The clarity and readability of Lhamon's prose, his obvious engagement with and love for the repertoires, and his command of the earliest primary sources make his linking of minstrelsy, vaudeville, "coon" shows, film, and MTV video immediate and compelling.

But *Raising Cain* is best understood as a Derridean deconstruction of minstrelsy: one individual's avowedly personal and idiosyncratic reading of the idiom's semiotic connotations.

Lhamon's particularly valuable contribution is to recognize topographical, geographic, linguistic, ethnic, bodily, choreographic, and cognitive boundary zones as providing liminal spaces in which identity, class, and social power could be contested and negotiated through ritualized performance—and to recognize that, in all the epochs of American popular musics, African American performance has been a vehicle for such renegotiation. Like Lott, he offers a sophisticated reading of minstrelsy's meaning to its audience, and identifies blackface as a tool white working-class youths deployed to simultaneously distance themselves from those immediately below them on the economic ladder, aspire to higher status, and critique that higher status. His semiotic analysis of minstrelsy's sound and physical vocabulary, its transgressive connotations, and its recurrence throughout U.S. popular music history, is poetic and persuasive but does not address the performance experience that ignited the blackface audience. He does, however, provide an argument through which blackface minstrels can be claimed as the first urban ethnomusicologists.[50] Lhamon's contribution to this book is epitomized in the following quotation, in which he identifies the improvisational, participatory practice that he intuitively recognizes: "Assembling Jim Crow . . . was hardly a sudden or whimsical event. Figuring out Jim Crow was a process, a practice, evolving for years over considerable territory."[51]

Lhamon's 2003 *Jump Jim Crow: Lost Plays, Lyrics, and Street Prose of the First Atlantic Popular Culture* provides a massive compilation of dozens of playscripts and hundreds of song texts; it may be thought of as the companion to his *Raising Cain*. Most useful for the present study is the lengthy introduction in *Jump Jim Crow*, which provides an effective and relatively succinct summary of Lhamon's perspectives. His fundamental thesis, and his argument for minstrelsy's continued relevance to U.S. cultural studies, is that the Jim Crow plays exemplify working-class resistance.[52] His detailed biographical sketch of T. D. Rice, for example, emphasizes Rice's earlier experience on the U.S. frontiers playing stock comic and ethnic characters and links to Cockrell's discussion of the early minstrels' transgressive lineage.[53]

Lhamon provides a nuanced analysis of black identity in the New World as a construction synthesizing pan-Afro-Caribbean elements.[54] Applying this sort of analysis to Mount's media—considering the factual immediacy of his experience of black-white musical interaction in both rural and urban contexts, and considering musicological analysis of his visual observation—

permits a new contribution to the literature on minstrelsy. These works reveal the breadth, range, and reach of African American approaches into a range of white cultural situations and provide a way of looking at black infiltration into white culture that is simultaneously musically accurate but that is not limited to verbal description or standard musical notation.

John Strasbaugh's *Black Like You: Blackface, Whiteface, Insult and Imitation in American Popular Culture*, like Tosches's *Country*, its spiritual forefather, is a collection of informal essays written for a nonspecialist audience.[55] Strasbaugh articulates the argument made more rigorously by Cockrell, Lott, Lhamon, and Mahar: that blackface masking, throughout all the epochs of U.S. history, as in its earlier European Renaissance and medieval manifestations, cannot be simply understood as pure racist caricature. Strasbaugh is useful in delineating the recurrence of the "blackface impulse" toward masking and ethnic parody that has effectively blurred class, race, and power boundaries in all periods of American popular culture, and his insight that "imitation plays a large role in how American culture is formed" is astute.[56] He also provide a concise and effective summary of blackface's long twilight retention in nooks and crannies of U.S. popular culture (fraternities, social organizations, festivals) and a long and effective exegesis of blackface elements in later fictional creations such as Uncle Tom, Topsy, and Uncle Remus.[57]

PERFORMANCE SCHOLARSHIP

Gerald Jonas's *Dancing: The Pleasure, Power, and Art of Movement* represents a small body of scholarly literature that is particularly significant here because of its detailed, consistent, and methodical performance analysis of *dance* and its semiotic meanings.[58] Jonas is especially useful for his clear articulations of the ways that the visual iconography of dance can reveal aspects of cultural synthesis and experimental identity: he comments directly on such synthesis in minstrelsy's historical melding of African American and Anglo-Celtic dances, making a particularly elegant analogy between West African aesthetics of "cool" and the Renaissance European *sprezzatura*.[59] He is also particularly effective at tying innovations and new fashions in dance style to contemporaneous cultural, social, and political trends—thus providing a particularly important analytical perspective for this book.

Some of the most directly relevant scholarship on the dance elements of minstrelsy's popularity comes from African—rather than U.S.—music specialists. For example, William P. Murphy significantly enriches and grounds insights about blackface's transgressive elements when he describes African dance as "a visible and invisible dialectic of power," pointing out that, in Mende society, "both an intricate dance step and an extraordinary political performance . . . evoke the wonder of a secret source of transformative power generating astonishing public effects."[60] Similarly, like Murphy's, Judith Lynne Hanna's insights, as an anthropologist specializing in African dance, are particularly useful.[61]

Marian Hannah Winter's "American Theatrical Dancing from 1750–1800" (1938) is an important forerunner to her 1947 essay on the Long Island–born African American dancer William Henry "Juba" Lane, and it exhibits the unique strengths that still make that later article an important foundation for a study of blackface performance.[62] Winter's close survey of primary sources confirms the exchange between various forms of Continental, Caribbean, Anglo-Celtic, and African American "characteristic dance" in the colonial United States—a stylistic exchange whose detailed analysis has largely eluded later scholarship. She points out that not only African American but also Anglo-Irish dancing were regularly imitated as part of urban theatrical entertainments—that *imitation* of these characteristic dances was central to vernacular theater long before minstrelsy began. Winter's essay becomes another confirmation that an imitative creole exchange was already occurring on the streets and in the working-class theatrical idioms of the new nation, long before the Virginia Minstrels in the early 1840s. This is an important foundation for the present study because it broaches the possibility of a much earlier and more widespread choreological component to the blackface synthesis than later scholarship identifies.

Henry T. Sampson's *Blacks in Blackface: A Source Book on Early Black Musical Shows* provides a needed corrective to the neglect of the African presence in early minstrelsy.[63] In a compendium of primary sources similar to Epstein's, Winter's, and Southern's, Sampson gives detailed biographical information on a number of significant African American musicians of the pre–Civil War period. However, due to the nature of his sources (playbills, unpublished autobiographical recollections, newspapers, and other public documents), and his emphasis on shows rather than on soloists, Sampson is uninformative regarding the earliest 1820s–30s performers from whom Dixon and Rice appear to have derived their repertoire and performance practice.

Thomas F. DeFrantz's edited volume, *Dancing Many Drums: Excavations in African American Dance*, includes a few items relevant to the current study. In his own essay, DeFrantz provides a good summary of terminological shifts in dance scholarship and the ways they reflect on development of black studies and related disciplines since the 1960s.[64] P. Sterling Stuckey's "Christian

Conversion and the Challenge of Dance" provides a thoughtful discussion of the implications of the "African body" as it has been appropriated, imitated, depicted, and distorted in U.S. popular culture, and of the "body knowledge" that dance inculcates but that has been resistant to traditional functionalist or text-based analysis.[65] Samuel A. Floyd Jr.'s "African American Dance and Music" is primarily a summary of African American scholarship (including his own) on dance, but he does make the insightful observation that "patting juba" is best described as dance, rather than as merely accompaniment to dance.[66] This insight is important in considering the subtler African musical details in Mount's dance iconography.

Lynne Faulkey Emery's *Black Dance in the United States from 1619 to 1970* complements Epstein and Malone by providing a useful and detailed summary of early references to African American dance in popular literature. The rich material she supplies includes, for example, Nicholas Cresswell's 1774 descriptions of banjo playing, singing and dancing in colonial Maryland; the observations of Dutch burghers traveling to see Negro dances in Pennsylvania and New York State, and of the seminal black dancers of Long Island, Albany, and Manhattan's theaters and Catherine Market.[67] Emery's expertise in dance idioms in turn permits interesting and relevant deductions regarding the early choreographic synthesis of African American and Anglo-Celtic dancing and thus provides useful tools for the present study.

Michael D. Harris in *Colored Pictures: Race and Visual Representation* explores ways in which musicology that seeks to relate cultural context to musical content must draw on analytical techniques, terminology, or methodologies from outside the realm of traditional musical analysis; his is thus an important philosophical rationale for this book.[68] He points out that because there is already a sophisticated and effective analytical method for looking at the "iconography of the black body" in American popular culture, there is no need for us to invent an idiosyncratic, less-sophisticated repetition of it.

Taken as a whole, the existing scholarship on minstrelsy provides essential foundations in methodology, analytical perspectives, and interpretive techniques, but crucial lacunae exist. These lacunae lie specifically in the areas of improvisation; performance practice; the Afro-Caribbean as opposed to European performance traditions that were simultaneously minstrelsy's central sources and most powerful attractors for a white audience; iconography; and the actual sound and participatory experience of the idiom as *performance*. This book addresses those gaps.

Notes

Chapter 1. Recovering the Creole Synthesis

1. Dixon's birthdate is contested, but Cockrell has it as 1801; see Dale Cockrell, *Demons of Disorder: Blackface Minstrels and Their World* (Cambridge: Cambridge University Press, 1997), 96 n9.

2. Cockrell, *Demons of Disorder*; Eric Lott, *Love and Theft: Blackface Minstrelsy and the American Working Class* (Oxford: Oxford University Press, 1993); William Mahar, *Behind the Burnt Cork Mask: Early Blackface Minstrelsy and Antebellum American Popular Culture* (Urbana: University of Illinois Press, 1998); W. T. Lhamon Jr., *Raising Cain: Blackface Performance from Jim Crow to Hip Hop* (Cambridge, Mass.: Harvard University Press, 2000). For an extended discussion of blackface scholarship, seen the appendix.

3. Edward P. Buffet, "William Sidney Mount: A Biography. The Story of Old Time Life in Brookhaven North Told Through His Pictures, as published by Mr. Buffet in the Port Jefferson Times from December 1, 1912, to June 12, 1924," typescript in the collection of the Long Island Museum of American Art, History, and Carriages, 93, emphasis added. Buffet also transcribes a good first-person description of Mount sketching cider making from life (57).

4. Buffet, "William Sidney Mount," 157.

5. Ibid., 167 and 168.

6. See Kevin M. Scott, "Rituals of Race: Mount, Melville, and antebellum America," PhD diss., Purdue University, 2004, for examples of this sort of analysis.

7. Reproduced in Lhamon, *Raising Cain*, 23.

8. See Scott, "Rituals of Race"; also Alfred Frankenstein, *Painter of Rural America: William Sidney Mount, 1807–1868* (Washington: H. K. Press, 1968); also Karen M. Adams, "The Black Image in the Paintings of William Sidney Mount," *American Art Journal* 7/2 (November 1975): 42–59; Frederick C. Moffatt, "Barnburning and Hunkerism: William Sidney Mount's *Power of Music*," *Winterthur Portfolio* 29/1 (spring 1994): 19–42; Lucretia H. Giese, "James Goodwyn Clonney (1812–1867): American Genre Painter," *American Art Journal* 11/4 (October 1979): 4–31.

9. Mount's name does appear once in the index of Cockrell's *Demons of Disorder* and once in that of Lhamon's *Raising Cain*.

10. As Cook says, "Our sensitivity to the inequities of power should not prevent us from acknowledging that this was . . . a dynamic cultural space shaped by a wide range of historical agents." James Cook, "Dancing Across the Color Line," *Common-Place* 4/1 (October 2003): 2.

11. But see the notable exception, discussed in chapter 4, of Robert Carlin, *The Birth of the Banjo: Joel Walker Sweeney and Early Minstrelsy* (New York: McFarland, 2007).

12. For a technical definition of liminality, and some of its first applications in the analysis of cultural performance, see Victor Turner, *The Ritual Process: Structure and Anti-Structure* (Ithaca, N.Y.: Cornell University Press, 1969), 128.

13. See Cockrell, *Demons of Disorder*, 31–36; also Robert Allen, *Horrible Prettiness: Burlesque and American Culture* (Chapel Hill: University of North Carolina Press, 1991), 33; also Shane White, "Pinkster: Afro-Dutch Syncretization in New York City and the Hudson Valley," *Journal of American Folklore* 102/403 (January–March 1989): 70.

14. Shane White, "'It Was a Proud Day': African Americans, Festivals, and Parades in the North, 1741–1834," *Journal of American History* 81/1 (June 1994): 19, 21.

15. For "signifyin,'" see Henry Louis Gates Jr., *The Signifying Monkey: A Theory of African American Literary Criticism* (New York, 1988); for the original locution "double consciousness"—the requirement that oppressed populations adopt multiple personae and experiential perspectives in order to survive exploitative situations—see W. E. B. DuBois, *The Souls of Black Folk* (New York: Forgotten Books, 1965), 4. For modern applications to the topic of this book, see Paul Gilroy, *The Black Atlantic: Modernity and Double Consciousness* (London: Verso, 1993), 126.

16. An invaluable resource in productively complicating the nature of black-white exchange is Roger D. Abrahams's seminal *Singing the Master: The Emergence of African American Culture in the Plantation South* (New York: Penguin, 1994), which examines a context—the slave-era South—in which the imbalance of power was still greater, but in which cultural exchange likewise flowed in both directions.

17. On the various evidence in current scholarship, see Paul F. Wells, "Fiddling as an Avenue of Black-White Musical Interchange," *Black Music Research Journal* 23/1–2 (spring–autumn 2003): 135–47; Chris Goertzen, "Fiddle Tunes and the Historic-Geographic Method," *Ethnomusicology* 29/3 (autumn 1985): 448–73; Chris Goertzen and Alan Jabbour, "George P. Knauff's Virginia Reels and Fiddling in the Antebellum South," *American Music* 5/2 (summer 1987): 121–44.

18. Victor Turner, *The Ritual Process: Structure and Antistructure* (London: Routledge and Kegan Paul, 1969); Victor Turner, *From Ritual to Theatre: The Human Seriousness of Play* (New York: Performing Arts Journals Publications, 1982); Clifford Geertz, *The Interpretation of Cultures* (New York: Basic Books, 1973); Erving Goffman, *The Presentation of Self in Everyday Life* (New York: Anchor, 1959); Barbara Babcock, "'A Tolerated Margin of Mess': The Trickster and His Tales Reconsidered," *Journal of the Folklore Institute* 11/3 (175): 147–86; Katharine Young and Barbara Babcock, eds., "Bodylore," special issue, *Journal of American Folklore* 107 (1994); Dell Hymes, "The Anthropology of Communication," in *Human Communication Theory*, ed. Frank E. X. Dance, 1–39 (New York: Holt, Rinehart, and Winston); Richard Bauman, *Story, Performance, and Event* (Cambridge: Cambridge University Press, 1986);

Henry Glassie, *Passing the Time in Ballymenone* (Bloomington: Indiana University Press, 1995); Richard Schechner, "Audience Participation," *Drama Review: TDR* 15/3 (summer 1971): 72–89; Jan Mukarovksy, *Structure, Sign and Function: Selected Essays by Jan Mukarovsky* (New Haven, Conn.: Yale, 1978).

19. See Jacqui Malone, *Steppin' on the Blues: The Visible Rhythms of African American Dance* (Urbana: University of Illinois Press, 1996); Marshall Stearns and Jean Stearns, *Jazz Dance: The Story of American Vernacular Dance* (New York: Da Capo, 1994); Robert Farris Thompson, "An Aesthetic of the Cool," *African Arts* 7/1 (autumn 1973): 40–43, 64–67, 89–91; Sule Greg Wilson, communication with the author, September 20, 2007; Christopher J. Smith, "I Can Show It to You Better Than I Can Explain It to You: Cuing in African American Improvisational Music," PhD diss., Indiana University, 2000.

20. Here see, for example, Sule Greg Wilson's work on the body languages implicit in the music and iconography of Thomas Dartmouth Rice's "Jump Jim Crow." Wilson, communication with the author.

21. See Karen E. Bond and Susan W. Stinson, "'I Feel Like I'm Going to Take Off!': Young People's Experiences of the Superordinary in Dance," *Dance Research Journal* 32/2 (winter 2000–2001): 53.

22. Cockrell, *Demons of Disorder*; Mahar, *Behind the Blackface Mask*; Hans Nathan, *Dan Emmett and the Rise of Early Negro Minstrelsy* (Norman: University of Oklahoma Press, 1977).

23. See Charles Keil, "Participatory Discrepancies and the Power of Music," *Cultural Anthropology* 2/3 (August, 1987): 277–78.

24. Lott, *Love and Theft*, 1996.

25. Michael Broyles, *Music of the Highest Class: Elitism and Populism in antebellum Boston* (New Haven, Conn.: Yale University Press, 1992).

26. Lhamon, *Raising Cain*, 1–55.

27. *Banjo Player (in the Barn)*, ca. 1855, oil on canvas, Detroit Institute of Arts.

28. Lhamon, *Raising Cain*, 141.

29. Scott, "Rituals of Race," 66.

30. Though there are loose pages, which juxtapose Anglo-Celtic and African American tunes, carefully interleaved within the handwritten manuscript. They are cut from printed tune books like those of Elias Howe, and they confirm the currency of both Anglo-Celtic and prototypical minstrel tunes in Long Island dance repertoires. Kate Strong Historical Library, Hawkins-Mount Family Papers, LIM, William Sidney Mount (Printed) Sheet Music box 2, catalog KSA031572, KSA031573, and KSA031574.

31. Pestcoe quotes a *Pinkster Ode*, published in Albany in 1803, which opens: "Now hark! the Banjo, rub a dub, / Like a washer-woman's tub; / And hear the drum, 'tis rolling now, / Row de dow, row de dow,. / The pipe and tabor, flute and fife, / Shall wake the dullest soul to life." Solomon Pestcoe, "Banjo History: Challenging The Myths," http://www.myspace.com/uncleshlomo/blog/292085161, accessed September 2007.

32. See Buffet, "William Sidney Mount," for Jones (71) and for Mathewson (181). The iconic portrait of a black fiddler playing for white dancing is in 1830's *Rustic Dance after a Sleigh Ride*, discussed in chapters 3 and 6.

33. A number of factors account for the presumption that minstrelsy was a New York–based phenomenon: on the impact of urbanization on dance, see Judith Lynne Hanna, "Movements Toward Understanding Humans through the Anthropological Study of Dance," *Current Anthropology* 20/2 (June 1979): 313–39; and Patricia Cline Cohen, with Timothy J. Gilfoyle and Helen Lefkowitz Horowitz, *The Flash Press: Sporting Male Weeklies in 1840s New York* (Chicago: University of Chicago Press, 2008), 54, on the New York press. As we see in chapter 6, the urban environment may have accelerated the process of dance synthesis and dissemination; see Judith Lynne Hanna, chapter 8, "The Urban Ecosystem of Dance," in *To Dance Is Human: A Theory of Nonverbal Communication* (Austin: University of Texas Press, 1979), 199–229.

34. See the anonymous (but attributed to Hawkins) printed handbill "'Big Red Nose, and How to Bleach It' . . . where a classic brawl is enacted between the bullying Big Red Nose and his agile little tormentor Pat, 'Hibernia's Son.'" Quoted in Buffet, "William Sidney Mount," 20.

35. A comprehensive survey of previous scholarship is contained in the appendix.

36. The paradox is neatly captured, for example, in the title of Lott's *Love and Theft: Blackface Minstrelsy and the American Working Class.*

37. See John Smith Kendall, *The Golden Age of New Orleans Theater* (Baton Rouge: Louisiana University Press, 1952), 130; quoted in Mark McKnight, "Charivaris, Cowbellions, and Sheet Iron Bands: Nineteenth-Century Rough Music in New Orleans," *American Music* 23/4 (winter 2005): 416. See also Henry A. Kmen, "Old Corn Meal: A Forgotten Urban Negro Folksinger," *Journal of American Folklore* 75/295 (January–March 1962): 29–34. On Rawley, see Lhamon, *Raising Cain*, 4.

38. Charles Dickens, *American Notes for General Circulation* (New York: Penguin, 2001): 48–49. For the flash press perspective on Dickens's visit to Almack's, see Cook, "Dancing Across the Color Line."

39. Washington Irving, *Salmagundi and Voyages and Discoveries of the Companions of Columbus*, vol. 5 of *The Works of Washington Irving* (New York: Co-operative Publication Society, n.d.), quoted in Nathan, *Dan Emmett and the Rise of Negro Minstrelsy*, (Norman: University of Oklahoma Press, 1962), 72.

40. Note the "Grand Trial Dance Between Nance Holmes and Suse Bryant" from *Whip and Satirist of New-York and Brooklyn*, June 24, 1842 (Cockrell gives this as from *The Libertine*). Cohen, *Flash Press*, 217.

41. The term *thick description* originates with cultural anthropology, and recognizes that social events—including performance—implicate multiple simultaneous communicative channels; hence, analysis needs to account for and describe such events' "thick" experiential textures. The canonic source is Clifford Geertz, "Thick Description: Toward an Interpretative Theory of Culture," in *The Interpretation of Cultures* (New York: Basic Books, 1973).

42. Cockrell, *Demons of Disorder*, 84, emphasis added.

43. Cockrell, *Demons of Disorder*, 156.

44. Ibid., 158ff.

45. Dena J. Epstein, *Sinful Tunes and Spirituals: Black Folk Music to the Civil War* (Urbana: University of Illinois Press, 1977, rev. ed. 2003), 347.

46. Catherine A. Shoup, "Scottish Social Dancing and the Formation of Community," in "Communities of Practice: Traditional Music and Dance," special issue, *Western Folklore* 60/2–3 (spring–summer 2001), 140.

47. Pete Daniel, *Lost Revolutions: The South in the 1950s* (Chapel Hill: University of North Carolina Press, 2000).

48. William Mahar, "Ethiopian Skits and Sketches: Contents and Contexts of Blackface Minstrelsy, 1840–1890," in *Inside the Minstrel Mask: Readings in Nineteenth-Century Blackface minstrelsy*, ed. Annemarie Bean, James V. Hatch, and Brooks McNamara, 179–222 (Hanover, N.H.: Wesleyan University Press, 1996), 179.

49. Southern overstates and oversimplifies, for example, when she says, "It is common knowledge that the white entertainers obtained their materials from blacks by listening to the songs and impersonating them," Eileen Southern, "Black Musicians and Early Ethiopian Minstrelsy," in *Inside the Minstrel Mask*, 43. Of course this is true, but the statement is incomplete: blackface performers did more than only "impersonate" (though this term itself has complex connotations, more effectively analyzed by Lott and Lhamon); if this were true, then blackface imitations of African American performance should have been accurate replications, a presumption that Southern's scholarship vehemently denies.

50. Lhamon, *Raising Cain*, 6.

51. The archival material is discussed in chapter 2. See also, for example, Elizabeth Kahn Kaplan, with Robert W. Kenny, and Roger Wunderlich, eds., *William Sidney Mount: Family, Friends, and Ideas, Essays by Members of William Sidney Mount Project* (Setauket, N.Y.: Three Village Historical Society, n.d.).

52. Benjamin Quarles, *The Negro in the American Revolution* (Chapel Hill: University of North Carolina Press, 1996). Epstein cites the presence of African American musicians in militia regiments, in both the South and the North, as early as 1725 (*Sinful Tunes and Spirituals*, 119ff).

53. See Robert A. Selig, "The Revolution's Black Soldiers," http://www.americanrevolution.org/blk.html, accessed October 27, 2012.

54. Nicolas A. Butler, archivist to the city of Charleston, August 22, 2007. Communication with the author.

55. Judith Lynne Hanna, "African Dance: The Continuity of Change," *Yearbook of the International Folk Music Council* 5 (1973): 171, emphasis added.

56. See, for example, Jacqui Malone, "Ethnic Historical Study," in *Dance History Research: Perspectives from Related Arts and Disciplines, The Proceedings of the Second Conference on Research in Dance* (New York: Congress on Research in Dance, 1979), 86–97.

57. Ralph Ellison, *Going for the Territory* (New York: Random House, 1986), 139–41; quoted in Malone, "Ethnic Historical Study," 2.

58. Malone says, "To many western and central Africans, flexed joints represented life and energy, while straightened hips, elbows, and knees epitomized rigidity and death." "Ethnic Historical Study," 11–12. See here also Berndt Ostendorf, "Celebration or Pathology? Commodity or Art? The Dilemma of African American Expressive Culture," *Black Music Research Journal* 20/2 (autumn 2000): 217–36.

Chapter 2. The Creole Synthesis in the New World

1. Bolster specifically articulates the ability of black sailors to cross "cultural and geographic boundaries." See W. Geoffrey Bolster, *Black Jacks: African American Seamen in the Age of Sail* (Cambridge, Mass.: Harvard University Press, 1998), 35. We may cite here also Michael J. Jarvis, "Maritime Masters and Seafaring Slaves in Bermuda, 1680–1783," in "Slaveries in the Atlantic World," special issue, *William and Mary Quarterly* 3rd series 59/3 (July 2002): 585–622, and Murphy on African dance as creator of liminal spaces: "The act of gathering itself adds intensity to social life. Gathering . . . for a meeting transforms that space into a dangerous arena of hidden mystical forces, both helpful and harmful." William P. Murphy, "The Sublime Dance of Mende Politics: An African Aesthetic of Charismatic Power," *American Ethnologist* 25/4 (November 1988): 572.

2. For example, Noah Ludlow, Thomas Rice's first theatrical employer, by the early 1840s had been involved in multiple theatrical ventures throughout the South, including Mobile's Royal Street Theater in 1843.

3. See Judith Lynne Hanna, chapter 8, "The Urban Ecosystem of Dance," in *To Dance Is Human: A Theory of Nonverbal Communication* (Austin: University of Texas Press, 1979), 199–229; and Murphy, "Sublime Dance of Mende Politics," "Practice in the theoretical framework of an aesthetic of the sublime is necessarily makeshift and purposively crafted, a form of artistry consciously shaped and adapted to the uncertainties and indeterminacies of the social world" (65).

4. Lott describes the observation and imitation of East River waterfront public performance by the early blackface practitioners as "fieldwork," an apt and apposite use of ethnomusicological terminology. Eric Lott, *Love and Theft: Blackface Minstrelsy and the American Working Class* (Oxford: Oxford University Press, 1996), 94. This imitation is also characteristic of the young-white reaction to later African American idioms; it is attested in the history of other black music styles, from ragtime through hip-hop, and also by the more contemporaneous evidence of the audience for the flash press. "Some of the pleasure was vicarious. Even a shy fellow who stayed in his boardinghouse could imagine himself as a blade making a sophisticated entry into a brothel parlor. *The printed pages allowed him to partake of, even create, a fantasized identity as a sporting man.*" Patricia Cohen, with Timothy J. Gilfoyle and Helen Lefkowitz Horowitz, *The Flash Press: Sporting Male Weeklies in 1840s New York* (Chicago: University of Chicago Press, 2008), 91, emphasis added. For Joel Walker Sweeney as "prototypical ethnomusicologist," see Robert Carlin, *The Birth of the Banjo: Joel Walker Sweeney and Early Minstrelsy* (New York: McFarland, 2007), 19.

5. For a detailed chronology on "Mungo" and other blackface characters in earlier English-language theatrical settings, see Dale Cockrell, *Demons of Disorder: Blackface Minstrels and Their World* (Cambridge: Cambridge University Press, 1997), 13–20.

6. See, for example, Ben Jonson, *The Masque of Blackness* (1605; printed 1608); Jonson, *The Irish Masque at Court* (1613; printed 1616); "Caliban" in William Shakespeare, *The Tempest* (1610–11); Henry Purcell, *The Indian Queen* (1695).

7. T. Allston Brown's 1874 account describes Pot Pie Herbert as "an actor of the West" singing "Back Side of Albany Stands Lake Champlain." T. Allston Brown, quoted in Charles Day, "Black Musicians and Early Ethiopian Minstrelsy," *Black Perspective in Music* 3/1 (spring 1975): 174. See also Dewberry, quoting an 1860 account that suggests that James Hewlett "anticipated" Mathews or that the latter got his soliloquies from attending African Grove; his description of a Grove performance of *Hamlet* is quoted in Jonathan Dewberry, "The African Grove Theatre and Company," in "Black Theatre Issue," special issue, *Black American Literature Forum* 16/4 (winter 1982): 131. Charles Mathews's memoir, *Mr. Mathews at Home* (London, 1824), is reprinted in Herbert Marshall and Mildred Stock, *Ira Aldridge: The Negro Tragedian* (London: Camelot Press, 1958), 40–41. See also Laura V. Blanchard, "The African Company Presents *Richard III*: A Play by Carlyle Brown," Richard III Society, http://www.r3.org/onstage/africa.html, accessed October 24, 2011.

8. Though it is beyond the reach of this book, this shift—to the imitation of urban, creole, and frontier folkways—may explain the relatively *late* date at which the banjo began to be played by whites in the North: though it was known among black populations in the North, it appears only to have begun to be played by Joe Sweeney and Dan Emmett and other blackface practitioners who learned the instrument from southern blacks.

9. Expertise in the African American expressive arts has often been a marker of cultural expertise and/or "insider" status. This tends further to support the idea of the blackface architects as prototypical "ethnomusicologists." See Hazzard-Gordon, who suggests that dance vocabularies can literally convey aspects of cultural identity and its constructed or intentional reinvention: "Certain neuromuscular patterns that attest to the cultural participation of the performer, verifying in motion the cultural identity and integrity of the dancer." Katrina Hazzard-Gordon, "African American Vernacular Dance: Core Culture and Meaning Operatives," in "African and African American Dance, Music, and Theatre," special issue, *Journal of Black Studies* 15/4 (June 1985): 432.

10. Roger D. Abrahams, *Singing the Master: The Emergence of African American Culture in the Plantation South* (New York: Penguin, 1994), 152, 157.

11. Howard L. Sacks, "From the Barn to the Bowery and Back Again: Musical Routes in Rural Ohio, 1800–1929," Phillips Barry Lecture, *Journal of American Folklore* 116/461 (summer 2003): 325; emphasis added. H. Sacks describes, for example, working-class white neighbors in Mount Vernon, Ohio, "asking for" Snowden family songs and for fiddle lessons.

12. Alexander Saxton, "Blackface Minstrelsy and Jacksonian Ideology," *American Quarterly* 27/1 (March 1975): 4. On Ludlow and Pinkster, see Cockrell, *Demons of Disorder*, 36, and Noah M. Ludlow, *Dramatic Life as I Found It: A Record of Personal Experience* . . . (New York: Benjamin Blom, 1966; orig. St. Louis: Ludlow, 1880), 62ff. For Cowell, and the Louisville origins of "Jump Jim Crow," see Ludlow, *Dramatic Life as I Found It*, 63–64. On "Jump Jim Crow" as disreputable, see Ludlow, *Dramatic Life as I Found It*, 67–68.

13. Cockrell, *Demons of Disorder*, 36.

14. W. T. Lhamon Jr., *Jump Jim Crow: Lost Plays, Lyrics, and Street Prose of the First Atlantic Popular Culture* (Cambridge, Mass.: Harvard University Press, 2003), 32.

15. Cockrell, *Demons of Disorder*, has Rice adding "Jump Jim Crow" to his characterization of Mungo in frontier performances of Dibdin's *The Padlock* (77–78); Ludlow, *Dramatic Life as I Found It* cites "his great fidelity in imitating the broad and prominent peculiarities of other persons, as was evident in his close delineations of the corn-field negro, drawn from real life" (327).

16. See John Strasbough, *Black Like You: Blackness, Whiteness, Insult and Imitation in American Popular Culture* (New York: Tarcher, 2006), describing T. D. Rice in 1828 hearing G. W. Dixon at the Bowery Theatre performing "Coal Black Rose" (73–74).

17. Hans Nathan, *Dan Emmett and the Rise of Early Negro Minstrelsy, 2nd ed.* (Norman: University of Oklahoma: 1977), 58–59.

18. Members of the multigenerational musical family the Snowdens, whose parents were born into slavery in Maryland, had emigrated to Knox County by 1827–28; H. Sacks and J. Sacks surmise that they had brought banjo and fiddle repertoire from "the Maryland slave culture that Thomas and Ellen had experienced in childhood," in the vicinity of St. Mary's River, which was precisely the same region in which Nicholas Cresswell (1774) had described the first banjo music (Howard L. Sacks and Judith R. Sacks, "Way Up North in Dixie: Black-White Musical Interaction in Knox County, Ohio," *American Music* 6/4 (winter 1988): 410. Emmett's "jig notebook" likewise contains tunes from the white fiddler Seeley Simpkins, and perhaps indirectly from the Snowden family; H. Sacks also posits "a field trip by a young Dan Emmett, possibly in 1834, when he returned home from the military," specifically for the purpose of collecting tunes from the Snowdens. Sacks, "From the Barn to the Bowery and Back Again," 320–21.

19. Ludlow, *Dramatic Life as I Found It*, 63.

20. Carlin, *Birth of the Banjo*, 19.

21. Ibid., 19. Chapter 4 confirms an early northern presence for the banjo among African Americans, but Carlin is correct that its use by white minstrels there appears to have been precipitated by the Virginian Sweeney's virtuoso performances in New York during the late '30s.

22. H. Sacks says he "formalized this musical vocabulary for a nationwide audience in his *Standard Drummer*, the manual adopted by the U.S. Army." H. Sacks, "From the Barn to the Bowery and Back Again," 317.

23. Oscar Reiss, *Blacks in Colonial America* (Jefferson, N.C.: McFarland, 1997), 125.

24. See Lhamon's comments on the significance of frontiers in the "revolutionary subtexts" of nineteenth-century arts: "The world of brotherhood and freedom can take place only in the oceanic friction . . . or on the river . . . in the woods . . . qualifiedly in the slave quarters . . ., or in the drugged imaginary." W. T. Lhamon Jr., *Raising Cain: Blackface Performance from Jim Crow to Hip Hop* (Cambridge, Mass.: Harvard University Press, 2000), 86. Perhaps the most eloquent and evocative example of the frontier = freedom trope in nineteenth century literature is the "light out for the territories" passage at the end of Twain's *Huckleberry Finn*: "and so there ain't nothing more to write about, and I am rotten glad of it, because if I'd a knowed what a trouble it was to make a book I wouldn't a tackled it, and ain't a-going to no more. But I reckon I got to light out for the Territory ahead of the rest, because Aunt Sally she's going to adopt me and sivilize me, and I can't stand it. I been there before." Mark Twain, *Huckleberry Finn* (New York: Harper & Brothers, 1896), 388.

25. This explanation would likewise link the popular response to minstrelsy with later white appropriations of cross-cultural musical syntheses: the riotous responses to the late-1950s "rock 'n' roll" films such as *Rock Around the Clock* and *The Girl Can't Help It*, the furor over the content and presentation of hip-hop stars in 1980s music television, and so on. *Rock Around the Clock*, directed by Fred F. Sears (1956; Sony Pictures Home Entertainment, 2007), DVD; *The Jayne Mansfield Collection (The Girl Can't Help It/The Sheriff of Fractured Jaw/Will Success Spoil Rock Hunter?)*, directed by Frank Tashlin (1956; 20th Century Fox, 2006), DVD. Mason describes this as the shift from a "social" to an "artful" performance frame; Jeffrey D. Mason, "Street Fairs: Social Space, Social Performance," in "Enacting America(n)s," special issue, *Theatre Journal* 48/3 (October 1996): 303–5.

26. Saxton likewise claims that the "life-style expressed in minstrelsy . . . had developed in middle Atlantic cities, moved west with the Erie Canal and urbanization of the Mississippi and its tributaries, and west again with the acquisition of California." Alexander Saxton, "Blackface Minstrelsy and Jacksonian Ideology," *American Quarterly* 27/1 (March 1975): 12–13.

27. Bolster, *Black Jacks*, 9 and 13. For Berlin's terminology, see "From Creole to African: Atlantic Creoles and the Origins of African American Society in Mainland North America," *William and Mary Quarterly* 53/2 (April 1996): 251–88.

28. Bolster, *Black Jacks*, 17–21. In an interview, Bolster specifically cites the presence of black sailors in all segments of the sugar trade: "men who cross-pollinated a variety of communities around the rim of the Atlantic, in an age when most black people were illiterate . . . moving between the West Indian islands, the Carolina low country, urban seaports like New York and Philadelphia, [and] metropolitan capitals like London." William Bolster, interview, 1997, SeacoastNH.com, http://www.seacoastnh.com/Black_History/Black_History_of_the_Seacoast/Black_Jacks/ accessed March 27, 2011. Jarvis, likewise, identifies eighteenth-century parallels throughout the Black Atlantic maritime experience, describing Bermuda runaways who escaped to South Carolina and Georgia, and trade between the Caribbean islands and the mainland colonies, including New England and "the coastal, riverine,

and intrabay fishing and transport boats of the Chesapeake and Lowcountry coast." Jarvis, "Maritime Masters and Seafaring Slaves in Bermuda, 1680–1783," 616–17.

29. Jarvis, "Maritime Masters and Seafaring Slaves in Bermuda, 1680–1783," 617.

30. W. Jeffrey Bolster, "'To Feel Like a Man': Black Seamen in the Northern States, 1800–1860," *Journal of American History* 76/4 (March 1990): 1174. We may note also the interesting story of Captain Paul Cuffe[e] (1759–1817); born Cuttyhunk, Massachusetts, who married a Wampanoag woman, made his fortune in Atlantic shipping, and became a leader in the Africa repatriation movement. James Sidbury, *Becoming African in America: Race and Nation in the Early Black Atlantic* (Oxford: Oxford University Press, 2007), 145–55.

31. Bolster, "'To Feel Like a Man,'" 1179, 1186–87.

32. Ibid., 1188, 1173.

33. See Peter H. Wood, *Strange New Land: Africans in Colonial America* (Oxford: Oxford University Press, 1996/2003), along with Bolster, "'To Feel Like a Man,'" on "creolization" in language, clothing, hairstyle, housing/gardening, and worship.

34. Wood, *Strange New Land*, 65–66, emphasis added.

35. Bolster, "'To Feel Like a Man,'" 1187.

36. Bolster, *Black Jacks*, 119. DjeDje describes analogous African-derived fighting techniques in the creole culture of Jamaica's Accompong Maroons; see Jacqueline Cogdell DjeDje, "Remembering Kojo: History, Music, and Gender in the January Sixth Celebration of the Jamaican Accompong Maroons," *Black Music Research Journal* 18/1–2 (spring–autumn 1998): 71.

37. Robert Carlin makes the apt observation that the likeliest point of musical transmission in tidewater Virginia, for example, would have been precisely between servants of contrasting ethnicities brought together by their masters' relocation and relocations. Carlin, *Birth of the Banjo*, 5.

38. Washington Irving, *Salmagundi and Voyages and Discoveries of the Companions of Columbus*, vol. 5 of *The Works of Washington Irving* (New York: Co-operative Publication Society, n.d.), quoted in Nathan, *Dan Emmett and the Rise of Early Negro Minstrelsy*, 72. "Hoe corn and dig potatoes" was specifically associated with dances imitating harvest movements; see Tracy C. Davis, "Christy's Minstrels (1857–61)," in *The Broadview Anthology Nineteenth-Century British Performance* (London: Broadview Press, 2011), 275. The reference also appears in the text of the early blackface standard "Sich a Gittin Up Stairs." Davis, "Christy's Minstrels (1857–61)," 274, n50.

39. For Ichabod as an African-influenced dancer, see Chadwick Hansen, "Jenny's Toe Revisited: White Responses to Afro-American Shaking Dances," *American Music* 5/1 (spring 1987): 9. On Newport, Rhode Island's 1,300-member African American population in 1755, see Melvin Wade, "'Shining in Borrowed Plumage': Affirmation of Community in the Black Coronation Festivals of New England (c. 1750–c. 1850)," *Western Folklore* 40/3 (July 1981): 211.

40. See Marilyn E. Weigold, "The American Mediterranean: An Environmental, Economic and Social History of Long Island Sound" (Port Washington, N.Y., and

London: Kennikat Press, 1974), 71. This is partly due to the fact that the slave trade was a major part of the Rhode Island economy. Reiss, *Blacks in Colonial America*, 75. Reiss also observes that aspects of the slave trade linked Upstate New York, the Atlantic coastal cities, and Manhattan, describing "large landowners" in the Hudson Valley using a "plantation economy similar to that in Narrragansett, Rhode Island" (83).

41. Lhamon, *Jump Jim Crow*, 43.

42. Marian Hannah Winter, *Juba and American Minstrelsy* (New York: Dance Index–Ballet Caravan, 1947), 224.

43. Berndt Ostendorf, "Celebration or Pathology? Commodity or Art? The Dilemma of African-American Expressive Culture," in "European Perspectives on Black Music," special issue, *Black Music Research Journal* 20/2 (autumn 2000): 221.

44. On the presence of both banjos and balafon in pre-Revolutionary America, see Wood, *Strange New Land*, 64–65.

45. Nicholas Cresswell, *The Journal of Nicholas Cresswell, 1774–1777*, quoted in Lynne Faulkey Emery, *Black Dance in the United States from 1619 to 1970* (Palo Alto, Calif.: National Press Books, 1972), 140.

46. Wade, "'Shining in Borrowed Plumage,'" 223.

47. John F. Szwed and Morton Marks, "The Afro-American Transformation of European Set Dances and Dance Suites," *Dance Research Journal* 20/1 (summer 1988): 30–31. English country dances such as the lancers were adopted both in Ireland (often in garrison towns) and in various Caribbean creole cultures: Jamaica, Antilles, Haiti, and Barbados.

48. See Thomas Ashe, *Travels in America performed in 1806* (London, 1808), 100, quoted in Nathan, *Dan Emmett and the Rise of Early Negro Minstrelsy*, 156 n33. See also Caroline Gilman, *Recollections of a Southern Matron* (New York, 1838), 76, quoted in Nathan, *Dan Emmett and the Rise of Early Negro Minstrelsy*, 156 n34.

49. Though it dates from a slightly later period, contemporaneous with Mount's maturity, the account of Solomon Northrup, a free man of color and fiddler kidnapped in Washington in 1841, contains several extended descriptions of his musical duties on Louisiana cotton plantations in the '40s; see Solomon Northrup, *Twelve Years a Slave, the Narrative of Solomon Northup, a citizen of New-York, kidnapped in Washington city in 1841, and rescued in 1853, from a cotton plantation near the Red River in Louisiana* (Buffalo, N.Y.: Derby, Orton and Mulligan, 1853), 216; at http://books.google.com/, accessed December 27, 2011.

50. On owners advertising the services of slave musicians, see Wood, *Strange New Land*, 64.

51. "Among most of these very different people . . . there began to appear during the 18th century one identifiable African American culture." Wood, *Strange New Land*, 59–60. See also Wood, chapter 6, "Building a Culture," 59–72; he calls music "one crucial starting point" for building a stable culture; "certainly no element was more central, or illustrates the process more clearly," (62).

52. Mary Chesnut quoted in Abrahams, *Singing the Master*, 137.

53. Ibid., 137. See also Nicholas Cresswell's report, from mid-1770s Virginia, cited previously, when "[a] couple gets up and begins to dance a jig (to some Negro tune)." Creswell, cited in Abrahams, *Singing the Master*, 138.

54. For archetypal examples, see Timothy Fields's 1829 account of the historical origins of a keelboatman: "Mike Fink, The Last of the Boatmen, And Sketches of Trappers among the Rocky Mountains," *Western Monthly Review* 3/2/ (July 1829): 15–19, at http://xroads.virginia.edu/~HYPER/DETOC/sw/fink6.html, accessed March 27, 2011. See also William Leggett, *The Critic: A Weekly Review of Literature, Fine Arts, and Drama* 1:167, at http://bit.ly/fudhxy, accessed March 27, 2011.

55. Nathan, *Dan Emmett and the Rise of Early Negro Minstrelsy*, 186.

56. For the hundreds of variants on "Jump Jim Crow," see Lhamon's massive *Jump Jim Crow*. For the Georgia Sea Islands variant, see Bessie Jones and Bess Lomax Hawes, *Step It Down: Games, Plays, Songs, and Stories from the African American Heritage* (New York: Harper & Row, 1972), 55ff.

57. Ludlow, *Dramatic Life as I Found It*, 392.

58. See Bolster, *Black Jacks*, 217, 189 n17. Northrup cites several Louisiana dance songs that appear to display relationships with various shanties, including "Old Hog Eye"; see Northrup, *Twelve Years a Slave*, 220.

59. Jarvis, "Maritime Masters and Seafaring Slaves in Bermuda, 1680–1783," 590.

60. "When they submitted, their officers were knocked on the head and every tenth man of the soldiers killed, and the rest shipped for the Barbados." Cromwell to Lenthall, September 17, 1649. *Writings and Speeches of Oliver Cromwell*, ed. W. C. Abbott (Cambridge, Mass.: N.p., 1937–47); quoted in Peter Berresford Ellis, *Eyewitness to Irish History* (Hoboken, N.J.: John Wiley, 2004), 115.

61. Thurloes, "Of the Seizing of Widows and Orphans, and the Destitute, and Transporting Them to Barbadoes in the English Plantations," quoted in John P. Prendergast, *The Cromwellian Settlement of Ireland*, http://bit.ly/fJCgND, accessed March 27, 2011. As is obvious, the inevitable result of this particular form of "solace" would be mixed-race children and a creolizing Afro-Celtic island culture.

62. Sharon Meredith, "Barbadian *tuk* Music: Colonial Development and Post-Independence Recontextualization," *British Journal of Ethnomusicology* 12/2 (2003): 82, emphasis added.

63. On small freeholders from Barbados emigrating to New England in the 1640s, see Reiss, *Blacks in Colonial America*, 67.

64. http://www.yale.edu/glc/tangledroots/Barbadosed.htm, accessed March 10, 2010.

65. See Warren R. Pinckney, "Jazz in Barbados," *American Music* 12/1 (spring 1994): 62. Meredith, "Barbadian *tuk* Music," points out the mainly African roots of *tuk* music in eighteenth- and nineteenth-century sources, saying "the most commonly reported instruments were drums, horns (conch shells or animal horns) and later fiddles," but also describing white Barbadians "dancing French and English *quadrilles* to the music of a band consisting of a fife or concertina, two flat drums and a triangle" (82 and 93).

66. Meredith, "Barbadian *tuk* Music," describes colonial fife & drum musics "throughout the Caribbean—in the Bahamas, St. Kitts, Jamaica, Trinidad, the Virgin Islands, and Guyana" (93).

67. Meredith, "Barbadian *tuk* Music," says that, in the Barbados militia, by 1747 "*all* the drummers and trumpeters, numbering approximately one hundred, were black" (85).

68. Jarvis, "Maritime Masters and Seafaring Slaves in Bermuda, 1680–1783," 604–5.

69. Ibid., 587.

70. Ibid., 585.

71. Ibid., 493, 598, 585, 588, 592, 694, 600.

72. Ibid., 593, 602.

73. Ibid., 603–4.

74. Ibid.

75. See Lamia Tewfik, "'I Arise and Go with William Butler Yeats': Cultural Dovetailing in Lorna Goodison's *County Sligoville*," *Irish Migration Studies in Latin America* (Society for Irish Latin American Studies, 2007), at http://www.irlandeses.org/0711tewfik1.htm, accessed March 1, 2011.

76. Tim Pat Coogan, *Wherever Green Is Worn: The Story of the Irish Diaspora* (New York: Palgrave Macmillan, 2002), 569ff; Joseph J. Williams, *Whence the "Black Irish" of Jamaica?* (New York: Dial, 1932), 17.

77. This association of the Irish with the cooper's craft is ubiquitous throughout the colonial Americas: in Andrew Barton's 1767 ballad opera *The Disappointment, or, The Force of Credulity*, a roman à clef set in Baltimore, the comic characters include "McSnip," a Scottish tailor; "Washball," an English barber; "Raccoon," who though based on a Baltimore hatter named Swan speaks in a dialect showing elements of both Jamaican creole and Pennsylvania Dutch; and "Trushoop," an Irish cooper. See Carolyn Rabson, "*The Disappointment* Revisited: Unweaving the Tangled Web, Part 1," *American Music* 1/1 (spring 1983): 19.

78. See Martha W. Beckwith, "The English Ballad in Jamaica: A Note upon the Origin of the Ballad Form," *Proceedings of the Modern Language Association* 39/2 (June 1924): 455–83.

79. DjeDje, "Remembering Kojo," 67–68.

80. Lewin says "the hips move circularly in a horizontal plane while the feet cover a small area in backwards, sideways, and turning steps." Olive Lewin, "Mento," Grove Music Online, Oxford Music Online, Oxford University Press, http://www.oxfordmusiconline.com/subscriber/article/grove/music/18418, accessed October 30, 2012.

81. Messenger says that "African cultural retentions and reinterpretations with Irish forms [on Montserrat] are most pronounced in the realms of music, song, dance, verbal art and the supernatural." John C. Messenger, "African Retentions in Montserrat," *African Arts* 6/4 (summer 1973): 56. He also points out the extensive overlap on Montserrat of African and Irish folklore and verbal art, including tales of and belief in mermaids, fairies, ghosts, witches, omens, and so on.

82. See John C. Messenger, "African Retentions in Montserrat," *African Arts* 6/4 (summer 1973): 56. It is conventionally understood that the *bodhran*, an instrument associated with seasonal "wren boys" celebrations, only entered the Irish dance music tradition in the twentieth century, but both the Montserrat *babala*, and George Caleb Bingham's 1846 painting *The Jolly Flatboatmen*, depicting an iron skillet played with the same technique, intriguingly complicate this presumption; *Flatboatmen* is discussed later in this chapter.

83. Julian Gerstin, "Interaction and Improvisation between Dancers and Drummers in Martinican Bele," *Black Music Research Journal* 18/1–2 (spring–autumn 1998): 126–27.

84. Dena J. Epstein, "African Music in British and French America," *Musical Quarterly* 59/1 (January 1973): 89.

85. See Roger D. Abrahams, "The Shaping of Folklore Traditions in the British West Indies," *Journal of Inter-American Studies* 8/3 (July 1967): 456–80; and Robert W. Nicholls, "The Mocko Jumbie of the U.S. Virgin Islands: History and Antecedents," *African Arts* 32/3 (autumn 1999): 49–96.

86. Epstein documents the ubiquitous *calinda* dance in Louisiana by 1758 and the Haitian *banza* by the end of the century, while also reporting black fiddlers playing for white dancing in Virginia by the 1690s. Dena J. Epstein, *Sinful Tunes and Spirituals: Black Folk Music to the Civil War* (Urbana: University of Illinois Press, 1977, rev. ed. 2003), 63–64, 83.

87. Ben E. Bailey, "Music in the Life of a Free Black Man of Natchez," *Black Perspective in Music* 13/1 (spring 1985): 3–12.

88. For "Natchez Under the Hill," see Knauff, *Virginia Reels* 1/11 (1839), cited in Chris Goertzen and Alan Jabbour, "George P. Knauff's Virginia Reels and Fiddling in the Antebellum South," *American Music* 5/2 (summer 1987): 143, n27.

89. Shane White and Graham White, "Slave Hair and African American Culture in the Eighteenth and Nineteenth Centuries," *Journal of Southern History* 61/1 (February 1995): 45–46, 64–64, 70–71. Elsewhere, S. White has articulated a persuasive argument that this "bricolage" of clothing and adornment "helped to distinguish the hours of work from the hours of leisure and . . . the master's time from the slave's" and permitted both slaves and free blacks to "construct their own subculture." Shane White, "A Question of Style: Blacks in and around New York City in the Late 18th Century," *Journal of American Folklore* 102/403 (January–March 1989): 31, 24.

90. T. Allston Brown's 1874 account explicitly sources "Zip Coon" in "a rough jig-dance, called 'Natchez Under the Hill.'" See Brown, quoted in Nathan, *Dan Emmett and the Rise of Early Negro Minstrelsy*, 186. See also "Coonjine" songs, discussed in chapter 6.

91. David T. Gleeson, *The Irish in the South, 1815–1877* (Chapel Hill: University of North Carolina Press, 2001), 14. This is precisely the same double-sided strategy Lott says northern minstrelsy served, which in turn argues for a continuity of motive and method between northern and southern cross-cultural behaviors.

92. Henry L. Taylor, "Spatial Organization and the Residential Experience:

Black Cincinnati in 1850," *Social Science History* 10/1 (spring 1986): 57, 64–65, emphasis added. The social exchange of working-class blacks and whites took place under arduous conditions and amid resistance from both sides; Reiss, *Blacks in Colonial America*, points out that perhaps the commonest exchange would have been between white and black workers or house servants (182–83). And S. White both confirms the mixed nature of New York's working-class neighborhoods and cites numerous examples of white men living with blacks or patronizing African American prostitutes. Shane White, "'We Dwell in Safety and Pursue Our Honest Callings': Free Blacks in New York City, 1783–1810," *Journal of American History* 75/2 (September 1988): 461–64, 458–59.

93. For the 1809 "flood of [Haitian] exiles arriving from Cuba," see Alan C. Turley, "The Ecological and Social Determinants of the Production of Dixieland Jazz in New Orleans," *International Review of the Aesthetics and Sociology of Music* 26/1 (June 1995): 114. This is the actual period when the Vieux Carré takes on a specifically Francophone cultural identity—which is in fact a Caribbean *creole* identity.

94. See Garnett Laidlaw Eskew, "Coonjine in Manhattan," Library of Congress Works Progress Administration manuscript (1939), 3, http://lcweb2.loc.gov/wpa/07070413.html, accessed March 10, 2010.

95. The same kind of interethnic liaisons, previously cited, that led to mixed-race populations in New Orleans ("Creoles"), Jamaica and Haiti ("Maroons"), and Florida ("Black Creeks" or "Black Seminoles"), resulted in a creole population in Appalachia ("melungeons"). Few of these mixed-race groups have been examined by musicological scholarship.

96. Gleeson, *Irish in the South*, 32–33.

97. James E. Winston, "Notes on the Economic History of New Orleans, 1803–1836," *Mississippi Valley Historical Review* 11/2 (September 1924): 200–02.

98. Ibid, 203.

99. Gleeson, *The Irish in the South*, 33.

100. Winston, 219–20.

101. See Daphne Spain, "Race Relations and Residential Segregation in New Orleans: Two Centuries of Paradox," in "Race and Residence in Americans Cities," special issue, *Annals of the American Academy of Political and Social Science* 441 (January 1979): 87.

102. Gleeson, *Irish in the South*, 58–59, 23.

103. St. Mary's had been founded in 1788, in what was then known as the American Quarter to distinguish it from the Haitian creole-dominated French Quarter. Irish immigration into the neighborhood precipitated the recruitment of English-speaking Irish priests to service the new congregants. See Gleeson, *Irish in the South*, 33–34, 45; and Roger A. Fischer, "Racial Segregation in Ante Bellum New Orleans," *American Historical Review* 74/3 (February 1969): 927. Fischer comments that, in an urban environment of comparably large and anonymous populations, "where whites and Negroes were brought together frequently as total strangers, white supremacy and black subordination were neither automatic nor implicit." Fischer suggests further

that this destabilizing anonymity, and the tendency of New Orleans domestic slaves to "roam freely throughout the streets," was the precise impetus for the enhanced legal interest in formulating Black Codes, and eventually, the institution of Jim Crow laws (928). For more on "Hilo" (a corruption of the Peruvian port Ilo), see Lucy E. Broadwood, Percy Grainger, Cecil T. Sharp, Ralph Vaughan Williams, Frank Kidson, J. A. Fuller-Maitland, and A. G. Gilchrist, "Songs Collected by Percy Grainger," *Journal of the Folk-Song Society* 3/12 (1908): 239; and many other versions.

104. See Gleeson, *The Irish in the South, 1815–1877*, 43. This pattern would seem to have been set early: Turley, "Ecological and Social Determinants of the Production of Dixieland Jazz in New Orleans," claims that Storyville sporting houses were "initially run by the Irish immigrants (ca. 1840) from the . . . Irish Channel" (111).

105. In Rhode Island, legal ordinances limited not only black rights, but also white interaction with blacks. Reiss, *Blacks in Colonial America*, 74.

106. Spain, "Race Relations and Residential Segregation in New Orleans: Two Centuries of Paradox" (1979), 83, 85. This sort of courtyard/compound architecture is consistent with the physical spaces and social dynamics between races throughout the Caribbean—further confirmation of the city's essentially creole culture.

107. See Thomas Fiehrer, "From Quadrille to Stomp: The Creole Origins of Jazz," in "The 1890s," special issue, *Popular Music* 10/1 (January 1991): 22, 28–29.

108. William W. Chenault and Robert C. Reinders, "The Northern-born Community of New Orleans in the 1850s," *Journal of American History* 51/2 (September 1964): 236–37, 247.

109. Joseph Roach, "Mardi Gras Indians and Others: Genealogies of American Performance," in "Disciplines of Theatre: Theory/Culture/Text," special issue, *Theatre Journal* 44/4 (December 1992): 461–62, 476.

110. Henry A. Kmen, "The Roots of Jazz and the Dance in Place Congo: A Re-Appraisal," *Interamericano de Investigacion Musical* 8 (1972): 9. Kmen points out that, ironically, Latrobe, a civil engineer, had come to New Orleans for the same reason as Irish canal workers did—and was killed by the same "Irish [yellow] fever," in 1820, as so many laborers likewise later were.

111. Kmen, "Roots of Jazz and the Dance in Place Congo," 10.

112. Ibid., 14. Tregle confirms this thesis: Joseph G. Tregle Jr., "Early New Orleans Society: A Reappraisal," *Journal of Southern History* 18/1 (February 1952): 25.

113. Tregle cites the *Louisiana Gazette* (Nov. 6, 1823), the *Mercantile Advertiser* (Oct. 29 and Nov. 4, 1825), the *Argus* (Aug. 15, 1829), and the *Louisiana Courier* (July 30, 1833) as examples.

114. Quoted in Fischer, "Racial Segregation in Ante Bellum New Orleans," 931.

115. Ibid., 933.

116. Nichols has been called "a man of no education" who had cut his teeth touring with Purdy Brown's Theatre and Circus: T. Allston Brown and Charles Day, "Black Musicians and Early Ethiopian Minstrelsy," *Black Perspective in Music* 3/1 (spring 1975): 78.

117. Eileen Southern, *The Music of Black Americans* (New York: Norton, 1997), 94. For Nichols, see Brown 1874, quoted in Day, "Black Musicians and Early Ethiopian Minstrelsy," 78ff. See also Henry A. Kmen, "Old Corn Meal: A Forgotten Urban Negro Folksinger," *Journal of American Folklore* 75/295 (January–March 1962): 32.

118. Kmen, "Old Corn Meal," has him splitting a summer 1840 bill at the Camp Street Theater with the Irish-American blackface entertainer Mick Saunders (31).

119. Kmen, "Old Corn Meal." For "Rosin the Beau," see the 1840 Account by Francis C Sheridan of hearing it sung on the Galveston waterfront "by a Negro deck hand who accompanied himself with his iron cotton bale hooks," quoted in Kmen, "Old Corn Meal," 29.

120. See Southern, *Music of Black Americans*, and Robert C. Toll, *Blacking Up: The Minstrel Show in Nineteenth Century America* (New York: Oxford University Press, 1974), 45. Brown's 1874 account claims that Rice "first jumped" in imitation of Corn Meal around 1829; Brown, quoted in Day, "Black Musicians and Early Ethiopian Minstrelsy," 78. See also Kmen, "Old Corn Meal," 66.

121. Julie Rehmeyer, "1848 Daguerreotypes Bring Middle America's Past to Life," *Wired* 18/08 (August 2010), http://www.wired.com/magazine/2010/07/ff_daguerrotype_panorama/all/1, accessed August 15, 2010.

122. See Eskew, "Coonjine in Manhattan": "Along the rivers that border Southern Illinois, Kentucky and the Southern States, Negroes gravitated instinctively to the river life" (3).

123. For Black Bill, see Emmett D. Preston, "The Fugitive Slave Acts in Ohio," *Journal of Negro History* 28/4 (October 1943): 438ff. For Emmett, see chapter 3.

124. Frederick Way and Carl Vitz's 1947 reconstruction of steamboat tables is cited in Rehmeyer, "1848 Daguerreotypes Bring Middle America's Past to Life."

125. See, for example, Lafcadio Hearn, "Black Varieties: The Minstrels of the Row," in *Lafcadio Hearn's America: Ethnographic Sketches and Editorials*, ed. Simon J. Bronner (Lexington: University Press of Kentucky, 2002), 171.

126. Hearn, "Black Varieties."

127. Ibid., 172–73.

128. For "Bohemian," see Merriam-Webster Dictionary, "2. . . . b : a person (as a writer or an artist) living an unconventional life usually in a colony with others," http://www.merriam-webster.com/dictionary/bohemian, accessed September 11, 2010.

129. See Cohen, *Flash Press*, 24.

130. Cohen, *Flash Press*, 30–37.

131. The origin of the term is Parisian, employed to describe the supposed attributes of Romani people thought to have come from "Bohemia"—though in fact North India.

132. See Lott, *Love and Theft*, 48ff. See also Laurence Hutton, "The Negro on the Stage," *Harper's New Monthly Magazine* 79/409 (1889): 137.

133. As an example: Joseph Tosso, born in Mexico of Italian parents in 1802, and educated at the Paris Conservatoire, lived in Cincinnati 1827–87 as a violinist, conductor, and businessman, and played "Arkansas Traveler" as one of his showcase

pieces. See Ophia D. Smith, "Joseph Tosso, the Arkansaw Traveler," *Ohio History* 56 (January 1947): 16–43.

134. See Abrahams, *Singing the Master*. Northrup, *Twelve Years a Slave*, also provides a detailed description of a Louisiana plantation mistress sponsoring and appearing as guest of honor at Christmastime slave dances (285).

135. African American slave-era names not infrequently were based in classical mythology (Pompey, Caesar, Brutus). However, there is also carryover from West African names, particularly in the case of fictionalized African American characters. Cuffee, a common name in blackface theatrics, is likely a transliteration of Kofi (from the Akan word for Friday—children were often named after the days of the week on which they were born). See, similarly, Squash/Quash (Rice's *Bone Squash Diavalo* (Akan: "Kwesi/Akwasi": "Sunday"), and possibly "Joe" himself (Akan: "Jojo"). See Philip F. W. Bartle, "Forty Days; The Akan Calendar," *Africa: Journal of the International African Institute* (Edinburgh University Press) 48/1 (January 1978): 80–84.

136. Hearn, for example, provides a detailed description of the Afro-Caribbean *calinda*, ubiquitous throughout U.S. riverine and maritime environments. W. K. McNeil, "Lafcadio Hearn, American Folklorist," *Journal of American Folklore* 91/362 (October–December 1978): 955ff.

137. See Lhamon, *Raising Cain*, quoting the reminiscences of actor Joe Cowell (32).

138. See Ludlow, *Dramatic Life as I Found It*; on Rice, xx, xxv, 327, 328, 396; on Rice's performances in Cincinnati, 393; in Louisville, 392–93; in Mobile, 331–32, 336, 452, 498.

139. Nathan, *Dan Emmett and the Rise of Early Negro Minstrelsy*, 160.

140. Ibid., 98ff.

141. Ibid., 108.

142. Ibid., 58–59. For the C. J. Rogers reminiscence, see Carlin, *Birth of the Banjo*, 58.

143. Emery, *Black Dance in the United States from 1619 to 1970*, 147.

144. See P. H. Gosse, *Letters from Alabama* (1859), 306, quoted in Epstein, *Sinful Tunes and Spirituals*, 185.

145. Pearson confirms African American boatmen on the Ohio as a conduit for the banjo's entry into Appalachian culture. See Barry Lee Pearson, "Appalachian Blues," *Black Music Research Journal* 23/1–2 (spring–autumn 2003): 30–31. See also William E. Lightfoot, "The Three Doc(k)s: White Blues in Appalachia," *Black Music Research Journal* 23/1–2 (spring–autumn 2003): 167–93, for the ongoing borrowing by white musicians from black banjoists.

146. See Bolster, "'To Feel Like a Man,'" 1173.

147. Bolster, *Black Jacks*, confirms that Douglass's was not an isolated experience, saying that "nearly one quarter of skilled runaway slaves in VA between 1736–1801 were mariners" (24).

148. Jeffrey D. Mason, "Social Space, Social Performance," in "Enacting America(n)s," special issue, *Theatre Journal* 48/3 (October 1996): 315, emphasis added.

149. As Lhamon comments in *Raising Cain*, "The river was both a boundary and a conveyance. Catherine Market [in New York], like all traditional markets paradoxi-

cally smudged that borderline and also reinforced it . . . [Public performance] at the Catherine Market addressed the issue of overlap. It appealed to several audiences who were finding different values in the dance at the same time. It was a yoking across perceived differences. . . . After all, appeal and exchange was what display in a market was about" (2–3).

150. See, among others, Lhamon, *Raising Cain*; Lott, *Love and Theft*; Cockrell, *Demons of Disorder*; Mahar, *Behind the Burnt Cork Mask*; Carlin, *Birth of the Banjo*; Christopher J. Smith, "Blacks and Irish on the Riverine Frontiers: The Roots of American Popular Music," *Southern Cultures* 17/1 (spring 2011): 75–102.

151. See Lhamon, *Raising Cain*; and Joann W. Kealiinohomoku, "Ethnic Historical Study," 86–97, in *Dance History Research: Perspectives from Related Arts and Disciplines, The Proceedings of the Second Conference on Research in Dance* (New York: Congress on Research in Dance, 1979), 95.

152. For example, Beard's *Western Raftsmen* (1846) was painted in the same year that Bingham's *Boatmen on the Missouri* sold, and in the same year that Bingham painted *Jolly Flatboatmen*. Gail E. Husch, "'Poor White Folks' and 'Western Squatters': James Henry Beard's Images of Emigration," *American Art* 7/3 (summer 1993): 26.

153. For *Flatboatmen* as "optimistic," see Nancy Rash, "George Caleb Bingham's 'Lighter Relieving a Steamboat Aground,'" *Smithsonian Studies on American Art* 2/2 (spring 1988): 13; Rash also provides a detailed iconographic discussion of the image's political symbolism, 20ff.

154. Aside from the *Flatboatmen* variants, see Bingham, *Western Boatmen Ashore by Night* (1854, Museum of Fine Arts, Boston); possibly painted in Philadelphia, one of whose participants plays the Jew's harp or "trump," an instrument associated with Anglo-Scots culture. See Catherine Hoover, "The Influence of David Wilkie's Prints on the Genre Paintings of William Sidney Mount," *American Art Journal* 13/3 (summer 1981): 29.

155. Such idealization may paradoxically help to explain the positive response to Bingham, and its perceived "lack" certainly accounts for the disdain with which Beard's *Western Raftsmen* was met, discussed later in this chapter.

156. Lucretia H. Glese, "James Goodwyn Clonney (1812–1867): American Genre Painter," *American Art Journal* 11/4 (October 1979): 10.

157. Rash, "George Caleb Bingham's 'Lighter Relieving a Steamboat Aground,'" 18.

158. I am indebted to musicologist and native Missourian Roger Landes for his original observation about this mysterious percussionist.

159. See John C. Messenger, "African Retentions in Montserrat," *African Arts* 6/4 (summer 1973): 56, on the "jumble drum"; see also Abrahams, "Shaping of Folklore Traditions in the British West Indies," 460, on fiddle/triangle/tambourine dance bands in St. Vincent and Trinidad.

160. See Mark McKnight, "Charivaris, Cowbellions, and Sheet Iron Bands: Nineteenth-Century Rough Music in New Orleans," *American Music* 23/4 (winter 2005): 408.

161. See note 82 in this chapter regarding the *babala*.

162. Nathan, *Dan Emmett and the Rise of Early Negro Minstrelsy*, 186.

163. C. J. Rogers's reminiscence is cited in ibid., 58; See also H. Sacks and J. Sacks, "Way Up North in Dixie," 409–10. H. Sacks, "From the Barn to the Bowery and Back Again," also emphasizes that such exchange was not limited to specific periods, but in fact had obtained since before the war (314–38).

164. Lhamon, *Jump Jim Crow*, 29–31.

165. In fact, in 1834 President Andrew Jackson (a harbinger of a new, frontier-based working-class political populism) was forced to call out federal troops to quell Irish riots on the Chesapeake & Ohio Canals.

166. Robert B. Winans, "The Folk, the Stage, and the Five-String Banjo in the Nineteenth Century," *Journal of American Folklore* 89/354 (October–December 1976): 419, 421.

167. For example, they identify the gradual supplanting of the old Anglo-Celtic fiddle tune types by "newly fashionable dance genres," both black (breakdowns and clogs) and Continental (quadrilles and cotillions). In Knauff's first volume, the presence of prototypical minstrel tunes such as "Natchez Under the Hill" reveals a parallel between the southern synthesis revealed in Knauff's collection and that documented in the North by Mount's materials, where the same tune appears. Goertzen and Aln Jabbour, "George P. Knauff's Virginia Reels and Fiddling in the antebellum South," 125.

168. Wells cites the Negro tunes "Pompey Ran Away" from James Aird's *A Selection of Scotch, English, Irish and Foreign Airs Adapted*. . . (Glasgow, 1782); "Congo—A Jig" in an eighteenth-century manuscript from the Bolling family of Virginia; and a "Negro Dance" published in *Riley's Flute Melodies* (New York City ca. 1814–16). Paul F. Wells, "Fiddling as an Avenue of Black-White Musical Interchange," in *Black Music Research Journal* 23/1–2 (spring–autumn 2003): 141ff. On a personal note, I was grateful to discover from Wells's research that "Black Joe" Brown (1750-?), a Revolutionary War veteran and freedman of mixed African and Native American parentage, who owned a tavern and the pond where I swam and skated as a child, was a fiddle player. See Linda Weltner, "Black Joe: A Mythical, Musical, and Unforgettable Man on Gingerbread Hill," *Marblehead Magazine* (n.d., http://www.legendinc.com/Pages/MarbleheadNet/MM/Articles/BlackJoe.html, accessed March 10, 2010.

169. Goertzen and Jabbour, "George P. Knauff's Virginia Reels and Fiddling in the Antebellum South," 128.

170. Wells, "Fiddling as an Avenue of Black-White Musical Interchange," 140.

171. David Chevan, "Riverboat Music from St. Louis and the Streckfus Steamboat Line," *Black Music Research Journal* 9/2 (autumn 1989): 164.

172. James Henry Beard, *Western Raftsmen* (1846). Oil on canvas, 27 3/4 × 36 in. Collection of the Diplomatic Reception Rooms, Department of State, Washington, D.C.

173. Husch, "'Poor White Folks' and 'Western Squatters,'" 19.

174. Ibid., 20. Rash, "George Caleb Bingham's 'Lighter Relieving a Steamboat Aground,'" cites negative initial reactions to Bingham's *Jolly Flatboatmen* (1846); this

criticism had shifted in St. Louis to accolades by 1847, and that "Boatmen Dance" was sung in celebration of the painting (22).

175. Husch, "'Poor White Folks' and 'Western Squatters,'" 28.

176. Ibid., 28.

177. See Robert Fulton, *A Treatise on the Improvement of Canal Navigation . . .* (London: I. and J. Taylor at the Architectural Library, 1796), http://www.history.rochester.edu/canal/bib/fulton/1796/, accessed October 30, 2011.

178. See Alex Roland, with W. Jeffrey Bolster, and Alexander Keyssar, *The Way of the Ship: America's Maritime History Reenvisioned, 1600–2000* (Hoboken, N.J.: John Wiley, 2008), 107–11ff. The career of Henry Shreve replicates in miniature this shift: he made his fortune developing and exploiting the Mississippi keelboat/flatboat trade after the War of 1812, but by 1814 was exploring steam, and in 1825 introduced steamboats on the Mississippi (131–33).

179. Peter Way, "Evil Humors and Ardent Spirits: The Rough Culture of Canal Construction Laborers," *Journal of American History* 79/4 (March 1993): 1398. See also Nathan, *Dan Emmett and the Rise of Early Negro Minstrelsy*, 54; quoting J. F. H. Claiborne, *Life and Correspondence of John A. Quitman* (New York, 1860), 1:42. We may note the link here to Nathan's description of the conduct of riverboatmen in the 'teens: from an Ohio River 1819 reference, he quotes "what are termed 'steam-boats,' 'snapping turtles,' and 'half-horse half-alligators'—a formidable set of fellows.'"

180. Way, "Evil Humors and Ardent Spirit," 1398.

181. See Peter G. Buckley, "The Place to Make an Artist Work," in *Mount and Music* (Museums at Stony Brook, 1984), 4–7.

182. "The Riches of Sight: William Sidney Mount and His World," catalog to the exhibit, Long Island Museum of American Art, History, and Carriages (2003), 2.

183. *American Beacon* (Norfolk, Va.), September 6, 4/1; quoted in Richard Hopwood Thornton, *An American Glossary* (New York: F. Ungar, 1962).

184. See Way, "Evil Humors and Ardent Spirits," 1407, on "alienation" and canaller identity.

185. Way, "Evil Humors and Ardent Spirits," 1407.

186. Ibid., 1408, 1401. For the transgressive masked "justice" of rural Irish Strawboys, see Henry Glassie, *Passing the Time in Ballymenone* (Bloomington: Indiana University Press, 1995), 282. For European mumming roots and "folk theatrical" elements of such festivals, see Cockrell, *Demons of Disorder*, 42–46. In linking the two, Cockrell describes a young, unmarried male clientele, elements of music, "barely contained" violence, music or sounds "that approach what nonperformers would call noise," "a dynamic of protest against social structures," "theatricals [with the potential of] unsettling social norms," and a general attitude of license and display.

187. Way, "Evil Humors and Ardent Spirits," 1422–25.

188. Lott, *Love and Theft*, 104. Anonymous, quoted in David Roediger, "'Labor in White Skin': Race and Working-Class History," in *Reshaping the US Left: Popular*

Struggles in the 1980s, ed. Mike Davis and Michael Sprinker (London: Verso, 1986), 287–308.

189. Alexander Saxton, "Blackface Minstrelsy and Jacksonian Ideology," *American Quarterly* 27/1 (March 1975): 6.

190. Ibid., 11.

191. See Lott, *Love and Theft*, for Mose the Fireman as exemplifying "the first US working-class subculture—the volunteer fireman bent on class travesty, the butcher *wise in the ways of cultural bricolage*" (81ff).

192. Between 1740 and 1803, African Americans came to represent 18 percent of the total seafaring population. See Roland, *Way of the Ship*, 87. As well, black and creole musicians were an essential part of Colonial and Revolutionary armies; the 1723 Virginia Militia Act stated that "Such free Negroes, Mulattos or Indians, as are capable, may be listed and emploied as Drummers or Trumpeters." Wood, *Strange New Land*, 63. Wood likewise mentions the account of black drummer Mat Anderson playing and teaching younger slave musicians at Thomas Jefferson's home (64). Bolster, *Black Jacks* confirms black presence in maritime recruiting as well, citing black drummers playing for rendezvous ("rondy") at seaport taverns (33–34). See also Bolster, "'To Feel Like a Man,'" 1177–78. For drummers marking gatherings, see Charles Rappleye, *Sons of Providence: The Brown Brothers, the Slave Trade, and the American Revolution* (New York: Simon & Schuster, 2006), 108. Thanks to Rich Remsberg for this latter citation.

193. Roland, *Way of the Ship*, 96–99, 145.

194. From the *Delaware Patriot And American Watchman* (March 11, 1828): "LABORERS 500 Colored Men dry work, on the PENNSYLVANIA CANAL. THE subscriber wishes to hire five hundred colored-men, to work on the . . . place. frequent quarrels which happen between Irish and Colored will be avoided at this place, as no Irish men are employed on this section of the Canal." Wilmington, Delaware, March 11, 1828, http://www.newspaperabstracts.com/link.php?action=detail&id=33925, accessed March 10, 2011. Such disputes were not restricted only within working groups: recent archaeological evidence suggests deadly conflict between Irish canallers and more-established residents on the Philadelphia Canal in 1832: William Watson, a professor at Immaculata College, has identified a gravesite in a place called Duffy's Cut (near Philadelphia), which he argues contains the bodies of Irish canallers murdered in a labor dispute; see Peter Loftus, "The Mystery of Duffy's Cut," *Wall Street Journal*, 14 April 2011, http://online.wsj.com, accessed March 10, 2011.

195. Lott, *Love and Theft*, 47–48; see also an 1876 Lafcadio Hearn anecdote describing "black roustabouts on the riverfront of Cincinnati dancing a quadrille to the 'Devil's Dream' (accompanied by fiddle, banjo, and bass), gradually transforming it into a Virginia reel, and then changing it again, this time to a 'juba dance' done to a shout-like call-and-response song." Hearn, quoted in Szwed and Marks, "The Afro-American Transformation of European Set Dances and Dance Suites," 33.

196. McNeil, "Lafcadio Hearn, American Folklorist," 955ff.

197. Hearn, *Lafcadio Hearn's America*, 47.

198. M. E. Barnes-Ostrander, "Domestic Music Making in Early New York State: Music in the Lives of Three Amateurs," *Musical Quarterly* 68/3 (July 1982): 355.

199. Ibid.

200. Nathan, *Dan Emmett and the Rise of Early Negro Minstrelsy*, 156.

201. Meredith, "Barbadian *tuk* Music," 91.

202. There are many other parallels. See Reiss, *Blacks in Colonial America*, 55.

203. See Cohen, *Flash Press*, 10.

204. Ibid.

205. For Dixon's career, see Cockrell, *Demons of Disorder*, 96ff. For the possibility of Dixon himself having profited directly from the sex trade, I am indebted to Dale Cockrell, conversation with the author, Society for American Music national meetings, Cincinnati, Ohio, 10 March 2011.

206. Cohen, *Flash Press*, 28.

207. See December 11, 1841, issue of the *Flash*. Paraphrased in Cockrell, *Demons of Disorder*, 96.

208. Carlin, *Birth of the Banjo*, 19.

209. Ibid., 4.

210. See Solomon Pestcoe, "'The Old Plantation'—A Banjo Roots Perspective," http://www.myspace.com/banjoroots/blog/425545009, accessed March 11, 2011.

211. Carlin, *Birth of the Banjo*, 20–21.

212. Ibid., 22–23.

213. Ibid., 24–26.

214. Ibid., 37.

215. Ibid., 46–47.

216. Ibid., 19.

217. See ibid., 38ff; iconography on 43.

218. Nathan, *Dan Emmett and the Rise of Early Negro Minstrelsy,* 98ff.

219. Ibid., 104. We might, for example, trace Emmett's experience to that of the archetypal "printer's devil," Benjamin Franklin.

220. Interview by Jeff Hatsough and Derrick Logozzo, "George Carroll: Marching and Field Percussion Historian," *Percussive Notes* (April 1996): 34.

221. Ibid., 93ff.

222. Nathan, *Dan Emmett and the Rise of Early Negro Minstrelsy*, 109. See also H. Sacks and J. Sacks, "Way Up North in Dixie," 409ff.

223. Nathan, *Dan Emmett and the Rise of Early Negro Minstrelsy*, 113, 110–11.

224. Ibid., 114.

225. Ibid., 115.

226. Ibid., 116.

227. Ibid., 118.

228. Nathan in ibid. provides useful transcriptions of playbills from the Minstrels' Boston run that confirm both the content of their repertoire and the ways in which their performances were framed; these also include a feature for Pelham as "A Brief Battering at the Blues"—a very early use of this term (119–20). In their 1843 tour,

the Minstrels played Cork, Belfast, Glasgow, and Edinburgh, in all of which cities troupes sprang up in imitation—the original source for the incorporation of the five-string banjo into Irish music. Carlin, *Birth of the Banjo*, 63. By 1844 there were even minstrel troupes in Australia. Nathan, *Dan Emmett and the Rise of Early Negro Minstrelsy*, 84.

229. Carlin, *Birth of the Banjo*, 59.

230. For professionalization, see Carlin, *Birth of the Banjo*, 67, quote at 66.

231. Of festivals such as Pinkster and 'Lection Day, Wade, "'Shining in Borrowed Plumage,'" contests the traditional interpretation that these were "imperfect" imitations, arguing instead that "A more accurate assessment would have been that there was much free and open exchange of cultural traits within the festivals by both blacks and whites" (218).

232. See Brian Klitz, "Blacks and Pre-Jazz Instrumental Music in America," *International Review of the Aesthetics and Sociology of Music* 20/1 (June 1989): 50ff.

Chapter 3. Long Island and the Lower East Side

1. On John Canoe/Junkanoo and related midwinter Afro-European syncretic celebrations in the Caribbean and mainland South, see Dale Cockrell, *Demons of Disorder: Blackface Minstrels and Their World* (Cambridge: Cambridge University Press, 1997), 38–46.

2. S. White describes the location of slave festivals like Pinkster and Negro 'Lection Day as existing "in small pockets along the coast and up the valleys of the major rivers." Shane White, "'It Was a Proud Day': African Americans, Festivals, and Parades in the North, 1741–1834," *Journal of American History* 81/1 (June 1994): 18.

3. Shane White, "Pinkster: Afro-Dutch Syncretization in New York City and the Hudson Valley," *Journal of American Folklore* 102/403 (January–March 1989), 68.

4. Kevin M. Scott, "Rituals of Race: Mount, Melville, and Antebellum America," PhD diss., Purdue University, 2004, 49.

5. *The Memoir of John Durang: American Actor, 1785–1816*, ed. Alan S. Downer (Pittsburgh: University of Pittsburgh Press, for the Historical Society of York County and the American Society for Theatre Research, 1966), 49–50. Quoted in M. E. Barnes-Ostrander, "Domestic Music Making in Early New York State: Music in the Lives of Three Amateurs," *Musical Quarterly* 68/3 (July 1982): 355.

6. New York is cited in a March 1737 piece in the *New York Weekly Journal*, describing a celebration in which "blacks danced to the music of drums, fiddle, and bangar (banjo)"; see Solomon Pestcoe, "'The Old Plantation'—A Banjo Roots Perspective," http://www.myspace.com/banjoroots/blog/425545009, accessed March 11, 2011. For New Jersey, see S. White, "Pinkster," 72–73. For Massachusetts and the direct quotes, see S. White, "'It Was a Proud Day,'" 16, 20. S. White argues persuasively that the gradual shift around 1800 to direct importation of slaves from Africa, rather than the Caribbean, may account for a particularly strong "African" element

in late northern Pinkster, found in words, behaviors, dancing, and instrumentation, including the "Guinea drum," a large log drum played by straddling and singing. S. White, "It Was a Proud Day," 23–24.

7. Barbara S. Glass, *African American Dance: An Illustrated History* (Jefferson, N.C.: McFarland, 2007), 62ff; Thomas F. DeFrantz, ed., *Dancing Many Drums: Excavations in African American Dance* (Madison: University of Wisconsin Press, 2002), 142ff.

8. S. White, "Pinkster," 73.

9. Ibid., 73.

10. See Joseph P. Reidy, "Negro Election Day and Black Community Life in New England, 1750–1860," *Marxist Perspectives* 1 (fall 1978): 102–17.

11. Wade cites "probable convergences of traits evident in both the African and European-American cultural pasts" and refers to William G. Piersen's 1975 dissertation, which "examin[ed] the festivals as an African-derived, European-influenced cultural phenomenon common throughout the New World." Melvin Wade, "'Shining in Borrowed Plumage': Affirmation of Community in the Black Coronation Festivals of New England (c. 1750–c. 1850)," *Western Folklore* 40/3 (July 1981): 218, 213.

12. Wade, "'Shining in Borrowed Plumage,'" 211–12.

13. Ibid., 227. See also DeFrantz, *Dancing Many Drums*, 143.

14. Cornhuskings, of the sort exhaustively analyzed in Roger D. Abrahams's seminal *Singing the Master*, were a significant event in the North, as well; see Wade, "'Shining in Borrowed Plumage,'" 214. Jarvis and others cite analogous festivals throughout the Caribbean in the same period: Note that Bermudian maritime slaves "frequently gathered by themselves to celebrate marriages, funerals and holidays . . . balls and gatherings . . . 'merry meetings and midnight festivals' [that] reflected a synthesis of European fashion and African and Native American traditions perhaps best exemplified by the costume, dance, and music of *gombay* dancers." Michael J. Jarvis, "Maritime Masters and Seafaring Slaves in Bermuda, 1680–1783," in "Slaveries in the Atlantic World," special issue, *William and Mary Quarterly*, 3rd series, 59/3 (July 2002): 610. Wood also points out shared esthetics with Native American music (drums and rattles). Peter H. Wood, *Strange New Land: Africans in Colonial America* (Oxford: Oxford University Press, 1996/2003), 62–67. On the impact of the "First Great Awakening," see Wade, "'Shining in Borrowed Plumage,'" who usefully refers to the "emergent" (i.e., "constantly emerging") nature of such festivals (216, 229). Hanna, similarly, describes dance as "continually becoming in the phenomenological sense." Judith Lynne Hanna, "Movements Toward Understanding Humans through the Anthropological Study of Dance [and Comments and Reply]," *Current Anthropology* 20/2 (June 1979): 317.

15. S. White, "It Was a Proud Day," 17–18.

16. Wade, "'Shining in Borrowed Plumage,'" 216.

17. S. White, "'It Was a Proud Day,'" 15; see also Wade, "'Shining in Borrowed Plumage,'" 24.

18. Jeffrey D. Mason, "Street Fairs: Social Space, Social Performance," in "Enacting America(n)s," special issue, *Theatre Journal* 48/3 (October 1996): 305, emphasis added.

19. Wade, "'Shining in Borrowed Plumage,'" 218.

20. Ibid., 218, 217, 213, 217.

21. See Reiss, who confirms the close proximity of masters and slaves in New England and the mid-Atlantic, and that New Netherland was a much more lenient place for slaves than later New England. Oscar Reiss, *Blacks in Colonial America* (Jefferson, N.C.: McFarland, 1997), 49, 80ff. For a detailed discussion of New York free blacks' occupations, living conditions, experience, and neighborhood proximity to whites, see Shane White, "'We Dwell in Safety and Pursue Our Honest Callings': Free Blacks in New York City, 1783–1810," *Journal of American History* 75/2 (September 1988): 456–64.

22. Manumission—the prohibition of slave importation—was passed in New York in 1788, with the 1799 "Law of the Free Womb" guaranteeing freedom to black children born after that year. In 1817, a ten-year limit was set for existing enslavement, guaranteeing freedom for all blacks by 1827. This pattern of gradual abolition was also paralleled in three Northeast states: Massachusetts, Rhode Island, and Vermont enacted manumission in the early 1780s, while Connecticut forbade slave importation from the 1770s; see Reiss, *Blacks in Colonial America*, 71. A result significant to Mount's own musical autobiography on Long Island is that, as Marcus says, "by the early nineteenth century, small communities of freed people had sprung up in Amityville, Eastville (near Sag Harbor), Three Mile Harbor (northeast of East Hampton), Bellport, Setauket, Huntington, Mastic, Greenport, and Miller Place." See Grania Bolton Marcus, *Discovering the African American Experience in Suffolk County, 1620–1860* (Setauket, N.Y.: Amereon House, Society for the Preservation of Long Island Antiquities), 11, in the collection of the Long Island Museum of American Art, History, and Carriages (hereafter LIM).

23. S. White also points out that this latter trade led, eventually, to African American ownership of the oyster houses and dancing cellars that were central to black urban identity and were eventually minstrelsy's first theatrical venues ("'We Dwell in Safety and Pursue Our Honest Callings,'" 454, 456, 467).

24. On a personal note, it was a matter of small but significant satisfaction, on several levels, to discover that my own patrilineal ancestor Robert Smith, of Smithtown, New York, had manumitted his natural-born children sometime after 1803. See Bradley Harris, *Black Roots in Smithtown: A Short History of the Black Community* (Smithtown, N.Y.: Office of the Town Historian, 1986).

25. Many mixed-race children were acknowledged by New York slaveowners during and immediately after manumission. Reiss, *Blacks in Colonial America*, 84.

26. See chapter 2.

27. Hans Nathan, *Dan Emmett and the Rise of Early Negro Minstrelsy, 2nd ed.* (Norman: University of Oklahoma: 1977), 61–62.

28. See Philip H. Highfill, Kalman A. Bunim, and Edward A. Langhans, *Tibbett to M. West: Actresses, Musicians, Dancers, Managers, and Other Stage Personnel*

in London, 1660–1800, vol. 15 of *A Biographical Dictionary of Actors* (Carbondale: Southern Illinois University Press, 1993), 393. Lhamon explicates the dance connection: "'Long Island Juba' . . . tagged the black dancers who crossed the East River from Brooklyn to Manhattan's Catherine Market to dance for money and eels in the challenge dances and cutting contests that Rice had observed as a boy." He also confirms an additional maritime and street-food connection: "the subtitle, 'Love by the Bushel,' referred to the setting—an oyster cellar furnished with bushels of oysters"; oyster cellars being precisely the urban drinking houses where working-class blacks and whites met, conversed, and danced together. W. T. Lhamon Jr., *Jump Jim Crow: Lost Plays, Lyrics, and Street Prose of the First Atlantic Popular Culture* (Cambridge, Mass.: Harvard University Press, 2003) 43. For *The Prize*, see the 1808 imprint by D. Longworth (Worcester, Mass.: American Antiquarian Society, 1969).

29. S. White cites "the impact on New York of refugees" from the Caribbean, particularly "French Royalists," after 1793 and confirms that black Haitian émigrés in New York were especially active socially, as political leaders and in antiabolitionist organizing. S. White, "'We Dwell in Safety and Pursue our Honest Callings,'" 448–50. A major character in Kipling's *Captains Courageous* is the unnamed "black cook," who "comes from the innards of Cape Breton . . . where the farmers speak homemade Scotch [and] whose folk run in there durin' aour [revolutionary] war." Rudyard Kipling, *Captains Courageous: A Story of the Grand Banks* (New York: Century Company, 1919), 54. This is confirmed more formally in Alfred N. Hunt, *Haiti's Influence on Antebellum America: Slumbering Volcano in the Caribbean* (Baton Rouge: Louisiana State University Press, 1988).

30. Hunt, *Haiti's Influence on Antebellum America*, 15–16.

31. Ibid., 30.

32. Ibid., 40. S. White "'We Dwell in Safety and Pursue Our Honest Callings,'" confirms that four in ten black males were laborers or mariners, and indeed often worked both occupations (453).

33. Hunt, *Haiti's Influence on Antebellum America*, 30. Hunt emphasizes, in fact, that "in the Mississippi Valley, especially in Louisiana," French Creole influence both antedated and survived the U.S. takeover of New Orleans and the Louisiana Purchase (37–38).

34. See chapter 2, n36, where Nathan quotes the "Hayti" reference in Washington Irving, *Salmagundi and Voyages and Discoveries of the Companions of Columbus*, vol. 5 of *The Works of Washington Irving* (New York: Co-operative Publication Society, n.d.); Nathan, *Dan Emmett and the Rise of Early Negro Minstrelsy*, 72.

35. Chadwick Hansen, "Jenny's Toe Revisited: White Responses to Afro-American Shaking Dances," *American Music* 5/1 (spring 1987): 9.

36. Irving, in Nathan, *Dan Emmett and the Rise of Early Negro Minstrelsy*, 372.

37. S. White, "'It Was a Proud Day,'" 23.

38. See Scott, "Rituals of Race," 66; and Lynne Faulkey Emery, *Black Dance in the United States from 1619 to 1970* (Palo Alto, Calif.: National Press Books, 1972), 141.

39. Norton 1862: 16–17, quoted in Howard L. Sacks, "From the Barn to the Bowery and Back Again: Musical Routes in Rural Ohio, 1800–1929," Phillips Barry Lecture, *Journal of American Folklore* 116/461 (summer 2003), 317.

40. Hunt, *Haiti's Influence on Antebellum America*, 45.

41. Ibid., 49–58.

42. Ibid., 67, 69.

43. Ibid., 71.

44. Of course, resident African Americans had provided valuable music services since long before Toussaint's 1801–3 revolution: black fiddlers were ubiquitous throughout the thirteen colonies. African Americans were likewise highly visible as drummers and fifers in colonial armies: recruited from the ranks of southern runaways by Hessian mercenaries, exempted from Virginia's Black Codes that otherwise forbade free blacks to serve in the Continental Army, and employed by the British army throughout the New World.

45. Buffet says they were Baptist; see Edward P. Buffet, "William Sidney Mount: A Biography. The Story of Old Time Life in Brookhaven North Told Through His Pictures, as published by Mr. Buffet in the Port Jefferson Times from December 1, 1912, to June 12, 1924," typescript in the collection of the LIM, chapter 2.

46. Scott, "Rituals of Race," 66.

47. Ibid., 44.

48. Buffet, "William Sidney Mount," 2–3.

49. Vera Brodsky Lawrence, "Micah Hawkins, the Pied Pipe of the Catherine Slip," *New-York Historical Society Quarterly* 62 (April 1978): 142.

50. Buffet, "William Sidney Mount," 18.

51. Leonard P. Curry, *The Free Black in Urban America 1800–1850: The Shadow of the Dream* (Chicago: University of Chicago Press, 1981), 2.

52. Ibid., 4–5.

53. Curry, *The Free Black in Urban America 1800–1850*, 16ff.

54. Reiss, *Blacks in Colonial America*, 124.

55. S. White, "It Was a Proud Day," 32, 34. S. White calls it a "precarious existence" for free blacks in these first years of the 19th century, facilitated by manumission and urban opportunity, but also swiftly eliciting white working-class resentment and persecution. S. White, "'We Dwell in Safety and Pursue Our Honest Callings,'" 445.

56. A persuasive argument for this interpretation of Zip Coon's origins is found in Shane White, "A Question of Style: Blacks in and around New York City in the Late 18th Century," *Journal of American Folklore* 102/403 (January–March 1989): 23–25. Middle-class "unease" (S. White's term) about the "assumed link between crime and smartly dressed blacks" is attested both by the newspaper record and by the enactment of laws aimed at restricting not only black-white interaction in private but also black congregation in public. See also Reiss, *Blacks in Colonial America*, 81, 82–83. Wade notes similar anxieties about cross-cultural exchange in the creolized Colonial festivals of Pinkster and 'Lection Day: the fear that "allying the blacks with the white lower classes in their rejection of the civil authorities . . .

threatened to create an epidemic of social deviance," Wade, "'Shining in Borrowed Plumage,'" 21.

57. Curry, *Free Black in Urban America 1800–1850*, 79.

58. Ibid., 34–35.

59. Scott cites De Voe's description of "Ned (Francis), a little wiry negro slave . . . another named Bob Rowley . . . and Jack, belonging to Frederick De Voo, all farmers on Long Island." *The Market Book; A History of the Public Markets of the City of New York* (Thomas F. De Voe, 1862), quoted in Scott, "Rituals of Race," 51–52. The "Bob Rowley" mentioned is "Bobolink Bob."

60. Pinkster "was celebrated at the market at Catharine Slip and, across the East River in Brooklyn, at the old market, until that was torn down in 1814." S. White, "'It Was a Proud Day,'" 21. On Pinkster Hill, see S. White, "Pinkster," 70.

61. Lawrence, "Micah Hawkins, the Pied Pipe of the Catherine Slip," 141.

62. Ibid., 143.

63. In ibid., Lawrence says that the collections "predominantly of popular light music: marches, dance tunes (hornpipes, reels, waltzes, strathspeys), popular song airs from hit operas, folk ballads from the various British Isles, and the patriotic (or 'national') songs that were the staples of most contemporary tune books: 'Yankee Doodle,' then at the peak of its perennial popularity, 'The President's March,' . . . and a profusion of pieces enjoying the ubiquitous title of 'Washington's March' . . . Several pieces having strictly local appeal are included" (146–47).

64. Lawrence, "Micah Hawkins, the Pied Pipe of the Catherine Slip," 147.

65. "Micah Hawkins original material," box 1, KSA9, Kate Strong Historical Library, Hawkins-Mount Family papers, LIM.

66. Lawrence, "Micah Hawkins, the Pied Pipe of the Catherine Slip," 161.

67. See Robert Fulton, *A Treatise on the Improvement of Canal Navigation . . .* (London: I. and J. Taylor at the Architectural Library, 1796), http://www.history.rochester.edu/canal/bib/fulton/1796/, accessed October 30, 2011.

68. Cook describes a "massive migration to the city" in the 1820s–30s, most of whose working-class single young men resided in boarding houses and cheap hotels. See James W. Cook, "Dancing across the Color Line," *Common-Place* 4/1 (October 2003), http://www.common-place.org/vol-04/no-01/cook/cook-2.shtml, accessed November 23, 2012.

69. Cook, "Dancing across the Color Line."

70. See, for example, George W. Clinton, *Journal of a Tour from Albany to Lake Erie, by the Erie Canal, in 1826, Buffalo Historical Society Publications 14* (Buffalo, N.Y.: Buffalo Historical Society, 1910); and Colonel William Leete Stone, *From New York to Niagara—Journal of a Tour, in Part by Canal, in 1829* (New York: Buffalo Historical Society, 1910).

71. Nathan, *Dan Emmett and the Rise of Early Negro Minstrelsy*, 50. S. White argues that the Zip Coon archetype—and earlier African American imitations of white folkways—contained an element of masked caricature reminiscent of the later cakewalk, which on the surface was derogated by whites as incompetent imitation,

but has subsequently been read as black caricature of white pretense ("'It Was a Proud Day,'" 28). On the cakewalk's intentions and associations, see Brooke Baldwin, "The Cakewalk: A Study in Stereotype and Reality," *Journal of Social History* 15 (1981/2): 209.

72. Nathan, *Dan Emmett and the Rise of Early Negro Minstrelsy,* 52–54, quoting J. F. H. Claiborne, *Life and Correspondence of John A. Quitman* (New York: N.p., 1860), 1:42. Daniel Emmett's claims for his original authorship of "Boatman Dance" notwithstanding, the tune probably came likewise from riverine culture: it appears as "Ohio River" in George P. Knauff, *Virginia Reels* 1/11 (1839), cited in Chris Goertzen and Alan Jabbour, "George P. Knauff's Virginia Reels and Fiddling in the Antebellum South," *American Music* 5/2 (summer 1987): 133, while Nathan, *Dan Emmett and the Rise of Early Negro Minstrelsy*, 192, identifies earlier, morris dance antecedents.

73. S. White cites a 1799 advertisement that calls a mulatto runaway slave "a great dancer ["Hazzard's Peet"] and a very quarrelsome fellow, and is noted as such in the negro dancing cellars in the city" ("'We Dwell in Safety and Pursue Our Honest Callings,'" 467).

74. Patricia Cohen, with Timothy J. Gilfoyle and Helen Lefkowitz Horowitz, *The Flash Press: Sporting Male Weeklies in 1840s New York* (Chicago: University of Chicago Press, 2008), 6–7, 10.

75. Ibid., 68, is one of a number of citations of flash men frequenting African American brothels.

76. Cook, "Dancing across the Color Line."

77. As Cook points out in ibid., "Although Dickens was a relative newcomer to Manhattan, he seems to have had little trouble finding Almack's."

78. Reproduced in Cohen, *Flash Press*, 19.

79. Cook, "Dancing across the Color Line."

80. Ibid.

81. Ibid.

82. In ibid., Cook notes: "The sheer scope of the flash industry suggests that antebellum sporting culture was a relatively pervasive phenomenon." There were well over twelve New York "flash" publications in the 1840s, many including correspondence from subscribers and "sports" in New Jersey, Long Island, Massachusetts, Pennsylvania, Maryland, Louisiana, and California.

83. See Heather Nathans, *White Folks Do Not Know How to Behave at Colored Entertainments: William Brown's African and American Theater* (Durham: University of North Carolina Press, 2003).

84. Cook, "Dancing across the Color Line."

85. Ibid.

86. The first classes of the African Free School were held in a building at 65 Cliff St. (near Beekman); the first structure belonging to the organization was opened in 1815 (after a fire at Cliff St.) at 245 Williams St. (near Duane); subsequent locations included 135 Mulberry St. (between Hester and Walker); 120 Amity St. near 6th Ave., and 161 Duane St. Among the churches important in the New York African

American community were St. Philip's Episcopal Church (Collect St. near Anthony and Leonard), which was founded in 1819 by abolitionist, newspaperman, and AFS graduate Peter Williams Jr.; Abyssinian Baptist (Anthony St., now Worth, west of Broadway); First Colored Presbyterian Church (Frankfort St., corner of William), organized in 1821 by Samuel Cornish, who left to found *Freedom's Journal* in 1827, and African Methodist Episcopal Zion ("Mother Zion"), located at Leonard and Church Sts. and founded by the Rev. Peter Williams Sr. in 1796.

87. For a fascinating and revealing period map of these locations, see http://www.scribd.com/doc/20114576/1785%E2%80%931835-ny-African-Free-School, accessed December 8, 2011.

88. Jonathan Dewberry, "The African Grove Theatre and Company," in "Black Theatre Issue," special issue, *Black American Literature Forum* 16/4 (winter 1982): 128.

89. Ibid.

90. Ibid., 129–30.

91. This costuming evokes Zip Coon and the iconography of minstrelsy. *National Advocate* (August 3, 1821), quoted in Dewberry, "African Grove Theatre and Company," 128.

92. Dewberry, "African Grove Theatre and Company," 129. Although Dewberry surmises that these "white rowdies" may have been "spoilers" hired by competing white-owned theaters, another interpretation of the evidence is that these rowdies were simply members of the middle- and working-class "flash" community acting out the volatile, transgressive behaviors they sought in their expeditions through black New York.

93. William Moncrieff's 1821 theatrical adaptation of Pierce Egan's comic novel *Tom and Jerry; or, Life in London* was a massively popular "picaresque" ballad-opera that toured throughout the colonies. *Obu* [Obi?]*; or, The Three-Fingered Jack* was a pantomime, using improvised and topical slapstick action and contrafact songs, that opened in London in the Haymarket in 1800. *Three-Fingered Jack* included topical songs such as "Mandingo King" and "The Poor Negro Woman" and alluded to the rebellion of Jamaican Maroons. See Tracy C. Davis, "Acting Black, 1824: Charles Mathews's *Trip to America*," *Theatre Journal* 63 (2011): 163, n2. See also Dewberry, "African Grove Theatre and Company," 129.

94. Dewberry, "African Grove Theatre and Company," 31–32, emphasis added.

95. See, for example, Thomas Southerne's 1695 *Oroonoko*, whose idealized title protagonist is Native American. Nathan, *Dan Emmett and the Rise of Early Negro Minstrelsy*, 4. Similar is the pseudonymous "Andrew Barton's" *The Disappointment* (1762), which like its British Shakespearean and ballad-opera inspirations, includes comic Yankees, Dutch, Scots, and Irish. See Carolyn Rabson, "Disappointment Revisited: Unweaving the Tangled Web," part 1, *American Music* 1/1 (spring 1983): 12–35. By the 1820s, such characterizations were favorites in frontier touring companies, as well: recall that Edwin Forrest played "Cuffee, a Kentucky Negro," in the play *The Tailor in Distress; or, A Yankee Trick*" in Cincinnati in 1823. Nathan, *Dan Emmett and the Rise of Early Negro Minstrelsy*, 35.

96. Nathan, *Dan Emmett and the Rise of Early Negro Minstrelsy*, 44–45.

97. Ibid.

98. Nathan here references the illustrations for Charles Hunt's "Life in Philadelphia" series from ca. 1827 (London); Nathan, *Dan Emmett and the Rise of Early Negro Minstrelsy*, 44.

99. Nathan, *Dan Emmett and the Rise of Early Negro Minstrelsy,* says Mathews "did not fail to visit the Negroes' own theater and witness a performance of *Hamlet*" (44).

100. Dewberry, "African Grove Theatre and Company," 130.

101. Cook, "Dancing across the Color Line."

102. Ibid.

103. Cook, "Dancing across the Color Line."

104. The classic citation is Amiri Baraka, *Blues People* (New York: Harper Collins, 1963), 86; but see also Ingrid Monson, "Doubleness and Jazz Improvisation: Irony, Parody, and Ethnomusicology," *Critical Inquiry* 20/2 (winter 1994): 283–313, and David Krasner, "Parody and Double Consciousness in the Language of Early Black Musical Theatre," in "Special Issues on the Music," *African American Review* 29/2 (summer 1995): 317–23.

105. Nathan, *Dan Emmett and the Rise of Early Negro Minstrelsy*, says that Dibdin, for example was adept at a wide range of ethnic/comic/dialog characterizations, including "English, Irishmen, Italian singers . . . Jewish peddlers" (24).

106. See "The Negro and his Banjer," in *The Wags, or the Camp of Pleasure*, 1790, cited by Nathan, *Dan Emmett and the Rise of Early Negro Minstrelsy*, 34–35.

107. Nathan, *Dan Emmett and the Rise of Early Negro Minstrelsy*, 6–7.

108. Nathan, ibid., also points out a shift from a more idealized Enlightenment or "primitive" characterization to a more comic, true-to-life, realist one; he says "in *The Padlock* [1768] encouraged by alcohol, he is delightfully insolent; whereas in *Blackbeard* ["a serio-comic Ballet of Action," 1798] . . . he does not hide the fact that a fight would not appeal to him as much as a drink" (15).

109. Mahar's further and fundamental deductive leap is to recognize that blackface texts probably represent a much more literal transcription of African American verbal and musical practice than it has been fashionable to presume, and he links the dialect mannerisms in the song texts with the actual sound of black vernacular speech in the period. William J. Mahar, "'Backside Albany' and Early Blackface Minstrelsy: A Contextual Study of America's First Blackface Song," *American Music* 6/1 (spring 1988).

110. In eighteenth-century theater, much the same language, costume, and even dialogue was applied indiscriminately to Native Americans, Creoles, or African Americans. As Nathan, *Dan Emmett and the Rise of Early Negro Minstrelsy,* points out, the music Dibdin composed "was no more Negroid . . . than was Osmin's Turkish in Mozart's *Die Entfuhrung aus dem Serail*" (22). Indeed, renderings of dialect in period playscripts argue for a generic "otherness" in ethnic characterizations: a character realized as "Pennsylvania Dutch" in one production might be contrarily

acted as New York African American in other; see, for example, "Raccoon" in Barton's *The Disappointment* (1762). Rabson, "Disappointment Revisited: Unweaving the Tangled Web," 13.

111. Nathan, *Dan Emmett and the Rise of Early Negro Minstrelsy,* essentially confirms this about Dibdin (34ff).

112. Tatham, "David Claypoole Johnston's 'Militia Muster,'" 11.

113. Nathan, *Dan Emmett and the Rise of Early Negro Minstrelsy*, 35.

114. Ibid.

115. In that respect, then, Mahar's analysis of the linguistic evidence represent an important model for the current study's analogous analysis of the *iconographic* and kinesthetic evidence.

116. Mahar, "'Backside Albany' and Early Blackface Minstrelsy," 23.

117. A photograph of Aldridge in blackface as Mungo is noted in Don B. Wilmeth and C. W. E. Bigsby, *The Cambridge History of American Theatre: Beginnings to 1870* (Cambridge: Cambridge University Press, 1998), 357.

118. Buffet, "William Sidney Mount," 21.

119. No "Enterprise Society" is mentioned in the Hawkins-Mount Family Papers. However, Barnes-Ostrander confirms his membership in a New York's "Euterpean Society"; see Barnes-Ostrander, "Domestic Music Making in Early New York State," 371. Buffet, "William Sidney Mount," 23.

120. Lawrence, "Micah Hawkins, the Pied Pipe of the Catherine Slip," 144.

121. Cohen, *Flash Press*, 6, emphasis added.

122. Russell Sanjek, *From 1790 to 1909*, vol. 2 of *American Popular Music and Its Business: The First Hundred Years* (Oxford: Oxford University Press, 1988), 162.

123. See Scott, "Rituals of Race," 34.

124. Nathan, *Dan Emmett and the Rise of Early Negro Minstrelsy*, 38, 44.

125. Notable predecessors were staged in Philadelphia and elsewhere by Benjamin Carr, Alexander Reinagle, Raynor Taylor, and "Andrew Barton," but with the possible exception of the pseudonymous Barton, none were native born.

126. This is of course the usual situation: because ballad operas typically reused familiar tunes in order to set new words, it was considered necessary only to supply those words, and a title indicating that the new words would be "sung to the tune of . . ."

127. Johns cites a letter from H. S. Mount to R. N. Mount describing the scenery and songs, see Elizabeth Johns, "The Farmer in the Works of William Sidney Mount," in "The Evidence of Art: Images and Meaning in History," special issue, *Journal of Interdisciplinary History* 17/1 (summer 1986): 272.

128. Micah Hawkins, December 7, 1824, letter. Quoted in Lawrence, "Micah Hawkins, the Pied Pipe of the Catherine Slip," 155.

129. See the earlier *The Disappointment, or, The Force of Credulity* (1767), by "Andrew Barton," whose comic plot had similarly turned on disguise, deception, and ethnic caricature, noted in Rabson, "Disappointment Revisited: Unweaving the Tangled Web."

130. Lawrence, "Micah Hawkins, the Pied Piper of Catherine Slip," 157, emphasis added.

131. Micah Hawkins, *The Saw-Mill, or, A Yankee Trick. A Comic Opera, in Two Acts. As performed at the Theatre, Chatham Garden, with distinguished success. Written and composed by Micah Hawkins* (New York: J. & J. Harper, 1824), Hawkins-Mount Family Papers, item 00.471.

132. "Brother Jonathan" allegedly originated, as did "Yankee Doodle," as a derogatory British term for colonials during the revolution. Various, probably apocryphal, sources for the name are extant, the commonest one originating in a George Washington anecdote about the skepticism and fiscal conservatism of Jonathan Trumbull (1710–1785), the colonial Governor of Connecticut. For "Royall Tyler," see Alan Buechner, "Royall Tyler [1757–1826]," in *The William Sidney Mount Museum Collection at Stony Brook* (New York: Sonneck Society, 1976).

133. See also "Royall Tyler [1757–1826]," in Allan Gates Halline, *American Plays: Selected and Edited with Critical Introduction and Bibliographies* (New York: American Book Company, 1978); Joshua Taylor, *America as Art* (Washington, D.C.: Harper & Row, 1976), 40; and Johns, "Farmer in the Works of William Sidney Mount," 271.

134. Johns, "Farmer in the Works of William Sidney Mount," 271–72.

135. Ibid., 273.

136. William P. Murphy, "The Sublime Dance of Mende Politics: An African Aesthetic of Charismatic Power," *American Ethnologist* 25/4 (November 1998): 567.

137. Lanman quoted in Buffet, "William Sidney Mount," 86.

138. Andrew Barton's 1767 ballad opera *The Disappointment, or, The Force of Credulity* is a roman à clef set in Baltimore. Comic characters include "McSnip," a Scottish tailor; "Washball," an English barber; "Raccoon," who though based on a Baltimore hatter named Swan speaks in a dialect showing elements of both Jamaican creole and Pennsylvania Dutch; and "Trushoop," an Irish cooper. See Rabson, "Disappointment Revisited," 19.

139. S. White, "Question of Style," 25–26.

140. Bridenbaugh 1973:40–41, quoted in ibid., 26–27.

141. "When your pappy Moved fromm de New-York city Bowery up to Genesee, Jake wanted me to stay behind [i.e., in New York] and marry him." Hawkins, *Saw-Mill*, act 1, scene 4, emphasis added.

142. Hawkins, *Saw-Mill*, act 1, scene 3.

143. S. White, "Question of Style," 23–44. De Voe (1862), 345, quoted in ibid., 33.

144. As well as the expanded use of the Caribbean-inspired bandanna in the early nineteenth century; see Shane White and Graham White, "Slave Hair and African American Culture in the Eighteenth and Nineteenth Centuries," *Journal of Southern History* 61/1 (February 1995): 70–71.

145. Lawrence, "Micah Hawkins, the Pied Piper of the Catherine Slip," 159.

146. See "Yankee Doodle Rides into Town," including texts of *Yankee Doodle, or, the Lexington March* (1775?), *The Farmer and His Son's Return from a Visit to*

the Camp (1786?), and *Yankee Doodle* (ca. 1708); J. Heywood Alexander, ed., *To Stretch Our Ears: A Documentary History of America's Music* (New York: London, 2002), 49–52.

147. Hawkins, *Saw-Mill*, act 3, scene 16.

148. Johns, "Farmer in the Works of William Sidney Mount," in an acute and closely argued art-historical analysis, makes this analogy explicit (275).

149. The letter is dated Jasper County, Georgia, January 17, 1841. For a trenchant discussion of "Possum Up a Gum Stump," see Nathan, *Dan Emmett and the Rise of Early Negro Minstrelsy*, 47.

150. For Mathews to Aldridge, see Scott, "Rituals of Race," 71, and Buckley, "Place to Make an Artist Work," 10.

151. Scott, "Rituals of Race," 75.

152. For the Hawkins manuscript book, see LIM, item KSA021192, no. 15; for the Kinkeldy reference, see the museum's archival typescript of his article of October 19, 1927, KSA021192, Hawkins-Mount Family papers.

153. An 1849 account retracing Dickens's trip to Five Points describes a band who are "black or blackfaced" and whose instrumentation includes "a fiddler, a trumpeter, and a bass drummer," who play "Cooney in de Holler." George Foster, quoted in Eric Lott, *Love and Theft: Blackface Minstrelsy and the American Working Class* (Oxford: Oxford University Press, 1996), 84. The same song is mentioned in Dickens's original 1842 account, quoted in Nicholas E. Tawa, *High-Minded and Low-Down: Music in the Lives of Americans, 1800–1861* (Boston: Northeastern University Press, 2000), 286. For the tune's pre-1830 provenance, see Mark Wilson, liner notes to *That's My Rabbit, My Dog Caught I: Traditional Southern Instrumental Styles* (New World Records NW 226).

154. Nathan, *Dan Emmett and the Rise of Early Negro Minstrelsy*, 48, n22s. See also James Kirk Paulding, *Letters from the South: Written during an Excursion in the Summer of 1816*, vol. 2 (New York: Eastburn, 1817), 90, http://bit.ly/hYIjY, accessed April 3, 2011.

155. Buffet, "William Sidney Mount," 24.

156. LIM, autobiographical notes and account of career 1825–1853 (16pp), [Jan 1854] items 0.11.3548, 0.11.3547, 0.11.3549.

157. Buffet, "William Sidney Mount," 26.

158. *Christ Raising the Daughter of Jairus*; *Saul and the Witch of Endor*, both reproduced in Alfred Frankenstein, *Painter of Rural America: William Sidney Mount, 1807–1868* (Washington: H. K. Press, 1968), plates 4–5.

159. Frankenstein, *Painter of Rural America*, 21.

160. Buffet, "William Sidney Mount," 26ff. Mount's various known addresses were, in 1827, 154 Nassau St.; in 1830, 15 Cherry St.; 1830–31, 71 James St.

161. WSM to Charles F. Morse, letter 1853, New-York Historical Society, Mss Collection, William S. Mount papers 1833–1868.

162. WSM to Robert Nelson Mount, letter May 29, 1930, New-York Historical Society, Mss Collection, William S. Mount papers 1833–1868.

163. WSM to Martin E. Thompson, (undated) letter, New-York Historical Society, Mss Collection, William S. Mount papers 1833–1868.

164. See Lynda Rose Day, *Making a Way to Freedom: A History of African Americans on Long Island* (Interlaken, N.Y.: Empire State Books, 1997). See also Richard J. Koke, *American Landscape and Genre Paintings in the New-York Historical Society: A Catalog of the Collection, Including Historical, Narrative, and Marine Art* (New York: New-York Historical Society, 1982), 1:3.

165. Buffet, "William Sidney Mount," 17.

166. Ibid.

167. From the first trade fair in 1828, instrument makers were represented: it may be that these early trade fair showings were one source for Mount's lifelong interest in instrument design. See Nancy Groce, *Musical Instrument Makers of New York: A Directory of Eighteenth and Nineteenth Century Urban Craftsmen* (New York: Pendragon Press, 1991), xviii.

168. See Catherine Hoover, "The Influence of David Wilkie's Prints on the Genre Paintings of William Sidney Mount," *American Art Journal* 13/3 (Summer 1981): 14.

169. Alan Buechner, "Music and Dance in the Paintings of William Sydney Mount" (typescript text of November 1976 presentation to National Meetings of the American Musicological Society): "the key to a fuller understanding of the paintings and the music and choreographic traditions which underlie them." Mount Research Articles, LIM.

170. Buechner, "Music and Dance in the Paintings of William Sydney Mount," 11.

171. See, for example, John Lewis Krimmel (1786/7–1821), cited in Kevin Scott, "The 'Negro Touch' and the 'Yankee Trick': William Sidney Mount and the Art of Race and Ethnicity," *Visual Resources* 24/3 (2008): 233; Krimmel's *The Blind Fiddler* (1812) seems to reveal direct influence on Mount's *Rustic Dance*. See also Hoover, "Influence of David Wilkie's Prints on the Genre Paintings of William Sidney Mount," 5–33. See also various works by Hogarth and Cruikshank; folk musicians and singers were popular elements in vernacular painting and "popular antiquities" as far back as Rembrandt and the Brueghels.

172. See George Washington Cable, "Creole Slave Dances: The Dance in Place Congo," *Century: A Popular Quarterly* 31/4 (February 1886): 519, http://memory.loc.gov/cgi-bin/query/r?ammem/ncps:@field%20%28DOCID%2B@lit%20%28ABP2287-0031-119%29%29, accessed March 10, 2011.

173. Margot Lieth-Philipp. "*Bamboula*: Historical, Ethnological, and Linguistic Evidence for a Forgotten Caribbean Music," *Ethnomusicology and the Historical Dimension* 59–70, papers presented at the European Seminar in Ethnomusicology, London, May 20–23, 1986 (Ludwigsburg, Germany: Philipp Verlag, 1989).

174. Pierre C. de Laussat, *Memoire su ma Vie Pendant les Annees 1803 et Suivantes . . . a la Louisiane* (Pau, 1831), 395, quoted in Dena J. Epstein, "African Music in British and French America," *Musical Quarterly* 59/1 (January 1973): n62.

175. Lafcadio Hearn, whose reports on postbellum African American practices are cited elsewhere in this book, described such dancing-and-drumming in his

article for the *Century* "The Scenes of Cable's Romances," *Century* 26 (November 1883): 45, quoted in Henry A. Kmen, "The Roots of Jazz and the Dance in Place Congo: A Re-Appraisal," *Interamericano de Investigacion Musical* 8 (1972): 12, n26. Explicit connections between the *bamboula* and *djouba*/juba appear in Julian Gerstin, "Interaction and Improvisation between Dancers and Drummers in Martinican Bèlè," *Black Music Research Journal* 18/1–2 (spring–autumn, 1998): 126, and the dance was still extant in the U.S. Virgin Islands in the mid-twentieth century, see Robert W. Nicholls, "The Mocko Jumbie of the U.S. Virgin Islands: History and Antecedents," *African Arts* 32/3 (autumn 1999): 60.

Chapter 4. Minstrelsy's Material Culture

1. The first three of our four paintings—*Just in Tune*, *Right and Left*, and *The Banjo Player*—are in the collections of the Long Island Museum of American Art, History, and Carriages (hereafter LIM). The fourth—*The Bone Player*—is in the Karolik Collection, Museum of Fine Arts, Boston.

2. Edward P. Buffet, "William Sidney Mount: A Biography. The Story of Old Time Life in Brookhaven North Told Through His Pictures, as published by Mr. Buffet in the Port Jefferson Times from December 1, 1912, to June 12, 1924," typescript in the LIM, 0.7.3527, 149; Kevin Scott, "The 'Negro Touch' and the 'Yankee Trick': William Sidney Mount and the Art of Race and Ethnicity," *Visual Resources* 24/3 (2004): 247–58.

3. See Donald L. Keyes, "The Sources of William Sidney Mount's Earliest Genre Paintings," *Art Quarterly* 32/3 (1969): 259–68.

4. For Mount as antiabolitionist, see Kevin M. Scott, "Rituals of Race: Mount, Melville, and Antebellum America," PhD diss., Purdue University, 2004. See also Frederick C. Moffatt, "Barnburning and Hunkerism: William Sidney Mount's *Power of Music*," *Winterthur Portfolio* 29/1 (spring 1991): 22. For minstrelsy as generically anti-abolitionist, see Alexander Saxton, "Blackface Minstrelsy and Jacksonian Ideology," *American Quarterly* 27/1 (March 1975): 3–28.

5. Scott, "Rituals of Race."

6. See Richard Cullen Rath, "African Music in Seventeenth-Century Jamaica: Transit and Transition," in "Third Series," *William and Mary Quarterly* 50/4 (October 1993): 700–726; and William J. Mahar, "Black English in Early Blackface Minstrelsy: A New Interpretation of the Sources of Minstrel Show Dialect," *American Quarterly* 37/2 (summer 1983): 260–85.

7. See Scott, "Rituals of Race"; Alan Buechner, "Music and Dance in the Paintings of William Sydney Mount" (typescript text of November 1976 presentation to National Meetings of the American Musicological Society); Alfred Frankenstein, *Painter of Rural America: William Sidney Mount, 1807–1868* (Washington, D.C.: H. K. Press, 1968); and others previously cited.

8. Buffet, "William Sidney Mount," observes and discounts the claim that the model was Shepard S. Mount (97); he also suggests that, while Robert Nelson Mount

sat for the painting (perhaps only to provide details of stance, body posture, hand position, and so forth), William Sidney did not reproduce his brother's features in it (112).

9. See for example the full-page advertisement for "Mr. Woodbury's Musical Works" in the *Musical Review and Choral Advocate* 4/1 (January 1853), LIM, KSA031554.

10. Schaus to William Sidney Mount, New York, letter September 1, 1852: "I would also give you an order for some large head same size about of—Just in tune—Right & left—&—Raffling—; the subjects to be something like the above and representing 'Negro playing the Banjo and singing—Negro playing with bones.' Quoted in Buffet, "William Sidney Mount," 191.

11. William Sidney Mount to Schaus, Stony Brook, letter September 9, 1852: "I will undertake those large heads for you—although I have been urged not to paint any more such subjects. I had as leave paint the characters of some Negros—as to paint the characters of some Whites." Quoted in Buffet, "William Sidney Mount," 192.

12. Scott, "Rituals of Race."

13. Buffet, "William Sidney Mount," 112.

14. The reality of such underreported rural-urban black-white musical interaction is confirmed by period sources: "In March 1737, a piece in John Peter Zenger's *New York Weekly Journal* reported on a Pinkster celebration, held in the fields outside of New York City, in which blacks danced to the music of drums, fiddle, and bangar (banjo)." Schlomo Pestcoe, "Banjo History: Challenging the Myths," http://www.shlomomusic.com, accessed November 23, 2012.

15. Buffet, "William Sidney Mount," 58–60.

16. Ibid., 149.

17. I am indebted to banjo scholar Robert Carlin for this observation regarding the cord's possible function. Carlin, correspondence with the author, February 15, 2012.

18. See Mary Jo Sanna Barron, "Singing for the Ancestors," *Black Perspective in Music* 13/1 (spring 1985): 95; also Olcutt Sanders, "The Texas Cattle Country and Cowboy Square Dance," *Journal of the Folk Music Council* 3 (1951): 23.

19. See Elizabeth Johns, "The Farmer in the Works of William Sidney Mount," in "The Evidence of Art: Images and Meaning in History," *Journal of Interdisciplinary History* 17/1 (summer 1986): 259, 266.

20. See Robert Carlin, *The Birth of the Banjo: Joel Walker Sweeney and Early Minstrelsy* (Jefferson, N.C.: McFarland, 2007), also "An Apprenticeship with the Ghosts," *Old-Time Herald* 5/7 (spring 1997); Robert Winans and Robert Carlin, liner notes to *Minstrel Banjo Style* (Rounder, 2009). Robert Winans, "Black Instrumental Music Traditions in the Ex-Slave Narratives," *Black Music Research Journal* 10/1 (spring 1990): 44–53; Robert Winans, "Early Minstrel Show Music 1843–1852," in *Inside the Minstrel Mask: Readings in Nineteenth-Century Blackface Minstrelsy*, ed. Annemarie Bean, James V. Hatch, and Brooks McNamara, 114–62 (Hanover, N.H.: Wesleyan University Press, 1996); Robert B. Winans, "The Folk, the Stage, and the Five-String

Banjo in the Nineteenth Century," *Journal of American Folklore* 89/354 (Oct.–Dec. 1976), 407–37; Robert Carlin and Elias J. Kaufman, "Minstrel and Classic Banjo: American and English Connections," *American Music* 12/1 (spring 1994): 1–30. Cecilia Conway, *African Banjo Echoes in the Southern Appalachians* and "Black Banjo Songsters in Appalachia," *Black Music Research Journal* 23/1–2 (spring–autumn 2003): 149–66. Pestcoe, "Banjo History"; "Banjo Roots: West Africa," http://www.myspace.com/banjorootswestafrica, accessed March 18, 2011, "Ekoting"; http://www.myspace.com/akonting, accessed March 18, 2011. Ulf Jagfors, "African Banjo Roots: The Akonting Lute, One Possible Ancestor to the Banjo," paper read at the Banjo Gathering, November 8–11, 2001, Williamsburg, Va.

21. Carlin, *Birth of the Banjo*, 20. See also Sir Hans Sloane's *A Voyage to the Islands of Madeira, Barbados, Nieves, S. Christopher and Jamaica* (London, 1707), "written in 1688, which depicts two Jamaican negro 'strum-strumps' with long necks and skin-covered gourd bodies," cited in Jay Scott Odell and Robert B. Winans, "Banjo," Grove Music Online, Oxford Music Online, Oxford University Press, http://www.oxfordmusiconline.com/subscriber/article/grove/music/01958, accessed November 23, 2012.

22. Carlin, *Birth of the Banjo*, 127.

23. Schlomo Pestcoe, "'The Old Plantation'—A Banjo Roots Perspective," http://www.myspace.com/banjoroots/blog/425545009, accessed March 18, 2011.

24. Herskovits to Little, quoted in ibid.

25. See Richard Cullen Rath, "Drums and Power: Ways of Creolizing Music in Coastal South Carolina and Georgia, 1730–90," in *Creolization in the Americas*, ed. David Buisseret and Steven G. Reinhardt (College Station: Texas A&M University Press, 2000), 113.

26. See Schlomo Pestcoe, "West Africa: The Wellspring of the Banjo's African Heritage," http://www.myspace.com/banjorootswestafrica, accessed November 10, 2012.

27. For Maryland, see the Rev. Jonathan Boucher, *Boucher's Glossary of Archaic and Provincial Words* (London, 1832), quoted in Odell and Winans, "Banjo." See also Dena J. Epstein, "African Music in British and French America," *The Musical Quarterly* 59/1 (January 1973): 76.

28. Pestcoe, *Banjo Roots*.

29. Carlin, *Birth of the Banjo*, 19; see Alex Roland, with W. Jeffrey Bolster, and Alexander Keyssar, *The Way of the Ship: America's Maritime History Reenvisioned, 1600–2000* (Hoboken, N.J.: John Wiley, 2008), 96–99, 145.

30. Carlin, *Birth of the Banjo*, 139, 140.

31. On William Esperance Boucher (1822–1899), see Carlin, *Birth of the Banjo*, 134.

32. The Boucher Company prided itself on those "scientific" advances it had made in banjo design, even donating instruments for display at congresses and expositions throughout the second half of the century. See Philip F. Gura and James F. Bollman, *America's Instrument: The Banjo in the Nineteenth Century* (Chapel Hill: University of North Carolina Press, 1999), 64.

33. See the stocking-capped Caucasian dancer, identified by Edward Buffet as farm laborer Tom Briggs, a member of Mount's Setauket circle of acquaintances, in *Haymakers*; the anonymous stocking-capped black coachman in 1830's *Rustic Dance*; and the frequent depiction of stocking-capped black dancers in various sketches.

34. Sule Greg Wilson, correspondence with the author, September 2007.

35. William Sidney Mount diary, quoted in Lance Mayer, and Gay Myers, *American Painters on Technique: The Colonial Period to 1860* (New York: Getty Publications, 2011), 200.

36. Buffet, "William Sidney Mount," 112. In 1850, Mount's uncle John Brewster lived in Brookhaven, on the South Shore of the Island, having been born in 1774, while the lawyer John Satterly, also resident in Brookhaven, was his contemporary (b. 1790). The Suffolk County census for 1840 lists a "Charles Freeman" living in Brookhaven, and the 1850 version lists what appears to be an extended Freeman clan in the same area, including both Charles (b. "abt 1815") and Charles M. (b. "abt 1845"). Most crucially for our purposes, the same 1850 census lists as part of this family "George Freeman," born "abt 1835." While this "George Freeman" would have been aged about twenty-one in the year of *The Banjo Player*, and thus not "teenaged," the sitter in the portrait could certainly be in his early twenties. http://www.rootsweb.ancestry.com/~nysuffol/1850cb2.html, accessed March 15, 2012.

37. Though Freeman's surname may be a coincidence, it is also distinctly possible that it was assumed postmanumission by a former slave—perhaps George's paternal relative?—and thus connects George Freeman particularly directly to the postrevolutionary ex-slave experience.

38. A similar 1845 Boucher instrument is held in the Smithsonian Institution collections: "Boucher Five-String Fretless Banjo," National Museum of American History, Kenneth E. Behring Center, no. MI*094764.

39. Pestcoe, "Banjo History."

40. See Winans, "Folk, the Stage, and the Five-String Banjo in the Nineteenth Century," 418.

41. Recent banjo scholarship (Daniel Jatta, Ulf Jagfors, Schlomo Pestcoe) has tended to confirm the strong influence of the *akonting* on the *banza/banjar*/banjo. See, for example, Daniel Laemouahuma Jatta, "An Akonting Report: The First International Conference on the African Origins of the New World Banjo," Mandinary Gambia: The Senegambia Center for Cultural Research and Education, 2006, http://web.comhem.se/abzu/akonting/opening.html, accessed November 2, 2011.

42. Additional substantiation for the claim that Mount is depicting the earlier, Afro-Caribbean, "stroke" style can be found in comparable illustrations in period banjo tutors: Tom Briggs's 1855 *Briggs' Banjo Instructor* depicts the stroke style, while the first description and depiction of "guitar" style fingerpicking on the banjo was only published in Frank Converse's banjo tutor, from 1865. See Carlin and Kaufman, "Minstrel and Classic Banjo," 6, 8.

43. I am indebted to African American dance scholar Sule Greg Wilson for posing the question that forced me to discover this answer. Wilson correspondence with the author.

44. Reiss points out, for example, the enhanced mobility and opportunity available to skilled slaves: coachmen, barbers, and so on. Oscar Reiss, *Blacks in Colonial America* (Jefferson, N.C.: McFarland, 1997), 130.

45. "One day he saw, to his amazement, a Negro 'driving a stage-coach . . . and urging his horses by different tunes on a fiddle, while he ingeniously fastened the reins around his neck.'" Mrs. Mathews, *Memoirs of Charles Mathews, Comedian* (London, 1839), 3:390, quoted in Hans Nathan, *Dan Emmett and the Rise of Early Negro Minstrelsy*, 2nd ed. (Norman: University of Oklahoma: 1977), 46 n18. See also Northrup, who describes a slave fiddler named Platt Epps playing while sitting on a mule. Solomon Northrup, *Twelve Years a Slave: Narrative of Solomon Northup, a Citizen of New-York, Kidnapped in Washington City in 1841, and Rescued in 1853, from a Cotton Plantation Near the Red River, in Louisiana* (New York: Miller, Orton & Mulligan, 1855), 217, http://books.google.com, accessed November 23, 2012.

46. Jarvis mentions that, in Bermuda (and likewise in other Afro-Caribbean islands), restrictions on the acquisition of property led slave sailors to "take pride in their appearance and spen[d] money on personal adornments"; he quotes the case of the sailor Josiah Saunders who "wore a gold 'ring-bob' in one of his ears." Michael J. Jarvis, "Maritime Masters and Seafaring Slaves in Bermuda, 1680–1783," *William and Mary Quarterly*, 3rd series, 59/3, *Slaveries in the Atlantic World* (July 2002): 609.

47. See Floris Barnett Cash, "African American Whalers: Images and Reality," *Long Island Historical Journal* 2 (fall 1989): 41–42; Grania Bolton Marcus, *Discovering the African American Experience in Suffolk County, 1620–1860* (Setauket, N.Y.: Amereon House, for the Society for the Preservation of Long Island Antiquities), in the collection of the LIM; and Marilyn E. Weigold, *The American Mediterranean: An Environmental, Economic and Social History of Long Island Sound* (Port Washington, N.Y., and London: Kennikat Press, 1974), chapter 5.

48. Lhamon, *Raising Cain*, cites the singer Bessie Jones's 1970s reminiscences of singing and dancing "Jump Jim Crow" in the Georgia Sea Islands folk tradition in the early part of the 20th century: "There were lyrics to the song. . . . However, the lyrics are only a fraction of the whole event. Clapping and slapping, double-timing and patting Juba, kicking and high-stepping, the staging and the lyrics were all part of dancing 'Jim Crow'" (181).

49. Don Herbison-Evans, "The Perception of the Fleeting Moment in Dance," *Leonardo* 26/1 (1993): 46, emphasis added; see also Wilson, correspondence with the author; and Robert Farris Thompson, "An Aesthetic of the Cool," *African Arts* 7/1 (autumn 1973): 41.

50. Dance scholars have commented, for example, on the unremarked *accuracy* of those "knee bones bent" and arms akimbo in the Jim Crow iconography; they have suggested that such body imagery, if understood as representing the body

moving through space, rather than a static pose, may in turn reflect the springy kinetic rebounding of Jim Crow's leaps and twists—its "wheels and turns." Wilson correspondence with the author; Thompson, "Aesthetic of the Cool."

51. There is fascinating archival and iconographic work to be done on the chronology and dynamics of the interplay between Anglo-Celtic and African American approaches to the percussive bones—we can anticipate that, as was the case throughout the whole of the creole synthesis, this contact was much earlier and much more extensive than has previously been documented.

52. Many of the great jazz drummers, for example, from Baby Dodds in the 1920s to Shadow Wilson in the 1960s, have been noted dancers, and the author well remembers in 1970s Cambridge, Massachusetts, hearing and playing with the late John "Mr. Bones" Burrill, who had learned the bones from watching 1930s minstrel troupes, and who, despite a twisted spine that made walking difficult, was not only a virtuoso percussionist but had also been a champion jitterbugger.

Chapter 5. Melody's Polyrhythmic Polysemic Possibilities

1. Eliot D. Chapple and Martha Davis, "Expressive Movement and Performance: Toward a Unifying Theory," *TDR (1988–)* 32/4 (winter 1988): 61.

2. See Curtis D. Jerde, "Black Music in New Orleans: A Historical Overview," *Black Music Research Journal* 10/1 (spring 1990): 22; Frederick C. Moffatt, "Barnburning and Hunkerism: William Sidney Mount's *Power of Music*," *Winterthur Portfolio* 29/1 (spring 1994): 40; Howard L. Sacks and Judith R. Sacks, "Way up North in Dixie: Black-White Musical Interaction in Knox County, Ohio," *American Music* 6/4 (winter 1988): 414; Robert B. Winans, "Black Instrumental Music Traditions in the Ex-Slave Narratives," *Black Music Research Journal* 10/1 (spring 1990): 52.

3. Hans Nathan, *Dan Emmett and the Rise of Early Negro Minstrelsy*, 2nd ed. (Norman: University of Oklahoma Press, 1977); Chris Goertzen, "American Fiddle Tunes and the Historic-Geographic Method," *Ethnomusicology* 29/3 (autumn 1985): 448–73; Chris Goertzen and Alan Jabbour, "George P. Knauff's Virginia Reels and Fiddling in the Antebellum South," *American Music* 5/2 (summer 1987); Paul F. Wells, "Fiddling as an Avenue of Black-White Musical Interchange," *Black Music Research Journal* 23/1–2 (spring–autumn 2003): 135–47, previously cited.

4. These include the Kate Strong Historical Library and the Kidder-Douglass Collection ("Letters, deeds, wills, tickets, sketches, diaries, journals and financial papers of William Sidney Mount, Shepard Alonzo Mount, Samuel Seabury, Ruth Hawkins Mount, Thomas Shepard Seabury, Bishop Charles Seabury, Ruth Frances Seabury Blydenburgh and Edith Blydenburgh. Also includes genealogy for the Mount, Seabury, Saltonstall and Blydenburgh families. Items of note include early financial records of the Bishop Charles Seabury, personal letters of William Sidney Mount, and pencil sketches executed by various family members"), Hawkins-Mount Family Papers, catalog numbers KSA10, KSA13, KSA21, KSA3, KSA9, Long Island Museum of American Art, History, and Carriages (hereafter LIM).

5. Robert Nelson Mount to William Sidney Mount, letter January 17, 1841, from Monticello, Jasper Co., Georgia: Robert Nelson describes "running away to Texas" because "my Class was principally made up with back sliding Methodists, and on that account it was called the Methodist Dancing School." Mount Letters, Hawkins-Mount Family Papers, LIM.

6. Robert Nelson Mount to William Sidney Mount, letter January 17, 1841.

7. Robert Nelson Mount, quoted in liner notes, Gilbert Ross, *The Cradle of Harmony: William Sidney Mount's Violin and Fiddle Music* (Smithsonian Folkways FW32379–206, 1976).

8. The LIM still owns his kazoo and the prototypes of the violins he designed, as well as several of his flutes and tin whistles in various materials.

9. C. Bishop to William Sidney Mount in Stony Brook, letter January 9, 1830: "I started this morning to come over and see you about assisting me at a public [dance] tomorrow night . . . the one I depended upon is obliged to disappoint me—It is probable there will be a large company . . . I engaged to get another player and I shall be very sorry to disappoint them I wish you (or your brother (if not engaged) would come if you can anyway, if not I would like to have you see Mr [Shep]Jones & him to come if he will." Mount Letters, LIM.

10. A number of LIM items include attributions to Shepard Jones: the manuscript inscribed "Music Book from Martin Titus. To Wm. S. Mount. April 1853" (KSA031628) includes "Jones Favorite" "noted down by G.L. Pfeffer, Esq" and "Stony Brook Hornpipe—Composed by S.S. Jones Esq.," while KSA032124, dated "Setauket Long Island February 1851," contains "Shepard Jones' Hornpipe." Found tucked into the paper backing of the framed version of *Dance of the Haymakers* is handwritten musical notation for "Shepard Jones's Hornpipe," further confirming that Jones is the depicted fiddler. Edward P. Buffet, "William Sidney Mount: A Biography. The Story of Old Time Life in Brookhaven North Told Through His Pictures, as published by Mr. Buffet in the Port Jefferson Times from December 1, 1912, to June 12, 1924," typescript in LIM, 71, identifies the "young man playing the fiddle" as Shepard Jones, though Buffet later quotes Henry Floyd Jones's identification of the fiddler as "John Henry Mount (or Henry J. Mount as he later called himself), a fifteen-year-old son of William's deceased brother Henry" (74). Jones was by all reports a heavy drinker and therefore perhaps not reliable: Buffet quotes "Mount's Advice to a Friend on the Drinking Habit" ("William Sidney Mount," 136).

11. See Buffet, "William Sidney Mount," 136.

12. Mount's handwritten musical notations include minstrel standards like "Jim Crow Polka" (KSA031492), "Mississippi Sawyer" (KSA031474), "Old Dan Tucker" (KSA032109), "Arkansas Traveller" (KSA032111), and many others. William Sidney Mount (Handwritten) Sheet music, box 1, LIM. For parallels in Sweeney's repertoire, see Robert Carlin, *The Birth of the Banjo: Joel Walker Sweeney and Early Minstrelsy* (New York: McFarland, 2007), 109–12.

13. For Latrobe's reportage in the Federalist period, see Shane White and Graham White, "Slave Hair and African American Culture in the Eighteenth and

Nineteenth Centuries," *Journal of Southern History* 61/1 (February 1995): 46; also Dena J. Epstein, "The Folk Banjo: A Documentary History," *Ethnomusicology* 19/3 (Sept. 1975): 358; Thomas F. DeFrantz, ed., *Dancing Many Drums: Excavations in African American Dance* (Madison: University of Wisconsin Press, 2002), 150; Michael J. Morgan, "Rock and Roll Unplugged: African American Music in Eighteenth-Century America," in "African American Culture in the Eighteenth-Century," special issue, *Eighteenth-Century Studies* 27/4 (summer 1994): 651; Henry A. Kmen, "The Roots of Jazz and the Dance in Place Congo: A Re-Appraisal," *Interamericano de Investigacion Musical* 8 (1972): 8.

14. Nathan, *Dan Emmett and the Rise of Early Negro Minstrelsy.*

15. A selected list of more recent scholarship citing Nathan includes Lawrence Gushee, "The Nineteen-Century Origins of Jazz," in "Selected Papers from the 1993 National Conference on Black Music Research," special issue, *Black Music Research Journal* 14/1 (spring 1994): 4; H. Sacks and J. Sacks, "Way up North in Dixie," 422; Cecelia Conway, "Black Banjo Songsters in Appalachia," *Black Music Research Journal* 23/1–2 (spring–autumn 2003): 154; Goertzen and Jabbour, "George P. Knauff's Virginia Reels and Fiddling in the Antebellum South," 133; and so on.

16. Robert Winans, "Early Minstrel Show Music 1843–1852," in *Inside the Minstrel Mask: Readings in Nineteenth-Century Blackface Minstrelsy*, ed. Annemarie Bean, James V. Hatch, and Brooks McNamara, 114–62 (Hanover, N.H.: Wesleyan University Press, 1996), 143.

17. For exchange of body vocabularies, see Saxton, "Blackface Minstrelsy," in *Inside the Minstrel Mask*, 73; Dale Cockrell, *Demons of Disorder: Blackface Minstrels and Their World* (Cambridge: Cambridge University Press, 1997), 84; P. Sterling Stuckey, "Christian Conversion and the Challenge of Dance," in *Dancing Many Drums: Excavations in African American Dance*, ed. Thomas F. DeFrantz, 39–58 (Madison: University of Wisconsin Press, 2002), 39–41.

18. Nathan, *Dan Emmett and the Rise of Early Negro Minstrelsy*, 189.

19. In addition, these printed transcriptions tended toward intentional simplification for the at-home, middle-class parlor piano market at which they were aimed.

20. Nathan, *Dan Emmett and the Rise of Early Negro Minstrelsy*, 182–89.

21. See, for example, S. White and G. White, "Slave Hair and African American Culture in the Eighteenth and Nineteenth Centuries."

22. See Winans, "Early Minstrel Show Music 1843–1852," 143.

23. As we have seen in chapter 3, he attributes the iconic "Possum up a Gum Stump" to the frontiers and "Clare de Kitchen" to the Mississippi. "Possum" (Nathan, *Dan Emmett and the Rise of Early Negro Minstrelsy*, 44). For "Clare de Kitchen," "Ole Jaw Bones," "Zip Coon," see Nathan, *Dan Emmett and the Rise of Early Negro Minstrelsy*, 186. Likewise, he says that "De Ole Jaw Bone" "was probably played and sung by Negro banjoists at a white frontier frolic in Tennessee in the early thirties"; while "Zip Coon," one of the earliest hits for Thomas Dartmouth Rice, is said to have been "taken from a rough jig dance, called 'Natchez under the hill,' and "De Boatman's Dance" is said to have been "chanted . . . [by] Ohio river boatmen."

24. Specifically, in discussing the early "Bonja Song" (ca. 1820) and "Coal Black Rose" ("late 1820s"). Nathan, *Dan Emmett and the Rise of Early Negro Minstrelsy*, 159. "Zip Coon" is linked to the "Glasgow Hornpipe" and "Post Office Hornpipe"; "Sich a Gitting Up Stairs" to a morris tune of the same title; "My Long Tail Blue" to the Scots "Jenny's Babee" and "Jump Jim Crow" to "I Wish the Shepherd's Pet Were Mine." Nathan, *Dan Emmett and the Rise of Early Negro Minstrelsy*, 170ff.

25. For ex-slave narratives, see Carlin, *Birth of the Banjo*, 4; the iconic traveler's report is that of Benjamin Latrobe (1764–1820), whose 1819 visit to Place Congo in New Orleans yielded firsthand description and sketches of music making; see Lynne Faulkey Emery, *Black Dance in the United States from 1619 to 1970* (Palo Alto, Calif.: National Press Books, 1972), 150, and Dena J. Epstein, "The Folk Banjo: A Documentary History," *Ethnomusicology* 19/3 (September 1975): 355. See also Jerah Johnson, "New Orleans's Congo Square: An Urban Setting for Early Afro-American Culture Formation," *Louisiana History: The Journal of the Louisiana Historical Association* 32/2 (spring 1991): 118–20.

26. See Roger D. Abrahams, *Singing the Master: The Emergence of African American Culture in the Plantation South* (New York: Penguin, 1994).

27. Lydia Parrish, comp., *Slave Songs of the Georgia Sea Islands* (Athens: University of Georgia, 1992).

28. In ibid., Parrish, publishing in 1942 on fieldwork conducted in the 1920s, describes the Georgia Sea Islands as providing a geographical link "between the Negroes of America, the West Indies and Africa" (v), and, in her chapter "Concerning Slave Songs and Their Preservation" notes that the Inland Waterway between the islands and the mainland was full of "sailing vessels from all parts of the world" (15).

29. Stills from Parrish's later ethnographic films are also included in the 1992 edition, including Snooks dancing "Juba" and Julia dancing "The Buzzard Lope." Parrish, *Slave Songs of the Georgia Sea Islands*, 66, 128. See also the extended discussion of these transcriptions in chapter 6.

30. But see William B. Smith, "The Persimmon Tree and the Beer Dance," *Farmer's Register* (April 1, 1838), 58–61, reprinted in *The Negro and His Folklore in Nineteenth-Century Periodicals*, ed. Bruce Jackson (Austin: University of Texas, 1967), 5.

31. Chapter 2 observes a similar "African" version of the creole synthesis in Barbados and Bermuda.

32. Parrish, *Slave Songs of the Georgia Sea Islands*, 80–84; transcription after Churchill's in ibid.

33. William Francis Allen, Charles Pickard Ware and Lucy McKim Garrison, *Slave Songs Of The United States* (Boston: Smith, 1929).

34. Chapple and Davis, "Expressive Movement and Performance," 67.

35. My analysis is deeply indebted to Nathan because of his remarkably detailed sourcing of minstrelsy's tunes, but, like that of Winans, significantly nuances Nathan's reconstruction of the music's sound and rhythm. It is also important to acknowledge here that such hypothetical rhythmicizations of transcribed music in no way intend its "improvement" or codification—in fact, quite the opposite:

these hypothesized reconstructions seek to recover essential and definitive rhythmic characteristics of early blackface music that significantly enrich and fruitfully complicate our understanding of how that music worked.

36. On the "Buzzard Lope" as a Georgia Sea Islands children's dance song, see Parrish, *Slave Songs of the Georgia Sea Islands*. Also cited in Nathan, *Dan Emmett and the Rise of Early Negro Minstrelsy*, 171.

37. Andrew Kuntz, Fiddler's Companion, http://www.ibiblio.org/fiddlers/OLDHA_OLDMRS.htm, accessed November 18, 2012.

38. Cecil Sharp quoted in William Lynwood Montell, *Grassroots Music in the Upper Cumberland* (Memphis: University of Tennessee Press, 2006), 193.

39. Parrish confirms that in performance, the lead sing "obeys [the text's] instructions and bends the knee far down with the rhythm of the words." Parrish, *Slave Songs of the Georgia Sea Islands*, 80.

40. See Charles Keil, "Participatory Discrepancies and the Power of Music," *Cultural Anthropology* 2/3 (August 1987): 277–78.

41. *Kinesics* is defined by dance scholar Judith Hanna as "the systematic study of learned body motion which has communicative value," see Judith Lynne Hanna et al., "Movements Toward Understanding Humans through the Anthropological Study of Dance [and Comments and Reply]," *Current Anthropology* 20/2 (June 1979): 313–39, 316. See also Joann W. Kealiinohomoku, "Ethnic Historical Study," in *Dance History Research: Perspectives from Related Arts and Disciplines* Proceedings of the Second Conference on Research in Dance (1970), 94–95, on "dance motor behavior."

42. Though there are many examples of such *grotesquerie*, Hearn's ethnographic accounts from Cincinnati and New Orleans have probably the greatest and most informative accuracy; see "Levee Life: Haunts and Pastimes of the Roustabouts," in *Lafcadio Hearn's America: Ethnographic Sketches and Editorials*, ed. Simon J. Bronner (Lexington: University Press of Kentucky, 2002), 48–49.

43. Nathan, *Dan Emmett and the Rise of Early Negro Minstrelsy*, 160.

44. Such contrafacta are somewhat outside the scope of this book, but they have been exhaustively cataloged and imaginatively unpacked in W. T. Lhamon Jr., *Jump Jim Crow: Lost Plays, Lyrics, and Street Prose of the First Atlantic Popular Culture* (Cambridge, Mass.: Harvard University Press, 2003).

45. For the Knauff reference, see Goertzen and Jabbour, "George P. Knauff's Virginia Reels and Fiddling in the Antebellum South," 133. ; for Nathan, see Nathan, *Dan Emmett and the Rise of Early Negro Minstrelsy*, 169.

46. See Nathan, *Dan Emmett and the Rise of Early Negro Minstrelsy*, 177.

47. See Nathan, *Dan Emmett and the Rise of Early Negro Minstrelsy*, 173. See also Kuntz, http://www.ibiblio.org/fiddlers/BI_BILE.htm, accessed March 10, 2010. For "Bow-Wow-Wow" as London music-hall song, see, for example, "Bow wow wow: a much admir'd song sung at the Anacreontic Society by C.M." ([New York?]: s.n., 1783?), Bodleian Library: Harding Mus. G 398.

48. It was also associated with teenage minstrel J. W. McAndrew, see http://memory.loc.gov/ammem/sm2html/sm2great3.html, accessed March 11, 2011.

49. See Carlin, *Birth of the Banjo*, 114.

50. This "interlock," the rhythmic placement of individual instruments' sonic attacks in silences left by other instruments' parts, sometimes inaptly (for an African context) described with the European term *hocketing*, is ubiquitous in African and Afro-Caribbean musics; see Lewin on Jamaican *mento*: "accents sometimes occur not in the melody but in the supporting percussion rhythms, clapping and stamping." Olive Lewin and Maurice G. Gordon, "Jamaica," Grove Music Online, Oxford Music Online, Oxford University Press, http://www.oxfordmusiconline.com/subscriber/article/grove/music/44476, accessed November 23, 2012.

51. LIM sources for the items in this list are as follows: (1) KSA031474, dated December 19, 1858; (2) KSA031628; (3) KSA032109; (4) KSA032110; (5) KSA032111; (6) KSA032112.

52. The inscription suggests that these pages were copied from the unidentified "Mr. Pfeiffer," who might be a Long Islander, given his German surname. The family name recurs throughout various items in Sheet Music Box 1, KSA031628 in the Mount collections: a George Edward Pfeiffer, retired from Mount's New York lithographic house, is mentioned as "remember[ing]" Mount in Buffet's 1920s serial biography, and several Pfeiffers are cited as contributors in the Cotillion repertoire list in Mount's hand cited elsewhere in this chapter, and as sources for other items in the manuscript collection, including the very old minstrel tune "Keemo Kimo." Buffet, "William Sidney Mount," 67, and LIM KSA031581 and KSA031628.

53. LIM KSA031572. Paul Wells, a specialist in nineteenth-century printed tune collections, confirms that these loose sheets come from a Howe publication: "The page with 'Fisher's . . . ' 'Hull's Victory' etc is from 'Howe's School for the . . . ' which was published in editions for violin, flute, fife, clarionett, and flageolet. All with the same musical contents; only the pedagogical sections were changed for each instrument. This was one of Howe's first series of tutors, originally published by him in 1843. When Ditson bought Howe out he re-copyrighted most or all of Howe's stuff, so there are lots of copies around with a copyright date of 1851." Paul F. Wells, communication with the author, January 13, 2011. See, for example, Wells, "Fiddling as an Avenue of Black-White Musical Interchange."

54. "De Banks of de Ohio," LIM KSA031576; "Julie is de Hansum Gal," KSA031577; and "Mary Lee," KSA031735. Paul Wells tentatively identifies Edward Baack as "one of those fingers-in-lots-of-pies . . . music entrepreneurs of the times. . . . I didn't know of him as a publisher . . . but obviously he at least dabbled in publishing." Baack was in business at 81 Fulton St. from 1845 to 1849. Paul Wells, communication with the author, January 2011. Though little is known about Baack as a publisher, he was likely at least modestly involved in printing materials for commercial sale in concert saloons; it was common practice for popular-song publishers to print palm-sized cards rendering the tune of the verse and tune and text of the chorus of new songs—their "pluggers" would then distribute the palm cards while singing, and promoting the songs in Manhattan's song saloons.

Crawford provides fascinating excerpts from such pluggers' autobiographical reminiscences; see Richard Crawford, *America's Musical Life: A History* (New York: Norton, 2001), 473–75.

55. LIM KSA031733.

56. See, for example, the Hawkins-Mount Family Papers, manuscript inventory, box V, LIM.

57. LIM KSA031581.

58. See Eric Lott, *Love and Theft: Blackface Minstrelsy and the American Working Class* (Oxford: Oxford University Press, 1996); W. T. Lhamon Jr., *Raising Cain: Blackface Performance from Jim Crow to Hip Hop* (Cambridge, Mass.: Harvard University Press, 2000); and Cockrell, *Demons of Disorder*.

59. Cowan quoted in Dorothea E. Hast, "Transformation and Community: Contra Dance in New England," *Dance Research Journal* 25/1 (spring 1993): 28, emphasis added.

Chapter 6. Akimbo Culture

1. Mary M. Smyth, "Kinesthetic Communication in Dance," *Dance Research Journal* 16/2 (autumn 1984): 19. On the liminality of participation, see Richard Schechner, "Audience Participation," *Drama Review: TDR* 15/3 (summer 1971): 72: "Inclusion and participation are not metaphors; they are concrete physical acts of the body."

2. See Victor Turner, *The Ritual Process: Structure and Antistructure* (London: Routledge and Kegan Paul, 1969), 182–83. Bond and Stinson add, "People in communitas experience a kind of flow, an unmediated absorption in a freely chosen event. There is a quality of celebration, a feeling of unbounded social euphoria." Karen E. Bond and Susan W. Stinson, "'I Feel Like I'm Going to Take Off!': Young People's Experiences of the Superordinary in Dance," *Dance Research Journal* 32/2 (winter 2000–2001): 74. See also Christopher Washburne, "Play it 'Con Filin!': The Swing and Expression of Salsa," *Latin American Music Review/Revista de Música Latinoamericana* 19/2 (autumn–winter 1998): 160–85.

3. Ray Allen, "Shouting the Church: Narrative and Vocal Improvisation in African American Gospel Quartet Performance," *Journal of American Folklore* 104/413 (summer 1991): 313–14.

4. The major source of ethnochoreological scholarship in this chapter is that body of literature that addresses Afro-Caribbean and African American dance. This focus, and the concomitant relative de-emphasis on African ethnochoreology, is both logistical and topical: logistical, because the subject of African dance is enormous and beyond the scope of this book; and topical, because this book is about specifically African American syncretic styles in the New World. A fundamental premise of my argument is that the creole synthesis was not "simply African," but a phenomenon that, like minstrelsy itself, reflected the admixture in New World of disparate African and European ethnicities and musical traditions. Examination

of the relevance of African ethnochoreology on the synthesis can only enrich our understanding but must await future scholarship.

5. See Eric Lott, "Love and Theft: The Racial Unconscious of Blackface Minstrelsy," *Representations* 39 (summer 1992): 25. Also: "Just as there can be explicitly ordinative discourse, there can also be insubordinate discourse: discourse that transgresses or inverts existing orderings, discourse that challenges the nation of fixed orders or the ordinative authority of another discourse." Robert G. Allen, *Horrible Prettiness: Burlesque and American Culture* (Chapel Hill: University of North Carolina Press, 1991), 34; also Dale Cockrell, *Demons of Disorder: Blackface Minstrels and Their World* (Cambridge: Cambridge University Press, 1997), 180.

6. Equally problematic is Nathan's 1962 description of the Jim Crow choreography, which is so tortuous as to be confusing rather than enlightening; Hans Nathan, *Dan Emmett and the Rise of Early Negro Minstrelsy*, 2nd ed. (Norman: University of Oklahoma: 1977), 77ff.

7. Sule Greg Wilson, conversation with the author, April 2009. I am indebted to Wilson (Carolina Chocolate Drops and Sankofa Strings) for this insight.

8. In the scientific literature, see the relatively recent scholarship on "mirror neurons" and action recognition, which has confirmed the actual physiological response, in the cortex and the body of the viewer, in response to observed motion (including dance). See Giovanni Buccino, Ferdinand Binkofsky, and Lucia Riggo, "The Mirror Neuron System and Action Recognition," *Brain and Language* (2003), http://www.elsevier.locate/b&l, accessed April 8, 2012. Thanks to Eliot Grasso for making me aware of this body of literature.

9. And further to the sense of communal connection which participatory dance can engender: "Dance is often a multimedia communication: performers moving in time and space are seen, sounds of physical movements are heard, odors produced by physical exertion are smelled, kinesthetic activity or empathy is felt, as is the touch of body to body, body part, and performing area." Paul Jordan-Smith, "About That Swing: 'Sleaze' Dancing and Community Norms at River Falls Lodge," in "Communities of Practice and Dance," special issue, *Western Folklore* 60/2–3 (spring–summer 2001): 198 (emphasis added); see also Judith Lynne Hanna, "African Dance: The Continuity of Change," *Yearbook of the International Folk Music Council* 5 (1973): 166; Ray Allen, "Shouting the Church: Narrative and Vocal Improvisation in African-American Gospel Quartet Performance," *Journal of American Folklore* 104/413 (summer 1991), 314; Dorothea E. Hast, "Performance, Transformation, and Community: Contra Dance in New England," *Dance Research Journal* 25/1 (spring 1993): 25. On "the body as the locus of 'shared somatic experience,'" see also Paul Jordan-Smith and Laurel Horton, "Guest Editors' Introduction," *Western Folklore* 60/2–3, Communities of Practice: Traditional Music and Dance (spring–summer 2001): 106. John Blacking was the originator of the latter term in "Towards an Anthropology of the Body," in *The Anthropology of the Body*, ed. John Blacking (London: Academic Press, 1977), 10.

10. Seebass adds "there is a kinaesthetic awareness immanent in the act of painting," and provides a useful analogy to Chinese calligraphic practice, in which the

resulting art works reveal the painter's physical technique and kinesthetic command at the moment of composition. Tilman Seebass, "Iconography and Dance Research," *Yearbook for Traditional Music* 23 (1991): 35.

11. See Arthur C. Cole, "The Puritan and Fair Terpsichore," *Mississippi Valley Historical Review* 29/1 (June 1942): 15–16.

12. See, for example, Judith Cobau, "The Precarious Life of Thomas Pike, A Colonial Dancing Master in Charleston and Philadelphia," *Dance Chronicle* 17/3 (1994): 230.

13. Though the mainstream of musicological scholarship has tended to treat research on dance history and iconography as a subsidiary field, a few previous studies, some minstrelsy-specific, have pointed the way: W. T. Lhamon Jr., *Raising Cain: Blackface Performance from Jim Crow to Hip Hop* (Cambridge, Mass.: Harvard University Press, 2000); Eric Lott, *Love and Theft: Blackface Minstrelsy and the American Working Class* (Oxford: Oxford University Press, 1996); Cockrell, *Demons of Disorder*; and Nathan, *Dan Emmett and the Rise of Early Negro Minstrelsy*. These four, for example, have all addressed issues of dance as a signifier: of resistance, ethnicity, community, and/or cultural retention. However, none of them is a dance specialist, and none has fully addressed the complex, difficult, slippery task of reconstructing the movement vocabularies that were a principal conduit for minstrelsy's popularity and dissemination, or of the insights such reconstructions can provide. Nathan, for example, though providing a useful compendium of minstrel dance illustrations, is out of his element in attempting either to analyze the body mechanics of these illustrations or to reconstruct the Jim Crow dance. Throughout his seminal text, *Dan Emmett and the Rise of Early Negro Minstrelsy*, Nathan's attempts to describe dance are clumsy and confusing (52–53, 70–77, 80–86).

14. Stephen Johnson, "Juba's Dance: An Assessment of Newly Acquired Information," *Proceedings of the 26th Annual Conference of the Society for Dance History Scholars*, Proceedings of the SDHS, 2003, 3, http://www.sdhs.org, accessed March 10, 2010. Johnson employs a "microhistorical" approach to historical dance that parallels Rauf's and Mahar's exegeses of Afro-Caribbean music and dialect.

15. Johnson, "Juba's Dance," 3.

16. Ibid., 4.

17. See, for example, "Zip Coon," Endicott & Swett, 1834, LC-USZ62-126131 DLC, http://www.loc.gov/pictures/item/00650780/, accessed November 25, 2012.

18. See, for example, Nathan's reproduction and discussion of an 1812 portrait of a meeting of Philadelphia Methodists *(Dan Emmett and the Rise of Early Negro Minstrelsy*, 82).

19. As Ostendorf says, "motor behavior and kinesthetics are particularly hard to address in the history of African American cultural expression." Berndt Ostendorf, "Celebration or Pathology? Commodity or Art? The Dilemma of African-American Expressive Culture," in "European Perspectives on Black Music," special issue, *Black Music Research Journal* 20/2 (autumn 2000): 220.

On the same "pelvic concentration" in the *Wukkin' Up* dance from Barbados, see also Sharon Meredith, "Barbadian Tuk Music: Colonial Development and Post-Independence Recontextualization," *British Journal of Ethnomusicology* 12/2 (2003): 89.

20. Ostendorf, "Celebration or Pathology?" 220–21. See also Jacqui Malone, *Steppin' on the Blues: The Visible Rhythms of African American Dance* (Urbana: University of Illinois Press, 1996), 11–12.

21. Thomas F. DeFrantz, ed., *Dancing Many Drums: Excavations in African American Dance* (Madison: University of Wisconsin Press, 2002), 184–85.

22. Seebass, "Iconography and Dance Research," 33.

23. Ibid.

24. See, for example, Richard Leppert, *The Sight of Sound: Music, Representation, and the History of the Body* (London: Diane Publications, 1993).

25. Seebass, "Iconography and Dance Research," 34, emphasis added.

26. "If the artist belongs to the same culture, and is a dancer, the kinemic elements will more likely be recognized and shown." Ibid., 35.

27. See, for example, a typeface employed on an 1843 London playbill for a performance by the Virginia Minstrels, in which the alphabetical characters are drawn as akimbo dancers. Reproduced in Nathan, *Dan Emmett and the Rise of Early Negro Minstrelsy*, 137.

28. Citations of African American "akimbo" stances appear in Charles Mathews's descriptions of Ira Aldridge at the African Grove Theatre (see *Mr. Mathews at Home*, quoted in Jonathan Dewberry, "The African Grove Theatre and Company," in "Black Theatre Issue," special issue, *Black American Literature Forum* 16/4 [winter 1982]: 131) and in Dickens's descriptions of Juba in 1842.

29. See Lydia Parrish, comp., *Slave Songs of the Georgia Sea Islands* (Athens: University of Georgia, 1992), 71ff.

30. Ibid., 79–81.

31. The bird (*Cathartes aura*) is found throughout the Americas.

32. See Parrish, *Slave Songs of the Georgia Sea Islands*, 111 n9; for more on the etymology of "John Crow," see Richard Allsopp, ed., *Dictionary of Caribbean English Usage* (Kingston, Jamaica: University of the West Indies Press, 2003), 314. For the photographs of the Buzzard Lope as danced in the Sea Islands, see Parrish, *Slave Songs of the Georgia Sea Islands*, 130. Glass specifically identifies the Buzzard Lope, in the Caribbean, as an African retention: see Barbara S. Glass, *African American Dance: An Illustrated History* (Jefferson, N.C.: McFarland, 2007), 55.

33. Parrish, *Slave Songs of the Georgia Sea Islands*, 114, 116; for photographs, see ibid., 66. Glass, *African American Dance*, similarly describes the *juba/jumba/majumba* complex in the West Indies (113).

34. Elements of this same singing culture are preserved in a 16mm film shot in 1963, featuring the singing ensemble organized by Lydia Parrish a generation before. Edmund Carpenter, Bess Lomax Hawes, and Alan Lomax, dirs., *The Georgia Sea Island Singers* (Film Images, 1963).

35. Henry Bibb, *The Narrative of the Life and Adventures of Henry Bibb, an American Slave Written by Himself. Pub. by the author.* (1850), 23, http://books.google.com, accessed November 23, 2012.

36. Lanier, 189, quoted in Dena J. Epstein, *Sinful Tunes and Spirituals: Black Folk Music to the Civil War* (Urbana: University of Illinois Press, 1977, rev. ed. 2003).

37. William B. Smith, "The Persimmon Tree and the Beer Dance," Farmer's Register 6 (Apr. 1, 1838): 58–61, reprinted in *The Negro and His Folklore in Nineteenth-Century Periodicals*, ed. Bruce Jackson (Austin: University of Texas, 1967), 5. See also Robert B. Winans, "The Black Banjo-Playing Tradition in Virginia and West Virginia," *Folklore and Folklife in Virginia* 1 (1979): 17, for another citation of the same account. Elizabeth Allen Coxe described African American church services in South Carolina about the time of the Civil War. At the Eutaw Plantation, "Every day of Christmas week, in the afternoon, the Negroes danced in the broad piazza until late at night, the orchestra consisting of two fiddlers, one man with bones and another had sticks with which he kept time on the floor, and sometimes singing." Elizabeth Allen Coxe, *Memories of a South Carolina Plantation during the War . . .* [n.p.; privately printed, 1912]; quoted in Epstein, *Sinful Tunes and Spirituals*, 144.

38. Mount reproduces a tune called "Black Toney's Juber" in his manuscripts; see Kevin Scott, "The 'Negro Touch' and the 'Yankee Trick': William Sidney Mount and the Art of Race and Ethnicity," *Visual Resources* 24/3 (2008): 241; while Emery quotes period sources that explicitly link Juba ("juber") and the banjo; Lynne Faulkey Emery, *Black Dance in the United States from 1619 to 1970* (Palo Alto, Calif.: National Press Books, 1972), 96.

39. Thomas Washington Talley, *Negro Folk Rhymes: Wise and Otherwise* (New York: Macmillan, 1922), 232–33. We may also note the close resemblances between this description and the visual details of Mount's 1830 *Rustic Dance after a Sleigh Ride*. Later in the same excerpt, Talley cites "Jump Jim Crow" as another example of a dance-song demanding body-percussion. See http://books.google.com, accessed September 13, 2010.

40. Samuel A. Floyd Jr., "African American Dance and Music," in *African American Jazz and Rap: Social and Philosophical Examinations of Black Expressive Behavior*, ed. James L. Conyers Jr., 117–30 (Jefferson, N.C.: McFarland, 2001), 119.

41. Particularly clear illustrations of middle-class body aesthetics can be found in period etiquette manuals and dance methods; the various methods for clog dancing contain numerous illustrations of an upright, elongated, and flowing spine and limbs.

42. This defiance has been a central focus in more recent studies of blackface's semiotic meaning; see in particular Lott (*Love and Theft*) and Lhamon (*Raising Cain*).

43. See Lyotard's "concept of the sublime" in postmodern theory: "to diagnose the aesthetic sensibility associated with the chaotic social forces and crisis of legitimation in the postmodern condition" Lyotard, 1984, quoted in William P. Murphy, "The Sublime Dance of Mende Politics: An African Aesthetic of Charismatic Power," *American Ethnologist* 25/4 (November 1998): 566. See also Schechner on

the tension-release dyad, which is central to expressive performance: "Performers specialize in putting themselves in disequilibrium and then displaying how they regain their balance psychophysically, narratively, and socially—only to lose their balance, and regain it, again and again." Richard Schechner, *Performance Theory* (New York: Routledge, 1988), 197.

44. See Charles Keil, "Participatory Discrepancies and the Power of Music." *Cultural Anthropology* 2/3 (August 1987).

45. Henry Louis Gates Jr., *The Signifying Monkey: A Theory of African American Literary Criticism* (New York, 1988); Robert Walser, "Out of Notes: Signification, Interpretation, and the Problem of Miles Davis," *Musical Quarterly* 77/2 (summer 1993): 343–65; and Robert Walser, "Rhythm, Rhyme, and Rhetoric in the Music of Public Enemy," *Ethnomusicology* 39/2 (spring–summer 1995): 192–217.

46. For "sublime dissonances," see Murphy, "Sublime Dance of Mende Politics," 565. Irish fiddle virtuoso James Kelly refers to the cross-rhythm, 2-and-4 accent in unaccompanied melodic playing as "the pulse" and insists on its essential contribution in Irish music, more commonly heard as 1-and-3 oriented. James Kelly, communication with the author, July 14, 1998. See also Murphy, "Sublime Dance of Mende Politics," who finds here the power that participatory discrepancies can provide in West African contemporary contexts; he calls instances of danced "charisma" "the eruption[s] that break through the regularities of the political world" (567). He also notes that in West African aesthetics politics and dance are considered to be analogous and complementary.

47. Murphy, "Sublime Dance of Mende Politics," says "The act of gathering itself adds intensity to social life. Gathering . . . for a meeting transforms that space into a dangerous arena of hidden mystical forces, both helpful and harmful" (572).

48. Rebecca Sachs Norris, "Embodiment and Community," in "Communities of Practice: Traditional Music and Dance," special issue, *Western Folklore* 60/2–3 (spring–summer 2001): 116.

49. Glass, *African American Dance*, 55ff. White describes this as "black kinesics"—Shane White, "A Question of Style: Blacks in and around New York City in the Late 18th Century," *Journal of American Folklore* 102/403 (January–March 1989): 35–36—and Kealiinohomoku as "dance motor vocabularies"—Joann W. Kealiinohomoku, "A Comparative Study of Dance as a Constellation of Motor Behaviors among African and United States Negroes," in Adrienne L. Kaeppler, *Reflections and Perspectives on Two Anthropological Studies of Dance*, CORD Dance Research Annual (New York: CORD, 1976), 86–97. On the specifically African American manifestations of such motor vocabularies, see Hazzard-Gordon, who cites "improvisational ability . . . isolation and movement of the pelvis, individual manipulation of other body parts such as torso, head, arms, phrasing ability, flat-footed movement style, flexed leg position, and percussive use of rhythm." Katrina Hazzard-Gordon, "African American Vernacular Dance: Core Culture and Meaning Operatives," in "African and African American Dance, Music, and Theatre," special issue, *Journal of Black Studies* 15/4, (June 1985): 432.

50. Glass, *African American Dance*, 16. See also Meredith's discussion of movement vocabularies in the Afro-Caribbean colony of Barbados ("Barbadian Tuk Music," 89).

51. Glass, *African American Dance*, 55.

52. Quoted in ibid., 101. Such dancing confirms transatlantic distribution of the Afro-Celtic creole synthesis: the term *Kroomen* references the *Kroo* (*crio*/"creole") sailors who worked the African coastal boats and ships. On Jamaica, see Richard Cullen Rath, "African Music in Seventeenth-Century Jamaica: Transit and Transition," in "Third Series," *William and Mary Quarterly* 50/4 (October 1993).

53. Meredith, "Barbadian Tuk Music," 82, emphasis added. See also Robert Schomburgh's 1847 description of dancing in Barbados confirms that, ibid.

54. Glass, *African American Dance*, 31ff.

55. Ibid., 107–8.

56. Robert B. Winans, "Black Instrumental Music Traditions in the Ex-Slave Narratives," *Black Music Research Journal* 10/1 (spring 1990): 51.

57. See Roger D. Abrahams, *Singing the Master: The Emergence of African American Culture in the Plantation South* (New York: Penguin, 1994), 137ff, and Winans, "Black Banjo-Playing Tradition in Virginia and West Virginia," 53–54.

58. Winans, "Black Banjo-Playing Tradition in Virginia and West Virginia," 53, emphasis added.

59. Benjamin Waterhouse (1816), *A Journal of a Young Man of Massachusetts, 2nd ed. Late A Surgeon On Board An American Privateer, Who Was Captured At Sea By The British, In May, Eighteen Hundred And Thirteen, And Was Confined First, At Melville Island, Halifax, Then At Chatham, In England . . . And Last, At Dartmoor Prison. Interspersed With Observations, Anecdotes And Remarks, Tending To Illustrate The Moral And Political Characters Of Three Nations. To Which Is Added, A Correct Engraving Of Dartmoor Prison, Representing The Massacre Of American Prisoners, Written By Himself*, http://www.gutenberg.org/files/27763/27763–8.txt, accessed August 8, 2009, emphasis added.

60. See William J. Mahar, "'Backside Albany' and Early Blackface Minstrelsy: A Contextual Study of America's First Blackface Song," *American Music* 6/1 (spring 1988): 3.

61. Kevin M. Scott, "Rituals of Race: Mount, Melville, and Antebellum America," PhD diss., Purdue University, 2004, 62. Scott does not provide specific identifications of "Bob," "Ned," or "Jack," but the implication is that he is referring to dancers name-checked in De Voe's 1868 *Market Book*, including "Bobolink Bob" Reynolds of Long Island.

62. Rath, "African Music in Seventeenth-Century Jamaica, 702–4; see also Mahar, "'Backside Albany' and Early Blackface Minstrelsy," on Black Ethnic Vernacular (BEV), 1–27.

63. Mahar, "'Backside Albany' and Early Blackface Minstrelsy."

64. The epitaph claims that "Anthony, though indigent, was most content. Though of a race depis'd, deserved he much respect. . . . Upon the Violin, few played as Toney play'd. His artless music was a language universal and in its

Effect-most irresistible." Quoted in Mahar, "'Backside Albany' and Early Blackface Minstrelsy," 13.

65. Mahar, "'Backside Albany' and Early Blackface Minstrelsy," 14.

66. Glass, *African American Dance*, 16ff.

67. Ibid.

68. Cockrell, *Demons of Disorder*, 4–7.

69. Glass, *African American Dance*, 16–22.

70. Ibid., 22.

71. Some scholarship suggests that this "polyrhythmic body"—which we discover ubiquitously in Mount's renderings of dancers—was viewed as the most exotic and potentially salacious element by European observers. See P. Sterling Stuckey, "Christian Conversion and the Challenge of Dance," in *Dancing Many Drums: Excavations in African American Dance*, ed. Thomas F. DeFrantz, 39–58 (Madison: University of Wisconsin Press, 2002), 46–47. Cockrell, *Demons of Disorder*, likewise links dance and sexual transgression in his account, from *The Flash*, of a Boston dance contest between two prostitutes (18). Lott describes blackface's creole synthesis as "gesturing toward a specific kind of political or sexual danger, and all constituting a peculiarly American structure of racial feeling" (*Love and Theft*, 18). Lott's commentary on minstrelsy's transgressive sexual semiotics are superb, but he is unable to link this same sexualized fascination to other, earlier colonial responses to black dance.

72. For the mimetic characteristics of the Buzzard Lope, see Glass, *African American Dance*, 55; also Parrish, *Slave Songs of the Georgia Sea Islands*, 66. The mimesis in "Jump Jim Crow" goes all the way back to Ludlow's origin myth—Noah M. Ludlow, *Dramatic Life as I Found I: A Record of Personal Experience* . . . (St. Louis: Ludlow, 1880; reprinted New York: Benjamin Blom, 1966), 392. On the cakewalk, see Malone, *Steppin' on the Blues*, on "derision dancing" (18).

73. In Enlightenment France, Germany, or England, a young person could learn dancing—as with deportment, music, fencing, or a language—as a means of accruing social capital that could provide valuable social or economic opportunity. In contrast, dance as a tool for social mobility was largely unavailable in West Africa; in fact, because of its associations with specific social, age, gender, or class groups, it tended to reinforce and reinscribe social bounds.

74. Nathan, *Dan Emmett and the Rise of Early Negro Minstrelsy*, for example, cites minstrels' use of "clogs" and "heel-taps" "from the early Forties on" (75).

75. Charles Keil. "Applied Sociomusicology and Performance Studies." *Ethnomusicology* 42/2 (spring–summer 1998): 3. See also Keil, "Participatory Discrepancies and the Power of Music," 277. As Progler puts it, in a statement that could be applied to virtually every aspect of music and dance performance practice addressed in this book: "The fundamental component of ensemble 'feel' in the African tradition is a product of the process of interaction required in group execution." J. A. Progler, "Searching for Swing: Participatory Discrepancies in the Jazz Rhythm Section," *Ethnomusicology* 39/1 (winter 1995): 29.

76. See Eric Lott, *Love and Theft: Blackface Minstrelsy and the American Working Class* (Oxford: Oxford University Press, 1996), 80 n35, figure 7 (81).

77. Samuel Woodworth, George Pope Morris, Theodore Sedgwick Fay, and Nathaniel Parker Willis, *The New-York Mirror*, vol. 10 (New York: G. P. Morris, 1832), 206. http://books.google.com/, accessed November 23, 2012.

78. Jordan-Smith and Horton, "Guest Editors' Introduction," 107–08, original emphasis.

79. Robert Carlin, *The Birth of the Banjo: Joel Walker Sweeney and Early Minstrelsy* (New York: McFarland, 2007), 68.

80. Recalling experiences in the Scottish Borders, Jeffrey Mark says "Anyone will appreciate [it] who has danced on the springy boarding of a barn floor, its surface beautifully polished by dragging hay across it." See Jeffrey Mark, "Recollections of Folk-Musicians," *Musical Quarterly* 16/2 (April 1930): 173.

81. Glass, *African American Dance*.

82. Buffet, "William Sidney Mount," provides a reasonably complete (if hypothetical and circumstantial) identification of the entire cast of characters, which tends to confirm the close relation of the painted image with individuals and scenes Mount knew well: "The standing spectator behind 'Shep' Jones is Horace Newtone, the woebegone man seated on the box at the left is Billy Biggs. The colored woman on the mow with her daughter beside her lived at the Seaburys" (71). The boy with the flail is identified otherwise as Jedediah Williamson, who later was killed and his name given to a brother. Buffett ends this passage with a solicitation for additional identifications, which also suggests that Mount's circle of subjects and friends was still part of Setauket memory in the 1920s.

83. In other works, Mount likewise borrows Jump Jim Crow imagery across the color line: the turned-away dancer in *Bar-Room Scene* (1833) provides a reverse image of the blackface posture and step; for more on the image's allegorical (but not choreological) meanings, see Scott, "'Negro Touch' and the 'Yankee Trick.'" It is pleasingly symmetrical, though probably felicitously coincidental, that the barn of *Barn Floor* reverses that of *Haymakers*, much as the various characters' ethnicities have been reversed; it is almost as if we are looking into the same barn, but from opposite sides.

84. A host of African American instruments—most notably the one-stringed percussion instrument called the diddley-bow—have so involved "playing on the wall."

85. Nicholas Butler, archivist to the Charleston County Public Library; communication with the author, July 25, 2006. I am indebted to Butler for this crucial observation.

86. Kealiinohomoku, "Comparative Study of Dance as a Constellation of Motor Behaviors among African and United States Negroes," 77.

87. Ibid., 73.

88. Ibid.

89. The ball-of-the-foot stances of *The Old Plantation* (1790s) may reflect an assimilation of Anglo-Celtic footwork, either on the part of the observed dancers, or on that of the unknown watercolorist.

90. The late date confirms Mount's continuing activity in life-sketching, even after infirmity and failing eyesight had caused him to abandon painting; see Buffet, "William Sidney Mount," 157.

91. See William Sidney Mount to Charles Brown, letter October 4, 1848; collection of New-York Historical Society, cited in Frederick C. Moffatt, "Barnburning and Hunkerism: William Sidney Mount's *Power of Music*," *Winterthur Portfolio* 29/1 (spring 1991): 19 n1.

92. The militia is a relatively common topic for vernacular painters of the period; see the James Goodwyn Clonney (1812–1867) drawing *Militia Training* (1841), reproduced in Lucretia H. Giese, "James Goodwyn Clonney (1812–1867): American Genre Painter," in *American Art Journal* 11/4 (October 1979): 12. Clonney frequented the same circles as Mount and was obviously indebted to him; see Clonney's *Waking Up* (1851), a virtually verbatim copy of Mount's *Farmers Nooning*.

93. David Tatham, "David Claypoole Johnston's 'Militia Muster,'" *American Art Journal* 19/2 (spring 1987): 4–15, 8.

94. Ibid., 8.

95. Ibid., 7.

96. See Peter G. Buckley, "The Place to Make an Artist Work: William Sidney Mount and Micah Hawkins in New York City," Museums at Stony Brook, September 1983, 10; Tatham, "David Claypoole Johnston's 'Militia Muster,'" provides a lengthy biographical sketch as part of an analysis of Johnston's comic militia sketches (4–15); see also Jennifer A. Greenhill, "'Playing the Fool': David Claypoole Johnston and the Menial Labor of Caricature," *American Art* 17/3 (autumn 2003): 32–51.

97. According to Tatham, the volunteer militias "also thrived as social organizations. Many sponsored lively seasons of dinners, dances, and other festive events. . . . Elective systems and the costs . . . ensured a degree of social uniformity" ("David Claypoole Johnston's 'Militia Muster,'" 8). Tatham misreads the social environments for "general" versus "volunteer" militia, presuming that volunteer militias were an urban phenomenon and general militias a rural one—this is an oversimplification, contradicted by Mount's sketch of a volunteer militia, drawn long after he had relocated permanently to Long Island.

98. Other Johnston works likewise employ theatricalized caricatures of the sort we find, for example, in Micah Hawkins, *The Saw-Mill*: the 1833 *Termination of a Militia Sham Fight* includes both Yankee "Brother Jonathan" and Irish immigrant "Paddy" stereotypes, though Tatham misses this. Tatham, "David Claypoole Johnston's 'Militia Muster,'" 12.

99. Tatham, "David Claypoole Johnston's 'Militia Muster,'" 12.

100. Ibid., 9.

101. Giese, "James Goodwyn Clonney (1812–1867)," 21.

102. Other Clonney works confirm his status as a close, sympathetic, naturalistic depicter of African Americans, as was Mount: see his sketch of black fisherman in the 1855 "What a Catch."

103. Giese, "James Goodwyn Clonney (1812–1867)," 18.

104. See Scott, "Rituals of Race," 33, 35. See also Lott, *Love and Theft*, on *charivari*, militia celebrations, and street parades (28).

105. Though it is interesting to compare the approximate body-postures, and the racial transformation of this sketch and the dancers in *Dance of the Haymakers* à la "Comb and Brush" and *Dancing on the Barn Floor*.

106. See Glass, *African American Dance*: on John Canoe's English-language roots, 67ff; on 'Lection Day in Connecticut, Rhode Island, Massachusetts, New Hampshire (all Atlantic maritime zones), 77; on General Training Day, 79, 83. Note also that James Goodwyn Clonney, *Militia Training* (1841), shows dancers à la "dancing for eels."

Conclusion

1. Hans Nathan, *Dan Emmett and the Rise of Early Negro Minstrelsy*, 2nd ed. (Norman: University of Oklahoma: 1977), 1962.

2. Dale Cockrell, *Demons of Disorder: Blackface Minstrels and Their World* (Cambridge: Cambridge University Press, 1997), 1997; Eric Lott, *Love and Theft: Blackface Minstrelsy and the American Working Class* (Oxford: Oxford University Press, 1996); William Mahar, *Behind the Burnt Cork Mask: Early Blackface Minstrelsy and Antebellum American Popular Culture* (Urbana: University of Illinois Press, 1998); W. T. Lhamon Jr., *Raising Cain: Blackface Performance from Jim Crow to Hip Hop* (Cambridge, Mass.: Harvard University Press, 2000); Robert Carlin, *The Birth of the Banjo: Joel Walker Sweeney and Early Minstrelsy* (New York: McFarland, 2007).

3. Hunter S. Thompson, *Fear and Loathing: On the Campaign Trail '72* (San Francisco, Calif.: Straight Arrow Books, 1973).

Appendix

1. Some of the material contained in this section may be familiar to readers; it is offered here in order to fill out the picture of minstrelsy scholarship, and perhaps further enrich the knowledge of those readers already familiar with it. Hans Nathan, *Dan Emmett and the Rise of Early Negro Minstrelsy*, 2nd. ed. (Norman: University of Oklahoma, 1977).

2. Dale Cockrell, *Demons of Disorder: Blackface Minstrels and Their World* (Cambridge: Cambridge University Press, 1997); Eric Lott, *Love and Theft: Blackface Minstrelsy and the American Working Class* (Oxford: Oxford University Press, 1993); W. T. Lhamon Jr., *Raising Cain: Blackface Performance from Jim Crow to Hip Hop* (Cambridge, Mass.: Harvard University Press, 2000); William J. Mahar, *Behind the Burnt Cork Mask: Early Blackface Minstrelsy and Antebellum American Popular Culture* (Urbana: University of Illinois Press, 1998).

3. Robert Carlin, *The Birth of the Banjo: Joel Walker Sweeney and Early Minstrelsy* (New York: McFarland, 2007), 19.

4. These phenomena not only recur in later popular-music syntheses but have also been not entirely absent from the history of more "formal" ethnomusicology.

5. Ethnomusicology itself is inevitably and universally an act of translation, historically enacted by an "observer" who travels "elsewhere" to witness "informants" making music as part of culture, and who then returns, eventually to explain—to translate—to outsiders something of the music's structure, function, and meaning in its original contexts. This is, at base, what ethnomusicology does. Ethnomusicology has sometimes yielded not only intellectual insight but also cultural exploitation; sometimes, conversely and more constructively, ethnomusicological scholarship has represented not only career advancement but also *cross-cultural* enrichment. The discipline in its best manifestations has enriched not only the opportunistic scholar's pocketbook, publication record, or curriculum vita, but also the dominant culture's artistic resources—and even, sometimes, the minority informants' economic opportunities.

6. Many but not all of these Long Island Museum of American Art, History, and Carriages (hereafter LIM) materials originate in bequests by Ward Melville and his estate, in the Kate Strong Historical Library, Hawkins-Mount Family Papers at the LIM.

7. An example of artwork not held by LIM is the *Banjo Player*, held instead in the Museum of Fine Arts, Boston, from which it seldom tours.

8. But see Patricia Cline Cohen, with Timothy J. Gilfoyle and Helen Lefkowitz Horowitz, *The Flash Press: Sporting Male Weeklies in 1840s New York* (Chicago: University of Chicago Press, 2008), for commentary from the flash press.

9. See Shane White, "A Question of Style: Blacks in and Around New York City in the Late 18th Century," *Journal of American Folklore* 102/403 (January–March 1989): 33–34, for De Voe's commentary on African American hair styles, which informs my discussion of Micah Hawkins's *The Saw-Mill* (chapter 3); Shane White, "Pinkster: Afro-Dutch Syncretization in New York City and the Hudson Valley," *Journal of American Folklore* 102/403 (January–March 1989): 74, for De Voe on slaves harvesting and selling street food on the Lower East Side; Kevin M. Scott, "Rituals of Race: Mount, Melville, and Antebellum America," PhD diss., Purdue University, 2004, 51ff, for De Voe on black farmers from Long Island, including Ned Francis and "Bobolink" Bob Rowley, in Lower Manhattan; see Lhamon, *Raising Cain*, 9, for De Voe on dancers engaged by merchants to attract trade.

10. Noah M. Ludlow, *Dramatic Life as I Found It: A Record of Personal Experience* (St Louis: Ludlow, 1880; reprint New York: Benjamin Blom, 1966).

11. See Elizabeth Johns, "The Farmer in the Works of William Sidney Mount," in "The Evidence of Art: Images and Meaning in History," special issue, *Journal of Interdisciplinary History* 17/1 (summer 1986): 257–81.

12. Mahar, *Behind the Burnt Cork Mask*, 1998.

13. See, for example, E. P. Thompson, "Rough Music Reconsidered," *Folklore* 103/1 (1992): 3–26.

14. Cockrell, *Demons of Disorder*, xiii, xi.

15. See Cockrell, *Demons of Disorder*, 33–37; and Dale Cockrell, "Jim Crow: Demon of Disorder," *American Music* 14/2 (summer 1996): 168; also Nathan, *Dan Emmett and the Rise of Early Negro Minstrelsy*, 118.

16. Cockrell, *Demons of Disorder*, 60.

17. This in turn has occasionally elicited rather biased critique that ignores the scope and value of Cockrell's contribution; see Thomas DeFrantz, review of Cockrell, *Demons of Disorder*, *TDR (1988-)* 44/3 (autumn 2000): 184–85.

18. See, for example, William J. Mahar, "Black English in Early Blackface Minstrelsy: A New Interpretation of the Sources of Minstrel Show Dialect," *American Quarterly* 37/2 (summer 1983), which analysis of blackface texts as transcriptions of "black English vernacular" is particularly effective in this area, because it seeks to work backward from *texts* in order to recover *sound*. However, Mahar's study does not contain musicological, iconographic, or performance analysis.

19. Cockrell, *Demons of Disorder*, 158ff.

20. The connections between these characters are not imagined: literary critic Henry Louis Gates Jr. describes the 1932 Our Gang/Little Rascals film *Spanky*, which contains a comic restaging of the novel, and in which actor Matthew "Stymie" Beard cross-dressed as both Topsy and Uncle Tom. See Henry Louis Gates and Hollis Robbins, eds., *The Annotated Uncle Tom's Cabin*, by Harriet Beecher Stowe (New York: W. W. Norton, 2007), xi.

21. This archetype enters the American semiotic landscape in the personae of the semi-mythical Ohio River keelboatman Mike Fink (b. 1770/1780?–ca. 1823), actor Fess Parker's (1924–2010) film portrayal of Daniel Boone (1734–1820), or, for that matter, Jimi Hendrix's (1942–70) 1968 "Voodoo Chile," as in the careers of a "white boy playing the blues," such as vaudevillian Emmett Miller (1900–1962), R&B artists Mac Rebennack/Dr. John (b. 1940) and Johnny Otis (b. 1921), and blues guitarist Stevie Ray Vaughan (1954–1990).

22. For "lore cycles," see Lhamon, *Raising Cain*, 281.

23. Carlin, *Birth of the Banjo*, 18.

24. William J. Mahar, "'Backside Albany' and Early Blackface Minstrelsy: A Contextual Study of America's First Blackface Song," *American Music* 6/1 (spring 1988): 1–17.

25. Thomas DeFrantz goes so far as to say that Cockrell's *Demons of Disorder* and Bean, Hatch, and McNamara's edited volume *Inside the Minstrel Mask* (which includes essays by Mahar, Cockrell, Lott, Lhamon, and number of other principal scholars) "all but ignore the African-derived performance imperatives that white minstrels imitated." Thomas F. DeFrantz, ed., *Dancing Many Drums: Excavations in African American Dance* (Madison: University of Wisconsin Press, 2002), 185. Mahar, in contrast, acknowledges that "there is every reason to believe that [Micah] Hawkins was familiar with other black performers in New York City and rural Long Island." Mahar, "'Backside Albany' and Early Blackface Minstrelsy," 184.

26. Dena J. Epstein, *Sinful Tunes and Spirituals: Black Folk Music to the Civil War* (Urbana: University of Illinois Press, 1977, rev. ed. 2003).

27. Robert Winans, "Early Minstrel Show Music 1843–1852," in *Inside the Minstrel Mask: Readings in Nineteenth-Century Blackface Minstrelsy*, ed. Annemarie Bean, James V. Hatch, and Brooks McNamara, 114–62 (Hanover, N.H.: Wesleyan University Press, 1996).

28. Saxton's "Blackface Minstrelsy," which is excerpted from his larger *The Rise and Fall of the White Republic*, echoes Lott, Lhamon, and Cockrell when he observes that the "bohemianism of the entertainment world" was a powerful attraction for several of the early blackface minstrels. Alexander Saxton, "Blackface Minstrelsy," in *Inside the Minstrel Mask*, 69.

29. The passage is worth citing at greater length, as Frankenstein recognizes the interrelated nature of Mount's interests, saying "Mount the inventor is inseparable from Mount the musician. At Stony Brook there is a vast amount of music in his hand. . . . The pieces involved are all dance tunes—waltzes, polkas, jigs, marches, schottisches—adapted to the fiddle. . . . Some typical Mountian fiddle tunes appear in the letters that passed between William and Robert [yet] all in all, William Sidney Mount is not a milestone in American musical creativity." Alfred Frankenstein, *William Sidney Mount* (New York: Harry N. Abrams, 1975), 80ff, emphasis added.

30. A partial exception to this is Scott, "Rituals of Race," which provides a useful close reading of race and class symbolism in Mount's paintings, and links this reading effectively to contemporaneous trends in politics and the arts. However, because Scott's method proceeds from culture studies and iconography, he does not address the kinesthetic and musicological information the works contain, or the insights they provide about nineteenth-century music-making and the creole synthesis.

31. See Catherine A. Shoup, "Scottish Social Dancing and the Formation of Community," in "Communities of Practice: Traditional Music and Dance," special issue, *Western Folklore* 60/2–3 (spring–summer, 2001): 140. Though Shoup is describing a different dance tradition, the term *centripetal* aptly confirms the inward-directed social cohesion that group dance can elicit.

32. There are many examples, found throughout the creole Caribbean, of Anglo-European music and dance forms being imitated, borrowed, mutated, and caricatured by Afro-Caribbean performers; the cakewalk craze of the 1890s is only a late, and particularly visible, manifestation of a much older parodic tradition. See Brooke Baldwin, "The Cakewalk: A Study in Stereotype and Reality," *Journal of Social History* 15 (1981/2).

33. David Cassedy, *William Sidney Mount: Works in the Collections of the Museums at Stony Brook* (New York: Museums at Stony Brook, June 1983). The LIM collections include not just primary sources on Mount, but also copies of much of the secondary sources, reaching back to the 1920s.

34. W. T. Lhamon Jr., "Every Time I Wheel About I Jump Jim Crow: Cycles of Minstrel Transgression from Cool White to Vanilla Ice," in *Inside the Minstrel Mask*, 276, 278.

35. Barbara Lewis, "Daddy Blues: The Evolution of the Dark Dandy," in *Inside the Minstrel*, 257–74.

36. Marian Hannah Winter, "Juba and American Minstrelsy," in *Inside the Minstrel Mask*, 223–44.

37. See also Marian Hannah Winter, "American Theatrical Dancing from 1750 to 1800," *Musical Quarterly* 24/1 (January 1938): 223.

38. William J. Mahar, "Ethiopian Skits and Sketches: Contents and Contexts of Blackface Minstrelsy, 1840–1890," in *Inside the Minstrel Mask*, 179, 180.

39. Eileen Southern, "Black Musicians and Early Ethiopian Minstrelsy," in *Inside the Minstrel Mask*, 56–57, 61–62.

40. Southern overstates and oversimplifies, for example, when she says, "It is common knowledge that the white entertainers obtained their materials from blacks by listening to the songs and impersonating them" (43). Of course this is true, but the statement is incomplete: blackface performers did more than only "impersonate" (though this term itself has very complicated connotations, more effectively analyzed by Lott and Lhamon); if this were true, then blackface imitations of African American performance should have been accurate replications, a presumption that Southern's scholarship vehemently denies.

41. W. T. Lhamon Jr., *Jump Jim Crow: Lost Plays, Lyrics, and Street Prose of the First Atlantic Popular Culture* (Cambridge, Mass.: Harvard University Press, 2003).

42. Lott, *Love and Theft*, 9, 14.

43. Peter Guralnick, *Sweet Soul Music: Rhythm and Blues and the Southern Dream of Freedom* (Boston: Back Bay Books, 1999).

44. This is particularly evident in those sections of *Love and Theft* in which he cites Richard Middleton and Fredric Jameson—two *literary* theorists—to describe the "musematic" versus "discursive" mutations of musical repetition (41, 94). This awkward adaptation of inapposite analytical methods to identify the participatory, experiential, bodily attraction of African American music making is not particularly effective.

45. Eric Lott, "Blackface and Blackness: The Minstrel Show in American Culture," in *Inside the Minstrel Mask*, 3–34.

46. Robert G. Allen, *Horrible Prettiness: Burlesque and American Culture* (Chapel Hill: University of North Carolina Press, 1991), 170.

47. In ibid., Allen writes about the relationship between cultural tropes and political power: "Cultural production does not occur on even terms among groups within society. Because society is ordered in terms of power relations . . ., cultural production expresses these relations" (31).

48. Mahar, *Behind the Burnt Cork Mask*.

49. Lhamon, *Jump Jim Crow*, 91–92.

50. In *Raising Cain*, Lhamon says performances by blackface minstrels "provided a *frisson* of danger and supposed authenticity . . . embodying the urban margin quite as much as they were evoking the plantation" (158, emphasis added). S. White confirms the likelihood that northern or urban black culture was the likelier source of minstrelsy's imitation: "Many of the constituent elements of the minstrel show may

have had their origins in white observations of northern black culture, particularly as displayed in the slave festivals and, later in the nineteen century, in the cities." Shane White, "'It Was a Proud Day': African Americans, Festivals, and Parades in the North, 1741–1834," *Journal of American History* 81/1 (June 1994): 26, emphasis added.

51. Lhamon, *Raising Cain*, 195.

52. In ibid., Lhamon says they "display how politically disfranchised and economically excluded Americans have long felt attraction for black ways of moving through trouble" (x).

53. See W. T. Lhamon Jr., *Jump Jim Crow*, 7–13.

54. Ibid., 4.

55. John Strasbaugh, *Black Like You: Blackface, Whiteface, Insult and Imitation in American Popular Culture* (New York: Tarcher, 2006). Nick Tosches, *Country: The Twisted Roots of Rock 'n' Roll* (New York: Da Capo, 1996).

56. Ibid., 33.

57. Ibid., 146–49ff.

58. Gerald Jonas, *Dancing: The Pleasure, Power, and Art of Movement* (New York: Harry N. Abrams, 1992). Also included in this small body of effective dance anthropologies on parallel genres might be Jane K. Cowan, *Dance and the Body Politic in Northern Greece* (Princeton, N.J.: Princeton University Press, 1990); Judith Lynne Hanna, *To Dance Is Human: A Theory of Nonverbal Communication* (Chicago: University of Chicago Press, 1987); Barbara Browning, *Samba: Resistance in Motion* (Bloomington: Indiana University Press, 1995); Yvonne Daniels, *Dance and Social Change in Contemporary Cuba* (Bloomington: Indiana University Press, 1995); and perhaps Jason Berry, Jonathan Foose, and Tad Jones, *Up from the Cradle of Jazz: New Orleans Music Since World War II* (Lafayette: University of Louisiana at Lafayette Press, 2009), and Christopher Waterman, *Juju: A Social History and Ethnography of an African Popular Music* (Chicago: University of Chicago Press, 1990).

59. Jonas, *Dancing*, 167.

60. William P. Murphy, "The Sublime Dance of Mende Politics: An African Aesthetic of Charismatic Power," *American Ethnologist* 25/4 (November 1988): 564, 567.

61. See Judith Lynne Hanna, chapter 8, "The Urban Ecosystem of Dance," in *To Dance Is Human: A Theory of Nonverbal Communication* (Austin: University of Texas Press, 1979), 171.

62. Marian Hannah Winter, "American Theatrical Dancing from 1750–1800," *Musical Quarterly* 43/1 (January 1938): 58–73. See also Marian Hannah Winter, "Juba and American Minstrelsy," in *Chronicles of the American Dance: From the Shakers to Martha Graham*, ed. Paul Magriel (New York: Dance Index, 1948; reprint New York: Da Capo Press, 1978).

63. Henry T. Sampson, *Blacks in Blackface: A Source Book on Early Black Musical Shows* (Metuchen, N.J.: Scarecrow Press, 1980).

64. See Thomas F. DeFrantz, "African American Dance: A Complex History," in *Dancing Many Drums*, 3–38.

65. Sterling Stuckey, "Christian Conversion and the Challenge of Dance," in *Dancing Many Drums*, 39–58.

66. Samuel A. Floyd Jr., "African American Dance and Music," in *Dancing Many Drums*, 119. Northrup provides a detailed physical description of the technique in 1840s Louisiana. Solomon Northrup, *Twelve Years a Slave, the Narrative of Solomon Northup, a citizen of New-York, kidnapped in Washington city in 1841, and rescued in 1853, from a cotton plantation near the Red River in Louisiana* (Buffalo, N.Y.: Derby, Orton and Mulligan, 1853), 219; at http://books.google.com/, accessed November 7, 2010.

67. Lynne Faulkey Emery, *Black Dance in the United States from 1619 to 1970* (Palo Alto, Calif.: National Press Books, 1972), 140, 141–42.

68. Michael D. Harris, *Colored Pictures: Race and Visual Representation* (Chapel Hill: University of North Carolina Press, 2003).

Index

CHRISTOPHER J. SMITH is an associate professor and chair of musicology/ethnomusicology and the director of the Vernacular Music Center at the Texas Tech University School of Music. A working musician, he also performs, records, and tours internationally with the medieval music ensemble Altramar and other bands specializing in Irish traditional music and pre-World War II blues and jazz.

Music in American Life

Only a Miner: Studies in Recorded Coal-Mining Songs *Archie Green*
Great Day Coming: Folk Music and the American Left *R. Serge Denisoff*
John Philip Sousa: A Descriptive Catalog of His Works *Paul E. Bierley*
The Hell-Bound Train: A Cowboy Songbook *Glenn Ohrlin*
Oh, Didn't He Ramble: The Life Story of Lee Collins, as Told to Mary Collins *Edited by Frank J. Gillis and John W. Miner*
American Labor Songs of the Nineteenth Century *Philip S. Foner*
Stars of Country Music: Uncle Dave Macon to Johnny Rodriguez *Edited by Bill C. Malone and Judith McCulloh*
Git Along, Little Dogies: Songs and Songmakers of the American West *John I. White*
A Texas-Mexican *Cancionero*: Folksongs of the Lower Border *Américo Paredes*
San Antonio Rose: The Life and Music of Bob Wills *Charles R. Townsend*
Early Downhome Blues: A Musical and Cultural Analysis *Jeff Todd Titon*
An Ives Celebration: Papers and Panels of the Charles Ives Centennial Festival-Conference *Edited by H. Wiley Hitchcock and Vivian Perlis*
Sinful Tunes and Spirituals: Black Folk Music to the Civil War *Dena J. Epstein*
Joe Scott, the Woodsman-Songmaker *Edward D. Ives*
Jimmie Rodgers: The Life and Times of America's Blue Yodeler *Nolan Porterfield*
Early American Music Engraving and Printing: A History of Music Publishing in America from 1787 to 1825, with Commentary on Earlier and Later Practices *Richard J. Wolfe*
Sing a Sad Song: The Life of Hank Williams *Roger M. Williams*
Long Steel Rail: The Railroad in American Folksong *Norm Cohen*
Resources of American Music History: A Directory of Source Materials from Colonial Times to World War II *D. W. Krummel, Jean Geil, Doris J. Dyen, and Deane L. Root*
Tenement Songs: The Popular Music of the Jewish Immigrants *Mark Slobin*
Ozark Folksongs *Vance Randolph; edited and abridged by Norm Cohen*
Oscar Sonneck and American Music *Edited by William Lichtenwanger*
Bluegrass Breakdown: The Making of the Old Southern Sound *Robert Cantwell*
Bluegrass: A History *Neil V. Rosenberg*

Music at the White House:
A History of the American Spirit *Elise K. Kirk*
Red River Blues: The Blues Tradition in the Southeast *Bruce Bastin*
Good Friends and Bad Enemies: Robert Winslow Gordon
and the Study of American Folksong *Debora Kodish*
Fiddlin' Georgia Crazy: Fiddlin' John Carson, His Real World,
and the World of His Songs *Gene Wiggins*
America's Music: From the Pilgrims
to the Present (rev. 3d ed.) *Gilbert Chase*
Secular Music in Colonial Annapolis:
The Tuesday Club, 1745–56 *John Barry Talley*
Bibliographical Handbook of American Music *D. W. Krummel*
Goin' to Kansas City *Nathan W. Pearson, Jr.*
"Susanna," "Jeanie," and "The Old Folks at Home":
The Songs of Stephen C. Foster from His Time to Ours
(2d ed.) *William W. Austin*
Songprints: The Musical Experience
of Five Shoshone Women *Judith Vander*
"Happy in the Service of the Lord": Afro-American Gospel Quartets
in Memphis *Kip Lornell*
Paul Hindemith in the United States *Luther Noss*
"My Song Is My Weapon": People's Songs, American Communism,
and the Politics of Culture, 1930–50 *Robbie Lieberman*
Chosen Voices: The Story of the American Cantorate *Mark Slobin*
Theodore Thomas: America's Conductor
and Builder of Orchestras, 1835–1905 *Ezra Schabas*
"The Whorehouse Bells Were Ringing"
and Other Songs Cowboys Sing
Collected and Edited by Guy Logsdon
Crazeology: The Autobiography of a Chicago Jazzman *Bud Freeman,*
as Told to Robert Wolf
Discoursing Sweet Music: Brass Bands and Community Life
in Turn-of-the-Century Pennsylvania *Kenneth Kreitner*
Mormonism and Music: A History *Michael Hicks*
Voices of the Jazz Age: Profiles of Eight Vintage Jazzmen *Chip Deffaa*
Pickin' on Peachtree: A History of Country Music
in Atlanta, Georgia *Wayne W. Daniel*
Bitter Music: Collected Journals, Essays, Introductions,
and Librettos *Harry Partch; edited by Thomas McGeary*

Ethnic Music on Records: A Discography of Ethnic Recordings Produced in the United States, 1893 to 1942 *Richard K. Spottswood*
Downhome Blues Lyrics: An Anthology from the Post–World War II Era *Jeff Todd Titon*
Ellington: The Early Years *Mark Tucker*
Chicago Soul *Robert Pruter*
That Half-Barbaric Twang: The Banjo in American Popular Culture *Karen Linn*
Hot Man: The Life of Art Hodes *Art Hodes and Chadwick Hansen*
The Erotic Muse: American Bawdy Songs (2d ed.) *Ed Cray*
Barrio Rhythm: Mexican American Music in Los Angeles *Steven Loza*
The Creation of Jazz: Music, Race, and Culture in Urban America *Burton W. Peretti*
Charles Martin Loeffler: A Life Apart in Music *Ellen Knight*
Club Date Musicians: Playing the New York Party Circuit *Bruce A. MacLeod*
Opera on the Road: Traveling Opera Troupes in the United States, 1825–60 *Katherine K. Preston*
The Stonemans: An Appalachian Family and the Music That Shaped Their Lives *Ivan M. Tribe*
Transforming Tradition: Folk Music Revivals Examined *Edited by Neil V. Rosenberg*
The Crooked Stovepipe: Athapaskan Fiddle Music and Square Dancing in Northeast Alaska and Northwest Canada *Craig Mishler*
Traveling the High Way Home: Ralph Stanley and the World of Traditional Bluegrass Music *John Wright*
Carl Ruggles: Composer, Painter, and Storyteller *Marilyn Ziffrin*
Never without a Song: The Years and Songs of Jennie Devlin, 1865–1952 *Katharine D. Newman*
The Hank Snow Story *Hank Snow, with Jack Ownbey and Bob Burris*
Milton Brown and the Founding of Western Swing *Cary Ginell, with special assistance from Roy Lee Brown*
Santiago de Murcia's "Códice Saldívar No. 4": A Treasury of Secular Guitar Music from Baroque Mexico *Craig H. Russell*
The Sound of the Dove: Singing in Appalachian Primitive Baptist Churches *Beverly Bush Patterson*

Heartland Excursions: Ethnomusicological Reflections on Schools of Music *Bruno Nettl*

Doowop: The Chicago Scene *Robert Pruter*

Blue Rhythms: Six Lives in Rhythm and Blues *Chip Deffaa*

Shoshone Ghost Dance Religion: Poetry Songs and Great Basin Context *Judith Vander*

Go Cat Go! Rockabilly Music and Its Makers *Craig Morrison*

'Twas Only an Irishman's Dream: The Image of Ireland and the Irish in American Popular Song Lyrics, 1800–1920 *William H. A. Williams*

Democracy at the Opera: Music, Theater, and Culture in New York City, 1815–60 *Karen Ahlquist*

Fred Waring and the Pennsylvanians *Virginia Waring*

Woody, Cisco, and Me: Seamen Three in the Merchant Marine *Jim Longhi*

Behind the Burnt Cork Mask: Early Blackface Minstrelsy and Antebellum American Popular Culture *William J. Mahar*

Going to Cincinnati: A History of the Blues in the Queen City *Steven C. Tracy*

Pistol Packin' Mama: Aunt Molly Jackson and the Politics of Folksong *Shelly Romalis*

Sixties Rock: Garage, Psychedelic, and Other Satisfactions *Michael Hicks*

The Late Great Johnny Ace and the Transition from R&B to Rock 'n' Roll *James M. Salem*

Tito Puente and the Making of Latin Music *Steven Loza*

Juilliard: A History *Andrea Olmstead*

Understanding Charles Seeger, Pioneer in American Musicology *Edited by Bell Yung and Helen Rees*

Mountains of Music: West Virginia Traditional Music from *Goldenseal* *Edited by John Lilly*

Alice Tully: An Intimate Portrait *Albert Fuller*

A Blues Life *Henry Townsend, as told to Bill Greensmith*

Long Steel Rail: The Railroad in American Folksong (2d ed.) *Norm Cohen*

The Golden Age of Gospel *Text by Horace Clarence Boyer; photography by Lloyd Yearwood*

Aaron Copland: The Life and Work of an Uncommon Man *Howard Pollack*

Louis Moreau Gottschalk *S. Frederick Starr*

Race, Rock, and Elvis *Michael T. Bertrand*
Theremin: Ether Music and Espionage *Albert Glinsky*
Poetry and Violence: The Ballad Tradition
of Mexico's Costa Chica *John H. McDowell*
The Bill Monroe Reader *Edited by Tom Ewing*
Music in Lubavitcher Life *Ellen Koskoff*
Zarzuela: Spanish Operetta, American Stage *Janet L. Sturman*
Bluegrass Odyssey: A Documentary in Pictures and Words,
1966–86 *Carl Fleischhauer and Neil V. Rosenberg*
That Old-Time Rock & Roll: A Chronicle
of an Era, 1954–63 *Richard Aquila*
Labor's Troubadour *Joe Glazer*
American Opera *Elise K. Kirk*
Don't Get above Your Raisin': Country Music
and the Southern Working Class *Bill C. Malone*
John Alden Carpenter: A Chicago Composer *Howard Pollack*
Heartbeat of the People: Music and Dance
of the Northern Pow-Wow *Tara Browner*
My Lord, What a Morning: An Autobiography *Marian Anderson*
Marian Anderson: A Singer's Journey *Allan Keiler*
Charles Ives Remembered: An Oral History *Vivian Perlis*
Henry Cowell, Bohemian *Michael Hicks*
Rap Music and Street Consciousness *Cheryl L. Keyes*
Louis Prima *Garry Boulard*
Marian McPartland's Jazz World: All in Good Time *Marian McPartland*
Robert Johnson: Lost and Found *Barry Lee Pearson and Bill McCulloch*
Bound for America: Three British Composers *Nicholas Temperley*
Lost Sounds: Blacks and the Birth
of the Recording Industry, 1890–1919 *Tim Brooks*
Burn, Baby! BURN! The Autobiography of Magnificent
Montague *Magnificent Montague with Bob Baker*
Way Up North in Dixie: A Black Family's Claim
to the Confederate Anthem *Howard L. Sacks and Judith Rose Sacks*
The Bluegrass Reader *Edited by Thomas Goldsmith*
Colin McPhee: Composer in Two Worlds *Carol J. Oja*
Robert Johnson, Mythmaking,
and Contemporary American Culture *Patricia R. Schroeder*
Composing a World: Lou Harrison, Musical Wayfarer *Leta E. Miller and
Fredric Lieberman*

Fritz Reiner, Maestro and Martinet *Kenneth Morgan*
That Toddlin' Town: Chicago's White Dance Bands and Orchestras, 1900–1950 *Charles A. Sengstock Jr.*
Dewey and Elvis: The Life and Times of a Rock 'n' Roll Deejay *Louis Cantor*
Come Hither to Go Yonder: Playing Bluegrass with Bill Monroe *Bob Black*
Chicago Blues: Portraits and Stories *David Whiteis*
The Incredible Band of John Philip Sousa *Paul E. Bierley*
"Maximum Clarity" and Other Writings on Music *Ben Johnston, edited by Bob Gilmore*
Staging Tradition: John Lair and Sarah Gertrude Knott *Michael Ann Williams*
Homegrown Music: Discovering Bluegrass *Stephanie P. Ledgin*
Tales of a Theatrical Guru *Danny Newman*
The Music of Bill Monroe *Neil V. Rosenberg and Charles K. Wolfe*
Pressing On: The Roni Stoneman Story *Roni Stoneman, as told to Ellen Wright*
Together Let Us Sweetly Live *Jonathan C. David, with photographs by Richard Holloway*
Live Fast, Love Hard: The Faron Young Story *Diane Diekman*
Air Castle of the South: WSM Radio and the Making of Music City *Craig P. Havighurst*
Traveling Home: Sacred Harp Singing and American Pluralism *Kiri Miller*
Where Did Our Love Go? The Rise and Fall of the Motown Sound *Nelson George*
Lonesome Cowgirls and Honky-Tonk Angels: The Women of Barn Dance Radio *Kristine M. McCusker*
California Polyphony: Ethnic Voices, Musical Crossroads *Mina Yang*
The Never-Ending Revival: Rounder Records and the Folk Alliance *Michael F. Scully*
Sing It Pretty: A Memoir *Bess Lomax Hawes*
Working Girl Blues: The Life and Music of Hazel Dickens *Hazel Dickens and Bill C. Malone*
Charles Ives Reconsidered *Gayle Sherwood Magee*
The Hayloft Gang: The Story of the National Barn Dance *Edited by Chad Berry*
Country Music Humorists and Comedians *Loyal Jones*

Record Makers and Breakers: Voices of the Independent Rock 'n' Roll Pioneers *John Broven*

Music of the First Nations: Tradition and Innovation in Native North America *Edited by Tara Browner*

Cafe Society: The Wrong Place for the Right People *Barney Josephson, with Terry Trilling-Josephson*

George Gershwin: An Intimate Portrait *Walter Rimler*

Life Flows On in Endless Song: Folk Songs and American History *Robert V. Wells*

I Feel a Song Coming On: The Life of Jimmy McHugh *Alyn Shipton*

King of the Queen City: The Story of King Records *Jon Hartley Fox*

Long Lost Blues: Popular Blues in America, 1850–1920 *Peter C. Muir*

Hard Luck Blues: Roots Music Photographs from the Great Depression *Rich Remsberg*

Restless Giant: The Life and Times of Jean Aberbach and Hill and Range Songs *Bar Biszick-Lockwood*

Champagne Charlie and Pretty Jemima: Variety Theater in the Nineteenth Century *Gillian M. Rodger*

Sacred Steel: Inside an African American Steel Guitar Tradition *Robert L. Stone*

Gone to the Country: The New Lost City Ramblers and the Folk Music Revival *Ray Allen*

The Makers of the Sacred Harp *David Warren Steel with Richard H. Hulan*

Woody Guthrie, American Radical *Will Kaufman*

George Szell: A Life of Music *Michael Charry*

Bean Blossom: The Brown County Jamboree and Bill Monroe's Bluegrass Festivals *Thomas A. Adler*

Crowe on the Banjo: The Music Life of J. D. Crowe *Marty Godbey*

Twentieth Century Drifter: The Life of Marty Robbins *Diane Diekman*

Henry Mancini: Reinventing Film Music *John Caps*

The Beautiful Music All Around Us: Field Recordings and the American Experience *Stephen Wade*

Then Sings My Soul: The Culture of Southern Gospel Music *Douglas Harrison*

The Accordion in the Americas: Klezmer, Polka, Tango, Zydeco, and More! *Edited by Helena Simonett*

Bluegrass Bluesman: A Memoir *Josh Graves, edited by Fred Bartenstein*

One Woman in a Hundred: Edna Phillips
and the Philadelphia Orchestra *Mary Sue Welsh*
The Great Orchestrator: Arthur Judson
and American Arts Management *James M. Doering*
Charles Ives in the Mirror: American Histories
of an Iconic Composer *David C. Paul*
Southern Soul-Blues *David Whiteis*
Sweet Air: Modernism, Regionalism,
and American Popular Song *Edward P. Comentale*
Pretty Good for a Girl: Women in Bluegrass *Murphy Henry*
Sweet Drams: The Worlds of Patsy Cline *Warren R. Hofstra*
The Creolization of American Culture: William Sidney Mount
and the Roots of Blackface Minstrelsy *Christopher J. Smith*

The University of Illinois Press is a founding member of the Association of American University Presses.

University of Illinois Press
1325 South Oak Street
Champaign, IL 61820-6903
www.press.uillinois.edu